AZTECS, ANDES, AND ARMADILLOS

A Grand Expedition Through Latin America

RED BAXTER

Published in Australia by Sid Harta Publishers Pty Ltd,
ABN: 34 632 585 203
17 Coleman Parade, GLEN WAVERLEY VIC 3150 Australia
Telephone: +61 3 9560 9920, Facsimile: +61 3 9545 1742
E-mail: author@sidharta.com.au

First published in Australia 2019
This edition published 2019
Copyright © Red Baxter 2019
Cover design, typesetting: WorkingType (www.workingtype.com.au)

Please contact the author at:
Box 112, Flemington, VIC 3031, Australia

The right of Red Baxter to be identified as the Author of the Work has been asserted in accordance with the Copyright, Designs and Patents Act 1988.

This book is a work of recall. The Author of this book accepts all responsibility for the contents and absolves any other person or persons involved in its production from any responsibility or liability where the contents are concerned.

All rights reserved. No part of this publication may be reproduced, stored in a retrieval system, or transmitted, in any form or by any means without the prior written permission of the publisher, nor be otherwise circulated in any form of binding or cover other than that in which it is published and without a similar condition being imposed on the subsequent purchaser.

Baxter, Red
Aztecs, Andes and Armadillos
ISBN: 978-1-921642-89-0
pp474

CONTENTS

The members of the expedition iv
Map, showing the route v
Colour illustrations .... begins after 252
Introduction 1
Preface 3

Part One   THE CENTRAL AMERICAN EXPEDITION

Chapter One	California	9
Chapter Two	Mexico	13
Chapter Three	Belize	39
Chapter Four	Guatemala	43
Chapter Five	Honduras	65
Chapter Six	Nicaragua	69
Chapter Seven	Costa Rica	75
Chapter Eight	Panama	81

Part Two   THE SOUTH AMERICAN EXPEDITION

Chapter Nine	Colombia	91
Chapter Ten	Ecuador	113
Chapter Eleven	Peru	165
Chapter Twelve	Bolivia	253
Chapter Thirteen	Chile	269
Chapter Fourteen	Argentina (Southbound)	301
Chapter Fifteen	Fuegian Patagonia	337
Chapter Sixteen	Argentina (Northbound)	355
Chapter Seventeen	Paraguay	389
Chapter Eighteen	Brazil	399

Suffix 435
Index 437

INTRODUCTION

For years I have had a wanderlust which has taken me all over the world, and have been urged so often to write a book, as the stories I related aroused a fascination in others, who wanted to hear ever more about my travels. I have found voyaging most rewarding, with few worries or unforseen expenses, even though I always travelled on a shoe-string with just a full backpack and die-hard self-confidence as my only security.

This particular journey began (in August 1980) and ended for me in Boston, Massachusetts, and is my account of a major expedition through Latin America in two distinct stages. The first part covers Central America, and after recuperating for a fortnight in Panama City the second part explores the great South American continent from end to end. If you anticipate travelling in Latin America, please be encouraged by this book. The countries present numerous challenges both social and natural. The very innocence of travellers in these corrupt and struggling countries is their own best security when faced with the peculiar demands of the various authorities. Apart from exasperation at the hands of crooked uniformed services, it is impossible to stay healthy for long with mediaeval sanitation and widespread sickness in every country. With common sense we overcame adversity and spent seven unforgettable months exploring remote areas as well as the more famous tourist spots, and took many thousands of photographs.

I have been a conservationist and an animal-lover all my life and at different times I have taken care of everything from tropical aquarium fish to Himalayan mountain bears, and Mexican snake-eating eagles to Hamadryad baboons. The whole expedition through Latin America was a wonderful chance for me to investigate scores of exotic species of fauna and flora, quite apart from the indigenous Indian races, Mestizos, Caribs and Creoles, Whites and Negroes, with cultures and traditions steeped in mystery.

PREFACE FOR THIS PRINTING

Four decades have passed since this enormous journey was undertaken, and recently the members of this expedition have rediscovered each other via modern media. The countries have changed politically: many dictators have gone, and oil, beef, drugs, timber, and other boom industries have brought a new mix of wealth for some, but continuing overwhelming hardship for the majority of Latin Americans.

I have continued to travel Latin America and globally, and this year I shall travel 1,500 kilometres up the Amazon again, a far cry from the few days in an Indian dugout: described in this book. Annette Leutert and Bernie Fischer have told me how they too have travelled on long adventurous journeys, roughing it all over the world. The erstwhile great difficulty in reaching the High Andes, Mt. Cotopaxi, Machu-Pijchu, the Paine Glaciers, or the Iguazu Falls is now eclipsed by luxury travel and hotels.

It has become easy to reach the once exotic destinations named in my book with $60,000 and a credit card. I covered the whole circuit from San Francisco down through Central and South America, all for $3000 and a tent. Doing it the hard way, visiting the remoter spots by routes less travelled remains infinitely more rewarding for the lifetime memories it conjures up. Also there is no angst from missing a flight or mucking up a hotel booking. The completely carefree immersion amongst the villagers along the way was for us all of the great rewards of this down-to-earth expedition. My especial pleasure was to see the animals and their habitats, not just the delightful baby guanaco at the San Sebastian border post in Argentine Tierra Del Fuego, which we all adored. Unfortunately the fauna, including birds and fish, and their habitats are being rapidly and systematically wiped out by mainly illegal logging and the march of agriculture everywhere. Soaring population, peculation, and grinding poverty remain the same.

Finally I thank Bernie Fischer for sharing his photographs here.

THE EXPEDITION MEMBERS

Central America

Switzerland	Kiki Albrecht, Brigitte Ott, Christoff Lüdin.	Denah Goldberg, Hans Marty,
Canada	Debbie Dahms,	Joan Treleaven.

Central and South America

Australia	Red Baxter (author), Rein Kamar (leader).	Frances Clifford,
U.S.A.	Frank Göhde,	Bill Carel.

South America

England	Stephanie Alcock, Ann Garnett, Dee Stace, Paul Wood (leader).	Diane Dupree. Joan Phillips, Tobin Roberts,
Switzerland	Gaby Colombo, Bernie Fischer, Sam Gamper,	Chantal Staub, Annette Leutert (organiser), Armin Russenberger.
Holland	Alice Limbeck,	Sandra Smits.
Australia	Kathy Barry.	
Austria	Maria Schmidt.	
Sweden	Rolf Carlsson.	
Germany	Manfred Weber.	

OUR ROUTE

PART ONE

THE CENTRAL AMERICAN EXPEDITION

'Even jade is shattered,
'Even gold is crushed,
'Even quetzal plumes are torn. . .
'One does not live forever on this Earth:
'We endure only for an instant!'

Song of the sage King Nezahualcoyotl of Texcoco.
(A.D. 1402 – 1472)

CHAPTER ONE

CALIFORNIA

I arrived in San Francisco across the enormous Yerba Buena Bridge and over the next week I prepared myself for the expedition ahead, due to start from this beautiful and easy-going city, but who can visit San Francisco without seeing the sights? Pier 39 is a must for visitors, and represents all that is best in this city of the beautiful people. It is more than just a double-decker wooden shopping precinct surrounded by nodding dinghies, with a fine view across to

Oakland and the Golden Gate Bridge. There are regular comedy diving and mime acts and fascinating shops to browse among where the artisans produce colourful arts and crafts in glass and wire, wax and copper. Close by, Fisherman's Wharf offers tempting aromas of seafood and has many restaurants and tourist attractions. Chinatown and trolley-buses and Russian Hill and the canyons of skyscrapers all provide indelible memories, but is the inhabitants of San Francisco who make it such a friendly place. People of all races, skateboarders and roller-skaters crowd the sunny streets.

In due course I liaised with the other 11 members of the expedition, including Rein, the leader, to organise our route through Central America as far as Panama City. Inevitably our best laid plans were subsequently confounded by persistent mechanical problems even though all our equipment and our van and trailer were purposely bought for the expedition and were well tested. The cost was split equally between us at less than $1000 each per month, and in addition to Rein and me the party was made up of Kiki and Denah, both young Swiss doctors, Brigitte, Christoff, and Hans, also Swiss who spoke very little English. There were Bill and Frances, both hardened travellers who had accompanied each other all over the world. Joan and Debbie joined us from British Columbia, and Frank, a New Yorker, has his own job on the expedition. As he declined to submit us to his cooking, he was elected Rein's deputy in charge of unloading all the equipment each evening when we made camp, and then stowing it next morning. The rest of us paired up as cooking teams, to do our shopping from local markets every day.

We intentionally spent little time in the United States and sped down the Pacific Coast, passing a few very brave surfers, for the water was too cold this late in the year and there was no end to the brown seaweed. We spent most of the first day becoming acquainted. Frances, Bill, Frank, Rein, and I would be travelling through the whole of Latin America during the next eight months, while the others were only going to Panama City. Bill in particular had an unbelievable life story, having travelled for years through virtually every country in the world on the lucrative proceeds of his career as a male model for Playboy. Incredibly his kit consisted of ex-U.S.A.F. khaki uniform, and for a hardened traveller to embark on an expedition across a continent riddled with complexes about Americans, the C.I.A. and military clothing, it was, to put no finer point on it, a dumb move!

Out of San Francisco we made steady progress to Santa Cruz, along Monterey Bay and into sensational countryside. For 65 miles after Carmel we went along the coastal edge of the Santa Lucia Mountains which are composed of small compressed chips and grains like cob or coarse sandstone, out of which the rain has washed fantastic runnels and slipways like vertical sandy streambeds. Our first lunch stop was by a river where the girls found a five-foot garter snake, and knowing the species to be harmless I picked it up, albeit gingerly. We carried on through rolling mountains clad in green, but this area around Morro Bay is semi-arid reliant on extensive irrigation to support a gamut of crops, especially artichokes. Santa Barbara lingers in my memory as a town which does not properly belong in the United states, as it has cacti and Mexican palms everywhere and an Hispanic populace and way of life. We skirted the Santa Monica Mountains Inland, thereby avoiding Los Angeles on our way to San Clemente. There was nothing in the desert to look at; not a single blade of grass grew here outside the few watered gardens, and we passed the time in conversation. Kiki and Denah formed a natural team, being lifelong friends, outwardly very kind and both newly graduated doctors. We camped in remote spots by night, preferably with a stream near at hand, and we had the option of sleeping in two-man tents, but Frank and I did not usually bother, choosing to sleep warmly under the stars with just our camp-beds. Every morning we drove to the next town for provisions, petrol, and water, but could not leave the van unguarded for an instant since the Mestizos steal everything they can lay their hands on, particularly if it belongs to a Gringo. We formed the habit of encircling the vehicle with our tents or camp-beds, and seldom rose later than dawn to make the greatest use of daylight, but this also served to give us more time in the evenings to set up camp in the twilight and to relax. It proved a good arrangement.

CHAPTER TWO

MEXICO

The United States of Mexico is an extremely mountainous and fairly dry country, half of it being over 3,300 feet above sea-level. In the north-west is the Mexican Sahara Desert and generally the centre of the country forms a high plateau, but the national territory is so large that it contains a wide range of terrains from tropical lowland jungle and steamy marshland east of the isthmus to high altitude moorland (páramo) and alpine vegetation above the tree-line at 13,000 feet. The population totals 70,000,000 of whom 20,000,000 live in the 20 square mile mountain basin forming the Federal District wherein lies the capital, Mexico City. Two thirds of the national population are Mestizo, a miscegenation betwixt the Spanish and the Indians, a quarter are Indian, and the remainder are derived from Negro, European, Arab and Chinese stock. Half the population of Mexico are minors. Life for the peón or landless peasant has always been hard, cheap, and feudal, no matter who the current landlord. Most are barely literate and live in homes of sticks and adobe to this day, without windows or facilities of any kind. Several dozen Indian tribes inhabit the country, each with its own tongue and many more have come and gone in Mexico's long history. Past cultures to have left their marks in different regions are the Olmecs, Toltecs, Matlazincas, Chichimecs, Huastecs, Itzás, Mezcalas, Tarascas, and even the Apaches. Tatters of their cultures show, through in customs and trappings. When, in 1519, Hernán Cortés led 500 heavily armed cavalry peacefully to Tenochtitlán, now Mexico City, capital of the theocratic Aztecs under the rule of Moctezuma, the Mayas were already on the decline. The next year Cortés returned with reserves and joined the forces with the Tlaxcalan Indians to defeat the warlike Aztecs. Mexico is full of ruins and pyramids and more are being discovered all the time, but in the deep south-east in particular Indian traditions and languages such as Nahuatl and Zapotec predominate. Present Mexican tribes and cultures include the Otomí, Tarahumara, Huichol, Cora, Nahua, Mazateca, Chinautec, Mixtec, Tzotzil, and Tzeltal.

We crossed into Mexico at Tijuana which is a real hole. The quality of souvenirs and bric-á-brac is the worst I have ever seen apart from a few articles like huge birdcages and saddles. Most of the thousands of tourists who come to this garish place are Americans who come to say they have been to Mexico. It is a filthy town, and I for one was glad to leave. The mountains in Baja California are drier and more weather-beaten than north of the border, and the Mexicans are dreadful litterbugs. Our first meal in Mexico was typical Mexican tacos on the beach at Rosarito. We filled our unleavened tortillas with salad, cheese, meat, and a hot guacamole (avocado and chilli) sauce. We considered La Bufadora was worth a visit for it has the biggest blow-hole on the Pacific Coast. With every surge of the ocean a huge spout of froth and vapour shot skywards out of a vent in the cliff, and. flecked the rockface and observers with spume as much as 150 feet above, and the force of it made the whole cliff shudder.

Once out of the United States, we learned to cope with very poor roads. Admittedly the situation is slowly improving, but to this day 90% of roads in Latin America are unpaved at best, and are very commonly criss-crossed by eroding streams, or are so badly cambered and pot-holed that it comes as a tremendous relief to reach the mainly macadamised surface of the Pan-American Highway. This is an ambitious project to build at least one good road link from Alaska to Tierra del Fuego, extensively financed by the United States. This is not to say. that the Latinos do not work on their roads; they are simply quite inefficient. Every few miles in Baja California we came upon workmen in small numbers refilling the deepest pot-holes with stones. Much further south the Peruvians proudly boast that theirs is the most modern road system in the world; and this may literally be true, for they bulldoze them all with fresh dirt after every rainy season.

Our first taste of Mexican cunning occurred at Bufadora, miles away from the nearest habitation. We had camped on the tip of a barren promontory, and true to form began to strike camp in the pre-dawn light, when a jeep could be seen by its one head-lamp picking a path along the stony cul-de-sac towards us. I was the only member of the expedition to speak reasonable Spanish, and when the two paisanos got out and walked towards us, we were bemused to see them carefully place some of the roadstones to one side of the track. They demanded money from us for using the dirt-road which they claimed to have built. They must have thought we were still wet behind the ears, or maybe they had succeeded in exacting a toll from Americans previously, but they had no right to our money and Rein sent them packing with a flea in the ear. Latin Americans have but one way of treating Gringos, which is with disdain. They know for a certain fact that every Gringo has $1,000 in his pocket, and they are duty-bound to part him from his money and preferably as much else as possible. As a result of their steadfastness and expertise at stealing, every traveller in Latin America loses a proportion of his luggage or valuables despite the best precautions.

Rein was a great natural leader, and had led expeditions all round the world. He was full of anecdotes, which he delivered with a wicked chuckle and in great style, at once both off-hand and vociferous. He was an Estonian, which probably accounted for his hard-hitting conservative radicalism. His outrageous disparaging comment on worldwide matters of politics and race fell on basically incomprehending ears, but his chief audience, the two Swiss doctors and the Canadian girls, demonstrated a complete ignorance of the social facts of life outside their own countries by laughing at his tirades. At the end of each day Rein and the girls regularly produced bottles of liquor, and sat on camp-stools amid the chirring of the cicadas and all the other sound of the countryside, and the good-humoured anecdotes needed little coaxing, or else the world's problems were solved while the tequila did its work loosening tongues and bringing enlightenment.

The high price of prickly pears as a fruit in the markets surprised us; after all they were plentiful and merely had to be scraped to remove the spines, but we found out first-hand just why they fetched such a premium. South of San Quintin on the desert Sierra San Pedro Martir, which was so steep and broken that the Pacific was obscured for much of the way, we stopped amid the scrub and cacti for lunch in 100-degree heat. Nearly every plant had vicious points, bushes, shrubs, and cacti alike, but I managed to harvest a basket of red and green prickly pears getting spiked everywhere in the process, and Debbie, Frances and I struggled to eat their sorbet flesh, but dozens of irritating unseen barbs stuck in our tongues and soft palates. The desert contains virtually no agriculture, just great quantities of xerophytes and specialist desert bushes, although it has a system of wide river beds containing narrow streams. We passed a cowboy moving his herd of mangy steers along the valley on our way inland from El Rosario. They seemed so out of place amid the many different species of cactus: squat ones, fat leafy ones, 30-foot tall spindle-branched ones, prickly pears, nopals and cirio (or candle) cacti up to 35 feet tall, and the biggest of all, the bulging saguaros. This is one of the loveliest spots on the globe, the Mesa de San Carlos, strewn with thousands of crumbly granite boulders as large as houses. The panorama of plateaux and mountainous hills strewn with innumerable rocks and dense with cacti growing like trees was spectacle never to be forgotten. We camped in the midst of this primaeval wilderness, and once the engine was cut the sounds of the desert took over. The desert is host to many animals, particularly lizards, coneys, dragonflies, dung beetles, and colourful insects, all preyed on by bats and birds, especially eagles and ravens; and walking alone, dwarfed by the cacti and huge loose boulders, I startled a fox into bolting. After a cloudless blue sky with 100-degree heat all day, a swift and fiery sunset faded to allow a perfect unimpeded panoply of stars to shine down, clear and bright, while the temperature plunged through 90 degrees by morning. In the tropics the sunsets are brilliant but quick, as there is virtually no twilight.

The following morning we reached Bahía de los Angeles on the Gulf of California, and stepped out of our air-conditioned van into 120 degrees Fahrenheit. The gulf water was warm and contained harmless jelly-fish, but this gulf is renowned for the many species of whales, sharks, seals, dolphins, and sea-birds. The whales and dolphins are protected in Mexican waters, and at this tiny village an American marine biology research station investigates the schools of finbacks and bottle-nose dolphins which swim up the coast every dawn within a few yards of the beach, where dozens of bedraggled brown pelicans infested with lice later sit bobbing up and down on the waves to ride out the noonday heat. In the evening they hunt for fish by skimming mere inches above the surface, holding their heads just like pterodactyls, and upon spotting a fish double back to dive and settle on the surface to eat it at leisure. Perhaps 600 people live in this little village which boasts an airstrip of hard sand along the beach road, and most of them are fishermen. We copied their example and set out our camp-beds right on the sand, as the humidity kept the temperature comfortably warm overnight. The largest boat belonged to the marine biologists, who told us that the finbacks and porpoises leap around its bow but leave as soon as humans enter the water. Throughout the afternoon we gathered brushwood for a beach barbecue which attracted a couple of yachtsmen bringing a bottle of tequila sauza, which kept us talking until nearly dawn, while the calls of a coyote and a feral cat could be heard in the desert.

The red orb of the dawn sun rose beyond the islands in the Gulf and immediately the heat increased and routed away the many strange insects which come out in droves by night, and the seething mass of fiddler crabs each with one big pink claw protruding from the wet tide-marked sand squirmed out of sight.

For two days we had been unable to buy petrol in the desert, and the little villages of Puerta Prieta and Rosarito had none, so it was inevitable that we should run out in the cactus desert at a very lonely mountainous spot. We were very lucky to be rescued within one hour, because traffic is not necessarily a daily occurrence in this isolated desert. Back on the road, for several miles we wondered at the identity of a curious double spire straight ahead. Upon closer inspection it turned out to be a monstrous modern art twin tower erected as a monument to the twenty-eighth parallel here in the middle of the desert. Joan was the first to photograph an approaching brown pelican, but it was very jealous of its private monument and attacked her legs, chasing her all over the place and making her screech hysterically. We all said it must have been going after her green outfit and taken her for a frog, but the pelican won the day and chased us all back into the van and tried to jump in too ahead of Brigitte, who had to leap for her life into the moving van and slam the door with pelican in hot pursuit.

The salt-mining village of Guerrero Negro derives its name from the miniscule blackflies which swarmed about us and bit like fleas, adding their misery to the dust and 110 degrees of heat. We all longed to jump in a cool river, and we had no choice but to drive past one in the oasis town of San Ignacio, nestled under the 6,000-foot Volcan de las Tres Virgines. There were over 10,000 date palms here and racks of thousands of yellow and orange dates were laid out to dry. We pressed on beyond Santa Rosalía in the mountains on a tortuous road winding steeply up and down, often with a sheer drop aside, before we could camp. It was worth all the waiting to reach a lovely broad beach, where we met a young Dutchman making his way round the world on a B.M.W. motor-cycle. During the expedition we met quite a few other travellers whose tips and experiences came in very useful for us and who invariably had great stories to tell. Driving for hours through the endless baking desert made the stops at isolated beaches such as Bahía Concepción all the more relaxing. Joan had the foresight to bring seawater soap, so we could all wash the desert dust from our hair.

The least natural moisture is made use of and south of Ciudad Constitución irrigated cotton fields succeeded the desert. Especially in the morning and evening, breezes were a constant factor here and raised clouds of flying dust for half an hour at a time. Once the sun had set bugs of all shapes and sizes flocked in their hundreds to the lights of the van. Fortunately none bit but they were still maddening as they blundered and crawled all over us.

Since Bill was a model, he spent hours each day in strenuous fitness training, and his lead was taken very seriously. All the girls did their exercises in a circle, but Hans and Christoff joined Bill. In the meantime a battle of wits, often personal, had developed betwixt Joan and Rein. Every morning Rein called out and taunted the Canadian girls who were always the last up, but Joan was a trade union secretary and an easy match for his declared chauvinism, and she had a ringing scornful laugh which never failed to rile him.

At last we reached La Paz at the southern tip of the world's longest peninsula and checked into a camp-ground with a swimming-pool and a laundry, both luxuries we had not expected and did not find again during the next six months. We held a barbecue and partied the whole night, half of us ending up in the swimming-pool ambushing passers-by.

From the minute the sun rose, the heat and the harsh stridulation of the cicadas were merciless, and we had our first encounter with a little transparent pink scorpion, (and to think we were fooling around in swimming costumes) while overhead a dozen buzzards were circling, much larger than the eagles we had seen in the desert. The first of many persistent problems occurred to our van as we set off, a universal joint broke up. Rein never gave up in his attempts to keep the van roadworthy, even if it entailed suspending himself under it to locate the problem while someone else drove on slowly. Back at the camp-site a six-inch scorpion closely skirted my bare toes and Rein and I captured it carefully in the butter-dish. It was a beauty and Rein kept it as a pet, and fed it live cockroaches which were common and not much thinner than the scorpion itself. The scorpion administered a couple of lightning-quick paralysing stings and overnight ate all but the wings and thorax. Thenceforth Rein slept on the roof of the van for safety: and he recounted the story of a girl on a trans-Africa expedition who found a very flat scorpion underneath her when she woke up, which had sought her warmth during a freezing Sahara night but was rolled on with its tail down, luckily for the girl. We got used to just lazing around for hours while Rein worked on the van. The weather was perfect, and we could sunbathe or explore the locality while we waited a couple of days for the ferry to the mainland. Swimming in the sea at Pichilingue was impossible on account of the jellyfish, including lethal Portugese men-o'-war, but it was made up for by the amazing languid antics of a couple of giant sea-turtles playing in a school of fish. The ship was packed with Mexicans, and we saw our first Indians in traditional highly coloured woven costumes, in utter contrast to the dreary and mostly dirty, ragged, Mexican clothes. The 20-hour crossing in stifling claustrophobic cabins was made worse by entirely unhygienic conditions typical of the Mexicans. When we visited major cities nearly every hotel we stayed at had extremely poor sanitation, and most had no hot water at all. We became quite accustomed to cockroaches and bedbugs by the end of the trip, not to mention stained and peeling walls, inadequate lighting, and a total lack of security.

The change of habitat could not be greater: from the harsh sterile desert of Baja California we passed into countryside tropical in its verdure where crops of all kinds abounded, particularly fruit orchards and sugar-cane, and cattle and horses grazed. The bounty was reflected in the market prices, and Brigitte and I did our shopping for half the price we had paid hitherto. We bought a dozen shark fillets for supper. Previously we had tried sea-bass at Bufadora, and again found that experimenting with new or unusual foods turned out very well. We certainly ate in style on this expedition. After Mazatlán the climate and topography also changed utterly. From here to Panama City tropical downpours, virtual cloud-bursts, were nearly a daily occurrence. On our way inland we passed beautiful lush cultivated valleys set against very high steep mountains, in which the sheer cliff faces were the only bare rock. It was not easy to find camp-sites now in this terrain, and we just had to keep going and take whatever came up. That first night off the boat we found a soft clay lay-by where we set up camp under a grey sky in which the stupendous lightning flashes were splitting the clouds, and thunder boomed in the mountains all around us. Within ten minutes we were in the midst of a tempestuous deluge. Brigitte and I cooked supper under a tarpaulin after dark while the others sheltered in the van. Kiki and Denah had erected their tent in a dry depression facing, uphill and found it half submerged in a muddy torrent, and so abandoned it to sleep in the van.

It was in this place that Montezuma's Revenge came upon us.

This affliction, alias the Aztec Quickstep, Colitis Amoebiani, or amoebic dysentery, affects approximately two thirds of the inhabitants of Latin America at any one time, and I did not know it then, but I was to suffer another eight months and spend hundreds of dollars on medical treatment; and I lost 60 pounds before I eventually shook off the infection.

After supper, while we were all busy in remote ditches, we discovered two hazards: six-inch long tarantula spiders, and truck head-lights exposing our indignity which caused much hilarity. The rain had virtually stopped, but I admired the lightning flashing all round without a second's pause. The road had been so hot by day that it was already bone-dry, belying the gurgling silty streams which ran in the gutters. We all spent the evening in the van, and upon going to our tents were greeted by the whine of mosquitoes and the brilliance of myriad stars in a washed clean sky, and we slept in the soggy chaos left by the rain.

We moved on towards Mexico City, sight-seeing along the way and stopped at Ixtlán del Rio to shop. Rein had so much trouble with polluted Mexican petrol that, once the nightmare of starting the van was over, he used to keep the engine running all day until we made camp. The van gave us one big problem after another and cost us about a fortnight in lost time altogether. It was equipped with air-conditioning which brought the temperature in the van down by 20 degrees, but when the outside temperature was 115 degrees Fahrenheit it did not seem like much, and we all wore just our swim-suits most of the time. We stopped for lunch at a spot overlooking Guadalajara, capital of Jalisco State and a city of 2,000,000 people. All round us obsidian fragments littered the ground. Generally we avoided cities, except the capitals, as little would have been gained in them and it would have meant negotiating hopeless traffic conditions, avoiding corrupt policemen, and searching ages for parking spaces.

The region is famous for its many small copper and opal mines, worked as family concerns. We made a stop at Magdelena, where we haggled for opals. The word soon got around and a couple of dozen dealers gathered about us, displaying all kinds of opals, some uncut, and others still embedded in rock bases with just one highly polished facet. Even young boys tried to sell us crude opals put in water-filled phials to enhance their reflections. Only Bill was serious about buying, and I acted as translator while he haggled. Black squares of velvet were held out to him, on each a collection of opals, scintillating in the hard sunlight, until he made his choice after examining them all. As we gradually climbed the winding mountain roads, we passed cultivated flood plains, for there were plenty of lakes and rivers, and in the diverse countryside agave cactus is widely grown as a crop, particularly on the mountain slopes where no other use can be made of the land.

In Baja, we had noticed the odd roadside shrine here or there in the desert where very few people lived. Here in Central Mexico they were much more common, at least one every ten miles, and oftentime a few were clustered together. They took the form of small kennel-like structures, with some flowers and a crucifix, and in all the different parts of Latin America they were regionally stylised. It took us a while to work out what they were, namely the gravestones of road casualties. This exactly bore out our own experience of Latin American macho driving. The traffic is notoriously dangerous, and road casualties are extremely high. Two characteristics in particular identify macho drivers, firstly they never give way, and secondly they always drive at top speed, and both these things are adhered to as a matter of honour, hence the extraordinary number of graves.

More and more I was falling under the spell of my illness, and felt like a pressure cooker, and so paid little heed, (or even slept through) many villages and small towns, and lush green mountains as much as 8,500 feet high where typical cowboys, or vaqueros, rode alongside the small herds of cattle, After the intense heat of the desert and the subtropical coast, Mexico City was relatively cool at 7,350 feet, but it was nevertheless in a cup-shaped valley, a big drab urban sprawl of 20,000,000 inhabitants with the worst air pollution on Earth and no respite from street noise. The local colour of the street markets and vendors was to be found everywhere, and so were the police. Entering the city, Rein was caught doing a U-turn and the police tried to fine him 500 pesos on the spot, but after a long hassle in which Rein insisted on a receipt, since he knew the money would go straight into the policemen's pockets, Rein threatened to complain to the Chief of Police.. Meanwhile we openly took down the displayed names and numbers of the group of policemen involved and they relented and let us go, Scot-free. As independence anniversary celebrations were about to start, it took us hours to find a hotel with 12 vacancies.

Throughout Latin America coffee is served in distinct regional styles. Here, for instance, white coffee is served in a floater nearly full of hot milk, into which the waiter pours a hot liquid so black and thick that a mere dollop is sufficient. Presumably the huge coffee-pot sits simmering on the hob while the brew gets stronger and stronger.

At six feet six tall, I stand a clear head and shoulders above the Latin men, and from this arose a singular hazard — shop awnings were at my head-height and were a constant nuisance. However I was not deterred from browsing among the market stalls, where I sampled the local foods.

For supper the group gathered in the Café Bolivar, quite a find by Frank, where the helpings were enormous, the cuisine international, and. the prices very reasonable. The only drawback was the long wait while our orders were cooked. We hit the town that night, and gravitated to the Plaza Garibaldi, the heart of Mexican night-1ife. Still at one in the morning street vendors were everywhere, also hundreds of wandering musicians in black uniforms. Their tight trousers are decorated with broad stripes made of chromed motifs such as cockerels or Aztec calendars with crossed rifles. These are the famous pistol-packing mariachis, who wear big sombreros and droopy, polka-dot, bandana bow-ties over their gala suits.

Initially intending to spend only a couple of nights in Mexico City, we ended up staying a week as Rein had problems non-stop with the van which he had to overhaul. Here it was quite literally 'non-stop', for the brakes failed the morning we were scheduled to leave. So it was back to sight-seeing, and in our street there was a famous covered market containing a wealth of Mexican souvenirs, particularly work in copper and silver from local mines, spinach-jade, stoneware, hats, and clothes. Our delay meant that we were able to join in the anniversary celebrations. Off our street in. an alley a spontaneous party erupted, and gorgeous blonde Brigitte, Debbie, Hans, and I danced the night away. It was a wild night, aided by a dozen tequila sauzas each. The Mexicans made way for us to dance while they watched deferentially for a while. They all showed great interest in Brigitte, who had a Marilyn Monroe figure, and did not give her a minute's rest all night.

The following night, having shaken off mammoth hangovers, Brigitte, Hans, and I went in search of the Independence Day, festivities in the Plaza de la Constitución. Everyone carried bags of confetti, and a few miscreants had flour, the idea being to throw it just as someone was talking and get it in his mouth. There must have been a quarter of a million people in the crowd, and being Gringos we. were fair game. We were smothered; one pretty girl had the cheek to take my stetson off before, dumping confetti over me. The fireworks display was all around us, stupendous in its proportions, with many set pieces which unfolded under centrifugal force. The ones which shot 500 feet high before bursting went up with such loud and forceful explosions that I could easily feel the blasts across the square as they shook my clothes. We bought confetti and gave as good as we got until our supply ran out, especially wary of. being asked the time, just a wheeze to make us open our mouths in reply. The street vendors were set up for trade all night; and we sampled the traditional corn-cob on a stick, spread with a little piquant butter. The ears of the corn were as big as fingertips and very tough and chewy like cattle cake: in fact we did not find any other variety in the whole of Latin America.

During our last hour in Mexico City, even as we were loading the van to go, a policemen unscrewed our front vehicle registration plate and said there was a 50 peso fine payable at the bank within a week for our plate to be returned. It goes without saying that the police regard all Gringos as stupid: it is a sport to fine them. We discovered that the confiscated plates end up in the hands of street sweepers to scoop up gutter garbage.

At last, we moved out into mountains up to 11,000 feet, high on our way to Puebla, the 'City of the Angels'. The mountains support a great variety of life, agriculture, and industry wherever the land, is flat enough. The drive was really pretty and the road wound to and fro around steep mountain clefts with patches of virgin woodland and much greenery, and on every hilltop there was a church. Puebla is renowned for its historical architecture as it was almost the first place in Mexico to be settled by the Spanish. A great many buildings have glazed tile roofs and façades. This old town is dominated by its churches and cathedral in common with most others in Central America. Here also was evidence of Moorish influence as at the Alhambra in Old Spain in the glorious State government building; many glimpses into doorways revealed interior courtyards, some lush with private wealth and others with gardens. The whole seventeenth century atmosphere of colonial Puebla, its tranquility, and beautiful whitewashed villas contrast with the faceless noisy urgency of Mexico city.

A little way to the south-west of Puebla is Atlixco, and to reach it we passed within sight of Mount Popocatépetl, an active volcano 17,887 feet high in the Sierra Madre. Atlixco is another uniquely beautiful town, renowned for its pretty and highly imaginative tilework from the sixteenth century which was surprisingly commonplace. Even the park benches were constructed with tiles arranged in patterns.

CHAPTER TWO   MEXICO

Pressing on south, I am left with memories of one of the most unusual plant forms I have ever seen; on those lush green mountain slopes, a virtual alien forest of candle cacti dominated the scenery, standing 35 feet tall amidst all the temperate bushes and squat trees. They looked quite out of place, and for miles the landscape consisted of this tropical greenery in a very steep terrain spotted with sharp peaks, and cleft by deep ravines. We were flabbergasted to see a bus charge past us on this sharply twisting road skirting the steep edge to overtake a truck and so disappear around a corner mere seconds before a jeep appeared coming the other way. Thank God the Mexicans are religious!

More and more we entered a story book land, and paused at a curious little farm whose stockades were living cacti, penning a variety of farm animals all with young. There were wobbly kittens, puppies, calves, chicks, ducklings, and a placid little donkey, while the farmhouse itself was an appealing thatched stick-built affair with a well trodden packed earth floor.

We camped that night in the most Brobdinaggian setting in the shadows of spreading corticate cacti, each as big as a house, quite dwarfing the van. As usual the sky was menacing and after supper a shower precipitated a quick cover up operation, which also served to put things out of the reach of local farmers and goatherds who come to ogle us with sullen uncomprehending blank faces. There was more vitality in the goats' expressions. Nearly every time we stopped, even on the remotest mountains, a band of peasants and their dogs would simply come and stare for hours. They just peered at the van or at the girls in their bikinis, and sometimes the urchins begged from us. When the undergrowth was a little drier we set out the camp-stools and chatted while the lightning flashed and flared without pause in the mountains on the horizon in a complete circle. We went and looked at a hairy theraphosid spider, as big as a tarantula and blood red with shiny black legs, and decoyed.it out of its charred hollow stump with a knock; and it charged out, vile and threatening, but sensing a trap it shot back to safety. just as quickly. Rather ambitiously I set up my camp-bed alfresco, with my mosquito-net tied up to one of the giant cacti, which had well formed lignified bark. It was dark at the time and I did not realise that a well worn track alongside my bed was a highway between two (of a network) of vast subterranean ants' nests. In the light of morning I observed them all round me, and the cleared empty areas of the nests were from ten to twenty feet across. Even before I was up, Rein had started the engine, setting fire to my luggage which had been slung under it during the evening shower.

After this poor start to the day, the scenery made up for it. It continued to be very mountainous with numerous streams and rivers which only filled a small portion of their beds. We passed herds of goats and cattle, and a harvest of maize and orchards of papayas, and the occasional vaquero on horseback. Everywhere the largest living things in these highlands were the arboreal branched cacti. With the remoteness of the district, it seemed also to remain in the Spanish colonial era. For instance, at Acatlán the architecture was in very good repair, having nearly perfectly preserved murals, stucco, and tilework, and a plethora of gold leaf decoration. The clothing and vegetable market here was unusually clean, in total contrast to the butchers' stalls where no attempt seems ever to have been made to clean any of the fly-blown surfaces or tools, which were covered in a blue-green fungus like plush velvet. This lack of concern was common in Latin America, a typical example of just how unhygienic the people are. South. of Acatlán the mountains of the Great Dividing Range became more arid, and in the crystal clear air, we could see across the valleys to mountains over 30 miles away. The view was so rewarding, and patches of scarlet and crimson blooms stood out on the magnolias brightly, and at other moments we saw clusters of cirio cacti, or the glistening golden dome of a church. From our vantage point we gazed down along a dry sandy river-bed where a dusty peasant moseyed his cows along. By now we had all recovered from the celebrations in Mexico City, and the buzz of polyglot conversation and Mexican music again filled the van. We were going great guns towards Tamazulapan, nosing into the Great Dividing Range which stretches all the way to Panama. The rocks had been serried by centuries of drainage erosion into a pattern of cracks and runnels, and these steep slopes were simply too much for the van. It broke down nearly every day for the rest of the trip: this time casting all four fan-belts. Naturally we did not have enough spares, but Rein's ingenuity shone through, and while all the rest walked ahead to the next town, he and I eventually solved the problem by turning the old belts inside out, only to discover we had lost a number of power circuits too.

Flat camping-spots in these philistine mountains were like proverbial duck's teeth:- impossible to find. After the breakdown at a hopelessly late hour we nosed down a narrow gravel track which became ever steeper and clearly went nowhere, but with no place to turn we ended up muscling the van and trailer back up the hill, the first of many times on the expedition. That night we strung our tents out along a razor ridge of sloping rock, where a forsaken wind-tortured tree gripped with tenacious serpentine roots, like living Japanese art. A freezing breeze blew across the peak, but Rein, Frank, and I ignored the storm-clouds and slept out. The inevitable curious peasants and their dogs showed such a close interest that the girls withdrew to their tents until dawn, emerging to a heavy dew.

Our next goal was the ruins at Monte Alban just out of Oaxaca de Juárez. This place name proved such a tongue-twister that it had us all in stitches and for months afterwards Bill still could not get it right. At least it was a big enough place for Rein to fix the engine while I accompanied Debbie and Joan to the market-place to act as their translator but ended up carrying the groceries to boot. We spent most of the day exploring the extensive ruins at Monte Alban, with its old temples, pyramids, tunnels, and famous tombs and chambers, The ruins date back at least 24 centuries and formed the

Sacred Capital of the Zapotec Culture built on a levelled mountain-top. When the tombs were excavated in 1932 enormous quantities of treasure were recovered, along with works of art, crystal, and alabaster; we were able to see ancient carvings in bas-relief and glyphs and calendar signs. Frank disappeared down some of the tunnels and re-emerged in unexpected places. Pressing on up higher and higher we wound our way around the mountainsides on the most tortuous track. Tropical storm-clouds gathered darkly on the peaks, shading the light sickly yellows and greys on the crops of sisal, luxuriant forest, and occasional sections of sheer brown rock with an unworldly soporific effect. This is a land where villages and isolated hamlets are hidden in the heavy verdure and thickets of scrub, thorn bushes, and cactus. It all supports an apparent wealth of animals: sand-lizards and brilliantly coloured insects, bright leaf shoot green grasshoppers, moths and butterflies, stray mules and oxen, eagles floating high in the sky, and in the evenings the bats became evident as they preyed on the bugs attracted by the lights of the van. In this region around Mitla (which translates as Place of the Dead) our hard-fought progress was very slow and the only camping-space to be found was on a dry river-bed in the humid heat. Our days were largely given over to pressing ahead, but in the relaxing calm of the evenings, serious and stimulating conversations brought us together like any close-knit family. Stories of our homes and backgrounds and travelling adventures frequently endured long into the night. Serious discussions about the mores of nations were hotly pursued while other evenings were spent in hilarity and ribald exchanges, particularly of a sexist nature. Rein never let up gently goading the girls chauvinistically or confounding Frank's ecclesiastical philosophising. With such perfect nocturnal temperatures in the tropics it seemed such a pity to have to sleep in a tent, but the alternative was to wake up soaked and thoroughly mosquito-bitten, as I discovered the hard way.

The first place of any importance in this remote rugged sierra was

Tehuantepec with a largely Zapotec Indian, population, a matriarchal society. The women had brightly ribboned and braided hair and square sailor's collars to their highly decorative clothes. We noticed as we passed from village to village in all parts of Latin America where the. Indians still subsist that the costumes identify the village they come from, by the mere shape or style of a hat or the weave and colour of their clothing, and yet others were identifiable by their jewellery. We set off north across the isthmus with the intention of exploring the Yucatán. Unbeknownst to us then, a cyclone was building up in the Caribbean and had been responsible for blotting out the sun over the past two days. It was very difficult, to pull off the road in these parts because it either winds along precipitous mountain slopes or in the plains is elevated between huge ditches or even swamps as a result of the tropical conditions. We found a welcome a few miles short of Coatzacoalcos at a Jewish settlement, where we stayed at their synagogue in the middle of an orange grove, and for the first time since leaving Mexico City we were able to wash. These Mexican Jews were very friendly but otherwise indistinguishable from Mestizos. Up before sunrise to be first at the well, I had the breakfast cooking before most of the others were awake, but drew a pack of dogs, and a magnificent 800-pound hog came and cast its greedy eye on my arrangements. The smell of food drew more animals including black wasps the size of stag-beetles.

Leaving the kibbutz behind the road threaded across an enormous swamp in which men were gathering reeds for thatch, and boys were fishing, and hundreds of thin white cranes stood stock-still waiting for their breakfasts to come by. This swamp extends most of the way round the coast to the walled city of Campeche. At Villahermosa, despite horrendous mosquitoes which attacked as soon as anyone stood still, we passed several well spent hours at La Venta museum park which contains huge Olmec (Rubber People) heads and stone statues of a negroid race and many caged animals from the Tabasco Jungle: alligators, caymans, peccaries, deer, monkeys, ant-eaters, jaguars, and birds. Just as fascinating and somehow awesome and scary was the sight of a huge column of ants ten feet across spanning the path, to one side of which was their nest and to the other an enormous tree with fern-shaped leaves which they were ascending in their tens of millions and returning with cut sections of leaves up to 20 times their size.

Meanwhile a little social drama unfolded in the market-place. Bill, a professional model for Playboy magazine, discovered a stationer selling spring-back loose-leaf files with his picture on. The incredulous salesgirl was overwhelmed when Bill gave her a signed memento. She was really quite bewildered because she understood nary a word of what he was saying, but a kiss broke down the language barrier.

Most people who wish to see the awesome ruins left by the Olmecs, Toltecs, Aztecs, Mayas, and others, fly between airstrips at all villages and major sites because the jungle roads are such a terrible ordeal and agonizingly slow-going. Our major aim on this expedition was to visit these ancient sites overland, and accordingly we allowed ourselves a full day at Palenques's impressive Mayan ruins. The weather was really playing tricks on us and within minutes of camping a high wind tore down leaves and twigs and the sky turned a deep grey, the harbinger of a virtual cloud-burst, so that we sought the shelter of a friendly pub which possessed but a single cassette of American music. I found a forlorn French couple from Mauritius and gave them my tent since I was still foolhardy enough to sleep out. That was one of our best evenings, drinking and dancing, while the barman became thoroughly intoxicated and plied us with olives and peanuts and chilli salad.

The next morning we visited the ruins very early to have them to ourselves in the clear dawn light. Of the buildings as yet reclaimed from the jungle, the two most impressive are the Palace Complex with numerous rooms and dark passages bearing frescoes and sculpted iconography and a high watch-tower, and the Pyramid

Temple of the Inscriptions which protects a funerary crypt well below ground-level containing the Sarcophagus of the Sun God, rendered world-famous by Erik von Daniken's interpretation of it as an astronaut taking off. The slab is huge, approximately twelve feet by seven and nine inches thick, and the crypt is now illuminated. The forest hems the site in densely on all sides and a team of workmen are employed full-time just to keep the undergrowth in check, excepting only the useful orange trees. By following a path into the forest, I came upon further ruins exactly as the jungle had claimed them, completely hidden from casual view by the trees growing out of them. Debbie and I spent much of the time in conversation sitting on a pyramid to take advantage of any slightest breath of cooling air in the battering sultry heat. The invariably warm midday rains arrived on cue and poured from a leaden sky for the rest of the day. Resigned to a soaking I made a tour of the remaining relics and found our French friends, Françoise and Laurent, in the museum. They were real pilgrims discovering Central America on foot, without tents, cooking facilities, or even sleeping-bags. We spent the whole afternoon confined to the van in purgatory under the onslaught of mosquitoes which did not let up even when we went to bed, and I slept with my beekeeper's veil on despite ridicule from the others. Thus it was I that was awake when a couple of intruders came by in the small hours and attempted to get into bed with Kiki and Denah. Rein and I saw them off, but Kiki slept through the drama fortified with alcohol, whereas Denah was scared speechless.

The cyclone was bringing so much flooding to the States of Campeche, Quintana Roo, and Yucatán that it was making world news and we learned of the delights in store for us in the trackless mangrove swamps of Belize. In the morning we packed up in the drizzling rain, bade farewell to our friends Françoise and Laurent, and so left soggy Palenque behind us. All day long we drove through the aftermath of the deluge, a flat drowned land which contains much natural swamp ordinarily. The road was frequently inundated, but Mexican drivers speed on regardless of invisible kerbs and potholes. In consequence we passed more accidents than hitherto, mainly buses and trucks up-ended in the ditches. We saw for ourselves that, when truck tyres wear smooth, some drivers simply nail on patches from disused tyres. It is a completely different world!

We stopped at Francisco Escárcega, a mere hamlet, for provisions but the street market conditions were so vile that we bought only vegetables. During the afternoon we reached the coast near Champoton and jumped into the waters of Campeche Bay which were clean and cool and in a dead calm. Any relief from the oppressive humid heat was welcome even at the expense of getting salty into the bargain. Further along the road we entered a plague of locusts which darkened the sky for several miles, but here I doubt they do severe damage as the land is so fecund. They were being preyed on in their thousands by swallows which flitted about inches above the road heedless of the traffic until it was nearly upon them, when they had to abandon their pursuit and flit neatly over the windscreens at the last instant.

Once again we were stuck for a spot to camp, and whereas even at the best of times spaces are few, here even those were waterlogged and unusable. At last we found a truckers' stop at the Edzná Ruins where the mosquitoes were merciless. After supper, followed by coffee laced with vodka or cinnamon to disguise the taste of the water purifier, we adjourned to the truckers' bar where an amazing variety of big insects visited us. A praying mantis proved most diverting; it was easily 7 inches long and very nimble on its feet to everyone's discomfort or hilarity, depending on whom the insect was alighting at the time. Only Rein and I durst handle it and the rest of the group thought us weird not be scared of touching insects and animals.

The night was truly the worst some of us ever spent in our whole lives. The voracious mosquitoes were so thick in my tent that their whine was never out of my ears. Putting on heavy clothes was no solution as the heat and humidity were insufferable and in any case

I was in a bath of sweat already. I tried sleeping on my hands to protect them, and wore my beekeeper's veil, and rearranged the gaps under my mosquito-net, and tossed and turned the hot hours away. I arose several times during the night and walked up and down the road to cool off. In addition the dogs and chickens set up such a hullaballoo, and as we were on a main truck route the pantechnicons thundered past all night, audible for miles in both directions. By removing the mufflers power is saved, and this is universal practice in Mexico amongst truckers and some car drivers.

We passed through Kabah Ruins on our way to see the Xiu tribal home of Uxmal (which means Thrice Sacred). Uxmal is still in a good state of repair with five frescoes of the Rain God and is inhabited by iguanas and snakes. There are so many hundreds of ruins and more are being discovered every year all over Latin America, and we planned our itinerary to see the biggest and the best. The weather continued so torrid that the sweat trickled off us in streams: there was no relief and we all smelled bad. There was another tropical downpour all afternoon which was spent at Mérida. It is impossible to get lost there as the streets are arranged in rectangles, with numbers in lieu of names, but they are very narrow and were virtual watercourses. We found a schoolyard on the outskirts of town, and it was the only spot we saw which was not at least ankle-deep in water, so we pitched camp there. At last the weather relented to a balmy perfection and as an added bonus was free of insects save the fireflies sparking all round. The wildlife in these jungles was completely new to us. Most of it is fascinating and beautiful, e.g. little brightly coloured salamanders, curious well disguised insects such as grasshoppers simulating light green leaf shoots, magnificent iguanas a foot across and four feet long, and all kinds of colourful birds, especially kites and other birds of prey. The unbroken jungle is also unbelievably varied with wild flowers adding vivid splashes of colour. Just as we were waking the first little children began to arrive at the schoolhouse for a seven o'clock start, and surrounded us with eyes agog and began to stone us.

We drove on through flat jungle to Chichén-Itzá where the most famous elaborate Mayan and Toltec ruins stand in jungle clearings half a mile square on either side of the road. Brigitte and I went shopping in the village and were grossed out beyond belief by the butcher's shop. Everything in it, walls, ceiling, slabs, even the knives, was covered in a quarter-inch carpet of turquoise mould and crawling with bugs and maggots. The knives and meat hooks had obviously never been washed. While we were there three hobbled pigs were dragged squealing off a truck into a back room for slaughter, but we opted for chickens which involved no cutting. It took the whole day to explore the ruins, dominated by El Castillo, a square pyramid with stairs up each side, decorated with a gaping plumed serpent. There is a large ballcourt with a grandstand and two towering walls each containing a projecting carved stone ring over 20 feet up. The captain of the losing team faced decapitation as carvings there show. There are numerous temples, pyramids, ballcourts, and palaces, with quite a few retaining original paintwork, and a unique round observatory complex. There are a great many statues, enormous stone serpents and were-jaguars, and one typical form of altar depicts a supine Toltec propped up on his elbows with his knees drawn up, while his hands hold a bowl on his stomach as he gazed sternly over his left shoulder to the plaza below. These reclining Toltec statues represent heart sacrifice and are also found at Monte Alban. The raised cemetery is lined with a carved wall covered in thousands of bas-relief skull masks. The market-place is marked by extensive stone colonnades which once held up a thatched roof. Whenever we explored old ruins Frank and I investigated the pitch dark twisting tunnels cut by robbers or excavators, but most of them turned out to be dead ends. My investigative urge got the better of me when I skirted a precarious broken ledge of the nuns' cloisters with a 30-foot sheer drop below me, only to find that the nuns' cells were easily accessible from the opposite direction. It was a timeless sensation to look out over the canopy of virgin jungle from the top of a pyramid and see the occasional ruined temple thrust above the tree-tops.

Today it was Bill's birthday and we made a big thing about it and had a proper birthday party with a cake, candles, and a card. Whenever one of us had a birthday, even under the most arduous of circumstances, we managed to drum up the basic components for a celebration. The weather was just right for it: the cyclone was receding into the Atlantic Ocean and we had another perfect evening, without insects.

When Frank and I took down our tent next morning, we found we had put it on a big, black, hairy spider. It was easily five inches across and in a bad temper, and when we let it go it charged us but went right on by to freedom. Later in the day we saw a migration of such spiders crossing the road, mostly even larger. By mid-morning it was clear we were in for blue skies and a hot dry day. For several days past, whenever the van stopped it had been festooned with laundry hung out to air, and today it finally dried out in temperatures in excess of 100 degrees Fahrenheit, while we explored the Mayan town of Valladolid. Our journey progressed through level exuberant jungle 20 to 25 feet high, with a great deal of agriculture, and even a gold mine. We passed small villages in jungle clearings with thatched adobe huts surrounded by stockades of low palings. Even in towns these were quite usual. We also saw an enormous snake, which might have been a python, crossing our path ahead of us. At Nueva X-Can we ventured onto our first dirt-road which cut through the jungle in a straight line due east to the extensive Cobá Ruins. (Eventually 17,000 of the 25,000 road miles we covered in 16 countries was on dirt-roads.) We were halted by road-builders who had apparently planted dozens of young palm trees in the road. Fortunately Frank had seen service in the jungles of South Viet-Nam as a road-building engineer, and he explained the paradox. The initial task the Mexicans had was to level the road, preparatory to paving it, by pattern drilling all the flat spots to the right depth. Then hard-core explosive is packed in the holes and sealed in with plugs of palm leaves until 100 yards is ready for simultaneous, blasting, and that is what we had seen. Since we regarded the road as impassable we piled out into 120 degrees of heat and sought refuge along forest paths, which were entirely hemmed in overhead and to the sides and were refreshingly cool, and we used our time to gather a stock of firewood. Eventually we could wait no longer and walked over the explosives while the van bounced over them with Rein at the wheel.

We stopped next at the Maya-Toltec ruins on the beach and cliffs at Tulum, dedicated to the worship of the Setting Sun. The buildings are all wider at the top than the bottom, and the main temple is quite impressive. The well preserved anthropomorphic wall paintings are easily discernible after eight centuries of neglect, despite the loss of small patches due to algae and erosion. A city wall of white stone encompasses the ruins, and the sights and sounds from a vantage point on the highest temple surmounting the cliff-top are of the surging Caribbean surf and a carpet of green jungle, both riffled by a fresh sea breeze. Tied up at one of the souvenir stalls hard by the ruins were a pair of kittenish furry coati-mundis with wiffly noses and dainty prehensile paws, but they were neither, tame nor defenceless as I tangibly discovered when one dug its incisors sharply into a knuckle. Coconut palms grow along the waterfront, and we cashed in on the incredibly cheap fresh coconuts. Brigitte definitely came prepared to spend a small fortune on souvenirs, large and small, and here it was an outsize woven blanket, which she proudly displayed to us.

CHAPTER THREE

BELIZE

Belize, formerly British Honduras, was still a British Crown Colony at the time of our visit, and is a tiny little country hardly opened up and not yet entirely explored. Heavy rains result in a mantle of forest over 90% of the country. Dense unpopulated mangrove swamps covers a fifth of the country, the littoral and north-east districts, but the western border with Guatemala is mountainous. Off the coast lies the second largest coral reef in the world, a major tourist attraction, particularly its islands, called 'cays.' The population of Belize is a mere 150,000, of whom half are Creoles, and a quarter are the indigenous Black Caribs and Mayas, who include the Kekchi Indians, a Mayan sub-culture with an independent language. The remainder are largely Mennonites, Arabs, Chinese, Waika Indians, and settlers from India and North America. The original settlers were British wood-cutters providing logs to make textile dyes, and exporting mahogany later on. To this day there are only eight towns in the country and 400 miles of dirt-road between them, but there are lots of waterways, which are navigable by motor-boat to a considerable extent. One of the banes of the country is its tempestuous weather, hurricanes and heavy rain. The country does not export much other than sugar, bananas, citrus fruits, and timber, and the national average income is less than ten dollars per week.

The Mexican border port, Ciudad Chetumal, is reputed to be a tax-free haven for electrical goods, but this proved a bad joke as prices were higher than in Europe or the United States. We met a bunch of British R.E.M.E. who had a decidedly low opinion of Belize. They had come from the British garrison at Belize airport and were in high spirits at the prospect of 24 hours leave over the border down Mexico way, and gave us a crate of English N.A.A.F.I. beer. As soon as we were in Belize the scenery changed to wetlands, zinicote and mahogany forests, and then continuous mangrove swamp. We made camp within an hour's drive of Belize City on a sandy strand surrounded by mangroves and swamp waters. This area had a lugubrious quality but the weather was perfect and only a few gnats were out to bother us. The people we saw were largely Maya Indians and Creoles, and their villages were unlike those in Mexico and were far more expansive, giving each home a couple of acres of cleared land. The houses themselves were constructed on stilts. The country is poor but it has enormous agricultural potential, and on the cleared wet pastures were herds of horses and cattle. It made a welcome change to hear radio programmes in English, the native tongue being Creole English. Hitherto the only English programme we could pick up had been the Radio Moscow propaganda aimed at an acquiescent underdog audience among the millions of disenchanted Latin Americans and other races.

Belize City, the former capital, is one huge shanty slum with sea-level ditches which serve as smelly slow-draining sewers, dependent on the tides to flush them out; and the population is largely composed of African Creoles, dirt poor and as squalid as their shacks. A guard was needed on the van as everyone was a potential thief. Many of the Creoles offered us dope or cheap watches and cameras stolen from previous tourists. Frank was robbed by a couple of them who forced him into a building, took his watch, and emptied his pockets while pressing a machete across his throat. Granted he looked naïve and timorous, but the town is the blackest hole I have ever seen and has a reputation for total lawlessness. I was appalled by the ignorance and complete lack of understanding displayed by the other members of the group, except Rein, regarding the locals wherever we went. In particular they felt condescending and patronising towards the 'poor' Mexicans and Belizeans, and constantly took 'cute' photographs of filthy children with sores and rotten teeth, or peasant women at stalls of low-grade fruit. They branded me as cruel for not sharing their pity for the thousands of beggars and scavenging dogs that searched us out. They frequently recalled how at Palenque I kicked at a mangy distempered mutt which was stealing meat from the chopping block while I was preparing it, and how at Chichén-Itzá I dispassionately put a badly mutilated bird out of its misery against their wishes. Apart from Rein and Frank, the others seemed entirely unaware of the risk of injury or disease they ran by encouraging advances from all and sundry people and animals, and yet they panicked at lacewings fluttering in their faces.

On the day we visited Belize City the local football teams were the star attraction and I helped a few penniless urchins sneak over the barbed wire fence into the grounds. After the foetid septic conditions of the city, the common interest was to go for a swim, and we left with a Negro boy as a guide who had been hanging around hoping for money. His open sexual advances towards Kiki and Denah caused much humorous giggling, but sensing I did not indulge his caprices, he kept giving me surreptitious kicks and punches which only increased the girls' innocent mirth. The boy directed us down a mud road onto the shore and into two feet of water, whereupon a couple of tall Creoles holding machetes emerged from the high reeds beside the path, which further alarmed Frank to say the least, but they helped us. We heaved and strained and eventually pushed the van out, at the cost of only a lost shoe or two in the deep puddle. The beach was a great disappointment, a clayey mudflat with fiddler crabs, human filth, and debris everywhere, some no doubt from the city but mainly as a result of the cyclone. Off the coast an almost unbroken coral reef and the cays prevent sewage from being adequately diluted and dispersed. We returned to town and I reclaimed my seat from the boy who was riding high on his popularity with the girls, who never comprehended for an instant they were merely objects to satisfy his image of his own virility.

The little s.o.b. still gave me sly punches and abuse from outside the van and the girls added their complaints to Rein that they wanted their friend to stay on the expedition to Panama. I never lived down my image as an ogre.

We had to change our plans owing to continuous serious flooding washing out the dirt-tracks to the north and south, and thus we went west towards Belmopan, the new purpose-built capital since 1970, but it too was cut off by road closures. Apart from the natural beauty and abundant luxuriance of the land, the Black population is completely sanguine about being one of the poorest nations in the world. We ran on through the savannah grassland, pine ridges, and high canopied forest, stopping at a secluded gravel pit close by a fast river a few miles short of the border at San Ignacio. The chance of a bath was not to be overlooked and we all went down to the swift Belize River, but the Swiss girls stood on the bridge and waited for the cover of darkness before washing. Although our stay in Belize had been somewhat marred by circumstance, the country is indubitably one of the most beautiful in the world with a healthy climate to match. For our last night there, Rein, Frank, and I slept out and the silhouettes and sounds of the forest closed in around us.

CHAPTER FOUR

GUATEMALA

Of the Central American republics Guatemala is the most Indian. Half the country is still virtually unpopulated including the northern third, the Department of El Petén, which was so impenetrable owing to dense hardwood forests, swamps, and mountains, that it took the Spanish nearly two centuries before they finally conquered the native Itzás in 1697. The land is still practically unused except for a little logging and the bleeding of chiclé, used as a base for chewing-gum. Most of the nationals are Indians, descendants of the Mayas and other cultures, and the western highlands are exclusively Indian territory and the loveliest part of Central America, full of steep volcanoes and jungles and the most colourful Indians in all America with scarcely any idea of profit in trade. They have their own languages, regional fashions, and semi-Christian pagan worship. About half the Guatemalans can read and write to some extent, and generally theirs is a very poor vegetable diet based on maize (cornpone and tortillas). The two great scourges of the nation are endemic diseases, such as amoebic dysentery, and earthquakes, both of which affect every generation. Coffee and cotton are the main exports, but the total reliance on agriculture is a thing of the past, as the petrochemical and mineral wealth is slowly being realised, and marble is being quarried in large amounts.

To reach the border we had only to cross the undulating mountain ridges of El Cayo District. We thought the roads in Belize were bad but in Guatemala we came in for a rude awakening. Right on the border the electronic ignition switch was shaken apart, and later in the day the exhaust pipe was twice shaken off and substantially battered out of shape, and for the second time a universal joint broke up; such was the condition of the roads. We drove through the blazing midday heat finding nowhere to stop until at last we pulled into a gravel quarry, which we seemed to do fairly often. At moments like these when the temperature soared above 100 degrees Fahrenheit, the van and bushes nearby were decked with damp clothing and sleeping-bags which got wet during the daily downpours or just due to the prevailing 85% humidity of the air. One became accustomed to smelly clothes and musty fungus on canvas and shoe-leather alike. The road from the border to Flores was a ribbon of clay 80 miles long, pocked and cratered everywhere, and by turns dry with choking dust or slippery as a mudpan with yellow puddles of ungaugeable depth. We arrived in Flores in torrential rain with a flat tyre and sick noises emanating from under the van: after all we had covered 4,500 miles. Debbie, Joan, Brigitte, and I went shopping in the market which was just a sea of silt underfoot and sheets of black plastic overhead and above the stalls. The food, particularly the greengroceries, was very cheap, and haggling over prices in a group was more fun than usual.

We were driving back the way we came to.be nearer the great Mayan ruins of Tikal when we discovered 'El Gringo Perdido', a camping-ground run by an American who had closed the place to go on holiday on the morrow. Rein did some smooth talking and we were admitted. The shady Lost Gringo camp-site was beautifully appointed with well kept lush green lawns and a restaurant on the shore of Lake Petén-Itzá, in the middle of which stands the island town of Flores. As we drove in we saw a deer and. could hear the strident calls of parrots. As usual I set up just my mosquito-net, but I was running a fever and collapsed on my cot until supper time. Afterwards as I lay in a dysenteric stupor I was vaguely aware of Kiki, Denah, Joan, and Rein talking into the night and passing around the whiskey as usual.

We allowed ourselves a whole day to explore Tikal Ruins. The heat and humidity were already extreme by the time we arrived at the customary museum at the entrance. This was the highlight of our tour so far as this greatest of Mayan cities covers a couple of square miles, far too great an area to be deforested, so that the ruins arise in small clearings in nearly unbroken high forest. The ancient city contained a major acropolis dominated on either side by pyramids surmounted by huge temples, and to either side were other buildings, palaces, and complex structures, including a few ballcourts for three-man teams, whose losing captain was sacrificed by the excision of his beating heart. The players wore yokes of rope from maguey briars around their waists as part of the ritual before, during, and after play. The whole place is amazingly well preserved, considering it was claimed by the jungle a millenium ago. There are carved walls and momoliths, raised paved roads, and a couple of hundred buildings. There is so much archaeological work to do that many mounds and ruins still have trees growing all over them disrupting the stonework, although a lot of work was in evidence.

The tallest ancient structure in the New World is here, a temple 215 feet high including the extremely steep man-made pyramidal base, as it was awesome to behold this tremendous 'Temple 4' rising out of the flat jungle a quarter of a mile away from where I stood. The ruins were so extensive that several hours exploration did not do them justice. From 100 feet up in the undisturbed panoply between the clearings was the constant noise of parrots and other birds and the howling of monkeys. The sizes and varieties of spiders and insects had to be seen to be believed. I saw little lizards everywhere, but when in the shade it was imperative to keep moving to avoid the agony of swarming mosquitoes. Ants of all kinds were present in their millions, anything from a hundredth of an inch to an inch in length, and all shades of red, brown, and black, even white! They bit like fury when I sat on them and they ran about in my underwear, but I had to laugh when Joan and Brigitte suffered the same indignity. We stopped at the museum which was the best yet with very fine examples of earthenware, and hand-worked bone and jade. There were pictorial friezes and inscriptions, finely carved gods and monoliths and a reconstructed tomb with its original bones and artefacts, and historical information.

So it was back to 'The Lost Gringo' for an afternoon of perfect weather, where we jumped in the lake and had a battle. Kiki, Denah, and Joan found a large dugout, and amid great hilarity Joan's attempts to bat me with the flat end of the paddle had the opposite effect, hitting Kiki on the head with the handle. You should have seen those girls paddle. They, didn't have a clue and really did not have their act together, and could not manage a straight line. I swam twice as fast as they could row, notwithstanding the tyre tubes around my midriff. Eventually I sank the canoe at which they started to caterwaul. We called a truce, and I went off to make friends with the exquisite slatey-headed Amazons, macaques, and scarlet macaws which lived in the thatched patio restaurant.

It rained virtually every day from the time we left Mexico City for the rest of the trip in Central America, and in the evenings this served to concentrate us all in the van, along with the creepy-crawlies attracted by the light. After a while I took no notice at all, because most of the time the biting flies and mosquitoes were absent. I think the late evenings were Rein's favourite time. He certainly nearly monopolised the discussions with the girls on every subject under the sun. Before we left the camp, we were shewn around its private menagerie, containing a variety of tame parrots, caymans, a charming two-year old ocelot, and other animals. The deer we had seen there was a pet so tame that it would feed out of our hands and let us stroke it. We drove to Flores on its island along a pontoon road across Lake Petén-Itzá to shop in a temperature of 105 degrees already by nine a.m.. In this extreme heat and humidity our lunches tended to be very light, but the stop presented a very important chance to dry out our clothes, and as the van became claustrophobically hot and stuffy, every chance to get out was taken. All day we pressed south along winding mountainous jungle tracks. The locals travel on foot or on horseback. We saw many horses and cowboys, often trailing several horses or mules behind them as pack-animals transporting sacks of maize. Even if a beast was lame or weak it still had to hobble on under a full four hundredweight load. We made good time all day, and passed a great rudimentary wooden bridges, temporary by nature, often with the concrete foundations of a new bridge abandoned pro tempore. Since we crossed into Guatemala we had not seen a paved road or even a flat stretch over 20 yards long.

Out of the blue at Dolores, a tiny village, we were stopped by a lancecorporal in the Guatemalan Military Police who asked to be given a lift a mile or so along the road to a military checkpoint. He showed his gratitude by ordering the six-man guard to surround us with machine-guns cocked and aimed. There followed an increasingly serious situation, no mere routine check. Guatemala's recent history has been extremely turbulent and reflects a vicious struggle, betwixt Socialism and Capitalism. At the time of our expedition

General García was the President and presumably the army, was a little nervous, but; I think that just plain greed and corruption at the barrel of a gun were the reason for what was simply armed robbery. The van, roof rack, and trailer were searched. Our passports were examined, but the N.C.O. was clearly illiterate as he studied as many of them upside-down as the right way up. Frank had his penknife and shoe-laces confiscated without a receipt or compensation as 'prohibited articles'!! The rest of us were allowed to keep our penknives and shoe-laces. The N.C.O. doubtless required the articles himself. He also dumped out Bill's green toilet bag and proclaimed that it was a prohibited military article by virtue of its colour, whereupon the young private who had been clambering about on the roof recalled four green bags, of which Bill and Frank owned one each and the others were mine. First these and then the remaining kitbags were emptied and searched, my poncho had been taken. All this had delayed us a couple of hours already, and Rein and I argued the toss many times with the pig-ignorant boorish N.C.O. The girls took it lightly to begin with and played hopscotch to pass the time, but the nastiness of the situation sank in when they were even refused permission to relieve themselves, and personal objects such as pottery figurines were trodden underfoot and broken, and reasonable requests and questions on our part fell on deaf ears. The stand-off lasted the whole day until an officer turned up in his jeep and I acted as spokesman. He was more reasonable and ordered our property to be returned to us, and we packed up and drove off, short only Frank's knife and shoe-laces.

We drove away through the late afternoon along a deteriorating road, but there were more signs of habitation. The going was extremely slow, and bumping over pot-holes and negotiating the oncoming trucks took considerable time and caution. Night fell while we were still sliding and jolting along this most primitive narrow clay track through San Luis. For the next hour we all kept our eyes peeled for a possible camp-site finally chancing upon a village football field with an absolutely ideal thatched shelter, which saved us the work of erecting tents. So we stayed and drew quite a crowd of peasants who stood at arm's length, watching us prepare for supper and bed. They were already up and among our things when we woke before dawn.

We moved out down a road so amazingly bad that we were obliged to get out several times and push or just walk past craters and slurry. The van bucked and heaved over the broken rocks and slid and lurched in the slippery clay and managed a top speed of 15 m.p.h. once or twice. We passed several little villages and a police check at a bridge, but all in all we made very slow time. The van grounded many times, the poor quality Mexican universal joint broke up, and we pulled into a little village while Rein fixed the damage. He reported that the exhaust system was also practically bashed to pieces. We had managed only 48 miles but at least we ended up early at a natural beauty spot, camping under the huge modern bridge over the River Dulce, the outlet from Lake Izabal into the Gulf of Honduras. The bridge was a wonderful feat of engineering, but is totally silent by night as no-one dares risk the ghastly roads then. We saw evidence of numerous accidents and spilt loads, but the commonest sign was a clear trail of oil down the road from split sumps. The stupid locals never learn that 'macho' driving here will cost them a new sump, or even a whole new truck, and yet they swung past us like lemmings over a cliff, which availed them no net gain as we caught them up at the next rickety bridge of wooden piles supporting a simple wooden platform with broken planks for the wheels to roll on and no sides. At some of the wider or deeper rivers we saw defunct or even sunken iron ferries.

We all swam in the river, and I very, nearly lost my life. I suddenly found myself seized by the current, passing along the bank at about 15 m.p.h., and barked my shin painfully on a submerged rock. I did not mind though; it was my salvation. Such a perfect opportunity to do our laundry was not let pass and our clothes were dry in minutes due to a hard breeze and the great heat. Our regular nightly discussions gave way for once to puzzles and guessing games such as charades, suitably aided by a bottle of Guatemalan 'Old Friend' whiskey. The night was made wretched by mosquitoes and I climbed into my sleeping-bag for the first time in ten days; just as well, as I discovered it had gone quite mouldy in the tropical humidity, with grey-green blotches. In the morning I was awakened by the honking of a gaggle of geese and at first I could not locate them, but then I was rewarded with the sight of a skein of a few dozen flying in perfect formation over the bridge. For an hour we bobbed along the remainder of the track through hilly jungles, but there was widespread evidence of tree felling, and royal palms were often left to dominate the scenery along with the few remaining very tall trees standing in rough useless hilly undergrowth. Then we reached the main road from Guatemala City to the Gulf of Honduras and the difference was amazing. We turned southwest and rode smoothly along to Teculatán where we stopped for lunch in the beautiful botanical plaza. The countryside we were then passing through consisted of rolling hills and the distant mountains of the high Sierra Madre with clouds on their shoulders. It was very pretty and green but there was no more virgin forest. The foot-hills were cut into low canyons, somewhat reminiscent of the Colorado and Utah Badlands, but here the land was free-range green pasture with occasional glimpses of cattle. We drove high into the mountains amid the thorny scrub and endured several police stops along the way without any unpleasantries — unless a six-dollar bribe to let us pass is considered unpleasant. We camped amongst the thorn bushes by a river, and were attacked by hordes or tiny biting flies which were not dissuaded by liberally applied insect repellant. Then I noticed the avenues of ants everywhere, particularly under my bed. Happily I found that a few drops of bug dope in their path was sufficient to turn them back. In any case I was rained out and resorted to Frank's tent during the night.

We made it to Guatemala City very early the next day, after cruising through beautiful and varied countryside, which changed from one mountainside to the next; sometimes arable, other times barely pastoral, fit only for coarse grazing. At the capital we discovered yet more trouble with the van — some of the tyres had been gashed on the terrible roads and had to be changed. The city is a huge, modern, and apparently wealthy metropolis, and some of its buildings are adorned with vast frescoes and mosaic scenes. Since the severe earthquake in February 1976, a lot of desolation has been visible to all visitors, but restoration has often been extremely good and has provoked fascinating architecture such as the blue and white Museum of Modern and Contemporary Art, constructed in utterly non-conformist bizarre shapes and curves complementing its hilltop setting in the Parque Aurora.

From time to time, since we could not possibly cover every famous ruin or cultural event we put it to the vote where we would go next; and so we reached a democratic decision to forgo lunch and make for Panajachel, on the shore of Lake Atitlán, one of the most beautiful lakes in the world, changing colours constantly, hidden by purple and olive green highlands and active volcanoes (after one of which the lake gets its name). The scenic view kept on improving all the time as the road became higher and distinctly more dangerous, and as we climbed further so it grew cooler, and the fragmented clouds collected and drifted between the mountain-tops like the trails of steam from the volcanoes. The climb was extremely steep and whenever the road passed over a bridge or close to the edge the view was panoramic and there was always a green mountainside looking down on us. Wherever we looked there were wild flowers, very tall trees, some very odd evergreens, and craggy sandstone cliffs left like scars marking past landslides. In the valleys we could look down on the chocolate brown rivers in flood, laden with the very dark rich earth from this region. We had climbed to nearly 8,000 feet when the van stalled due to lack of oxygen, and by this time it had begun to rain. There was nothing for it but to push the van. All afternoon, at every steep bit we got out in the rain and pushed, soaked and shivering. Even so the view was so spectacular that we forgot our discomfort and eventually ended up walking several miles through incomparable picturesque vistas over the hills and pine woods and volcanoes towering up to nearly 11,500 feet. We passed several Maya-Quiché Indians who came out of their isolated hovels to gaze at us and grinned at the jocular novelty of watching Gringos walking past in the pouring rain. Having struggled right up to the summit we climbed back in the van, but descending the steep gradients finally wore out the brakes which reeked appallingly, so we climbed in and out like yo-yos. Eventually Rein drove several miles ahead to reach a lower level and left us all to stroll down the mountain and thus we encountered four German travellers in two cars. Known to each other they had met by chance and were celebrating their happy reunion with a few drinks. We learned from them we were still ten miles short of Panajachel. We had no idea that Rein had left us to walk, and Joan, supposing she had only to round the next corner, had left her dress in the van to keep it dry. I found a four-foot by two-foot leaf to help cover her confusion as there was considerable local traffic on the road as well as pedestrian Indians. The Germans declined to give any of us lifts, so that by the time we caught up to the van we had climbed so many steep hills that we were ready to drop, by which time also the rain had stopped and our clothes had dried on our backs. The clouds engulfing us were so low that the mountains we were surrounded by were lost to view, and although Lake Atitlán was very close below us it was lost in a grey blanket. Two hundred yards further on, at a sharp turn, we came upon the scene of a serious accident: two of the drinking Germans who had sped past us in the rain were now sitting despondently on what remained of their wrecked rented sports car. They had a suffered a high speed collision head-on with a colourful local bus also a total write-off, now well and truly wedged in the ditch. Most of the passengers were standing staring all round the sports car. In this country traffic offences are covered by criminal law, and for a certainty the two men, still chugging beer would be jail-bound as bankrupts in the very near future. Jails in Latin America are notoriously dreadful, but Gringos are given particularly short shrift resulting in rampant extortion of bribes from the relations of the poor miscreant, who may even be innocent. The money is supposed to provide better conditions for the prisoner or a bribe to let him go, but the relations are milked to the maximum, and none of the money benefits the prisoner.

Inevitably on such a long trip there was a phantom farter. It was one of the Swiss girls, but she admitted to it, and many times a day as the noxious fumes reached our nostrils we loudly exclaimed her name in chorus. She took it very well and at last she explained she could not help it, as she had once had an operation which affected her self-control. At dusk we pulled onto the shore of Lake Atitlán at Panajachel, and by chance had arrived on market day. We were all delightfully surprised by the sheer size of its market selling mainly works of art, handicrafts, silver and jewellery, brightly decorated clothes and tapestries and blankets. The homespun clothing of the men and women was the most colourful and varied I have ever seen. Every bodice, shawl, dress, shirt, jacket, and pair of trousers was fantastically and ornately embroidered in coloured patterns. Being Saturday night the locals were living it up and dance music and firecrackers sounded until way after midnight. The beach offered us no haven but we found a camp-ground in the town centre, that is to say, it had a cold water spigot and offered the shelter of a high hedge.

Climbing out of Panajachel next morning we only travelled a mile before we had to get out and walk again. However the view over the lake and beautiful beaches with lovely villas and hotel sites made up for it. Across the placid lake were several conical volcanoes, the highest of which, Atitlán (11,489 feet), was capped with an eerie halo of white cloud. Along the lake-shore are over a dozen Indian villages, some named after the Apostles. Walking on we came up to a 400-foot waterfall, broken into a series of splashing cascades, but loveliest of all was the song of the nearly extinct quetzal bird, the national emblem. The bird is rarely ever seen, but is hunted for its glorious plumage, especially its magnificent trailing tail feathers. The young have an incredible means of self-preservation from the moment they hatch in their nests built over water in the dwindling rain forest around the lake: when danger threatens they climb out of the nest and drop into the water. Even the featherless chicks can swim instinctively. Their song is just as strange, and consists of a clear descending cadenza of notes, sounding midway between a squeaky axle and a peal of glass bells, almost a trill. The last surviving quetzals share the lake with another unique bird found nowhere else, the poc, which is a large flightless water-grebe. We did a repeat of the previous day, climbing in and out of the van on these almost impassable inclines to Chichicastenango, right in the centre of the Maya-Quiché highlands whose inhabitants are splendidly attired. The men wear a short-waisted highly embroidered jacket and knee-length britches in black, a colourful woven sash, and an embroidered bandana called a mecapal around their foreheads, while the women wear huipiles, the local flouncy blouses, with red embroidery and black or brown skirts with dark blue stripes. The preponderance of red in Mayan weavings reflects their belief in its power against the evil eye. Sunday market, draws crowds from all over the highlands, and Indians walk as much as 100 miles bearing loads sometimes larger than themselves. It was the biggest and best market I saw in the whole continent and is centred in the main plaza, 200 yards square and spreads out onto the church steps and into the winding cobbled alleys of white houses with bright red title roofs. Perched up in the mountains there were fine views high over the valley from the outer street corners. The market traded mainly in hand-woven textiles, tapestries, clothes, and wall hangings, and all in the brightest colours. There were also stalls selling excellent leatherwork, decorated machetes, fruit and vegetables (some quite strange, e.g. sweet bright pink bananas), meat, pottery, and bric-á-brac. On the steps of the Santo Tomás church, shored up since the 1976 earthquake, there was a flower market and smoke wafted from incense burning as part of pagan Indian rituals, which involve scattering flower petals to one of their Mayan gods. The pressing throng began to ease in the afternoon just as the sun showed its face for the first time that day. Without expensive camera equipment I could not hope to get any frontal shots of the Indian costumes, each one being different from every other. We could have spent days here, and some of us planned to return privately when the expedition was over. Joan's hobby was weaving and naturally she bought quite a variety of loomwork as did we all, and examined our purchases and declared them to be of very fine quality and in rare styles which are normally impossible to find. We had bought them mainly for the visual impact of the rich dyes and native Indian designs and motifs.

The van made a valiant effort to manage the mountain roads once again, but by now we had perfected the art of jumping from the moving van before it stalled, and Rein established a shuttle service, taking three journeys up the mountain, first with the luggage, then with the trailer, and finally fetched us up. The van developed a new fault, a ruptured tank, spilling a couple of gallons of fuel per hour. Considering Rein spent hours each day fixing the van, which always broke down over a ditch or puddle, he never lost his cool; but his problems were only just unfolding because mechanical problems nearly scuppered the expedition as we fell further and further behind our schedule. After supper our regular discussion group polished off a fresh bottle, of rum this time, but Montezuma's Revenge had struck down the entire company and temperance was considered the cure. The point was seriously being discussed while the rum was speedily being knocked back, the irony of it going completely over the heads of our bibulous women.

Now we had to make up lost time, and rose early, packed up, and had breakfast within half an hour of sunrise, but true to form with oxygen starvation the van lasted only as far as the next steep hill. I took the chance to walk on ahead, and for the next hour I slipped through a time warp. Apart from the tarmac road, the Mayas seem to have kept everything in their traditional ways. The colourful clothes and the wooden or adobe thatched huts provide a link with the forgotten past. The little children shrieked with surprise and delight as I passed their shacks and fetched others to come and see. They were either taken by my bushy red beard, or great height, or perhaps my shorts, here a taboo which attracts a heavy fine. All the Indians are very pleasant, though the girls are shy, but every one of them greeted me. The road wound around a mountainside and I could discern the irregular cultivated flat patches of maize and other crops amid the pine forests. The reverie ended when the van caught me up. We made good time to Chimaltenango, our shopping stop at the native market, and again were entranced by the brilliant colours and typical sounds. The men here wear woven skirts with or without calf-length trousers, and if they have no mule carry huge loads on their backs with the strain taken by the mecapal strap around the forehead, and walk bent double under packs which may be twice as big as themselves.

    We drove all afternoon towards the Honduran border and it rained a good deal on the way giving rise to a new aspect of the mountains: the peaks were draped in mantles of mist which resembled deep snow, and little fragments were detached by the breeze and floated along giving an unreal impression of white ack-ack smoke. Everywhere were the wrecks of crashed vehicles, which had been put to good use by the locals as hen coops or firewood stores, and one upturned van served as a family home. We camped outside Chiquimula, and it being Brigittes's birthday, in addition to making up a card for her, Bill and Frances served up bananas flambéed in whiskey to celebrate the event. This attracted a larger than usual cluster of children, who were far less shy than most of our quotidian audiences.

We elected to take a renownedly dangerous short cut direct to Copán in Honduras, arguably our downfall, but the van never arrived so most of us missed seeing the magnificent Mayan ruins there. The sheer ruggedness of the extremely poor road made it the bumpiest and most hair-raising part of the trip. We travelled on a track hugging the mountain on one side and overlooking a sheer drop on the other. Going around the outside of a hair-pin bend we met a truck coming down. We passed more by luck than judgement without a chance to hit the brakes. The road worsened the further up we went, and before long we found ourselves trudging through the muddiest sections and up the hardest inclines, and wading the rivers just in case the van should be tipped by the rain-swollen flooded streams which were quite numerous and all without bridges. A mere four miles from the border we rounded a steep bend and stopped. Ahead of us a pick-up van was stuck two feet deep in the middle of a 35-foot ford. We pushed it out and made one of our democratic decisions as to whether we should chance it or turn back. Committing ourselves, we unloaded the trailer and carried all the articles across. Rein then rapidly drove across quite successfully only to get stuck on the muddy bank. With a few heaves we got going again and several streams and muddy slopes later stopped outside a police checkpoint at the little village of Caporja. The engine died: it had had enough; and Rein diagnosed a defunct fuel pump. He lay in the inevitable puddle to fit a new pump but that did not help. Next Rein declared the problem to be a faulty carburettor, somewhat more serious, so while he tickled its private parts we set up camp.

I declined a tent, preferring to fasten my poncho taut like a lean-to, which the village children found most bizarre. All afternoon Rein dismantled and reassembled the carburettor and finally declared it sound. Upon starting the engine there was a terrific explosion filling the van with sheets of flame and setting it ablaze. Panic-stricken we rushed around for water, even reconstituted milk, and put it out. Every time Rein started up the engine, more flames flared up, indicating a backfire. Rein diagnosed either a cracked piston or a faulty-valve, work enough for two days. We all found plenty to occupy our time, exploring the village with its three shops, playing cards, mending clothes, or just reading and talking. I was very sick with amoebic dysentery, but at the time I still attributed it to the high levels of Chloromine T purifier Bill was putting in our drinking water, because it has the same effect and kills off all organisms in the gut indiscriminately. I took the advice of Bill and the two doctors, Kiki and Denah, and went on a futile fast to let my insides settle down. It was in fact exactly the worst thing to do and an increased diet and a lot to drink would have been much the better thing.

The village square like so many others contained a spreading ceiba (or kapok) tree. These trees reach enormous sizes and can live for centuries and it is quite likely that a number of villages were settled originally in the shade of their vast ceibas, which have a spread of 100 feet. The males of the village gradually filled the square as their working day was done and took their ease just standing around or sitting on the thick twisted roots of the ceiba tree. And so we found ourselves the focus of attention of the whole village, who watched whatever we did, a semi-circle of blank-eyed Mestizos. Pigs and dogs and chickens and ducks ranged freely, and occasionally small groups of cattle were driven through the village by young boys with dogs. One boy in particular, about ten years old, had been expertly cantering around bareback on a large bay, going about his business in the village and was later seen riding behind a herd of cattle with a switch in hand, which he used to split the herd and drive each half to a different destination. While we watched, a crowd of unwashed children climbed an orange tree and gathered skirts and shirts full of fruit, but disturbed a wasps' nest and fled. A tiny little tot was badly stung on the head and the whole village hooted with laughter at her. The reckless cowboy took his switch and whacked at the nest and obviously destroyed it. He ran off dancing and wildly flapping his bare arms around his head and was clearly stung many times, and as he retired scratching down the street, he maintained a consciously dignified expression while glancing sidelong at the villagers, hooting with derision at him too.

After dark I started one of my green cold-chemical lights, which totally amazed the locals who use sap-soaked tapers of pitch-pine, or log fires (or flashlights if they are lucky) after dark, but for the most part they simply learn to do without. I started a game for the village boys by hurling the lightstick high in the air and for an hour they chased it all round the square with shrieks of delight, blundering into tents and tripping over roots until they were tired, and then solemnly returned it to me. Staying amongst these dirt poor people and seeing how they lived in apparent happiness was for us all a deeply moving experience. They had never heard of telephones, or sanitation, or listened to a radio, and in common with the great mass of the Latin population are 800 years behind Europe in terms of social developments. We pulled straws to do an hour's guard each on the vehicle, and Kiki and I drew the last, watch which caused her a little embarrassment as everyone was aware she regarded me with some uncertainty, quite unnecessarily. When the discussion group broached bottles of rum and whiskey, it was my cue to hit the sack. Kiki and I were woken at four o'clock and there was already a cacophony at this hour. Cockerels were crowing and dogs were barking at each other, and among the tents pigs were grunting and squealing as they fought over cornhusks. The majority of the village was up before dawn, and incongruous with the pitch darkness were the sounds of neighbours greeting. each other or peasants clearing the phlegm from their throats and spitting in the street.

On the second day Rein took the engine to pieces and declared nothing had broken but that heavy carbon and dirt deposits had caused a lot of our troubles, and that two more days cleaning of parts was called for. Consequently we collected firewood to cook on to save fuel, but I was feeling worse inside and I was additionally stricken with migraine and spent the day in bed. Straws were drawn for a fresh guard roster and Denah and I drew the 1:30 watch that night.

Rein finished rebuilding the engine on the third day, but since the battery had been flattened by using the lights at night, we still could not start it. Shopping in this village was very haphazard: it was so small that we just bought everything it had to offer every day and worked out a menu around that. There was no meat for sale and so we used up our emergency tinned rations. My condition continued, to decline: I felt lousy and nauseous and spent another day in a fever and my eyes burned. As I was ill I was given the first watch.

By the fourth day my condition had ameliorated a little and my headache had gone. With Copán being so close, Kiki, Denah, Hans, and Christoff went off to Copán Ruins over the border on a day-trip, as their Swiss passports required no visas to cross the border in either direction. I decided on a walk back to the river for a bath about three miles and was glad to get out into such tranquil mountain scenery. Around me the peasants were working the fields and the little boys followed their cattle, and I startled a number of beautiful birds and butterflies as I trod silently in the road dust. I was lucky enough to catch a lift back up the mountain on the back of one of the iron ore trucks, which carried their loads through to Honduras every hour or so. The van had become an embarrassment to the police as they were due for an inspection today, but it stayed put with inert transmission on top of its other problems. Even linking the battery to a Guatemalan Army jeep did not start the engine. We also discovered that the rear brakes were jammed, so after supper we had a conference to discuss our plight, the outcome of which that; Debbie, Joan, and Brigitte opted to leave the expedition and go on together in the morning, while the rest of us would go back. I drew the 1:30 a.m. watch with Brigitte, and it was quite amusing to see her in a tizzy the whole time. For 90 minutes she kept the flashlight on and constantly swept it over the whole square on anything that moved, be it a dog or a pig or even the locals walking through their own gardens to pee. I asked her why she was so scared, and she said she thought the locals would try to rape her!

On the fifth day just as we were waking a flat-bed truck drove into Caporja from Honduras and spelled salvation for us. We negotiated a lift to Chiquimula for the van, luggage, and ourselves less the three girls for 75 quetzales (about $100) which Rein was far from pleased about. Brigitte kissed us all good-bye and we gave the girls a big cheer to send them on their way. The van was loaded onto the truck with much heaving and straining on our part while a villageful of macho hombres stood around and watched and all gave us plenty of conflicting instructions in rapid Spanish, while some of their wives helped us push, but not one of the men lifted a finger to help us. We tore down the camp, climbed aboard, and were off, leaving the empty trailer with the police (though that was no safeguard). Everyone else sat in the van and faced backwards, but I stood on the side wall of the truck which allowed me a clear view of the mountains in all directions. The truck was used to carrying 25 tons of iron ore and all up we weighed three tons. The driver must have owned the truck because his driving was unusually good and he took it easy on the very bad road. The weather was fine and the air so clear that the most distant mountains could be seen in detail. We passed all the villages and fords and steep valleys that we had negotiated with such care going up, and every so often I had to duck swiftly to avoid an overhanging magnolia or olive branch. I had some most exhilerating moments perched high on the edge of the truck watching the wheels skirting corners mere inches from plunging precipices. The scenery was so rich and awe-inspiring of exotic green shadow-mottled mountains, and every once in a while a buzzard soaring on high. When we arrived at the outskirts of Chiquimula we stopped at a truck repair yard where I acted as an intermediary interpreter. The illiterate mechanics were of the opinion they could do the work: a stronger starter motor would solve the problem of too much compression. So we unloaded the van again while the Latinos looked on.

Meanwhile on the other side of the road an amusing drama was acted out for nearly an hour. To start with a cattle truck was slowly edging along the road with an enormous Brahmin bull tied up close behind it by the horns while a second lasso was being kept taut by a young cowboy riding ten yards behind. The bull actively resisted every inch of the way but the truck was steadily drawing it along at walking speed. The bull was shaking its head and bracing its legs, only to skitter and slide along the tarmac. About half a dozen young men were walking alongside the bull, supposedly encouraging it to keep going by shouting at it and tapping and prodding it with their sticks. Suddenly they all stopped and began to go in reverse. The cowboy turned his horse around and kept urging it on, yet for all the effect it had on the bull the horse might just as well have saved itself the effort. For a few yards the bull backed up, but it seemed to prefer 'kicking against the pricks' (to quote a Biblical expression) and sidled around until it was alongside the truck and pulled against the motion with all its might, and occasionally adopted a strong stance and jostled the truck up and down for good measure, with its shoulder and horn under a ledge on the truck, which did not stop, but steadily reversed for 100 yards. Eventually the truck backed up to a tree, with the big white bull fighting all the way and not uttering a sound. For five minutes nothing seemed to happen, the truck stood still with the exhausted Brahmin braced stolidly against it, inert and unyielding. The two ropes around its horns were next made fast around the tree and the truck moved around so that the back opened onto the top of a natural earth ramp. At last it became clear what the men were doing, namely, taking advantage of the ramp to get the bull in the truck; but would it go in? Not on your Nelly! For a quarter of an hour they pushed and pulled it, swore at it, yanked its tail, and threw sand in its eyes. The bull capriciously feinted or kicked at them and by degrees was forced towards the back of the truck and was clearly furious as it snorted and stomped and pawed a good deal. After a lengthy stalemate a red T-shirt was fluttered in the bull's face. That did the trick, it charged the T-shirt and landed up neatly penned in the cattle truck. The cowboy recovered his lassos, the men climbed onto the truck, and off they all went.

After supper we discussed our agenda in the new light of events and decided to fetch the trailer, so Hans, Christoff, and I opted to wake early and accompany Rein back to Caporja before dawn. The trip up the mountains was no problem for the van which was running better than ever. We picked up the trailer, much to the chagrin of the local police who had taken rather a shine to it, and to the amusement of the villagers, neither of whom expected us crazy Gringos to return. We had driven most of the 50 miles back down the mountains when, on the outskirts of the remote village community of Los Planes, the van again lost all compression. Thereat Hans and I set out walking briskly through the mountains to find help. For an hour it was really great to be out in the elements, but we were given a lift on a 'bus' consisting of an open Toyota pick-up with a central handrail, and it was already carrying a complete football team standing cheek by jowl, and we packed in like sardines and were taken as far as the open road when the driver sped up and I lost the first of my hats in the breeze. I found a truck-driver and went back with him (in his Sunday best) to our van and he towed it down the mountain back to the mechanic's yard.

We were running out of things to do to pass the time until Frances taught us how to play 500, an Australian card game, which I took a liking to and won every hand. Finally we had a temperate evening with only coffee, good music, and conservation. It made such a pleasant change. The next day was a scorcher, and the sun roasted us from a clear blue sky. I thought how envious all my friends in northern climes would be since they struggle to get any tan they can while we could not help but turn brown as berries. Most of us took the opportunity to explore Chiquimula, a typically colonial town with the usual enormous aged ceiba tree affording shad for the street vendors in the central plaza. Its church, ruined in the 1765 earthquake, has been preserved as an historic monument. Rein declared he had discovered the cause of all the van's problems at last, a worn out nylon pulley on the camshaft, and triumphantly went off to Guatemala City with Kiki and Denah to order a new one flown in from North America. It was as hot as any sauna, and with time to kill I took a stroll along the river and discovered a dump of off-cuts from a sawmill, unlimited firewood which improved our lot since we had run out of gas. The sandfleas at our camp-site were considerably worse than mosquitoes since they were silent and bit a visible hole out of the skin which itched furiously for days afterwards, making life miserable for us in the evenings. They usually went for the calves and I notched up hundreds of bites during our ten days in the region and bear permanent scars on my ankles as a memento of Guatemala.

Since we had no choice but to stay put the following day under the merciless heat of the sun, the time dragged. I produced one of my more spectacular meals, chicken tikka, a Pakistani-style barbecue, and for a while it broke the boredom which had descended on the six of us remaining.

After a terrible night during which my complaint wrought havoc with my vision in some unexplained way, I took no part in the day's events, but excitement was evident at the prospect of departing finally. Rein returned and did indeed fix the van this time, just before dusk. Notwithstanding the late hour we crossed into Honduras and camped right there at Nueva Ocotepeque, the frontier-post, in the middle of the night.

CHAPTER FIVE

HONDURAS

For a country almost as large as England, Honduras has a very small population, a little over 3,000,000 of whom 90% are Mestizo, and once again part of the country is virtually unpopulated, this time the eastern half, particularly the Mosquitia Plain except for the Caribbean littoral, and the Bay Islands which are English-speaking. The country is very mountainous with a high rainfall, and almost half is covered in broad-leaved forests especially of oak, and also softwoods such as pine. When the Spaniards arrived they found an Indian population of Mayan and other cultures; the Hortis, Hicaques, Lenchas, Payas, and Chorotegas. The Spanish were chiefly concerned with extracting silver and established their capital at Comayagua, but the current capital, Tegucigalpa, was founded then as a gold-and-silver-mining camp. The name is Indian for 'Silver Hill'. The country is very poor, and over two thirds of the whole population are agricultural labourers and make use of mules and ambling ox-carts. The main exports are coffee and bananas, but communications and transportation are rudimentary, except along the Caribbean Gulf and the Pacific Gulf of Fonseca.

We drove on very early through the lovely soft dawn light. It made all the difference to the scenery and when, as today, the terrain was one of open mountains closely hemmed around us with the road paralleling a swirling river below, beyond which pocket handkerchief fields on the further slopes were separated by a thin covering of trees, the beauty of it all was impelling. We were stopped numerous times by the various authorities who ordered us out of the van and examined our passports. Once the van was fumigated inside and out by a man carrying an apparatus akin to a flame-thrower. Billows of chemical smoke gushed out with a roar. Another time Rein had to pay a $25 bribe as we were missing the registration plate the police stole in Mexico City. Our only mechanical problem occurred when we hit a rock full-tilt and that not only destroyed the tyre but also the wheel hub, but other than that we made good time along the Western Highway to San Pedro Sula, the major town in Western Honduras and a real hole. There were no interesting old buildings, only a modern industrial sprawl sitting in the searing tropical heat and humidity.

It was a considerable relief to move on again in the cool of the van. We passed through very pretty scenery on our way south, gradually leaving behind the dense tropical forests of pine and oak, carpeting the mountains up to 6,000 feet high. The further south we went the lower we dropped, reaching dry treeless savannah near the capital. The road was full of surprises. Apart from goats and cattle and ox-carts, there were lots of pot-holes, sudden ditches across the road, dips and humps, and of course, traffic accidents. This was the Northern Highway, the pride of the limited Honduran road network, but it took us almost to Tegucigalpa by the time we made camp. Tropical sunsets enriched our memories of the expedition. Almost every evening a phenomenal wealth of colours blazed around the western sky. Having lost so much time in Guatemala a number of us were now holding on to useless aircraft tickets, and so we spent the day in Tegucigalpa reviewing our arrangements, and were struck by the sheer numbers of armed soldiers in the streets. The city contains a lot of attractively coloured and stuccoed colonial houses turned in on central patios. The whole city is built on the slopes of El Picacho, a mountain which dominates it and its sister town, Comayagüela, attached to it across the Choluteca River by four bridges. The enormous covered market in Comayagüela was a great attraction with its outstanding native handiwork. Up in the city is the grandiose Presidential Palace and the barracks for its armed guards. Luxury goods from the developed world (mainly the U.S.A.) were for sale at horrendous prices. (An eight-ounce bar of chocolate cost ten dollars.) Joan had left us a letter to say she was flying out this very morning and that Brigitte and Debbie had flown out a couple of days previously.

At last I thought I was responding to treatment because I felt well for a day, but I was wrong. My state of health was the overwhelming factor governing my enjoyment and my sociability or otherwise towards the rest who never complained. When we continued south, Rein covered the ground as fast as possible and thus we nearly drove past one of the frequent police checkpoints. The police tried to fine us $50 for not stopping at the stop light. Rein politely pointed out there was no such stop light, and in any case he would not pay a fine without a receipt. The police demanded his driving licence to confiscate it, so Rein gave them his expired one instead, retained for just such an emergency; but it helped that the licence was in English, and Rein pointed out the expiry date as the date of issue and we left very fast. The children in Honduras were particularly friendly towards us, and wherever we stopped they immediately appeared on the spot selling handfuls of fruit, or crisp sun-dried plantain slivers, and other kickshaws. Universally the adults stared gloomily at us in the van and the only ones who spoke to us were the beggars, and they pestered us at every opportunity with the cheek of the Devil, especially when we were preparing food, loquaciously insisting we feed them too. Frank always gave them something, which encouraged them all the more. We became completely accustomed to the breezy hills with views fading into blue sweeps which had certainly proved such a powerful conversation piece much earlier in the expedition. Now we were more tired, what with setting out before the stars had faded from the sky and driving on until the light was quite gone before setting up camp under starlit skies once more.

Not having the freedom to choose the best camp-site we settled for a Dutch barn with a flat cement floor. Upon entering Frances stood rooted to the spot with horror at the sound of a loud insistent hissing. My flashlight revealed quite a few large toads to be responsible, so I shooed them away. They were not the only novelty; all evening we thought the menfolk in their houses 100 yards away were whistling at the girls or for their dogs, but it persisted and Denah guessed it was the frogs piping. I was kept up all night again, but it had a good side to it because the air was so clear that the familiar constellations and planets hung just above the tree-tops.

CHAPTER SIX

NICARAGUA

Nicaragua is the largest country in Central America, (Mexico being included in the North American continent). 90% of the population of 2,5000,000 is largely condensed into one twelfth part of the country, the lowlands along the Pacific Coast. This region has a rich alluvial soil from its two dozen or so volcanoes, some of which are quite active. The best known of these are Coseg̈uina, jutting into the Gulf of Fonseca, and Momotambo, facing the capital across Lake Managua. Once again the terrain is responsible for dissuading settlers. The centre of the country from end to end forms a range of mountains, higher in the north where it is named the Cordillera Isabella. The Caribbean shore-line is drenched with rain brought across by the prevailing easterly winds and is heavily forested with rosewoods and hardwoods such as black walnut and mahogany. This area including Mosquitia in Honduras is called the Mosquito Coast, but the name comes from the Miskito Indians who inhabit the rain forest still. In fact the British (bringing African slaves from Jamaica) settled here first at Bluefields and Greytown, and came for the timber. The population along this coast after a century as a British Protectorate still speaks English. The Conquistadores moving up from Panama settled the Pacific Coast in 1519, interested chiefly in Indian gold. They made León their capital, though Managua now holds that honour. The population is of very mixed origins, but four fifths are Mestizo and about half are basically literate. The nation's history is an amazing account of destruction by civil wars, invasions, and earthquakes. The country produces export crops of coffee and cotton, and half the inhabitants work on the land. Lake Nicaragua is a huge body of freshwater along the Pacific side which is drained by the San Juan River through dense jungle along the Costa Rica border into the Bay of San Juan del Norte to the east. The lake is 92 miles by 32 and contains sharks which swim up from the Caribbean Sea. It also contains alligators and snapping terrapins.

At the border-post in Guasaule Honduran money-changers pressed around us eager for business. Bill made a right nuisance of himself with every dealer, insisting on looking at every single banknote so he could select the newest and cleanest ones. With fresh stamps in our passports, we were anxious to go and extricated Bill from the black marketeers but were quickly overhauled and stopped by a border guard. Bill had evidently struck a deal without understanding the terms and still owed a money-changer several dollars and the soldiers were backing the marketeer, but Bill was not about to give way. Quite an ugly confrontation developed until Frances stepped forward and paid the guy out of her own pocket. We still did not go far; on the Nicaraguan side we were kept waiting for hours. It is a ploy regularly used by the corrupt officials who invent all sorts of delays so that a big bribe might be offered them to hurry things up, whereupon the difficulties instantly evaporate and everybody achieves satisfaction. After the farce of allegedly fumigating the van with a hand-operated perfume-puffer, it was clear that we were viewed with some degree of disfavour and were kept in limbo for hours. We spent the time with a Norwegian couple who were travelling by bus, but whose tips and recommendations about the best locations to visit turned out entirely superfluous. Nicaragua had recently suffered a take-over by the socialist Sandinista guerrillas reversing 50 years of free enterprise, and it was clear to us that the new authorities meant to be tough, not just with us but with everybody. We watching while the goods vehicles from Honduras were entirely unloaded and searched. We noticed how the clerks and boy-soldiers, and police and customs officials still found it novel to call out good-humouredly, "Comrade" or "Brother", and gave each other the clenched fist salute and pats on the shoulder.

We ended up with an unwelcome passenger, a very sour customs functionary who said he only wanted to go a little way with us. We were in no position to argue as he had appropriated the vehicle's documentation. His presence killed off all conversation: by now we had had a bellyful of anti-Gringo treatment and cussedness. The man showed no sign of wanting to get out anywhere and ordered us to keep driving. In another way I was glad of the silence and the chance to sleep and escape the pain inside me until woken at Chinandega, our only stop in Nicaragua, to hear the customs man, out of pure bloody-mindedness, trying to order Rein to keep driving. He lost that argument. It was my turn to do the shopping, but I was in another world; I was so sore and sick that despite the colossal heat I was shivering, and my sight was so badly affected that I had the general illusion of being drunk. Thankfully, Frank offered to come with me and carry the shopping. Before we went off Rein and I tried once more to quiz the laconic official and asked him to leave, but instead he used his authority to order passing cars to block us in. He tried to involve the army but the military patrol was quite antipathetic towards him, at which point Frank and I left the scene. When we returned it seemed, by all accounts, that our predicament had stirred up a heated argument involving the army, police, and some civilians who spoke English and took our part. Nevertheless the customs man wielded the strongest authority and won the day, but at last he made it clear what he wanted, effectually to prevent us leaving the main road and to see us off Nicaraguan soil with the least delay. As capitalists and imperialist dogs we were personas non gratas in their fine liberated country.

On we went through the heat of the afternoon and during the intervals when I was not comatose I glimpsed at the scenery, all flat pasture to the distant horizon which had a ridge of mountains and conical volcanoes. The tallest of these, Santiago Volcano, is double-crested and had a plume of steam issuing from its summit. Suddenly due to the extreme heat, one of the tyres exploded and we rode on the rim until we came to a garage where we could change it. We drove on without respite late into the night until we reached the Costan Rican frontier at Peñas Blancas, which was quite naturally closed, and camped right there in an apparently abandoned shanty town, disturbing some hogs sleeping in the shelters. I did not care. I just went straight to bed. Kiki diagnosed malaria which I was beginning to suspect since treatment for dysentery had proved entirely ineffective.

The night on the border was very hot and made unbearable by clouds of mosquitoes, forcing us to rise early. At dawn a crowded bus arrived full of café proprietors with all their wares, who had come to convert our shanty dormitories into bustling custom-post restaurants catering to the truck-drivers who had to stop here. As soon as they saw us they began to jeer, "Gringos". The propagandists had indoctrinated them well, and for not an instant did they leave us alone. For the most part they seemed quite content to stand in a semicircle within a few feet of us and simply stare. Kiki and Denah were reduced to tears because they could not shake off the persistent young men who pursued them to the toilet and surrounded them when they changed out of their night clothes.

It was a great pity that we were brusquely ushered through Nicaragua in a single day because we did have a plan to visit particular places, not least its capital, Managua, destroyed by an earthquake in 1972, and the lakes and famous chain of volcanoes, some of them active and as high as 5,240 feet. Although we did make up some time, the point came home to us just how arbitrary and unstable most of the Latin American countries are in their headlong struggle to catch up to the standard of living experienced in the developed world. It does form a part, however unwelcome, of the challenge that the continent holds for the adventurous traveller.

CHAPTER SEVEN

COSTA RICA

Costa Rica came as quite a contrast to us after travelling among peoples with olive complexions. The population is still Mestizo, but is virtually White, often with freckles. Out of a population of 2,000,000 only 5,000 are Indians, and there are descendants of the Chinese labourers who built the railways, and of the Black slaves. Since 1823 San José has been the national capital, which title was held by Cartago in the years prior to independence (in 1821), when the whole of Central America belonged to Mexico. As with Honduras, the Spaniards from Panama moved up the Pacific and settled on the Nicoya Peninsula before venturing inland to the Talamanca and

Guanacaste Mountain Ranges, already settled by sedentary farming Indians of the same names. The highest peak is the Chiripó Grande which attains a height of 12,537 feet, and several of Costa Rica's volcanoes are still active, and both coastal lowlands give way to swamps and marshes the closer they approach Panama. Two fifths of the country is forested and the rest is urban or farmed; none is wasted. Along the Caribbean coastline it rains six days a week, and is now being developed as a National Park. The land is ideal for coffee which was the first boom crop, brought in from Cuba. Today agriculture has been diversified and Costa Rica also raises cacao, abacá (Manilla hemp), African palms, bananas, sugar-cane, and cattle. The road and rail networks are very extensive for a Latin American State, though decoratively painted oxcarts are still commonplace and are something of a national emblem. This, little country is an exemplar for Central America: the army was abolished in 1948, and the country is a genuine democracy with the highest per capita income in Central America (assessed at $1,500 in 1978).

We entered Costa Rica in anticipation of seeing a much more pleasant country and liberated population which is the most literate and enjoys the highest standard of living in Central America. Personally I did not get off to too good a start. While making use of the custom-house facilities, two beggar boys (operating on the sure-fire principle of bursting in on men with their pants down) tried their trick on me, barricaded the cubicle shut from within, and shouted at me for money. I was so angered by this unwarranted breach of privacy that I gave them both backhanders to the head they would never forget and sent them packing.

We drove down the Pan-American Highway which runs the length of the country and made a stop at Liberia, a neat, clean, cattle town which Denah recognised from a previous visit, and so knew where to take us for the best milk shakes. Outside the towns the country looks quite European with large lowland cattle estates. Further on the Highway runs through hilly forests, replaced in many areas with plantations of coffee and bananas. Our expected midday tropical downpour lasted for hours. Typically the rain comes straight down as though poured from a bucket and is a regular feature every day of the rainy season. Starting at Liberia the road was good for the first time since leaving the U.S.A. and I slept as much as possible, too sick even to notice my surroundings. Police stops were just as frequent as in previous countries, but instead of demanding a bribe, the policemen conducted their business with a smile in a friendly and intelligent way. The change was also quite markedly noticeable on the radio, which was an important factor considering we spent at least half of each day in the van. A little point like up to date music or a refreshing attitude made all the difference to our frame of mind. One thing was impossible to come to terms with, the sheer wall of heat and the extreme humidity for days or weeks on end. It was just like living in a sauna, the sweat poured off us; and it all became so overpoweringly oppressive at the worst of times that I, at any rate, found my breathing laboured and asthmatic. The nights would have been cooler had it not been better to swelter under the protection of an eider-down to thwart the mosquitoes. We made camp at San Antonio close enough to the capital to give us a full day there.

We drove into San José in beautiful weather and wasted an hour in the maelström of traffic looking for a place to park. The parking problem in all Hispanic American cities is difficult to appreciate unless one has actually experienced it first-hand. The towns developed before the trucks and motorcars arrived and in most instances the streets are too narrow to allow parking, and so the car-parking fraternity who use the kerbs try to keep one step ahead of the police, handing out parking-tickets like confetti. That accounts for only half the problem. Owing to the enterprise and audacity of the thieves and car strippers (who include the police) parking even where permitted in the streets is still unwise — locking the doors does not safeguard the wheels or muffler. The answer is to put the vehicle in a privately guarded walled yard and pay the guard a little extra to stay awake or, as we always did, leave one of the group with the vehicle full-time. To our utter amazement Hans and Christoff came upon Debbie and Joan in the street. They were staying at the poshest hotel San José had to offer, which they had thought to be their final fling before flying out that very day, and so they rejoined the expedition. They told us our van would never have made it to Copán Ruins if we should have succeeded in fixing it at Caporja. The country road was worse, if that was possible, on the Honduran side of the border and their bus bounced off the road and they were stuck for hours, until two bulldozers, themselves in serious trouble, managed to drag it along the track.

San José is fairly hilly so that sight-seeing involves some effort and San José (and also Rio de Janeiro which some of us reached months later) has a well deserved reputation for having some of the most beautiful women in the world. It also boasts some famous architecture, especially the National Theatre, a deliberate exact copy of the French original in Paris, complete with marble staircases, frescoes, statuary, and a foyer decorated in gold. All over the city there are fine public buildings in the traditional Spanish style and acres of flower beds and parks, making it, in my opinion, the finest city in Central America, set in the most charming rural environment.

We continued south-east into the mountains of the Continental Divide to our camping spot on the Talamanca Ridge, over 11,300 feet up according to Frank's altimeter. It was a most useful device, also incorporating humidity and temperature gauges, and very often we would turn to him for a reading on one or other of these statistics, since we endured one extreme or another every day. Climbing away from San José we passed big sugar plantations, and children were ready with plastic bags full of cut and peeled lengths of cane for sale. So clear was the mountain air that it was possible to spy the oceans on the horizons (not both at the same time) no more than 80 miles off. The great altitude meant the night was really cold, and despite continuing to fast I was still forced to get up continuously after dark. At first light I observed a shiny bottle green hummingbird and remained stock-still while it investigated me. It was the size of an English robin with a long, delicate, curved beak and it did not hum but sounded like a moth trying desperately to fly through a screen. While I watched, it hovered and examined each blossom in its constant search for pollen and nectar.

We had a straight run to the frontier at Paso Canoas, and although it was yet rather early for the midday downpour it came as an outright cloud-burst. We wasted almost an hour at the checkpoint kicking our heels just watching an amazing quantity of water fall. Visibility was reduced to within a few feet while the roadway was turned into a water-race inches deep. Just as suddenly the rain ceased and the opposite side of the road returned to view, and steam rose from the jungle and the stones and the tin roofing in billows everywhere.

CHAPTER EIGHT

PANAMA

The strategic position of Panama has always shaped its fortunes. Since 1500 when Vasco Nuñez de Balboa reached Panama its use as a transit point for mules bearing captured treasure ensured its importance. In 1513 Balboa with 190 men looked across the isthmus to the Pacific and proclaimed the land for Spain. Later it was for many years a Department of Colombia, until well into this century. The population of Panama is nearly two million, inhabiting only a quarter of the country, mainly the Canal Zone and the Pacific Coast west of Panama City. Mountain ranges run the length of the country with only one break (in the San Blas Range) which forms the Canal Zone 10 miles wide. There are lowland shelves on both sides of these ranges and the Caribbean shore in particular receives very heavy rain, though the whole country gets plenty with the result that deep tropical jungle lies over three quarters of the land. Of the 60

Indian tribes the Spaniards exterminated all but three: the Cuñas of the San Blas Archipelago and Territory, the isolated Chocóes of the Darién Gap, and the Guaymíes of Chiriquí and neighbouring Costa Rica, each with its own language. English is widely understood throughout the country and especially in Panama City which has a population of 500,000, The main social problem in the country is one of squatters who account for a quarter of the population, but generally public services are very good. The Darién Gap is one of the last unexplored and challenging regions of virgin jungle and swamp in the world and forms nearly half the country. The Pan-American Highway stops at Chepo 30 miles east of the Canal for the time being. Panamanian money is identical with American money, coin for coin, though there is no separate paper money and currency is called balboas instead of dollars which makes money matters very simple.

From the border to the Canal Zone the Highway is paved with concrete slabs which were badly in need of repair as the rain had undermined them. Bouncing over the holes was too much punishment for the trailer which shattered a spring and clattered along behind us all morning. By now we were blasé about mechanical problems — we had had so many — and left off repairing it until we reached David, the capital of Chiriquí Province. The market at David contained many saddlery and horse-tackle stalls. There were hundreds of articles of meticulous workmanship, and I wondered who would buy such beautiful saddlemongery, horse-brasses, and decorations. A lot of locals' horses did have intricately patterned saddles and plaited leatherwork for show. The journey along Panama began through steaming-hot, flat, lowland jungle, and traversed hundreds of mountain streams. Fencing erected around gardens and fields along the way consisted of living trees, obviously planted as green staves with every intention of rooting. These hedge-fences looked most peculiar, like rows of even palings four feet tall with bushy green tops. Now and then mountains appeared above the jungle to the north of us, especially immediately after leaving the frontier

CHAPTER EIGHT   PANAMA

when we had a view of the extinct Barù Volcano, jutting boldly up to 11,000 feet, overlooking plantations of coffee, bananas, and fruit, notably orange groves, and gardens full of flowers for which the area is famous.

As we went east towards Panama City the terrain became more agricultural with cattle, and fields of grain sprouting amazing ant-hills as tall as a man appearing quite misplaced. Apart from camping a night we did not stop again in the isthmus until we reached our final destination. There was no point since it teemed much of the way, and peering through the rain the view was only of rice paddies or sugar-cane and cacao crops and more jungle. Quite suddenly we found ourselves among a flurry of American military vehicles, and looking around us saw we were in the Canal Zone with American military camps and road-signs in English, for the first time in over 7,000 miles. After the decline in our fortune during the last week or so, returning to civilisation really perked us up. Just as unexpectedly we rounded a corner to be confronted by the Panama Canal and spontaneously raised a cheer. We had made it! We walked along the 'Bridge of the Americas' which is over a mile long and whose central span is an unforgettable suspension bridge higher than the world's tallest ships. A few minutes later we climbed out of the van for the very last time and checked into our hotel, and for some of us this was the end of the expedition and for others the launching point on a much tougher and altogether quite major venture taking in a circuit of South America. As for me, I had no choice but to seek hospital treatment, and a fortnight of it cost me my every last penny.

Panama is a very romantic city associated with buccaneers and Wars of the Spanish Maine, treasure ships and historical struggles. A good deal of evidence remains for the tourist to seek out, but over the past century the fortunes and development of the city (and in fact the country) have depended upon the Canal (opened in 1914) and the Panama Railroad for 61 years before that. Now the city has additional attractions, a booming tourist industry, and the cheapest duty-free trade in luxury goods south of the United States, with the result that Central Americans invade the city at Christmastide.

We all had business to attend to but reconvened for a last supper together and a night of dancing before the group dissolved. Christoff was the first to leave the next day, but the rest of us stayed together for another night out on the tiles. In quick succession, Hans, Kiki and Denah our two doctors, and Debbie and Joan from British Columbia, all departed overnight which left behind an emotional hollow. The rest of us had plans to continue the adventure in South America, and when Frances, Bill, and Frank took a taxi to the airport I could see no point in keeping on my expensive air-conditioned hotel room and moved to a much more basic pension house in the fish market area. It lacked even a window, but I was travelling on a shoe-string and I would sooner the doctors had what was left of my money than the hoteliers. In the meantime Rein had the problem of disposing of the van, because there is no road connecting Panama to the South American continent. The Cuñas from San Blas wear even more stunning costume than the Maya-Quiché Indians in Western Guatemala. It consists of intricate 'molas' or decorative appliqués forming the fronts and backs of their woven blouses. In addition they wear broad headbands, anklets woven in situ to halfway up the shins, skirts, and sometimes armbands complete the costume. The whole outfit in bright and dazzling colours may take a year to finish and is worn with thick pendulous gold rings through the nose and ears. A few Indians who visited the city were the most colourful sight on the street, and even though they are very short of stature they are uniquely handsome and look like Ancient Egyptians.

On my attendances at the Santo Tomás Hospital I used to gaze out over the Gulf of Panama where dozens of freighters and tankers lined up for miles waiting to enter the Canal. I watched them from a promenade in front of the hospital where an enormous and imposing monument to Balboa shews him peering out to sea from his lofty perch, a marble globe on the shoulders of an Oriental, a Caucasian, a

CHAPTER EIGHT PANAMA

Polynesian, and a Negro. The city has quite a few statues erected to past dignitaries, and even one of a Brahmin, bull, but no visitor can forget the brightly painted buses. They are owner-operated and no two are alike. The drivers deck them out inside and out with rainbow tassles which flutter in the breeze. Naïve custom paintwork of comfortable rural scenes forms the background for the destination wording all over most of the front windows. Film stars, vintage cars, puppets, cartoon characters, and zany caricatures are hand-painted on. Messages adorn the backs and sides and each window bears a different name, sometimes that of a saint, and the name of the bus itself is high on the side, and may be either male or female, or even neuter, such as 'The Devil's Chariot'. On the tank cap covers were painted slogans like 'Drink Diesel' or 'Blood of Life'. Inside and out the spaces were filled in with patterns and linework, and this even extended to decorative curtains being painted in the windows, making it difficult to see out but velvet curtains were more common, mere fringes with tiny balls and tassles of twisted thread.

Since I detected I was on the mend, I commenced to try out the most highly recommended restaurants and discovered there were an awful lot. For Panamanian flavour, the outdoor pavement cafés were the most enjoyable, and actually cost less because of the lack of air-conditioning. Right out of the blue I received a telephone call at my hotel, and this was amazing as no-one knew I was there: nevertheless it radically affected my plans for South America. It was from a girl seeking information about the proposed expedition. Her name was Ann, and I was able to give her the particulars of the rendezvous that she wanted. We met only once in Panama before she went ahead to Colombia, but on the strength of it I subsequently changed my route and rejoined her and the others in Bogotá. In fact there were two sister expeditions commencing a week apart with Rein taking the second one. I had looked forward to being on his crew, but jumped ahead instead to join Ann on the earlier one. By staying a fortnight in the poor Santa Ana region of Panama, I gradually learned how the beggars worked at their living. Just like tomcats each had a territorial walk which took a few hours to complete and passed business premises where the patrons were pestered for alms, the most favoured localities being restaurants and markets where the beggars could accost people actually handling food or small change — since it made no difference to them. After a few days they recognised me and learned to leave me alone: I was nearly as poor as they were.

With the old set dispersed I soon struck up a new set of friends to see Panama with, in particular two travellers, Marlene, a tall Dutch girl, and Arvi, a beautiful dark Israeli. We made plans to take the ferry from Balboa to Taboga Island on a day-trip. Toboga Island is about 12 miles out into the bay and is famous for its uncounted wild flowers in a carpet covering the island year-round. The island has only one foot-path, and the ferry journey out to it is half the fun, going down the last bit of the Canal past the American naval installations and under the Bridge of the Americas, among the tuna-fishing boats and shrimp smacks and dinghies out of Balboa Yacht Club. The next day we took a cab to the ruins of Old Panama a few miles from the city which was sacked and looted in 1671 by the pirate Captain Henry Morgan, who subsequently governed Panama for the British since the Spanish were so scared of him. The tumbledown ruins of the Cathedral are now overgrown with moss and the old garrison has been attractively landscaped. The Panamanian Military Riding Academy is right next to the ruins and the horses drew the girls like bears to a honey-pot. Everyone warned us very strongly to beware of the snatch-thieves who prey on tourists in the park, and a cavalry officer was so concerned for our safety that he escorted us to the bus stop in full dress uniform, complete with sword, high riding boots and spurs, and waited until we were aboard and saluted in the old Prussian fashion before departing.

That was the first day in six weeks I did not have a stomach-ache, and I judged I was finally able to leave. The cost of medical treatment had been very high and had left me without even the cabfare to Panama Airport, so therefore, risking the uncertainty of arriving at the right place, I caught a bus for Tocumen village 20 miles away for a paltry 30 cents which delivered me right at the airport with hours to spare. A large group of Japanese, all nondescript and similarly dressed in grey business suits and carrying identical hand luggage, were bowing politely to each other and providing the shoeblacks with a bonanza. The shoeshine boys had mastered the art of sporadically loosening and tautening the polishing cloth to make a very authentic snapping sound. They could repeat it with either hand so skilfully that they played the shoe like a drum in elaborate syncopations. The Japanese looked down and laughed and having been put in a jovial mood gave more generously for the shine. The boys always did a good job, sitting on the floor talking among themselves at their level while the Japanese talked over their heads, and when it was time to present the second shoe the shoeshine boys tapped on their little platforms with the polish tins but never spoke to their clients.

PART TWO

THE SOUTH AMERICAN EXPEDITION

CHAPTER NINE

COLOMBIA

Colombia is an enormous country and extremely diverse in every regard. Its population of 25,000,000 is largely concentrated in the cool Andean highlands which occupy roughly the north-western half of the country. The population is extremely varied in its origins, containing blood mixes of all races, and pure Negro, European, and even East Indian communities, as the country has always had an attraction for migrants envisaging a bonanza just ahead. East of the Andes are the basins of the Amazon and Orinoco and the Llanos further north, firm flat grazing land. The Andes rise in four great ranges or cordilleras running vaguely north to south, with the highest peaks up to 19,000 feet occurring in a separate far northern group, the Sierra Nevada de Santa Marta, but considering Colombia sits astride the Equator, the 16,000-foot snow-line at these low latitudes is higher than most of its mountains and volcanoes. The first settlement by the Conquistadores took place in 1500 at Santa Marta, but their pursuit of gold, still plentiful in the rivers today, led them north from Quito to found Bogotá in 1538 in the heart of territory inhabited by the Chibcha-Muiscas, the only sedentary Indians in the country, who raised crops but no livestock. The Spaniards rapidly captured and enslaved them, and in those days Bogotá was just a central trading point but it is now the capital with over 4,000,000 citizens. Later settlers moved further north to the area around latter-day Bucaramanga, where the attraction was chichona bark. In the pre-Columban era other Indian cultures included the Tairona, Quimbaya, Sinú, and Calima, and today there are 398 tribes in Colombia. The fiercest of these are the Motilones on the far north frontier with Venezuela who shrink their visitors, particularly the missionaries who persist in trying to Christianise them. Poor diet and bad health is the usual lot of most Colombians; infant mortality is very high, and half the children receive no primary schooling, but an even greater problem is caused by the barrios clandestinos, or shanty towns, which have sprung up around the cities without any facilities whatsoever. Colombia's largest export-earner is its traffic in contraband drugs on which the government is claiming a crack down. Colombia is the world's greatest supplier of arabica coffee, and has the most prodigious coal reserves in Latin America; and apart from supplying emeralds and gold has an enormous potential in gems and precious metals as yet untapped.

At Barranquilla's decrepit airport I was hassled by plain clothes policemen who thumbed through my documents and gave me the third degree. Luckily being English and having no objectionable visa stamps I was released, but I subsequently learned that many young people are refused entry for the most trivial of reasons, such as being Australian, or just sheer Latin American bloody-mindedness. The Barranquilla police are notoriously unpleasant towards

CHAPTER NINE   COLOMBIA

travellers, and plant drugs on them and then impose spot fines. It is their method of augmenting their incomes. The rendezvous for the expedition was the Hotel Victoria, and the squalor and slum conditions, and the heat and decayed colonial architecture on the way there did little to encourage me. I shared a room there with Barry, an Australian, who was also embarking on the expedition led by Rein, which I would have been party to had I not received a note at the hotel from Ann inviting me to travel ahead and join the expedition which had set out from Barranquilla a few days before. I heard from Barry that she had already been beaten and robbed while sight-seeing on her own. During the course of the next few days the other members of Rein's expedition arrived, almost all girls, bedecked with jewellery, with permed hair-styles, and money and passports sticking out of open pockets. Apart from the impossibility of keeping their hands and complexions ladylike on a five-month wilderness expedition, unless they learned to be more security-conscious they ran the risk of losing their valuables and possibly their ring fingers too. Thieves here are outright cut-throats, brazenly bold, and trip you up to pull your boots off. Otherwise armed gangs regularly use razors to cut the rucksacks from travellers' backs and resistance is foolhardy and pointless. The cafés in Barranquilla sell a large range of tropical fruit juices, many of them local varieties which are unknown elsewhere, and are available as milk-shakes, or sorbets, or served as 'gaseosas'. There were too many to try them all, but with hours of tropical rain every day I enjoyed quite a few in the company of Barry and others in the nearby cafés.

To catch up with the earlier expedition meant taking a roundabout bus route via Santa Marta and Bucaramanga to Bogotá, which was a scheduled run of 28 hours, but the driver shaved six hours off this time. Before leaving I sent a telegram to the British Embassy in Bogotá giving my estimated time of arrival, as coaches are renowned for breakdowns and very long delays in the mountains not least due to frequent military and police harassment. The journey began over a sand-bar north-east along the coast where the forest came down onto the beach, and the saltwater lagoon had killed half the trees which stood with tall white trunks and branches poking out from the greenwood in a tissue of swamps. White storks with long crests waited immobile on low stumps peering steadily into the swamp waters. Later we passed a fishing village where the men and boys, were paddling their long outrigger dugouts away to sea to fish with rod and line. The Sierra Nevada de Santa Marta could be seen darkly rising above the thunder clouds a long way ahead. The road was badly pitted but the bus-driver tore along at maximum speed swerving strongly to avoid the holes, but only some of them; we quite often suffered jarring bumps. I had been exhorted to stay awake and keep an eye on my luggage but I was in no condition to do so, and snoozed on and off until we approached Bucaramanga. As we descended thousands of feet into the city the lights disappeared and reappeared around the corners, an experience akin to landing by plane, complete with popping ears. During the rest-stop my luggage attracted some boys who were surprised to.be addressed in their own tongue. I told them about other continents which they had never heard of, and they candidly told me they made their livings as pickpockets and baggage thieves, but that I was their friend, and they, would keep the others away. When my bus came in I made sure of a window seat above the luggage compartment. When dawn came I could scarcely believe my eyes, the mountains opposite were so high as to completely blot out any glimpse of the sky through the bus window short of peering, up with my cheek pressed against the fogged pane, and way way down at the bottom of the gorge which the sunlight had not reached I could see a winding grey ribbon. I had to look a while before I was sure it was a river, (a tributary of the Magdelena) and not a road as it was several thousands of feet below. I was so concerned at the likelihood of the bus being precipitated over the unprotected rim of the road ledge that I could not take my eyes off the lie of the land. The driver used his horn at every possible opportunity and overtook all vehicles bar none. He drove that bus like a. racing car and frequently passed other traffic on the wrong side. He seemed to take it personally when he caught up with another bus driven in a like manner, but after jockeying for position for half an hour finally secured the lead. The customs officials, police, and military all made their brusque checks en route, and one passenger, a Colombian peasant, was arrested and removed from the bus without his luggage. We crashed only once, thankfully at the end of the journey in Bogotá, and I carried all my luggage in some, trepidation looking out for the infamous gangs of armed men who rob travellers, but reached the haven of the hotel rendezvous safely. Annette, the organiser of these expeditions, had arrived only minutes before me from San Francisco whence she had seen us off nine weeks before. We were too tired to explore the red-roofed city, the architecture in its old quarter, and the coaeval plazas and splendid churches, and put all that off for another day. We found a seafood restaurant specialising in widow-fish, remarkably good to eat, and caught up with each other's news. As the organiser of the whole expedition she had been receiving desperate tidings from Rein. Apparently he was enmeshed by red tape in Panama getting the van off his hands and was starving because the banks could not trace his money. Meanwhile his Panamanian and Colombian visas had expired so Annette had had to telex him an airline ticket to Ecuador and Peru that morning. Apart from medical and language difficulties, travellers in Latin America are faced with an all-embracing problem of handling red tape, which is frustrating even when it is not stacked against them deliberately.

We devoted the following day to sight-seeing beginning at the old Presidential Palace of immaculately clean stonework, with armed guards and security cameras set back from the street behind high wrought iron palisades. All the neighbouring blocks were slums, though most of the colonial buildings and statues of luminaries were clustered together in a fairly small area and it made a very historic setting to take a walk in. We dived down a low corridor into a quaint old-fashioned café which doubled as a modern-day gambling den. At a height of 8,600 feet Bogotá spreads out on the skirt of Mount Montserrate, whose peak is attainable up a funicular railway climbing at 81 degrees to a convent and a popular picnic area with the best views to be had of the district. One of the major streets is Avenida Jiménez de Quesada, named after the city's founder, which runs crookedly through the middle of the city down an ancient riverbed, and it is along this street that scores of emerald dealers trade at the pavement cafés with their paraphernalia of tweezers, jewellers' eye-pieces, magnifying glasses, and twists of paper, cautious of synthetic laboratory forgeries. The Plaza Bolivar is the very heart of the city with a statue of its namesake, the Great Liberator. It is surrounded by grand old buildings with broad eaves and carved doorways, though on its northern edge the new Municipal Palace of Justice is just as imposing. Owing to the altitude it was necessary to proceed fairly slowly to avoid feeling light-headed; not did it help that the city was daily drenched in rain, ever our cue to divert to a new well recommended restaurant.

In the morning, Paul, the expedition leader, found us at the hotel and so we finally joined, the others who were already out exploring the metropolis. The truck was much larger than I had expected, an ex-military vehicle purposely rebuilt with coach seating, a high ceiling and a kitchen area. It had stowage space inside and out and behind it was hooked up a colossal trailer, designed to take all our luggage, tentage, and bedding. We found the others at the mind-blowing and unique Gold Museum where over 18,000 items of pre-Columban gold are displayed together with other precious earthenware and stoneware objects and funerary scenes. Considerable efforts to enlighten the visitors are made, including film shews, guided tours, charts and explanations of Colombia's heritage of gold and the history of its tribal use and techniques which are still practised to this day, not least the 'cire perdue', or 'lost wax', method of manufacturing vessels, by which means firm wax separates the internal and external clay moulds while they set hard, and then the molten wax is poured out and gold in. The greatest display was in a strong-room so crammed with thousands of golden artefacts, cataracts of nose- and ear-rings and necklaces, that the room was bright with the reflected radiance of priceless gold on all sides, and every bit of it irreplaceable.

Back at the truck I met Ann who introduced me to the others. Tobin had volunteered to be the barman rather than submit us to his cookery, and likewise Rolf had abstained from cooking and served as handyman. Once again Frank was in charge of the baggage, along with Manfred, and they built up their muscles with all the hard work it involved. Sam did a great job as our storeman despite his lack of Spanish, and except for Paul, who drove, the remaining 18 of us formed cooking partnerships while Sandra also served as a nurse. I teamed up with Ann who did not have a partner as yet, but Bill (vying with Sandra) tried to assume overall dominance of the group and cooked at every meal, and the partnership system was quite unclear for several weeks as he selected helpers on the basis of whomever was nearest at the time. It seemed odd to sit facing each other across tables in the truck, and most of the seats faced backwards to make the best use of the space available.

Not far from Bogotá in the midst of rich dairyland is the town of Zipaquirá and on the side of a mountain above the town a road tunnel leads into a rock salt mine so vast that it contains 400 miles of galleries and although it has been excavated for longer than recorded history, it still contains enough salt to satisfy world demand until the end of next century. An amazing cathedral has been carved deep within the mine, and the blackness of the salt lends immensity to the cathedral, though the vaulted roof is only 75 feet high. Huge hawsers encrusted with crystals of white salt were bound around the 20-foot thick columns and more white salt was visible as stalactites hanging in clumps and as a coating on the roof. One room off to the side was deliberately designed to demonstrate perfect accoustics, so that if one stood in the centre and spoke, or even whispered, the instant echo made one's lungs quiver, a sensation not unlike an electric shock. The circular wall and hemispherical dome had a highly polished surface of black salt about ten feet from the centre of the room. The cathedral was built on several levels with transepts, aisles, statues, and altars, the main altar being an 18-ton black salt monolith, and fluted alcoves which spread out the gleam of powerful arc-lights hidden inside their bases. Walking around the back of the altar, Ann and I surprised a local red-handed, desecrating it with a hammer and chisel, splitting off handfuls of salt for souvenirs, and she guiltily thrust some chunks into our hands. When we returned to the light we could see it contained crystalline gold and veins of green and red minerals streaked through it. The last part of the cathedral we saw was the Nativity Scene carved out of the bed-rock of salt, as was everything else except the massive cross. The ground and roadway for hundreds of yards from the mouth of the tunnel was peppered with leached salt, and a local soda industry has been developed near the mine which serves several factories.

Leaving Zipaquirá behind the truck climbed higher and higher into the mountains with its engine grinding passing a number of villages and clustered houses. Some wealthy people live here in brick-built retreats next to simpler adobe abodes: although the colour bar is not legal it was evident throughout our stay. The terrain we were negotiating was very fecund and as much as possible was cultivated. Fields were ploughed on slopes as steep as 60 degrees and all kinds of vegetables were grown, livestock was raised, and plantations of fir trees filled in the non-arable uplands. Every inch of the land basins was in use, even in the highest plateaux where only the waterlogged central dips were flat. The menfolk in particular wore colourful ponchos which they held over their faces at our passing to avoid breathing in the choking cloud of dust kicked up by our eight tyres. We passed a sumptuous leather market where cowhides in various natural colours had been cut and stitched together like overlapping tiles into shaped and circular patchwork rugs up to ten feet across. We wound on through these mountains, the Eastern Cordillera, passing large ponds and a riot of varied vegetation, and tall tropical grasses in areas of savannah, yielding to palms and blue-green fir-trees. There are no real seasons in this region, climate being a matter of altitude, and we continued until a few minutes before sunset, and the wild flowers and leaves of all tints made it look like an Ontario autumn. All along the route trees were in brilliant red and orange blossom and after a kaleidoscopic evening we trundled down a mud track through a musty dense spruce plantation to emerge on the edge of a lake where a llama was nibbling at the turf, completely unperturbed by our presence. A chorus of frogs serenaded us all night. Armin made a bonfire at every opportunity and had a blaze going in moments, and we sat round it to supper. Ann and I had spoken to Tobin for most of the day. He exuded the aura of a typical successful Englishman and was always very smart, though he tended to lose his pipe quite often. He had been raised on boats which led him into a specialist field of journalism. Since Ann had also devoted years of her life to yachting in the Atlantic and Caribbean, and had written for a nautical almanac, they had a good deal in common to discuss.

That night the rain came in torrents, of course, and after a parsimonious breakfast we pushed the truck back up the muddy track using our sandmats, and returned to Bogotá for provisions since the shops had all been closed the previous day, a Sunday. We drew up at Unicentro, the largest shopping mall in the continent, built with North American money, incorporating fancy curtain fountains and other special effects. In South America it was even more imperative to guard the vehicle, and two people were needed outside to watch over it. Here Frank and I stood guard and it was our first chance to talk in a while. Frank was a very deep philosophical thinker, and had a peculiarly jaundiced view of humanity. His oblique deductions always seemed tangential to the facts of the matter, but there was no doubting his sincerity. He told me then that the crew was simply not organised as a team and that the cooking was a massive failure, as the meals were inadequate and unrecognisable. In fairness to Frank the menu was up to the cookery teams who had to cope with whatever South American foods were available; we had no means of keeping food cold, and most of us had not cooked for 23 people on a small stove before, but both quantity and quality improved after a week or so. As regards the disunity of the members, it was largely the result of the English/German language barrier again and the differences between our social backgrounds, and subsequently our common hardships drew us a little closer together. Nevertheless Frank had hit the nail squarely on the thumb, to coin a phrase, and his dry sagacity had more than a grain of truth to it.

We set off for San Agustín in its mountain fastness, and during the afternoon the usual tropical rain poured and the fog wiped out the view. It was on such occasions that the family plan layout in the back of the truck with four people to a table came into its own, and we could play chequers or cards. There was an interminable backgammon feud 'twixt Annette and Tobin because she was invincible which got under his skin. The light was already quite faint when we dropped down from the splendid mountain heights into a long gorge, to my mind far more imposing. The sides of this gorge rose virtually sheer, yet wherever trees and palms and xerophytes or life of any kind could put down roots it lent some colour to the rock face. At one point where we stopped for water at a brook, I was amazed to see a worm well over an inch in diameter; it looked more like a bicycle inner tube. Another manifestation which indicated clearly how moist the tropics are was that the telegraph lines were frequently festooned with shrouds of green, perhaps a lichen or fungus or Spanish moss which found a purchase in the strands of the cable and must have easily tripled its weight. The canyon went on for miles following the Magdelena River and the view ahead was most impressive even under, the sickly yellow filtered light which threatened rain: the mountains rose like walls at least 1,000 feet high on either side for many miles. At last we rose out of it into a slightly flatter landscape and driving after dark we arrived at a closed camp-ground. Paul prevailed upon the owners to open up and we quickly discovered the swimming-pool with a fast slide which sent us into hysterics. Rolf had established himself as the expedition humourist, a master of wit and repartee even in English, not his mother tongue. He was also a talented musician and had brought along his ukulele and recorder. I know I always enjoyed listening to him playing, but out of consideration for the others' dislike of his music he usually found a perch some way off. For many days he slept past the unequalled scenery in the Andes, which was treated as an idiosyncracy, but in fact he had the same trouble as I, so I could sympathise. It was Sandra's birthday, and Stephanie, our artist, made a birthday card on which we all contributed our messages, and we gave her a fresh cream birthday cake. The temperature was perfectly equable despite the altitude but all evening flashes of lightning approached from the north and the rain finally broke up the party.

Paul had calculated that to reach San Agustín in a day would require a 4:30 a.m. start. Indubitably the passengers in the cab always had the best view, coupled to which they could select the cassette music and had the benefit of a heater, and all this added up to a privileged position which rotated but involved the extra duty of map-reading for Paul. Today Ann and I took our turn in the cab. Paul was an outstanding driver as he unfailingly respected the group in the back and avoided the least bump in the road, and he drove slowly around every town or village to give us a good long view, whether we stopped there or not. When we did hit a bump at high speed, it used to throw us high out of our seats against the canvas ceiling. Paul had rigged up speakers in the back, and although there was no public address system, he occasionally prepared taped messages and played them through. He had also fixed up a buzzer, and by means of a code he understood why those in the back required him to stop. He was a virtuoso actor and entertainer to boot, and had recorded several tapes of radio dramas based on previous expeditions he had led, and one on a wildly adapted Agatha Christie novel, and another on a nineteenth century caricatured safari; and all were farces and had the whole company in stitches. He played most of the voices and narrator and had excellent sound effects, and during the trip he made more tapes using us for the different characters, and often poking fun in such a way that we could not help laughing at ourselves. Most of all he shouldered full responsibility for all the difficulties we endured at checkpoints, frontiers, and in the towns.

As we pressed on south the gorge widened out gradually into two ranges of mountains enveloping a very prosperous fertile valley and centre of population. Some of the ranches were elaborately and expensively built, evidently the preserve of the rich, which contrasted with the much commoner plain stick and adobe houses along the roadside. During the course of the day the slow damp start gave way to bright heat dissipating all the clouds and causing the valley to shimmer in a flameless blaze. For many miles we approached a huge conical volcano in an extremely high snow-clad sierra with a blanket of white cloud emanating from its peak, drifting down like carbon dioxide past the snow-line where the clouds left the mountain and streamed away in a pennant. The road frequently wound along above a river or crossed very silty swollen streams. Where it entered a small town I noticed a cluster of large black vultures, cara-caras, not condors, the national emblem. Thereafter we saw them everywhere, soaring and wheeling in the sky or else standing on banks and verges peering at the road, waiting for carrion. Ann pointed out tall earthen structures in the pastures so oddly contorted by erosion or assault by mountain tapirs that they could have been abandoned, for they were termites' nests, some reaching a height of ten feet, though most were only four feet high. In fact they doubled as ventilation stacks, built high to act as chimneys and draw drying air out of the subterranean chambers. It was not clear what the occupants found to eat other than fence-posts as the trees in the area were pretty thin on the ground and at least

100 yards away. For thousands of miles throughout Central America Brahmin cattle were the only kind to be seen except for the occasional North American horned steer. Now we were seeing oddly coloured Brahmins with brown or even black hides, but all became clear when herds of English cattle were also seen mixed in with them, evidently to produce a hybrid strain suitable for the climate.

In just this one country the change of scenery was amazing from valley to valley. For instance, rice was being grown in the flooded flat areas, while giant agave was cultivated and other cacti were naturally dispersed, but they were less than man-sized. It was curious to look up from the paddies and see the pocket handkerchief fields of sugar-cane raised on the steep slopes. The most curious feathery bamboos grew in beds of up to half an acre, reaching heights of 30 feet and more. Consequently it was used as a building material in many of the country areas; and the bamboos, the paddy fields, and the sharp snow-tipped volcanoes and mountains created an overall impression as of Japan. We climbed right up to a mountain pass which afforded us a spectacular view of the silvery Magdelena River snaking through the gaunt mountain massifs, and everywhere were flowers the colours of fire. We passed through Neiva, the local capital set in a coffee-growing zone, and it was to this city that Pizarro's lieutenant, Sebastián de Benalcázar, properly Belalcázar, the Moorish-Spanish city of his birth in Estremadura, pursued his 25-year quest of El Dorado in 1539. Travellers to Neiva never forget its huge and curious statue of two naked cloud-borne Indians, a hunter and huntress with a spectacled bear, spearing a plunging Centaur and a Conquistador, who was further impaled on an industrial machine, while the Arabian horses escaped their flying arrows. Its interpretation is that the Colombians were reclaiming their country from the Colonials just as the Ancient Greeks drove out the Centaurs from their land. The length of the valley the colours of the trees and thick scrub caught our eyes, as many are hosts to epiphytes and bright red orchids, or are rubescent poinsettias or poincianas.

Men working with hand-tools on the road were an indication we were drawing near to the village of El Gigante, named after its gigantic ceiba which has given shade for a millennium, also known as the God tree, actually a kapok or West Indian cotton tree. Above the bole the trunk was 40 feet around and 100 feet high and its branches spanned 170 feet giving shade to the square of this sleepy little village which boasted a couple of small oil-wells, whose donkey-engines kept the machinery bobbing up and down like dabbling ducks. Hobo, the next village, had an even larger ceiba in its main square, and beyond Hobo alien stone shapes and deep pockmarks ate way back into the sandstone face, making it bizarrely crooked, and spacing out the tropical flowers. It was still light when we set up camp at San Agustín, but we were 5,660 feet up and the temperature plummeted after dark. The next day it was the turn of Ann and me to cook, and up so high in the rarefied atmosphere the Andean sun blazed down, so we decided on a simple cold lunch. When catering for.23 people all running backwards and forwards through the tiny galley, and allowing for individual food fads, simple meals do not exist, but Ann was ever the perfectionist, and with her gourmet approach and my patience we managed alright while the midday rains came and flooded the tents with three inches of water in less than an hour.

In the Valley of the Statues nearby, hundreds of figures representing people, gods, rats, and other beasts have been erected at over a dozen sites. Some have been carved into the mountainsides, as though guarding sacred locations. Archaeologists are not agreed as to the origins of these relics nor the forestal culture which produced them. To see them for ourselves involved hiring horses for a day, and we set out bright and early on fairly diminutive hacks. My boots would not fit in the stirrups designed like cups for the toes, so I removed them in transit and was much happier with muddy feet; and I never suffered a twinge of saddle-soreness but rather enjoyed the therapeutic rocking in the saddle as we rode along tracks and bridle-paths visiting selected locations of the enigmatic pre-Columban statues. The first we saw were named the Queen and the Eagle, and typical of the human statues the Queen bore fangs in her grinning mouth while the Eagle had a serpent in its beak. Ann gave me her camera for safe-keeping in the pack slung from my pommel, the last we ever saw of it: some lucky local bagged it at an unguarded moment while we were off studying the strange statues on foot. The second site contained a tiny statue, the Little Queen, for which we did not even bother to dismount.

I caused everyone to fall about in hysterics when we came to a steep (I mean <u>steep</u>, as a church steeple) hill going down. The track followed ditches four feet deep zigzagging awkwardly back on themselves all the way down. At first my miserable nag refused to descend so I tried dismounting to lead it down, but it bucked and snorted and shied at me, refusing even that. In considerable anxiety I remounted and the guide applied his whip to my horse's rump and so it did reluctantly advance very slowly, not along the ditches as all the others had, but along their very rims. I kept up an anguished conversation with the horse, so frightened was I of it stumbling on the soft edge of turf. Bill was laughing so hard that the tears were popping from his eyes. I made it though, by leaning way back in the saddle and virtually standing on the stirrup-plates. Diane, thoroughly at ease on her mount, knew how to ride well and galloped backwards and forwards all day. It was her finest hour and she had a well trained obedient horse, but others were not so fortunate. Tobin was left far behind; his horse turned out a real slow-poke, but not before it had given Bill a blood-letting bite on the thigh, and later on Bill was kicked off his horse by another. Not his day, obviously!

We rode across some unforgettable open country for a couple of hours and out onto a very rocky promontory, picking our way sharply down for half a mile. My little horse stumbled a number of times and found itself staggering helplessly sideways towards the edge of the bluff more times than I care to remember, but arrived at the narrow tip of the spur where we all dismounted. By climbing down over the face of the outcrop we found some huge exposed rocks carved in situ with figures on all sides like dice, long worn, smooth by the weather. Even the rock carvings were secondary to the commanding view from that natural vantage point. On the opposite side of the gorge splendid cataracts were tumbling hundreds of feet while scarcely touching the mountain, and distantly below riders were visible like ants on a thread which was a track going for miles in either direction through this rolling green landscape. The constant breeze blowing along the canyon filled our shirts with an exhilarating coolness in answer to the burning heat of the sun. No doubt the Ancient Indians had chosen this wild spot to carve the images of their gods in the side of the mountain because of the interaction of the elements here.

We made our way back up the crest and set off down a new leafy path crossing a muddy river on a platform of logs. My horse sank a cannon bone straight through into the soft ooze and I was neatly swung under its head, but I chivvied it on and with an effort it recovered and made the crossing. We visited more sites, and one involved walking the horses upstream along a gluey bed of mire and boulders since the jungle came impenetrably right to the banks. Holes in the bed had been developed by horses using the track for ages past and at every footfall the horses' hooves gurgled in the deep mud sockets. Here my tired steed finally collapsed under me, pitching me backwards head over heels into the wallow. Fortunately that was our last stop and we only had a couple of hours downhill walking to return to San Agustín. Meanwhile Ann left on a wild goose chase making door to door inquiries about her camera, but she had a terrific welcome at every home. The Indian peasants could not believe it, as they had never before been honoured in this way by a White person, and insisted on spreading their table-cloths and serving her refreshments. I walked back from the camp-ground to help her and several miles out I found her horse hitched by the roadside, and came upon her miles further on again. It took us till well after dark to reach camp, in perfect time for a chicken barbecue for which the sandmats were used as grills, something we often did over wood fires.

The next day we took the road to Popayán, and the sun favoured us, lighting up the waterfalls tumbling down the sometimes vertical slopes covered with shining greenery and tropical flowers. We passed through another narrow winding canyon and the road climbed gradually up one side, sheer above and below the road's edge straight down to the river. When we began the ascent the kerb was only ten feet above the swift grey waters but several miles further on we were hundreds of feet above them when we met a truck coming down. The road was but a single lane wide and fortunately the other truck had to back up since ours had a trailer. All day we moved through the most variable countryside, where coffee plantations were replaced by paddocks full of dark-eyed Zebu-cross cattle, the Zebu strain being imported from India as it can tolerate the tropical heat and humidity. We were still driving through these highlands full of flowers and birds when we broke into the cloud layer. We were yet in the gully made darker and gloomier by the thunder clouds that evening, and passed a few lone small-holdings. Camping-spots were not to be found until we reached, the Puracé National Park at 11,400 feet, the habitat of many unusual animals and birds, and the condor was the only one of these I subsequently saw. In the park is the snowcapped and smoking cone of Puracé Volcano, 13,000 feet high, which supplies heat to sulphur springs on its side at Pisimbalá, and we followed the road until it bifurcated, one leg going on to the sulphur mines and the other to the thermal baths. The sulphurous stench and invigorating cold hit us as we climbed out of the truck. We pitched the tent 50 feet above the truck and supper was a barbecue in a curious open circular kraal another 100 feet up. Zigzagging along the path in the pitch darkness required a slow cautious tread for fear of stepping clean off the mountain.

Breaking camp next morning, my hands froze into numbness and were revived by a dip in the hot sulphur spring. Back on the road conversation thrived: even the normally comatose Rolf kept his ears and eyes alert during the anecdotes. Rolf usually wore a hood while he slept which made him look like Santa Claus with his curly white beard and moustache and toymaker spectacles. Ann took an infectious pleasure in the scenery, and habitually took copious notes every hour every day throughout the trip, and we often pointed out details to each other. Although everybody spoke good English, Dutch and German were often used for privacy. All the while we were driving through scenery whose likeness we would never see again, range upon range of mountains endlessly backing each other up, dominated by the Nevado del Huila, 18,871 feet high, and it was amazing to look high above the clouds to see the horizon. It was not long before we reached Popayán in its peacefull garden valley, and Paul drove slowly round the city, also founded by Belalcázar, allowing us a leisurely look at the rococo Andalusian architecture in which the whitewashed houses have two storeys with enormous eaves (giving at least four feet of cover) and an infinite variety of black iron grids and stone balconies, and all with private patios at the rear. We stopped in Parque Caldas, the main square, full of tall trees, and bordered on one side by a grandiose old white church, with an oecumenical school for boys and a convent for girls. The city had been the seat of the colonial aristocracy, and a preserve of the Spanish, so that today it has a White population. The neighbouring Pijao Indian women may be identified by their black shawls and brilliant Skirts. Diane and I stood guard over the truck, and as always happened, people took a close interest in it and the trailer with all its extras, tools, ancillaries, and modifications, probably the sturdiest truck they had ever seen. Diane spoke Spanish with a clear Castillian accent, and being a friendly, amenable girl and very good-looking, she was quickly surrounded by townsmen, and she always spoke as much by gesticulating with her arms as with actual words. I found I usually attracted a band of children who were not the least bit shy of me. I must have presented a bizarre image to them, not least because

CHAPTER NINE   COLOMBIA

I stood a clear head and shoulders taller than any of their menfolk, and I wore the zaniest multicoloured jeans which were almost made from dozens of patches depicting scenes and activities from many States and walks of life.

Literally every hour's driving brought us to wild new country, in subtle ways different from anywhere else we had passed. There were many plants we had never seen before, e.g. tree-ferns like 12-foot palms with long fine leaves sprouting in all directions. There were more stands of the huge bamboos, which had long feathery side-shoots like 35-foot asparagus. Palms stood beside pine trees in tight copses or as lone sentinels along the mountain ridges, and we had to crane our necks to see them 1,000 higher up, and sharp-leaved agave and crops of sugar-cane grew in steep fields in clefts between the cordilleras as much as 4,000 feet deep. We covered most of the distance as far as Pasto on the Pan-American Highway, somewhat of a prestige project in Colombia, with a paved surface covering the 200 miles, and concrete structures shoring it up in the clefts in the mountains or else it disappeared down tunnels to reappear in the next tremendous valley revealing a whole hour's motoring at a glance. Villages were rare and surrounded by fields approaching the vertical, and the terrain grew even more rugged and the scale of measurements simply soared to vast proportions. The River Cauca scribbled in quicksilver at the nadir of the valley flashed back the sunlight without betraying the direction of the current, and when we descended to bridge-level we saw it to be 100 feet broad and bubbling over the rocky bed only a couple of feet deep at most. We camped there on a crumbly cliff 80 feet above the river, and the infrequent passing trucks made stones patter down on us in miniature landslides. We were at only 5,000 feet and so enjoyed a balmy evening and used the sandmats as gridirons again to cook on. It was Sam's birthday which was ceremoniously observed with a cake, and a 3-D card which Stephanie made. Since we would be crossing the border next day we had one of our regular meetings and Paul let us know the options ahead of us, which he did about once a week. In the dark of night the river could be heard rustling along, and coupled with propinquity of the stars evoked powerful feelings of nostalgia.

We arose while the sky was yet starlit, and downing Bill's usual leathern pancakes were on our way before Venus had faded from the sky. In those remote mountains the dawn chorus of birdsong was surprisingly loud in the absence of any other sound. Again we ascended the high sierras between mountain walls so lofty that no sky was visible through the window, a place where the dawn light develops gently before shafting suddenly over the mountain-tops. Paul was pretty good at matching the cassette music to the mood or scenery, and for a mountain arena like this he selected the Daphnis and Chloe Overture. We overtook a petrol tanker on a steep incline, and looking back were flabbergasted to learn it was driven by a small boy about nine years old, standing up to reach the controls. All day the sky remained a deep azure and the scenery was the same as yesterday's with alternatively mountains on all sides of us when we descended to 5,000 feet, or range upon range of sawtooth peaks when we went over passes at more than twice that height. As we ventured nearer the Equator the mountain greenery faded to a barren golden, leaving the high pinnacles sterile at the mercy of the weather, which caused small landslides daily, sometimes presenting motorists with massive boulders to be negotiated. A road-gang works year-round with a bulldozer to tip debris over the edge of the abyss and pack in pot-holes with hand-tools, and we passed these men later on.

We reached Pasto on a broad fertile plateau 8,530 feet up, but it sits near the smouldering Galeras Volcano another 4,780 feet higher. The Indians wear quaint bowler hats and coloured ponchos, and they live in adobe huts and raise cattle. We stopped at Ipiales amid three active volcanoes, where Ann and I found a crowd, all male, watching a gambling game like bagatelle. The money changed hands very fast while a couple of old men rolled outsize steel marbles down a 25-foot course at a target board with holes in it. We returned to the truck in the plaza, only to find the town band, dressed in mufti, giving an impromptu request concert, while the locals admired them with happy expressions on their creased and leathery faces which told of a life of hardship. We passed a training bullring and grandstand, built of wood, on the outskirts of the town as we went down the hill to the border-post at Tulcán, which is actually on the natural Rumichaca Bridge over the River Carchi. A road race held us up for an hour as the bridge formed part of the circuit. We did not know it then, but Rein was there watching the race, half-starved without money, and seeing the truck approaching which spelt his salvation, he tried to meet us but the authorities would not let him pass. The passport inspector, having watched the race for an hour, asked us to wait a further hour while he had lunch. (This ploy means, "If you pay me an extra $20, and give me a gift, I will let you through right away." Paul never paid the bribe normally extracted from groups.)

CHAPTER TEN

ECUADOR

Ecuador was the smallest South American country we visited, but it was one of the most interesting and we stayed a disproportionately long time. Two fifths of its 7,000,000 population are pure Indian, and the same number again are Mestizo, and the rest are other races and blood mixes including the descendants of African slaves. The Andes run through Ecuador in two chains containing dozens of volcanoes among the other peaks. Two of the giants are the extinct Chimborazo, 20,577 feet high, and Cotopaxi, 19,498 feet high and still active. Between the cordilleras are ten valley basins separated by lesser mountains, and in the north, south, and west of the country are productive lowlands, while to the east lies the Oriente in the Amazon River Basin. Most of the Andean highland is covered with grassy páramo (or moorland) more as a result of poor usage than lack of opportunity to develop it. Within the last decade Ecuador has lost its total dependence on agriculture for its exports: though it is still true that coffee, cacao, bananas, and sugar occupy over half the workforce, oil and natural gas have been discovered in the Oriente which has resulted in the building of roads into the jungle bringing settlers; and now Ecuador is a member of O.P.E.C., second only to Venezuela as an oil exporter from South America. Close on three quarters of the land area of Ecuador is clad in tropical jungle, and most of the children still do not attend school. Ecuador was already a separate country before Pizarro and his Conquistadores overthrew it, and it formed roughly the northern Kingdom of the Incas with Quito as its capital. Pizarro's task was rendered remarkably easy for him as the Incas of Quito were involved in a civil war with those of the southern Kingdom. Guayaquil is actually the largest city in the country with a population in excess of 1,000,000. It is also the main seaport, and the leading centre of commerce and light industry: Ecuador has no heavy industry.

The cemetery at Tulcán has become famous for its fantastic topiary, and here the skill of the artist in clipping the bushes to resemble other plants, animals, and geometric shapes has reached its apogee. Finally on the move, we all remarked on the cold (due to being 10,000 feet up) so close to the Equator, but far more noteworthy was the total change of scenery on this side of the border. We had entered a cold barren desert of creamy grey volanic rock and ash. Only the valley floor yielded any crops and the isolated hamlets depending on this frugal supply were inhabited by poorly dressed Negroes, descendants of the Jesuits' slaves transported in the seventeenth century.

CHAPTER TEN   ECUADOR

Despite high rainfall, over 50 inches in the wet season alone, jungle cannot grow here because the rock is too porous, and manages only thorn scrub with solitary palms and pine trees. The spartan territory gradually developed into the most enormous mountains with permanent snow. Below the snow-levels the peaks were ravaged by erosion scars running down the slopes opening out into alluvial fans, and in the evening light appeared entirely bereft of life other than occasional trees seen in silhouette in the moister clefts. We camped beside Lake Yaguarcocha, the so-called 'Lake of Blood'.

In the clear light of the day we could see across the valley to the enormous mountain on the other side with tiny fields demarcated by ash-brick walls going high up the mountainside nearly to its summit several miles away, while many houses and shacks dotted the whole landscape. The day turned out glorious with only a few cotton boll clouds hugging the snowy pinnacles and sometimes the glistening snow-fields many acres in extent. Throughout the Ecuadorian Andes waterfalls were so common that they scarcely raised any interest in the group, even though some rills came hurtling and cascading from great heights, splitting the greenery with silver lines as they dropped between their bushy banks, which slowly revealed them and then hid them from sight again as we passed by. We reached the high cloud-forests, and the mists rolling thickly past the crowded trees lent the forests a mystical magic. Even up here there were villages, high and cold, with such strange inhabitants, short stocky Indians wearing ponchos in their traditional colours and narrow-brimmed bowler hats, and all barefoot. The little children ran along the stony road behind us without appearing to feel the stone bruises on their tough leathery soles. The villages are mainly comprised of adobe buildings, some very well finished and appointed, proving it entirely the equal of brick for regular housing, and at no cost as it is freely available from the laval mud in these parts. Panama hats are made in villages here in Ecuador, and all over Colombia, Costa Rica, and Honduras, of shredded fibre from a cloud-forest plant. They were given their name by travellers sailing through the Panama Canal and seeing them there for the first time.

Statues are generally few in Latin America, save for the statesmen whose likenesses are to be found in all the capital cities. It was thus refeshing to see in open countryside a larger than life yoke of oxen pulling a simple plough in the hands of a peon. Soon after we saw exactly this method in use between rows of maize. Sometimes oxen and at other times horses, or one of each, are yoked together to draw a plough of wood. I noticed a number of such wooden ploughs leaning up against a hedge growing atop an adobe wall. Hedges are often planted to protect the soft walls from the rain, and agave cactus or some other scratchy plant is favoured. We passed hundreds of fields of alfalfa, but the variety of crops was enormous. In this country tagua nuts (the fruit of palm ferns) are a major export from the coastal hills, as is cacao from the natural levees on the flood plains. Even further south on the Peruvian border African palms are raised as a crop, but up here flowers are also grown by the Indians as a sale crop. The fields ranged from pocket hankerchief size to whole sections of the mountainsides and for the first time since leaving Tijuana in Baja California we saw blossoming shrubs and ornamental trees and flower beds in people's gardens, which often contained fruit trees, especially bananas and mandarins. We encountered luxury homesteads and 'haciendas' on the outskirts of large towns or remote in the most beautiful tracts of wilderness. The haciendas are so attractive and surrounded by stables, outhouses, cloistered patios, even swimming-pools and courtyards. Their architecture is rich with colonnades, fancy decorative carpentry and brickwork, ornate window grills over complicated shutters, fresh paint and curved coloured roofing tiles. Some people in Ecuador are very, very rich and this tiny handful monopolises the country's wealth. The majority live at subsistence level, especially the Indians, few of whom earn any money whatever.

About midday 15 miles north of Quito we crossed the Equator, and naturally it was a big event, so we stopped there quite a long time. Being so high up, nearly 8,000 feet, it was colder than we had expected the Equator to be. 15 miles away the magnificent snowcap of the slumbering giant, Rucu Pichincha, pierces the sky. Marking the Equator was a signpost giving latitude 0° 00' and a six-foot concrete globe. There is a second monument marking the Equator on another road, but both are about half a mile out. By this time, Ann, Rolf, Tobin, Frank, and I had become a particular set of friends but not exclusively, and Bill had assumed the role of self-imposed guru, chief cook, and physical fitness instructor. He was a very willing worker, taking overall charge of every task that came up, but very early each morning his enthusiastic approach rudely shattered our slumbers when he blew shrill blasts on his U.S.A.F. rescue whistle which he followed with a piercing falsetto greeting. It was almost too much to bear and his influence did not go down well, but his self-agrandisement was taken in good humour to begin with as part of his character, and Bill certainly was a character. Other than a very few of us, everyone used to nod off to sleep and miss the scenery.

Shortly before we pulled into Quito we saw three mountain goats; one black, one brown, and one white. In retrospect that seems likely enough, but at the time it was surprising to see wild goats. We planned only to provision ourselves for an excursion into the Amazon jungle, and for me that meant the opportunity to see the wildlife which includes jaguars, cougars, tapirs, ant-bears, falcons, owls, flamingoes and other grallatorial birds, monkeys, parrots, and a lot more. In the countryside near Quito there were so many new plants to observe; the cycad palms and tree-ferns were both shaped like fountains with their leaves bursting forth in cascades all round. Elsewhere the immensely tall royal palms towered above the thin forest, and there was standing deadwood with quantities of epiphytes sprouting all over it, and high forked conifers with just tiny crowns of green. In Quito it fell to Ann and me to guard the truck and we attracted the attention of a couple of members of the Peace

Corps, in fact its senior representatives in Ecuador. The Peace Corps is deeply involved in this country, but the couple would not enlighten us as to what the Corps actually did. That was secret. Quito is one of the loveliest cities in South America and is set in a dip at the base of the dormant Rucu Pichincha Volcano. Quito lies in a basin in the Central Valley between the two Andean cordilleras, and the peaks around it include noble chains of volcanoes. One of the peaks is that of Mount Chimborazo, the eighth highest mountain in the continent, but its summit is the point of the Earth's greatest radius when taking into account the world's equatorial bulge. The rainfall at Quito in the wet season adds up to 52 inches, but the city's environs are not dense equatorial forest because the substratum is soft porous ash.

Moving south-east into the jungle on the start of our excursion among the meandering tributaries of the Amazon in the Ecuadorian Oriente, we underwent another police search, and at last the message had sunk in by common understanding that it was unwise to speak to the authorities, and especially no-one should admit to any knowledge of Spanish. The check passed off without event and we travelled up to the high mountain pass near Papallacta village and we camped there in the freezing cold at 12,400 feet. Just as we were setting up camp, a huge, dense, grey, thunder cloud rolled up the mountain like a living entity and engulfed us briefly before passing on. Hundreds of frogs kept up their strident calls all night in the dripping undergrowth. By the time we arose, the temperature had dropped to two degrees below zero and hoar frost stiffened the flysheets so they could stand by themselves, and. it sparkled all around us on the ground, bejewelling the spiderwebs. A dawn chorus of invisible birds twittered in a hundred different sharps and flats and I went in search of them. The freezing mountain-top was covered in low bushes and I could only see little hopping birds and a couple of condors gliding high in the sky. Joining Rolf, I stood and looked at a vast and awesome peak shewing over the nearer mountains, covered in a dazzling coat of snow burnished to an emphatic brilliance

CHAPTER TEN ECUADOR

by the morning sun. This was Mount Antisana, an extinct volcano 18,720 feet high, renowned for the huge snowfalls it receives and for its great glaciers.

Leaving the location, we had only jolted a few miles down the uneven track when a sudden loud hiss indicated a puncture. We could not stop there even though the view was glorious overlooking a lake, for it was much too cold and we descended several thousand feet to the warmer air of Papallacta village. We all piled in to help, and for the others it was the first time they had seen a truck wheel taken apart and the tube changed. The volcanic road dust was choking, but for thousands of miles we drove on dust-roads and became quite used to it, even though it coated everything with a film of dirt. After an hour's work, Paul, Sam, Frank, Bill, Tobin, and I ended up smothered in powdery clay. Another first for most of the group was when they watched Paul fill the diesel tanks by means of a hand-operated pump, one more sign of the underdevelopment in these countries. By lunch time we had dropped sharply down into true luscious Amazonian jungle with streams and pools everywhere, and dripping moisture on the spongy sphagnum and damp epiphytes swathed the branches. We were in a riot of undergrowth: bluish green fungi, trumpet-shaped flowers, and every kind of tree surrounded us. Yuca, a tree root, and naranjillas, orange fruit related to the tomato, are harvested here for sale, and the jungle climate is eminently suitable for a lot more food plants which we saw as we went along, together with an enormous variety of ferns and palms, deciduous and evergreen trees, thousands of flowers, and all colours of foliage, bright reds, rich purples, and blossoms in startling yellow. Even the rocks were covered with colourful lichens, and tree trunks were splashed in all colours, ranging from pristine white through browns and greens and even mauve. A fungus was the oddest vegetation there; it was silver-grey and quite floppy like elephants' ears. All afternoon we advanced along the rather soggy gravel track built by an oil company opening up the Oriente, and we were making the same journey as hundreds of entrepreneurial Ecuadorians to this pioneer frontierland, who have razed plots in the forested plains to produce coffee, okra, cacao, tropical fruits, hearts of palm, also animal skins, fish, and timber. For as long as there was a road we were not into the tribal hinterland but in the territory of the semi-civilised Quechua Indians, a docile people converted to Roman Catholicism with its local missions becoming as large as villages. The head-hunting Jívaro Indians had their territory a little way to the south, but their ways have been mended and only a section of the tribe, the 'Jívaros bravos' are still completely independent and unapproachable deep in the forest.

Towards the end of the day Rolf and Tobin, after putting their heads together for a while, burst into an uproarious comical drinking chorus in the bass register and gave everyone a laugh. It became the theme song for the expedition, half in German, half in English. Early in the evening we arrived at Misahuallí, where the wide Misahuallí tributary (itself a major river) joins the River Napo which in its turn drains into the Amazon 600 miles downstream. The Misahuallí has a fine sandy beach used as a dock. My top priority was to take a bath after days of tropical weather without access to a dab of water, and the rushing Misahuallí waters felt as though they had just come off the snow-fields. There are two well known river guides in the village, Douglas Clarke, a lepidopterist, and a Mestizo called Hector, and Paul arranged with the latter for two expeditions into the jungle starting in the morning. Hector put us up in an enormous open-sided thatched cabin, complete with all modern conveniences. It was a great deal better than most of the hotels we stayed in at other times, and snuggled into the jungle out of sight and sound of the rest of the village. Most of us went bathing in the tropical moonlight, with only the sounds of the jungle and the chill of the water assaulting our senses. Paul and Hector arranged a fairly festive evening for us with taped music, Hector owning a private generator to provide electricity for lighting and a fridge.

CHAPTER TEN   ECUADOR

The most outstanding memory of the day is of the odd termites' nests fixed about five feet up many tree trunks. Brown and slightly lumpy, they were made of excavated wood material and saliva, and each nest was 15 inches high and mammiform, halfway encompassing the trunk. Lying in bed the jungle noises were loud around us, various birds and monkeys were sounding off and, unhappily, many species of insects buzzed annoyingly. The most peculiar insect of all was a pupa Bill found with luminous green 'eyes' which glowed brightly, as did a third luminous spot, this time scarlet. The pupa was an inch and a half long by two thirds broad, and when disturbed its lights went out and it flipped violently away. I burned a mosquito coil but it served more to evoke memories of my life in Asia than to keep at bay a jungleful of pestilential anopheline mosquitoes. Fireflies kept flashing over our heads, and the river added its soothing burble to the general eternal whisper. Hector provided a nightwatchman, a deaf mute who became as drunk as a lord and suddenly woke us all in the early hours by turning on the lights and music at full blast and smashing beer bottles. The poor fellow was very lonely, and Tobin fetched Hector to deal with the man, who was uttering pathetic squeaks. The generator was cut and we all went back to sleep, though the night was colder than I would have associated with Equatorial Amazonia.

In the morning we split into two expeditions, a walking party and a canoe party. The walkers endured the greater hardship, wading across rivers waist-deep, risking leeches, piranhas, and alligators, and also night walks and cold to reach their camping-spots, one being the village of a semi-civilised tribe of Indians. Most of them, if not all, sacrificed their shoes which rotted on their feet. They made an early start with Hector, initially by canoe. Paul did not go on either excursion as someone had to guard the vehicle, which also required a great deal of work. 11 of us, Maria, Sandra, Frances, Ann, Frank, Bill, Tobin, Rolf, myself, and a couple of young Frenchmen, took our places on benches in a one-piece 45-foot cedar dugout canoe, powered by a 40 b.h.p. outboard motor. There was considerable excitement as Paul saw us off. Ann and I had expected hot steamy jungle, such as the walkers were experiencing, but instead as we made 30 knots downstream, the strong breeze forced us to wrap under my poncho to keep the spray off. The jungle around Misahuallí is full of every sort of insect, but few biters, and loveliest of all are the flies and beetles with metallic sheens in purple and emerald and vivid crimson. The moths and butterflies of Amazonia are quite properly of world renown; they are all sizes and colours with the most strikingly intricate designs on the wings, and others had oddly shaped trailing wings or glittering abdomens, and some had pure white furry bodies the size of mice. One in particular had a wingspread the size of a dinner plate with eye markings on outlined wings in pastel green.

Our friendly guide, Demacio, was a Guaraní Indian from another area downstream but he spoke Spanish. He was a very cheerful young man with gaps in his smile, and the ability born of long practice to walk along the gunwales of the rocking canoe. The motorised dugout was infinitely better than any Venetian gondola. The Napo is about ten feet deep and 500 yards wide, much more in places, with islands and sand-bars all along it, and many rocky or sandy beaches. While Demacio sat in the bow or slept a lot of the time on the huge pile of luggage we had brought along, the boat-owner stood at the tiller reading the river ahead of us and swerving the canoe to avoid obstacles invisible to us in the muddy brown water, and evidenced only by the faintest turbulence and lines on the surface. Dead trees of all sizes were commonly embedded amidstream. Very often just one branch remained sticking a little way out of the torrent, and wagged up and down like a serpent cutting through the surface. These dancing trees were amazing to watch, while some trees formed temporary islands for a few months or years, snagging tangles of flotsam and jetsam and providing a habitat for hosts of grasses, cacti, moss, orchids, and even other trees to grow on.

Along the beaches we could see Indian families prospecting for gold, all working hard, but we were puzzled by their instruments and behaviour. Wherever other tributaries joined the River Napo we rode rocky rapids and spray flew up from the slapping prow. The vegetation along the shores appeared fairly low with trees up to 100 feet, especially the immortelles, breaking the monotony. This region of the Amazon Basin is semi-cultivated by Quechua Indians in the main, with all kinds of useful plants like pawpaws, lemons, coffee, cacao, dates, bamboo, and lianas being encouraged and a great deal of sugar-cane and all kinds of palms are planted. Red, yellow, and white flowers added colour everywhere, brightening up the infinite shades of green. When we embarked the sun was shining and the light penetrated the forest walls, but for at least an hour we sped through a heavy downpour, at which Ann took shelter under my poncho for the rain was chilling. Just like a shutting door the dull weather closed out the visual effect of the bright warm jungle. The river served as the quickest highway and dozens of dugouts plied to and fro, some employing outboards, and others paddles or punts, and ranging in size from 10 to 50 feet long. Many dugouts were beached by lone houses or missions and small villages. An hour out of Misahuallí we came upon a scene reminiscent of Mark Twain's era, a 'floatel' looking quite like an old Mississippi Riverboat Queen, three storeys high and painted red and white, but without the smoke-stack and paddle-wheels, nestled close by the shore at the confluence of a tributary with the River Napo. Across this tributary was the most amazing yet simple suspension bridge bearing an oil pipeline slung under a foot-path, and at either end cranelike geodetic scaffolds (like V's sticking out above the low jungle) supported a few simple cables. When the sun came out again it lit up the jungle and gave it renewed warmth, energy, and vitality. Endless stands of palms with fan-shaped foliage vied with mimosa and philodendrons and all kinds of ferns. There are so many varieties of palms and ferns and orchids and trees that it is not possible to identify any one against the mass. Fern palms and tree-ferns appear so similar, and pine trees may be very low and flat, spreading out fine leafy fans just like the fronded ferns.

A close view of the date palms reveals the dates (from the female flowers) grow higher up the trunks than the three massive tusk-shaped pods, which open up and shed their outsides to expose whiplike strands bearing hundreds of yellow male flowers the size of peas. Once the pollen has blown away these fall in showers onto the ground below. Immense ceiba trees dot the forest, but seem to grow no leaves, only the fluffy kapok shewing fawn at the tips of the branches. The silk-cotton bolls are harvested, though additionally ordinary cotton is grown here, alongside tobacco, breadfruit, mangos, quinoa, pineapples, tamarinds, and many herbal plants with lovely aromas from their leaves, and from place to place we saw mauve blossom on the native jacarandas. Every tree was taken advantage of by a host of creepers, parasites, spider plants, and epiphytes, including many varieties of orchids, identifiable on close inspection by a water-filled bulb in the stem. Lianas hung everywhere we looked, and very common were great trailing plants with flowers like laterally arranged clusters of vivid pink and orange shrimps, which split to reveal dark green and scarlet fruit the size of marbles. In the sky and tall trees were fish-eagles and other birds of prey, and along the surface of the River Napo little blue and white swallows and black and yellow swallowtails skimmed with great expertise and alacrity catching insects or tip-tilting their beaks to scoop a little water.

The huge banana-shaped fruit of the fast-growing cecropia tree is soft and tasty and attracts many birds and monkeys. The golden-collared toucanet (Selenidera reinwardtii), with other toucanets, also green and gold tanagers (Tangara schrankii), vermillion and paradise tanagers, and white-lipped tamarind monkeys relish the cecropia fruit. 130 feet up the foliage forms a ceiling with the forest giants forging further still towards the rain clouds, and at every level thimble-sized puddles of collected rain-water, form miniature aquatic gardens full of life; tiny tree-frogs and insect larvae hide among leaf stems and bromeliads, aeroids, orchids, and lianas, trailing down into the misty murky shadows. Here the river flows along only 800 feet above sea-level and has to go another 2,500. miles to reach the Atlantic Ocean, and it actually flows perceptibly uphill for the last 2,000 miles, resulting in only a tiny fraction of the water ever reaching the ocean and breaking out of the permanent cycle of evaporation and precipitation in thunderstorms which accounts for the rest of the water. For months on end the countless rivers may lie in flood trapped in a virtual sponge 1,500,000 square miles in extent, alone incorporating a third of the world's birdlife, over 2,000 species of fish, and tens of times as many types of trees than may be found in Europe.

After pressing on downstream for six hours we reached the sleepy Indian village of Coca, and returning this journey was to take us more than twice as long with both outboard motors going. Coca is very small and almost entirely shanty but for the naval base and the customs cum police checkpoint where we all had to produce our passports. It is connected by a foot-path to Misahuallí, and is one of the few centres of importance in the Oriente. Ragged squealing children played in the river by the pontoon docks, and the naval personnel kept arriving and departing in their high-powered dugouts, but they never sit for fear of soiling their pristine white smartly pressed uniforms; even their white shoes were immaculate. When the canoes rock or start up the sailors never lose their balance, but stand facing forwards as the craft moves through the current, and lean into the corners to counterbalance the centrifugual force. At Coca the set meal was the same at both its simple cafés, overpriced egg on rice with coca-cola, so I spent my money on several dozen bread rolls and hands of bananas at a cent apiece, avocados at two cents apiece, and tomatoes at three cents apiece. As a jungle expedition we had virtually no common provisions and everyone brought his own.

We only spent an hour at Coca because we had to hasten as far as possible downriver by sundown, and we moved out wide with great caution for at Coca the River Napo is joined by its major tributary, the River Coca, and this created standing waves higher than the sides of our dugout. Pollution in the form of chunks of white froth floated along around us and lingered over the sand-bars, and wherever the current was stilled the froth formed natural signs marking areas of shallow draught, so aiding navigation, though the more permanent sandbanks had been staked. Demacio told us the river had had this froth on it for generations whenever the water was high. Little whirlpools and 'boiling' eddies showed where branches or irregularities in the rocky, river-bed posed a hazard. Gossamer strands and tangles drifted gently down from overhanging boughs, and the river-banks continuously brought new images to mind. Occasionally the outboard screw choked on the sandy bottom, and in the precious seconds of silence which followed Ann and I listened keenly for the sounds of the jungle over the burble of the Amazon passing us by and the quiet undertow of conversation in the boat. The cicadas' shrill song came over clearly but only a. little birdsong was distantly audible, and there was no wind to rustle the leaves. Ann pointed out a black ibis feeding in the shade along the bank, and elsewhere an Amazonean umbrella bird, named after its high black crest plumage, was visible in a heliconia tree shaking its head and inelegant pendulous wattle. The faint birdcalls which we could hear best were the coarse squawks of the frugiverous cock-in-the-rock birds, of which the males construct lekking platforms for reasons of courtship dancing: all this feather-rustling renders them conspicuous to high-flying predators, so they are careful to display their orange plumes safely beneath the dense canopy of leaves. Birds were easiest to spot when we disturbed them, as when we passed close to shore and startled a grey-capped flycatcher (Miozetetes granadensis) into flight, and a green jay spurred into the air stridulously sounding the alarm. We also wondered at an antediluvian species, cumbersome hoatzins which are reminiscent of the archeopterix and flew in a series of heavy dips. The variety of birds was a source of constant wonderment, not least for their diets; e.g. the oropendolas share a nectar preference with many butterflies and monkeys, and in so doing fertilise the flowers. The black-tailed trogon is another bird which trades nectar and pollen for cross-pollination from the self-same flowers, and may be readily identified by the way it flicks its tail up and down.

The jungle is vast and sparsely inhabited but nearly all its people live along the shores of the mighty Amazon and its tributaries. All the time we passed tiny villages or houses built of split cane or date palm unrolled with an axe like crude veneer for the walls and floors, standing on high stilts for protection and coolness, and also to provide shelter for the motley domestic animals scratching around in the dirt underneath. Clusters of Indians and their children stood and watched us but made no sign of greeting. East of Coca the river was the sole highway and everyone owned a dugout, be it a short two-man affair or a long, heavy, passenger type requiring motors, serving the community as buses serve a city, carrying produce under a spray-washed tarpaulin in the bow and people on regular benches behind. We observed with great curiosity a boat apparently being burnt ashore with thick smoke rising amidships. We could not comprehend why a dugout should be thus treated and I surmised to Ann that it was being caulked. In fact I was not far out, and later we tackled Demacio about it and he told us that dugouts are hardened and made more waterproof and durable by lighting fires inside the hulls to temper them. As many of the dugouts have built up gunwales, the gaps need to be pitched at the same time, and this is what I had recognised. The dugout serves its maker for the rest of his life, gradually wearing out and going spongy as it rots from the outside, and whenever deemed necessary it is scraped so that the hull is slowly thinned down. All along the river-banks we noticed extraordinary white nests shaped like elongated pear-drops hanging utterly exposed from the outermost tips of the highest branches. These nests belonged to the shy oropendolas and were woven like baskets two to three feet long and nine inches across at the widest point, and dangled and swung conspicuously but completely invulnerably against the pink blossom and the blue of the sky. From the water the jungle appeared to us an unyielding phalanx of trees, broken only here and there by the foliage of an acacia, with finely divided tremulous leaves, or the large star-shaped leaves of the cecropia; trees were festooned with brilliant begonias and red-flowered vines, exhaling a subtle perfume, climbing above the lower trees to reach for the sunlight. The jungle is tenanted by jaguars, and kinkajous (also nocturnal carnivores but not averse to eating the pods off the bean-trees), porcine capybaras, deer, collared peccaries, and tapirs, an ancient species related to the rhinoceros and equally adapted to life in the rivers and on land, with elephantine trunks for scenting and foraging. Monkeys, sloths, and a variety of reptiles from the seldom encountered 30-foot monster serpents to frail lizards cohabit here: typical of the monkeys are the subspecies of titi monkey which will make do with any food available, whether it involves catching insects or garnering fruit, especially figs, and young leafy fronds; and rivalling the titi for the figs are squirrel monkeys and spider monkeys and the black capuchins and red wakari monkeys, all of which have prehensile tails, a feature unique to New World animals. Elsewhere white capuchin monkeys have learned the art of opening palm-nuts by smashing two together. The three-toed sloths have a curious symbiosis with a species of moth, which infests their fur while they are up in the trees, along with green algae which serves to camouflage the painfully slow animals from harpy eagles. The sloths' toilet habits require them to descend to ground-level every few days, when the moths all stay behind to lay their eggs in the dung; and the newly hatched moths complete the cycle by rising into the forest canopy in search of fresh hosts. While the three-toed sloths live discreet quiet lives, other animals go to a great deal of trouble to show themselves off; especially the band-tailed manakins whose agility in the trees allows them to play and dance with complete abandon. The smallest of all monkeys is the pygmy marmoset which seems so cuddly with a startled look on its baby face and big, round, eyes. In the trees dwells a paradise of birds: the snow-crested bellbird whose alarm cry is like the chime of a clapped bell, gaudy toucans long of beak, oilbirds, ghostly white herons, trumpeter birds, great egrets, and the boss of them all, the king vulture which has vivid colouring, especially a livid blue breast. Parrots and parakeets of all shades and sizes are the noisiest of all the forest-dwellers, and the largest of these are the scarlet macaws and blue macaws which have immensely powerful beaks to crush nuts and seeds. Many smaller seeds are swallowed whole with fruit and pass through the birds to be dropped miles away from the parent tree, and typical of these are the pods of balsa trees, also figs. White-bellied parrots, the quite rare hyacinth macaws (light purple in colour), and curious motmot birds all make quite a racket about their rights to eat in the strangler figtree. But insects were the dominant element, masters of the dank earth; army ants, tumecas, an inch long, had dreadful stings as well' as bites and attacked anything that moved, willy-nilly. There were other, ants which we had seen before in almost infinite numbers which defoliated the trees and carried the leaf fragments down into the earth to fertilise the fungus gardens on which they lived. There are species of termites and ants which have adapted to a cryptobiotical existence inside certain trees, trading shelter within the tree for protection of the tree from leaf-eating insects. For instance some melastome plants provide special chambers, or. domatia, for their resident ants; and the triplaris, or ant tree, is filled with azteca ants, utterly vicious and a centimetre long, and from place to place in the tree are special knot holes to let the ants in and out practically, anywhere in the entire tree down to its tiniest twig. Then there are mosquitoes which bring tertian fever, while the night-kiss of the female anopheles brings malaria. Endless flies, beetles, cockroaches, crickets, butterflies, preying mantises, terribly armed wasps, minute jejenes flies, a veritable plague of insects bothered us whenever we were still, and the worst of all were the sweat-bees, stingless bees searching perpetually for exudate and settling all over us, and particularly our eyes and nostrils and. in our hair.

As the evening sun drew lower directly behind us, the lighting effect grew more vibrant and colourful, changing the jungle by the minute. The slanting sunlight penetrated the river-banks dripping with tropical vegetation, sometimes atop bare mud or clay cliffs up to 20 feet above the river. One common type of tree particularly caught the light due.to the whiteness of its bark which I believe was the result of masses of lichens growing all over it. Quite suddenly at the passing of the day a strong gust blew up rocking our dugout and making branches and palm leaves thresh about. Ann was quite concerned for our safety, but the wind died out abruptly a few minutes later. How strange it was! Once the wind had settled down the river became smooth as glass and yielded the most perfect reflections of a darkening sky over the sunset-lit jungle. Especially pretty were the low flat clouds strung out all around the horizon leaving an empty dome of blue. All day long our guide had been in a hurry and now opened the throttle to a more urgent tone. It was not possible to navigate by night and we were miles short of our destination. The silhouettes of the trees, particularly the taller ones above the general pell-mell of foliage presented us with a wholly new romantic aspect of the jungle. Depth was lent to the vegetation now only by watching the branches and leaves slide across each other over our heads as they were all the same black against the navy sky.

At last, sore and stiff, we arrived at our refuge for the night. There was no dock: we just ran aground and scrambled up a high slippery bank. The stilt-house was entirely constructed of date palms, including the springy floor boards which were the opened out circumferences of the trunks, and the thatched roof which some Indians take the trouble to plait for longevity. I quickly set up a corner for Ann and me as there was obviously a shortage of bedspace, put up my mosquito-net and lit mosquito coils for all the dubious good it did, besides which the thatch was riddled with fat red cockroaches. On the ground below a number of jungle fowl (the ancestral forerunners of the domestic chicken), Muscovy ducks, white-lipped peccaries, and mongrel dogs all contributed their sounds to the twilight chorus and the perpetual chirring of insects. There was an open raised hearth also constructed of date palm with a sheet metal base in lieu of a hearthstone and the cooking range consisted of a couple of logs laid along the five-foot length of the fire-place at a suitable height above the flames. Sandra and Bill, self-appointed rival leaders of the expedition as a whole, volunteered to take charge of catering, and the dearth of provisions led to a heated argument betwixt Sandra and Frank. Budgetting for the expedition, with expenses varying from day to day, meant balancing the cost of food against the quantity, and the female majority opinion had always been in favour of small meals. The guides had their own food but Sandra offered to feed them from our scant common provisions which would certainly not last out the morrow.

There were a couple of shot-guns stuck in the thatch wall, one being an antique hammer-action 20-gate. The Indian who built the house and another one 20 feet away assured us that despite the fire-arm's desperate condition it still worked. I examined it and found it fully functional, whereas the wooden parts of the other one had all rotted off. Guns are used here to hunt dangerous animals, particularly the big cats and snakes (among which are pythons, boa-constrictors, and anacondas) which very occasionally raid the settlements, or to take as protection against sudden attack by crocodiles up to 20 feet long during organised baby crocodile hunts with spears to satisfy the demand from paying tourists. Demacio told Ann and me the Indians despise this hunting for sport because they love the animals and live in harmony with them. With the guns was a machete, put away by the simple expedience of sticking the blade through the wall up to the hilt. Since Bill was cooking it was clear we would have a couple of hours to wait for supper, so Ann and I went down to a clearing by the river and were swallowed up by our romance and the exotic sights and sounds of it all. We spotted constellations and planets which we recognised but our attention was rivetted to a beautiful glimmering off to one side of the sky, at that point completely obscured by cloud. This faint light was more or less constant but flickered more brightly every few seconds. We were both reminded of the Northern Lights but this was due to a monumental equatorial electric storm miles beyond earshot whose lightning was illuminating the cloud canopy over a great area of jungle. After a simple supper the others discovered the shortage of accommodation and Manfred ended up sleeping on a table. In the middle of the night he must have moved because he tipped the kerosene candle all over Bill and Frances, who made such a hullaballoo one would think the sky was falling in.

Long hours before dawn the miserable cockerels began to crow. How we wished them dead! Once again the night had been very cool and the floor too hard for comfort. While breakfast was on the go, Demacio and the owner answered questions Ann and I put to them about-the food being grown around the house. The main staple of the Amazonian Indians is the manioc, a plant with slender grey stems which support compound leaves and grow head-high: and when this plant is pulled up a large tuberous brown root with a brown bark-like integument weighing a pound or two is attached to the stem. The tuber is ground into cassava flour and the sweet manioc can be eaten without worry, but the bitter manioc contains prussic acid poison which must be removed by grating and washing the root. The Indian had a Brazil nut tree, and a thicket of sugar-cane, also coffee with tight little clusters of berries turning red and delicate pinkish white florets. Pineapples were growing but were not very plump on the dark forest floor. Demacio pointed out the shoot of next year's fruit growing at the base of the pineapple. There were red pepper bushes, and an extremely aromatic coarse grass which is traditionally steeped in boiling water and the brew drunk socially. There were bananas and plantains, and once again I saw brown termites' nests on the banana palms, and I studied them close up. Termites were crawling in an orderly highway up and down between the nest and the ground, but the tree was not harmed. We discovered a snail-shell as big as a baseball but only Frank displayed any interest.

All day the weather was gloomy and the forest completely lost its appeal, but worse, the boatmen had difficulty navigating and we ran onto a mudbank and all had to jump out and push. Nervous talk of alligators and piranhas arose, but clad only in our underwear we heaved the dugout to deeper water and were soon under weigh again. Quite an adventure! There were a few scarlet macaws in a tree overlooking the river and despite the overcast sky they cut a splash of red 200 yards away. We arrived at an Indian small-holding where we had our lunch, and the Indian woman who lived there brought out some hot yuca and plantain she boiled for us. Both were very bland dry eating. Meanwhile Demacio paddled the dugout the half-mile across the river to ask the woman's husband to act as a guide for us. Since the River Napo is so wide the guide had built a house on either bank and it took Demacio well over an hour to fetch him. In this time the Indian woman offered to sell us some hides she had prepared from a couple of jaguars, also agoutis (which have a predilection for fallen Brazil nuts), and she showed us some porcupine quills. The jaguars had diminished their livestock and her husband had gone after them with his knife. Little piccaninnies played with the goats and bush dogs in the low spaces under the house where the stilts formed the framework of a pen. Smoke was curling up through the rafters, and beside her home stood a fairly large grove of bananas: but I shall always remember the location most of all for the hundreds of different butterflies attracted to the clearing in the forest in front of the hut. Their bold markings were every hue and tint, resplendent and gorgeous, clouds of-fluttering colour. It was only when one settled and began flashing its wings as a signal to the others that the intricacies of shade, design, and camouflage became clear. Local moths and butterflies include heliconids and carniverous species, taking advantage of every niche in the ecology, and some butterflies even drink the tears of caimans and turtles. The larval stages are just as diverse as the imagos, and caterpillars have assumed very realistic disguises to avoid being eaten: some have aggressive spiky fur, and others eye-spots and dangerous aspects, or else look like twigs or even spring to safety when under threat.

By and by we crossed to the Indian's second home. He was evidently a well contented man in the fulness of his years, with all he needed to satisfy his every requirement close to hand. His time was spent cultivating a grassy garden and improving his large homes. He showed off some of his treasures to us; the foot-long spiny tail barbs of sting rays, the most feared of all the Amazonian poison fish, as it has the habit of resting on shallow sand-banks where it may be stepped on quite easily. There are a great many dangerous fish in these waters, the most renowned of which is the red-bellied piranha, Serrasalmus nattereri, usually about a foot long and whose interlocking triangular teeth are so sharp that they can chomp through a foot and the boot as well with one bite. There are 25 species in the Amazon with various specialisations, but they all attack at the slightest hint of blood or commotion in the water. Six species additionally eat fruit and then spread the seeds over thousands of square miles during their migrations. The electric fish also eats the fruit of the assaí palm which it shocks out of the trees with burst of 350 volts. Paiche are predatory, but only on other fish, but not for nothing are they otherwise known as giant redfish as they reach lengths up to seven feet and weights up to 15 stone, the largest freshwater fish in South America. Pacú are related to the piranha and they are fruit-eaters and roam long distances, and are of importance in the propagation of strangler figs. A particular danger to people is the whale candirú, which is a man-eating fish found in schools in the

River Madeira, a tributary of the Amazon but one of the six largest rivers in the world (by volume) in its own right.

The Indian had a very much more impressive trophy, a boa-constrictor skin over 25 feet long tacked up along two walls of his house. The boa had turned man-eater so he had been compelled to stalk it and had killed it with a single spear thrust to the heart, after sacrificing one of his goats as live bait, because after engorging itself the snake could only move sluggishly, leaving an easy trail and was too lethargic to defend itself. Anacondas are aquatic boas, and present little threat to the Indians, eating fish and small animals for the most part. Capybaras are highly favoured in this regard and are the largest of all rodents, growing more than three feet long but fall prey to the anacondas when they go into the rivers or even close to them, for an anaconda can strike from the water like lightning, first biting its prey to take hold and immediately throwing coils around it and dragging it underwater. The anaconda (Eunectes murinus) is the subject of many myths about its size but the longest actually measured was 37½ feet in length and weighed over three quarters of a ton, which are world records nevertheless. For humans the deadliest Amazonian snake is the bushmaster, and an encounter with one of these venomous snakes is generally fatal for they are commonly seven feet long. The Indian had planted all kinds of fruit in his garden and lovely flowering trees and shrubs, and a vegetable plot. We picked ripe papayas and lemons as big as cantelopes. As we went along he and Demacio pointed out trees and plants which provided the family with all the fresh food and drink they wanted. We heaved up a knobbly and very contorted bush which resembled elderberry somewhat, but whose thick swollen roots formed the edible part, just like cassava. This was yuca. We sampled chocolate fruit which is sweet and red, like cherries but with a sour after-taste, and spat out the hard pink pits which are cocao beans, or cacao. We filed along a jungle trail for a couple of hours, sweating and panting in the steamy torrid semi-darkness. The sky was virtually blotted out, and the ceiling of lush foliage was much closer than the crowns of the tallest trees which were lost to sight above us, even when we stood and peered straight up their trunks. Some light did filter vaguely through the canopy and reach the foreboding depths of the interior. At one point we stopped to sample heart of palm, previously known to me only as an expensive epicurean delicacy, and no wonder, since to provide each epicure with his gourmet dish involves chopping down a 40-foot date, palm to extract a mere 15-inch splinter from near the top of the tree. This tree is the black chonta palm, and Pizarro's myrmidons were shot at by Indians using hardwood bows made from it: the Indians called it the 'Tree of Life'. Later the jungle guide cut down an entirely nondescript tree, but on holding up a section he poured water into his mouth, and he passed it around for us all to drink. It had the faintest vegetable taste but was otherwise pure.

In the late afternoon we arrived at a high open hut whose steeply slanting roof came down to within five feet of the ground along its length and the ends and the sides were left open. It had a sleeping-platform under most of the roofed area, and a bare earth hearth and log stools. It was the Indian's fishing lodge which he had only recently constructed and would last a lifetime before mouldering away. I immediately set up our mosquito-net as bed-space was again at a premium, while the first fishing expedition went out. Demacio and the Indian took us all in turn to fish for our supper in the lagoon, or cocha, as the old ox-bow lakes of the flood plain are called. Our cocha was typical of the majority and had black water, darkened by the tannin from the leaves rotting in the stagnant water. At last it fell to Ann and me to go out with Demacio after all the others had returned empty-handed. When it came to boats Ann was in her element, and seated precariously in a tiny, old, and very rotten dugout, leaking like a collander through much-patched cracks, Demacio gingerly paddled the horribly unstable log out into the lake. We were hemmed in tightly by a dark frieze of tall trees and the light was

CHAPTER TEN   ECUADOR

almost gone. It was so placid on the little lake, as still as a mill-pond, that we could hear the water dribbling and squirting in through the leaks. Nothing stirred except for an occasional twitch on the Indians's bamboo rod, and he paid not the slightest heed to the rising water-level in his dugout which I believed in imminent danger of sinking altogether. Ann's job was to bail. Meanwhile I hung my fishing-line out with a piece of raw chicken as bait and waited ages without result. Ann kept on asking her questions and both Indians kept on catching fish using fresh fish as bait. I tried that and, hey presto! I caught a large piranha. More and more fish were landed, large lorons, corvinhas, and perros, as well as more piranhas. (Perro is Spanish for dog, though these were nothing like the familiar dog-fish but nasty-looking monsters the shape of loofahs, all fin and bones and about half mouth — that was the half we looked at before slinging the deadly denizens back, for they had dozens of aciform teeth). The piranhas we caught were the red-bellied variety, as big as dinner plates and very beautiful in life with basically pink sides, and their scales glitter and scintillate like slightly yellow diamonds. Even after they were caught the piranhas were vicious as they bit repeatedly at anything with their razor-sharp teeth. The other fish were dispatched by stunning them with the paddle to recover the hook, but the piranhas were left alone to suffocate before the Indian guide durst touch them, when he beat them frequently about the head to be certain of stunning them. It took a lot of blows for them to stop gnashing their formidable teeth, and at the earliest opportunity the guide carefully sliced off their lower jaws with a sawing action, pressing their threshing bodies firmly onto the chopping block which made their large blood red pop-eyes bulge in a most grisly way. After the jaw was severed, the tongue still worked up and down bleeding redly, and ghastly angry eyes sought out the torturing hands while the hook was worked free. When the jungle guide was removing a piranha's jaw it bit this thumb savagely, so to clean the wound he squeezed out a few drops of blood into the lake, and the surface raged with excited piranhas. These fish are such swift and efficient attackers that in the time it took to lift the bamboo rod, they had eaten the tail half of a loron on the line. We caught 16 fish — I caught two piranhas and two lorons — and the forest guide scaled and gutted them in his dugout with declared pleasure, while keeping his bare foot on the fishing-pole and a baited line in the water, ever ready for more.

It was quite dark when we triumphantly presented our catch to the group who had entirely relinquished any hope of fresh fish and had resorted to opening the tinned sardines, but it was just as well since the boiled yuca needed the rich tomato sauce to render it swallowable. Demacio and the guide cooked up the yuca and fish over the flames in a common bucket holding back the heat with a lid of banana leaves. The result was delicious, especially the piranhas, and it all went, even the broth. No-one minded that the lake water was a clear brown and retained its woody taste which made our tea taste peculiar. Suddenly, as though exclusively for the benefit of Ann and myself, a white-tipped sicklebill humming-bird swung up to a heliconia flower in front of us, investigated it with its beak arced into a quarter circle, then backed off and zoomed away. Earlier, alone with the Indians on the water, we had seen an Amazon kingfisher hover above our battered canoes eyeing our catch or maybe just the fish below the surface all around, but either it could not see well enough into the black waters or else it had had its fill already, for it did not-dive. Perhaps Amazon kingfishers do not go for piranhas. We packed the sleeping-platform like dominoes, while Frances left with the Indians carrying a flashlight and a trident whose prongs were barbed three-inch needles arranged in a close triangle. None of us had a good night's sleep, for it became quite cool and we could not escape the piping of frogs or bats. It is hard to say which we were hearing for there are so many hundreds of species of either, and there is such a burble of gentle sounds muffled by the trees. One kind of bat (Trichops cirrhosus) has such good hearing that it selects its

CHAPTER TEN ECUADOR

meal, a frog, by its mating call and so never goes after, the poisonous ones nor any of the larger ones which would eat it instead. We were aroused at midnight by the hunting party returning with their quarry, a banded white benign crocodile with a crested tail, speared, clean through the pelvis. It was about a yard long with bright feline eyes glinting steely at us hemming it in, a mere baby. Had it been a black crocodile the Indians would have flayed it, not out of colour prejudice here — black ones are edible. As it was the poor thing was unceremoniously hung up in a sack overnight for its own safety. The word crocodile is the family name; the ones in South America are more specifically known as caimans or South American alligators, and they are very beneficial to the fish population-as they return basic nutrients into the water to maintain an ecological balance. Due to the trade in garish caiman hide toys mainly for American tourists, these animals are directly threatened and with their demise the fish are dramatically disappearing. Apart from Man their only natural enemy is the anaconda.

At the crack of dawn the guide continued his fishing, and was rejoined by Demacio, but not before he and I took the crocodile down to the water's edge. At first the reptile showed no interest, so we put it further in and gave its tail a tap: it shot off like a rocket diving steeply into the brackish lagoon. Ann and I frankly doubted it would survive firstly such a wound, and secondly the piranhas. While we were packing up, the jungle guide's mother and wife came padding near naked into the clearing to carry back the fish, dozens of them, which they cleaned prior to departing ahead of us. On our way back along the trail we stopped to admire a colossal and spectacular red flower, quite similar to a tight posy of rhododendron blooms, and later sucked and chewed on lengths of natural sugar-cane. Ann asked Demacio which trees were used to make the huge dugouts, and he told us the largest ones were of cedarwood, because only cedars were massive enough, and shorter ones were also made in other hardwoods. He took us to a giant cedar and pointed out that for years an Indian family had had their eye on this tree which would yield a couple of 50-foot dugouts from its trunk and several smaller ones from its branches, together with many cords of wood. We also stood at the base of an extraordinary ceiba tree, ten feet across above its widely buttressed bole, shortly before arriving back at the Indian's garden.

From there we turned up a lesser tributary to a Catholic Mission, run by nuns wearing black and white habits and head-scarves so that only their faces and hands were visible despite the great heat and humidity. The lawns were neat and spacious with well-arranged beds of flowers and roses. The Mission had a private museum of Indian artefacts. Demacio translated the curator's account of each item, but the others showed no interest and Ann (asking questions) and I had the museum to ourselves. The contents were up to 400 years old, made by the Auca and Guaraní Indians, and included large funerary urns, blowpipes and darts reflecting their development through the ages, and a ferocious viper's head pickled in a striking pose. The Mission church was quite unusual. For a start the altar was an old war canoe, and the church walls were built of logs standing on end, not vertically, but slanting outwards, and the high thatched roof overshadowed the gables with broad pointed eaves. The church floor was just bare damp earth.

After this side-trip we started back in a great hurry adding a second outboard motor, through warm sunshine all afternoon until the sun set. The dugout fairly sped along sending the spray flying. We were still short of our destination but it was too perilous to proceed after dark so the boatman put ashore at the nearest habitation, a hamlet with a banana plantation and the most unbelievably dense thickets of the tall bamboos we had seen all through the Oriente. Actually the majority of it was rotten and crumbled like eggshells as I walked through it. We set up our bedding and nets in a dingy one-room schoolhouse, again on stilts. The place was seething with cockroaches, but I did not tell Ann that as she would have freaked out. Demacio cooked our supper from jungle foods once more, and all around little children assembled just to look at us, shyly agog with coy expressions visible in the firelight. Standing alone with Ann at the landing-point, the moonlight on the Amazon picked out the swirls and flurries of fish snapping at insects leaving only telltale bubbles drifting by. There was not a sign of the twentieth century; we could have been in any era, and shared at that moment a common knowledge of the security the Indians have felt in the warmth and fertility of the jungle.

In the morning Ann and I sat in the bow, and with no-one in front of us we felt isolated from the others since we could hear nothing behind us but the drone of engines beating together. We disembarked again at Coca where Ann and I just caught the end of a wedding ceremony. The bride was dressed entirely in white and wore an imported wedding gown complete with a veil and brand-new snow white plimsolls. We hurried up the hill to find the church and noticed the roads were cobbled in simple patterns, on which blankets were spread for coffee and cacao to dry and darken in the hot sun. We crossed the River Napo over a bridge which also served to support a pipeline as oil has been discovered in the environs of Coca. We wanted to take a closer look at some very modernistic shell-shaped buildings, but found they were out of bounds in a military zone. There are no beggars among the Indians and the houses at Coca were all made of date palm with ornately plaited banisters and walls. Ann always set off at a great pace to explore any village or town we stopped at, and located the craftsmen and backstreet folk whom she quizzed enthusiastically in her very pigeon Spanish which was often unintelligible, but the nationals loved her sheer vitality and ingenuity. No-one else on the expedition displayed such a deep interest in the underbellies of the localities we visited but stuck to cafés and well-frequented business and tourist premises.

From Coca we pursued the river upstream once more at a great speed and soon had to come ashore for more fuel. The petrol station, as on any other South American highway, doubled as a café. The petrol was stored in jerrycans and while the Indians saw to the motors we were enraptured by the tame monkeys running around free. Soon after this stop we pulled onto a pebbly beach where an Indian family was prospecting for gold. The womenfolk were clearing aside the bigger rocks and stones to gain access to the brownish grey alluvial loam underneath. Meanwhile the man used a wooden trolley which had two sloping trays inside, zigzag-fashion, covered with baize. On the top was a sheet of metal perforated with a dozen or more holes the size of a dime, onto which was scooped ten pounds of sandy earth plus an equal amount of small pebbles (up to an inch in diameter). The traditional gold-pan was then used to dish water over the sand and pebbles a quart at a time. The Indian stirred this about with his hand until all the dirt had fallen through. The little pebbles serve to block the holes so that the sand is not washed through in a rush carrying the specks of gold right out of the system. Having flowed through the runcible platform, the water and sand washed over the first oblique baize tray, which drained onto the second one, and in turn emptied into the river. The principle is that on these slight inclines the gold-dust falls out and sticks in the coarse cloth, which is subsequently rinsed in the gold-panner's dish. The Indian demonstrated the use of his trolley, and showed us how he swirled the gold-laden silt in the panning dish, letting most of the water and dark alluvium spill over the edge. Finally he carefully centred the residue, tilted the dish slightly, and dribbled a few drops of water on the pan. Magically the sediment slid off the gold-dust which gleamed in an unbroken smear three inches wide nearly to the rim of the gold-pan. The Indian told us it was half a gram of gold-dust, the fruit of a day's labour for which he would receive (the equivalent of) nine dollars in Misahuallí. He explained that he panned for gold when there was no work in the banana plantations, and for the Indian gold-panning is an age-old tradition and thus he was exempt from paying the statutory licence fee that other Ecuadoreans pay. The

CHAPTER TEN ECUADOR

old women take great pride in selecting the best beaches and it is a source of kudos amongst them to know exactly where to find the richest gold-fields as not all the tributaries are gold-bearing, and this information is held as a great secret to be passed on from mother to daughter, so that the distaff side will always have this security against destitution. We made a collection for him in gratitude for divulging his secrets.

We zoomed back to Misahuallí in very quick time, with several hours of daylight lift, which I put to good use swimming, or rather floundering, against the current of the River Napo. The port captain at Misahuallí had a couple of young howler monkeys tied on leashes outside his office. They were great fun and extremely playful and tangled their leads helplessly together but squealed when I sorted them out. The walking party returned at nightfall with horrendous news of the great hardships they had suffered, but they all seemed very happy about it, excepting Armin who had lost his glasses wading chest-deep across a river. Hector, our host, prepared a farewell feast for us and brewed up an amazing herbal tea over an open fire. It was naturally alcoholic, and was potent and delicious, and whenever the lid was lifted volatile flames blazed for an instant. There were a number of guests, and Ann and Tobin were very interested in why an evidently erudite American lady should have found her niche married to a Missahuallí man. , It was a very rewarding debate: the lady was an expert on orchids and an amateur painter and led the most leisured way of life in the pursuit of her art and cultural interests. The party ended very late, except for Frank who fell victim to a tummy bug picked up in the jungle. Most of the others were to follow in the next few days. I already had it, and my pills from Panama did not cure me, but merely lessened my suffering.

At Ann's suggestion we took a different and very attractive longer route back to Quito. The truck returned to the main road via Tena the way we had come. Tena is the rather quiet dignified capital of Napo Province within sight of the extinct Sumaco Volcano,

12,813 feet high. Once again we found ourselves gradually gaining height, and we reached Puyo by mid-morning on the River Verde, a town which looks like a piece of the old Wild West. Since Bill was shopping and always had an inflexible menu in mind before seeing what was actually available, it gave us a good two hours here. Ann and I rushed off and explored the little stores, and we found a gunsmith at work who invited us to examine his stock in which he took a homely pride, along with his other product, machetes. We stopped at stalls the length of the street, and rounding a corner beheld the most enormous market stretching throughout the town with stalls set up on both sides of the streets. In such situations Ann emulated Lewis Carroll's Red Queen; she sped on stopping frequently but never arrived anywhere better than before. She was hunting for cheap boots but they were even more expensive here than Stateside. Indian markets always contain some kiosks cooking local specialities, and here Ann led me to an Indian woman frying fish and yuca for just a few cents. Nearly all of us bought big, sweet, red bananas at three cents each. Approaching lunch time found us driving parallel to the Eastern Cordillera of the Ecuadorian Andes, and with the sun beaming down on the snow-clad mountains the view through a fringe of gum trees was very stirring. We saw Tungurahua and all grew excited at the sheer size of this volcano and the majestic proportions of its snowy cone. Ahead of us a storm was raging and moving our way, so Paul abruptly made an early lunch stop, just in time before the rain set in for hours. Thunderstorms transform the colours of the Andes in a very interesting way and lend qualities of threatening vitality and power.

All day long we drove through a wonderland of waterfalls cannon-balling over high cliffs: I never saw so many waterfalls in my life as along the sharp deep canyon from Mera to Baños. There were dozens of them, dripping, tumbling, and squirting out of the rocky hills above the Pastaza River. Our mountain road hugged the slender lip high up the Pastaza Canyon, and wound up the very edge of the precipice (several times passing under overhangs) with no lateral room to spare. It was a comfort to know that Paul was driving: he was a tall fit man of considerable intelligence tempered with modesty and a pleasant attitude towards the expedition members, both severally and individually. He always managed to be neat and clean, spoke in an Oxford accent and never, swore, and no matter what he turned his mind to, whether changing a tyre, addressing a meeting, solving others' grievances, or negotiating these treacherous road conditions, he did it in style, creating in the rest of us total confidence in his ability to cope. The rain was thinning as we drove under a massive rock outcrop which, became a dark tunnel and we pulled up beyond it in a lay-by, constructed as a viewing point opposite the massive Agoyán Falls, six miles from Baños whose height was not especial but the force of this great quantity of thundering white water pouring into a pond below raised a permanent billowing cloud of mist and spray more in keeping with Niagara. Naturally Ann meanwhile was probing the nooks and crannies of the nearby shop and bar where corn-cobs were drying on a mat, and she was engaged in inquisitive conversation with the Indian shopkeepers who were happy to respond. This region around Baños is where the best aguardiente comes from. Aguardiente is one of Ecuador's better known strong liquors, together with pisco and traga de caña. The Ecuadoreans even produce a very cheap dry wine from bananas.

After this the landscape changed without losing any of its prettiness, and while the road descended the agricultural valley itself grew higher and increasingly populated. The heights were of very dry, porous, laval ash and supported the meagrest grazing and even the various sorts of cacti were stunted, but the lower down the mountain slopes we looked the richer grew the crops, especially the fruit trees. Not an acre was wasted, and houses were dotted around, each separate from every other as though there were 5,000 small-holders occupying the valley. To make the most efficient use of the available water, extensive irrigation channels and conduits led all over the place. Ann and I recognised rice as a major crop, and Christmas trees were another on the arid areas, and hedgerows of tens of thousands of tall straight gum trees gave vital shade everywhere. We camped off a sidetrack just south Ambato, 'the Garden City of Ecuador', with the smell of eucalyptus in the air, and the soft gurgling of water in open stone channels all around us.

When we awoke a Salasaca Indian was soaking a black and white poncho she had just made depicting remarkably stylised animals. She said she was shrinking it for market and proceeded to spread it out flat on the grass. We drove the few miles into Ambato where Ann, quite agitated, left us to go on a 500-mile side-trip through several highly acclaimed resort towns, ruins, and the most famous autoferro (railcar) route through the Western Cordillera from Quito via Riobamba to Guayaquil. We pressed on north to Quito through Latacunga passing Cotopaxi only a few miles to the east, the world's highest active volcano, with a permanent snow-line at 16,170 feet. A protected herd of llamas grazed its slopes where there is also a N.A.S.A. satellite-tracking station. Paul dropped us off right at our hotel without stopping the engine, even though we had to unload virtually the entire contents of the truck and trailer: the traffic police in their elaborately ornamented uniforms do not let any vehicles stop in the narrow congested streets on pain of a hefty fine. Diane, Stephanie, Rolf, Manfred, Tobin, and I shared a dormitory. Generally in the cheaper Latin American hotels dormitories are the rule and single rooms can be hard to come by. Gradually more of us were succumbing to illness, and my condition was certainly worsening anew. A lot of us searched for a laundromat but could not find one in Quito; in fact we found none in South America. Worse than that the hotel washerwomen seemed to have a monopoly, since when they finished each day they cut off the hotel water supply. Some of us did our laundry in hand-basins and hung it out to dry overnight, but by morning the best items of clothing had been stolen off the line in the internal courtyard, quite feasibly by other guests. Gaby, Manfred, and I all lost our best garments. It was an unhappy reminder that nothing was safe from theft anywhere in the hotel unless it was locked away in the strong-box.

At 9,350 feet Quito is the second highest capital in South America, but it is still set among encircling mountains whose slopes are covered with a patchwork of corn-fields. Francisco Pizarro took the city from the Incas in 1532 shortly after he helped Atahualpa from Quito win the Inca civil war by conquering his brother Huáscar from Cuzco, the erstwhile capital, establishing Quito as the new capital of the Inca Empire. Quito is only .15 miles from the Equator but we arrived during the rainy season which made it quite cold at times. Old Quito in the south-west of the city retains a lot of its charm; the streets follow dipping cobbled ravines traversed by stone viaducts, and the low houses are whitewashed with red tile roofs. Quito, in common with all the towns we travelled through, has its cockpits: cock-fighting is a very popular gambling sport.

For supper that first evening Dee, Kathy, Tobin, Rolf, and I walked through the old city looking for a congenial restaurant, and occasionally dived into little places such as chandler's or print-shops. Quite by chance we struck upon Salón Italia, which was warm and, more importantly, cheap, and gave huge helpings. It served exquisite duck in tamarind sauce and enormous hamburgers, the house speciality for only 50 cents. Dee chanced a 'ponche', which turned out to be a delicious eggnog with nutmeg, served hot in a tall glass. Rolf and I split away from the rest and pursued a most devious route back to the hotel. Well, to be honest we were lost and found ourselves by the Machángara River which flows through the Indian quarter.

In the morning, as I said, I discovered my laundry stolen and waited for the Indian washerwomen to give them the rest, but I established myself in an armchair to watch over it while it dried since it was, seemingly, either that or losing it. Tobin and I went out for breakfast which we bought at a street kiosk and consumed with the curious local 'café con leche'. The cup is brought brimming with hot milk, and one adds cold black essence from a jug on the table. I did not get any further than breakfast when my illness confined me to the hotel along with some of the others. Tobin, Rolf, and I returned to the Salón Italia for more duck with tamarinds and other good fare, and well-fed settled down to ardent conversation. Coming out into the yellow streetlight, Rolf and I stuck with Tobin to return to our hotel, and 600 feet above the city a garish winged angel picked out in electric light bulbs looks down from Bread Roll Hill. The angel is not visible by day against the scaffolds which support it, and the aluminum statue of another winged angel holding a serpent on a chain stands close by. The angels despoil the site of an ancient Inca temple and observation tower.

The following day was market day, and old colonial streets we had earlier wandered down were a confusion of wood and cloth stalls and kiosks. Every day we were in Quito (or any capital city for that matter) we went to the main post office and haggled and argued for our mail. It often took a bribe to extract it from the Mestizo women handling it, who would deny its existence vehemently even after shewing it to us until money was paid over. I think it is a fair assumption to say that only a third of our private mail got through. Rolf and I came upon the most ornately overdecorated churches which were decked With literally tons of gilt and dozens of icons, seraphim, cherubim, and other religious statuary. There are 86 churches in Quito and in many every square inch of the interior is heavily decorated. Most, if not all, of the churches have side-altars devoted to various saints, and the largest of all, the San Francisco church and monastery, has a high altar of gold. Throughout the major cities of the colonial era the Spaniards built the loveliest churches and filled them with most precious treasures, as well as employing intricate stonemasonry and wood-carvings and a wealth of fine materials. Even though I considered many of the façades and interiors overwrought with riches and details to the point of obsession, they were fantastic examples of craftsmanship and fine architecture nevertheless and just took

CHAPTER TEN   ECUADOR

my breath away. Some are powerfully lit by arc-lights and spotlights and others rely on sunshine or feeble candles to reveal curious details in the church paintings such as diptychs or skulls or pious expressions. We looked down over the colourful Indian market in the wide Avenida 24 de Mayo from El Carmen Alto convent; there was so much movement, and endearing urchins played on the dirty pavements. The communal food stalls had roast 'cuy' for sale, i.e. guinea pig, which is widely eaten in tropical South America. We examined the wares, and studied an old bootmaker working with an awl and last he had made himself, and next a business trading in musical instruments which Rolf began to play. He could never walk past a music store but had to try out the woodwind pipes and local variations on a guitar.

We had spread the word about our Salón Italia discovery, and ended our sight-seeing there to book a room for tonight and told them to have plenty of duck in tamarind sauce, also Pekin duck (which they serve in their own inimitable fashion with a rich gravy), and of course lots of créme caramels, ponches, and hamburgers which were so good there. It rained heavily all afternoon as usual, but that suited me fine: by now I was developing an allergy to my medicine so that the cure was almost as bad as the complaint. I made a new friend in Quito, Mark, an Australian, who joined us for supper, making our party 15. The others had not believed us that the helpings were so generous and could not touch half their orders, but I was locked in earnest conversation with Mark, who was relating his wanderings all over the world and was now working his way back home. I did not realise it then, but the friendship of one evening with this Australian completely changed my life, for I subsequently took him up on an offer of hospitality and settled there 'down under'. By morning Ann had returned to Quito frozen cold, so we rushed off to 'do' Quito anew for her benefit, starting at some of the stalls of Indian knitwear where we haggled hard for a pair of llama wool gloves, and we did quite well, knocking the price down to 50 sucres (just over a dollar). At another stall we tried naranjilla juice which was very refreshing with an amazing taste which seemed to contain a whole fruit cocktail.

    I learned from Ann that Rein and Barry and their group had arrived at her hotel, the Gran Casino, and they plied us with questions about the jungle which they were about to visit next. Diane was in charge of our expedition town account, as she was a bank clerk, and like a paymaster she doled out money all round whenever we stayed in a city for us to book into any hotels of our choice. Again most of us hied to the Salón Italia; it was such an amazing find and excellent value for money. I went on to the Gran Casino, the focal point for the seediest Gringos staying in Quito a little while. Everyone looked like a career drop-out, passé liberals without a single redeeming quality. Doubtless they all had superb anecdotes to relate, but they were all of a type; down-at-heel tow-headed dreamers running out of youth, entirely careless of their sloppy clothes and dishevelled hair, and living as though next year (or next month) was too remote a concept to dwell on. Ann's room mate, Ida, and another girl recently back from the Galápagos Islands, came in and gave us a very interesting point of view on the Ecuadoreans. It turned out, as I had always suspected, that (street) vendors have one price for locals and another three times as high for Gringos. Ida could pass as an Ecuadorean and also had found out first-hand that the rich upper class in Ecuador lives the life of Riley, quite divorced from the general lot of the other 95% for whom they do not care a fig and entirely avoid. I heard stories like this about most other countries in South America.

    Our last morning in Quito, Ann, Tobin, and I took advantage of the sunshine to go sight-seeing. The streets were thronged with people, and the Indian women were especially well-dressed under multiple layers of heavy clothing in bold slabs of colour, with variations in the ornate trimming along skirt hems, and piles of cheap golden glass bead necklaces entirely hiding their necks from their

CHAPTER TEN   ECUADOR

shoulders to their ears. They looked super in their clean clothes, topped off with shapeless colourful head-cloths or trilbies. We started out round the little back streets, and bought empanadas (little meat pies) and tropical fruit as we went. Tobin led us to his favourite café, La Ronda, which served delicious strong cappuccinos in great big cups, which we drank while watching the streets scenes through the open door. Ann's interest was in the famous old churches, particularly La Compañía church which has a high altar of solid gold and ten gold-plated side-altars. $10,000,000 worth of its treasures are locked away in bank vaults between special festive occasions. Another church, in the Monastery of La Merced, has Quito's oldest clock built in 1817, the twin to that in Westminster Abbey (known erroneously as Big Ben, which is actually the hour bell). All the churches were resplendent in gold leaf, ornamentation, murals, and frescoes. Paintings depicted in gory and graphic detail the various Satanic punishments for sinners, and also the Day of Judgement. These two huge paintings bore a lot of studying as they were so full of vignettes and separate instances. At the post, office we bought amazing aerograms which are printed with five scenes and cost the same as a single postcard. I left Ann sitting taking notes amid the bustle along a typical Old Quito street with houses built in the old colonial style of whitewashed stone or adobe brick, with windows protected by curlicued bars under overhanging eaves as wide as the pavements below them. In our hotel there seemed to be no way of predicting when the water would flow, or an even rarer occurrence, when it would be hot, and this set a precedent for all the dubious hotels we subsequently visited. Quito will always stay in my mind as a city of churches with rich wood carvings, graceful arched stone porticos, and a Cathedral with green tiled cupolas in the main plaza.

    Dee, Kathy, and Rolf had left us for the now 650-mile side-trip to Guayaquil which Ann had taken, but their main reason was to take the autoferro railcar which offers unparelleled views of the high Andes. Meanwhile the rest of us drove north out of Quito through the Indian suburb of Calderón, plunging down the startling Guayllabamba Gorge and up the other side into an oasis village renowned for its groves of avocado trees. We climbed through the mountains into a semi-arid dusty region of páramo, or high altitude moorland with stiff clumps of grass and a very little scrub brush offering poor grazing. The scenery worsened to become the starkest, most unyielding mountains in the Andes, before improving with irrigation at Cayembe. Ann spotted the autoferro above us, a 24-seater electric car which she and the three others had taken. It was rocketing along at great speed, but being a narrow gauge (three feet six inches) it lurches scarily around the corners. Cayembe has been developed as a show-place, with rich dairyland producing cheeses, but after reaching it we climbed and climbed gaining great long distance views of the far high mountains collared with cloud in the Western Cordillera, seeding rain clouds shewing silver linings against the sun. Plantations of gum trees Spread out evenly over the mountain slopes but virtually no agriculture was in evidence. Erosion carved the most curious shapes out of the laval rock sides of the road in irregular slits and scars. Occasionally these pits had developed into deep caves or great crooked sears gashing the cliffs. We branched off to follow a soft narrow track still being cut out of the páramo by a bulldozer, and the truck kept lurching to one side in the soft tilth, and each time my heart leapt into my throat as I thought we were goners for sure, destined for the thundering river hundreds of feet below. Paul was only looking for a spot to turn the truck around so that we could camp.

At supper Chantal's birthday was celebrated with a delicious chocolate and orange pudding which Annette and Armin made for her. Our location was above natural hot sulphur-bearing springs-directly beside the river feeding into steaming pools in the Chillos Valley. Everyone took the opportunity to laze in these therapeutic sulphur baths, which were a wonderful relaxant and tonic, and the pools were stepped down in wide shelves until they reached the bottomless spring itself where little bubbles rose up and tickled us as they brushed over our skin. In the sky the moon was full and so amazingly bright that the whole gorge was lit up and we could hear the river waters crashing and chuckling over the rapids just feet away but out of sight. The humidity kept the night warm for only the second time in a month of travelling, but the mosquitoes came out in droves. We arose at four to reach the colourful Indian Saturday fair at Otavalo on time. We drove out of the páramo into the Province of Imbabura, and the mountain scenery became more opulent all the time as we entered a fertile valley with a lake below us, surrounded by tiny little fields separated from one another by living hedgerows of planted stakes, or fibrous agave cactus on curious adobe walls built from huge slabs.

As we approached Otavalo the houses appeared fairly modern and had political slogans daubed on many of them, exhorting the messages of Che Guevara and other revolutionary mottos. These Indian highlands have for centuries been farmed under the huasipungo system and the Indians lived as slaves on large ranches, a system now being replaced by co-operative farms. The Indians still exist at subsistence level, but their lot is gradually ameliorating, and many of them live by their traditional crafts. They have distinctive clothes, and the men wear very short bell-bottom white trews, dark blue ponchos, and as often as not a pork pie hat over their long black braids. Most go barefoot, and we passed many on their way to the fair carrying simply ENORMOUS loads on their backs, held in place by leathern straps around their foreheads. Doubled up under their loads they could not always see their way, but nor could they afford to stop, so they barged and shuffled wearily along. Many of them were tiny, well under five feet tall, and they looked so haggard and careworn that it was impossible to guess their ages. Nursing mothers had the looks of 50 and 60 year olds, brought about by the strain of extreme hard work and the effect of ultra-violet rays from the sun, unfiltered at this high altitude. Otavalo is at 8,300 feet above sea-level and is in a region with several picturesque lakes accessible along a welter of old trails.

First of all we visited the animal market and auction, which was a treasure-house of human expressions. There were scenes of pigs with rings through their noses being led on lianas, or children whipping along a mule or calf. There were no corrals or pens, just a field where the wheeler-dealing, the bargaining, and hubbub went on from four till eight in the morning. Uniform with markets worldwide, there were trilby-hatted countrymen talking through stilled teeth clenching cheroots, clutching pens and papers, apparent middlemen and agents profiteering from the animal trade. Chicken and sheep were very few, but they were there among the mules and llamas and other domestic breeds. The majority of the locals were missing teeth, sometimes most of them, yet they smiled broadly just the same while they stared at us and our truck.

The two main markets, trading in wool and produce, were in the town itself where the buildings had thick walls washed in pastel colours with small windows, typical old cool houses, with green plants and lichens growing all over the roof-tops of orange tiles. On my way to the clothing market, whom should I encounter but Arvi, my Jewish friend from Panama City with such a tale to tell of the rugged basalt Galápagos Islands on the Equator, once the haunt of privateers and whalers, and more recently a dire penal colony. She told me of the unique and strange wildlife there with no instinctive fear of Man. In the market Ann and I found several more people we knew from Quito and Panama and Dee, Kathy, and Rolf caught up with us after their side-trip, sporting various souvenirs, particularly Rolf in a thick llama wool balaclava which made him look more than ever like a pixie. The Indian wares included wall decorations and woven tapestries and llama wool jackets and all sorts of clothing bearing native designs in all colours. There were bags and blankets and pullovers with fringed edges. Apart from the woven and knitted goods, there were stalls of the local voluminous glass bead necklaces, and large silver coins dating back to Napoleonic times and beyond. These were snapped up by Bernie, who was a numismatist, as they sold here for less than the silver premium back in Switzerland. There were displays arranged on blankets of wooden carvings including a tagua skull, earthenware, coils of maguey and cabuya (aloe) ropes, second-hand goods, and all kinds of bric-á-brac laid out on the cobbles to show off to the customers. Beyond the rather commercialised cloth market, meat and vegetable produce was being sold in a section by itself. Indian women were hunkered down amid little pyramids of fruit, skimpy little bundles of herbs and vegetables, talking hard and letting their wares sell themselves. The 'meat' was entirely unrecognisable. The peasants eat <u>every</u> organ of their animals, even cuts the Gringos could never even look at, such as feet, ears and intestine. The Indians think nothing of chomping on a dog's jaw and spitting out teeth, hopefully the dog's. Here the Indians were most reluctant to allow tourists to photograph them and turned their backs, but if they supposed their pictures had been taken they vociferously argued for money or tried to open the camera. Ann tried to snap an old meat (?) vendor who picked up some hot polenta and slung it at her. Mostly it was the older women who resented being photographed; the younger ones often posed. The colourful Indian jamboree at Otavalo makes it second only to Chichicastenango market in all of Hispanic America.

Joan was severely ill, so we returned to Quito to take her to the American Hospital Voz Andes, and Dee, Kathy, and Rolf opted to keep her company. As we left we passed a circus and fun fair which had a troupe of elephants, and we all saw them but Ann who must have looked straight through their legs. We drove past them again, but still she did not see them much to her chagrin. The hospital had taken some finding and led us a wild goose chase the length of Quito shewing us the considerable slums and squalor which typify the poverty in the city. We were still driving at nightfall, through the rain, until we reached Mount Cotopaxi, and set up camp in the dark in a great hurry. Not feeling too well myself, partly due to altitude, I fell asleep quickly to a serenade of frogsong. We seldom indulged in a lie in, but since we were not going anywhere else on the morrow we did not arise until dawn, which only served to allow the local peasants time to form a larger audience. We drove on during the morning up through the heavy mist and low cloud continuing our ascent of Cotopaxi. The páramo changed gradually from entirely semi-desert scrub where the dews were very heavy, through a belt of mountain brush to an amazing variety of little high-altitude plants and stiff clumps of couch-grass right up to the snow-line. As we climbed the lower slopes of the volcano, we had occasional periods of clear visibility and saw the variegation in the colour, texture, and thickness of the geological strata, sometimes folded in loops and humps. We followed a brick red seam of haematite, and a broad chalky band, and layers of rock in ash grey and other colours. Once in the clouds we were lashed by drizzle or sleet, and the road grew worse with sudden dips, until at last we reached a guarded gate at the entrance to the Cotopaxi National Park where a shivering phlegmatic troop of soldiers announced with sang-froid that we were unwelcome since we did not have government authorisation to see the mountain. This was apparently a very new regulation designed to cash in on the few tourists who make it thus far up the mountain. They gave Paul the address of an official with a rubber stamp back in Quito who would decide whether we could be allowed in or not, another example of typical Ecuadorian efficiency at work to foil even the best prepared traveller. Once Paul had turned the truck about the soldiers relented, sensing we would not pay them a bribe in any case, and allowed us in.

It was very difficult to see anything, what with heavy condensation and intermittent sleet and hail lancing against the panes, but through it all Ann and I were picking out the lovely flowering plants which manage to survive in this harsh mountain terrain. The main vegetation of the páramo was quitch in huge spiky bunches, and rough twiggy bushes, but as we ascended into the really high ground above 15,000 feet, it was covered with a white lichen which bore a semblance to a dusting of snow, interspersed with a few mounds of green which I supposed to be species of worts. We could drive no higher than 15,100 feet and hung on (outside) to the upper edge of the truck while Paul parked it at an insane angle like a careened ship, and jumped off into deep volcanic pumice granules. The rocks and pebbles higher up the slope were all colours, a collector's dream, and being laval were very lightweight. We tramped upwards through the freezing wind, which whipped up tiny ice particles, stinging our cheeks and hands, but the climb made us so hot that we had to undo as much clothing as possible. The ash was extremely difficult to trudge through, and with every plodding step we sank into it and slid back a little, and slowly and laboriously toiled up the ridge of the mountain. There was a hut 650 feet up on top of the ridge, but by this time Ann had already turned back to make a botanical survey of the flowering plants on the shoulder of the volcano at 14,500 feet. After a rest at the shelter many of us found our second wind and struggled on up again into the first snow which succeeded the gritty lava fairly quickly and allowed us a firmer footing. To celebrate the achievement Bill and I exchanged snowballs but kept on climbing. I caught up with the group ahead of us including Frank whose altimeter read 17,000 feet at that point. He was making heavy weather of it, floundering and sliding at every step. I taught him how to kick his toes into the crisp snow for the most secure footholds. Poor Frank explained that due to vertigo he durst not look around, so he had just kept on puffing upwards. A dense cloud slowly sank onto the volcano, limiting visibility to about 100 feet. I descended by wrapping my waterproofs tightly around me, secured my spectacles safely in an inner pocket and tobogganed down a snow-field, starting out on my back. I got helplessly out of control as I picked up speed and rolled over a few times, and at one point I shot off into thin air over a lava crag and soon after reached the end of the snow. I was quite unable to check my velocity and careered headlong down the mountain on foot, lurching dizzily, barely managing to keep my feet landing under me. When the hut came in sight I pulled up with a knee-twisting slither and caught my breath again. Composed but exhilarated, I passed an ascending party of Japanese mountaineers with an air of dignity, and moments later on weak legs I again unintentionally resorted to charging on down the soft brown moraine helter-skelter, but the only time I stumbled I found it was impossible to get hurt as I crashed sidelong into the loose sandy ash in an ungainly flurry, all gloves and boots and stetson. Climbing out of the blizzard into the welcome warmth of the truck, lunch was ready, but cups of tea had to be held as the truck was sideways on a 35-degree gradient.

As we descended the volcano we stopped awhile at some lagoons where birds were flitting hither and thither, proving that even at this barren cold altitude there is a complete ecosystem. Ann was already there with a large posy of diminutive wild flowers in all colours, and told me she had seen a humming-bird (at 14,500 feet)! We walked the mile back to camp over the amazing tundra páramo with its specialist flora able to withstand permanent cold. There were lots of llama fewmets but not one llama in sight. By the time we had returned to base the dense icy mist had overtaken us and we put up the tents as fast as we could to get under cover of shelter. Meanwhile Paul went off with the truck to set up a driving course and invited all those interested to try it. He was looking for someone to take over if he should fall sick miles out in the Styx. Half of us tried it and manoeuvered the truck to and fro through his imaginary garage walls. It was great fun but bitterly cold with a blanket of fog playing tricks on our eyes. Several of us complained of the effects of altitude, nausea, lassitude, and debilitation, known collectively as soroche. Certainly I did and found relief only in sleep, but one of the symptoms is insomnia, and in the middle of the coldest night so far I got up, and not a breath of wind fanned the sleeping mountain. To my astonishment I disturbed an owl nesting in a hummock of coarse dead bunch-grass, and it let out a screech as it fluttered away in a panic.

CHAPTER TEN ECUADOR

The still morning air trapped a chilling cloud clammily around us while we had our breakfast. Then in a matter of a minute the sun dissipated the bank of mist and revealed the volcano east of us, brilliantly highlighted by the soft morning illumination, a must for our ardent photographers. The descent from Mount Cotopaxi took us back through the changing altitude-related foliage, which was almost tropically dense at the base of the volcano. Where the landholders have separated their fields they have very often built walls of the laval rock. For days Ann and I had been perplexed as to the construction of these walls which run everywhere criss-crossing the countryside. They are made either from slabs two feet square or of blocks twice the size of house bricks, as are many of the dwellings. We returned to Quito through the ever changing terrain in which the only constant was the light grey laval earth, and the semi-arid appearance of the land. Crops, mainly potatoes and tobacco, were growing in large neat fields and extensive plantations of red gum and Christmas trees made some use at least of the inhospitable rolling hills.

Our purpose in Quito was, of course, to pick up the others, but this allowed us several Hours in the city, and Ann and I huffed and puffed up the steep Bread Roll Hill, topped off by an observation tower, passing an enormous public wash-house and laundry and a building we believed to be a prison. From the top there were panoramic views of the whole city, which was easily twice as big as we had hitherto envisaged and far from being on one edge, the hill was plumb in the middle of the metropolis. At the foot of the hill in the old Indian quarter we discovered a covered market which had large windows, a Nisson roof, and two storeys, each opening onto a different street-level. At one end there was a huge overhead altar aglow with burning candles and neon lights honouring a tawdry mannequin amid vases of flowers, mostly withered and bent. The Indians here, in common with the descendants of the Mayas of Central America, combine idolatry with Christianity, and frankly their lot is very hard and I, for one, do not blame them for hedging their bets.

When Paul collected us all again, Joan was much better, but was still in shock from the doctor's bill! Our journey south took us back over ground already covered via Latacunga, Ambato, and Riobamba through pouring rain for most of the way, stopping only once at an ice cream shop we had 'discovered' a week before, where we had our final view of Mount Cotopaxi before it was quite swallowed up in the clouds. The scenery changed so quickly from region to region. Of the three main towns along our route Ambato was the prettiest with many lovely customised houses for the very wealthy, and popular as summer homes of the richest Guayaquileños. All were different and large even by Western standards. In Latacunga we passed well laid out parks with topiarised bushes, fashioned like balls and fans and tiered wedding cakes. In the countryside we often glimpsed a hint of blue in the leaves of many of the plants, and passed through areas of lush green minutes before canyoned, old, arid hills with streams which fed the peaceful Colta Lagoon. In the space of a mile Ann pointed out thousands upon thousands of large light brown leaves drying on racks. It was tobacco. We saw many great volcanoes soaring into the snow zone, in particular Chimborazo, Altar, Carihuairazo, and smoking Sangay, the most active volcano in the world. We camped after dark on the bank of the foaming River Chanchán which was noisy enough to cut out the sound of traffic, but in the light of day woke to find our camp-site particularly beautiful. We were in a tiny little valley 100 feet wide with grassy banks just south of Tambo. Along the other side of the brook light traffic was using the Pan-American Highway, and just beside us on our side ran a spur of the narrow gauge track of the autoferro, which came clattering up the line from Cuenca as we were having breakfast, a modern 30-foot long grey trolley-coach, quite devoid of passengers. Bill produced his usual greaseburgers for us: his breakfast menu seldom changed, it was either leathern pancakes or these things — fried bread sodden with warm cooking oil, dipped lightly in egg and spread thickly with butter (and sometimes a drip of syrup). Either menu was as efficacious as castor oil.

When we left we noticed the Southern Sierra, which we had entered after dark, was fairly, agricultural although basically arid, by dint of irrigating the alluvial fans. Many basic foods, but thousands of hectares of potatoes in particular, were grown in highly banked ridges, the troughs being the irrigation channels; and surprisingly there were paddy fields of rice. The population of the Southern Sierra seems to live in tiny thatched adobe huts in places often little bigger than dog-houses, but even the dogs had their separate kennels in this style. As the ground was uneven in many places the homes were built on rickety stilts and nestled in behind flowering red and green barricades of cactus. Such dwellings blended well with the countryside, but in the shanty towns the same houses crowded together looked horrible. As we drove through this agricultural valley we passed trees general to the tropics, pawpaws aplenty, African date and oil palms, coconuts, rubber plants and balata trees (the latex from which is used as a substitute for gutta-percha), aloes, bananas, and spodilla (the chicle tree), tagua nuts, even coffee, also scrub and thorn trees, lignum vitae, brazilwood and divi-divi (whose pods are used in tanning), the woods becoming thicker till in places the countryside was dominated by them. Now and again a tree ablaze with candle flames would catch the eye, which on closer inspection proved to be a roost for sieges of white egrets. Persistence paid off in our quest to learn how the lava was made into walls in large slabs from two to four feet square. Ann pointed to Indians using an upright wooden vessel as a mould into which the laval clay was poured in situ. Once the material hardens the boards are removed and with the passage of time the sun bakes the walls rock hard.

The Ecuadorean army was much in evidence, and quite apart from the checkpoints we saw barracks fairly often, with soldiers exercising and marching ever so shabbily, and worse, a great many wore mufti, indisguishable from the public at large. By and large the Central and South American armies are composed of teenagers, judging by observation. Wherever there was water for crops there were also the usual ungulates, sheep, goats, donkeys, and Zebu-cross cattle mixed together, having to contend themselves with the nearly bare areas devoid of irrigation where the blocks of granite and rocks were gathered into heaps. Belying their abject poverty these subsistence farmers kept their gardens and homes very pretty and neat. Leaving the Cuenca Valley we climbed swiftly to such an altitude that we were over a sea of cloud with the peaks of the Western Corillera peeping above it, exactly the view one has from an airplane. There were still trees up there, tamarinds with their leguminous pods and pink flowers. In the mountains we saw how the Indians dealt with nits and head lice: three children sat picking through each other's scalps, and when they found a mite or louse or tick, they ate it with relish, sometime squabbling over who should have it.

We passed the most curious necropolises in the most unlikely places. From a distance they took on the appearance of miniature, walled, Ancient Islamic cities, with numerous domes and blocks of apartments, though closer inspection showed the latter to be square chambers for funerary urns, and the domes to be the roofs of tiny rooms each big enough to allow a doorway into a store for probably ten coffins (apparently above ground). Access to any cemetery was through an ornate iron lychgate. Every cubicle or tomb was painted a different colour and decorated with flowers and a crucifix. The better cemeteries were nicely set out imitating parks with trees and whitewashed boulders carefully located in lines. We pulled into the filthy village of El Triunfo for our shopping, and the place reeked of rotting garbage which just lay in the streets. Never was a place more fly-blown. The village was notable for the cacao and coffee-beans spread out to dry in the sun on large reed mats. The cocoa smell was vaguely fruity, as the beans start out moist and pink inside a long pod, cushioned in a sweet flesh which is good to eat. Python, jaguar, goat, and other hides for sale hung on display. During our walk Ann and I found a mattressmaker stuffing palliases with straw. We could have walked a lot longer as Bill was shopping, and always took twice the time allotted, which got on everyone's nerves, not to mention the delay which was made up by cutting hours off our sleep.

From El Triunfo we pressed on into the hazy mountains, past houses of bamboo, every one of which was adorned with a television antenna. Incongruous with the region we saw families of white Aylesbury ducks in the streams. We stopped for lunch at a sugar plantation, the whole countryside along the Jubones River being devoted to raising sugar-cane. Apart from the hundreds of mosquitoes the place was memorable for the mobile haystacks which trundled along the road and materialised into vastly overloaded sugar-cane trucks, carrying crushed canes up to 20 feet long piled on higgledy-piggledy, so that they trailed on the ground and off the sides and over the bonnets as well, almost hiding the trucks. Brick factories were quite a common sight, but for a long time all we saw were the yellowish grey lava bricks drying in the sun. They were different from red bricks, and were less durable not being kilnfired, and were actually thick tiles, ten inches by seven by two. Here our observation was rewarded, for we watched an oven being built. The fuel was the dry crushed sugar-cane, and this was set ablaze and the bricks to be fired were stacked around it, demonstrating that the ovens were temporary devices only. We drove into the night to get as close as possible to the frontier and pulled into a coffee plantation with an inquisitive herd of cattle. The weather was so good that we had an impromptu party with the coffee grower and his wife. In our sack of cassette music we had plenty of stirring stuff and danced in the light of the truck until we were exhausted. Paul challenged Tobin to a dancing duel, 15 rounds of three minutes each. It was a real Bill Tidy affair; they waltzed at each other, hopped, shook shoulders, every round in a different style, including karate and boxing, Russian, Flamenco, and belly dances. Paul was also the referee but Tobin still vanquished him by a fall and a knock-out.

CHAPTER ELEVEN

PERU

Peru is the third largest country of Central and South America, but in terms of our expedition it was the most important country, in large part due to the influence of the Incas. The country is naturally split into three basic geographical zones, the first of these being the crowded Pacific seaboard. This is a strip of desert reaching inland to the Andes, usually not very far, a mere ribbon extending from the Gulf of Guayaquil to Chile. Almost half the populace lives here in several dozen oases, some large enough to support major cities, and surrounded by a total area of 2,500 square miles of irrigated land in the valleys of 52 desert quebradas tapping the Andean snowmelt and flowing into the Pacific Ocean. Of these less than one in five flow through the drought months of the 'summer'.

Conventional seasons do not exist in Peru, which alternates between wet and dry seasons, and climate is largely a matter of altitude, and along the coast is governed by the cold Peruvian Current sweeping north beside the hot desert. Anchovetas (Engraulis ringens and Cetengraulis mysticetus), which are not anchovies, have been a major food source for thousands of years, attracting huge flocks of guano birds, and these have provided enormous quantities of dung to fertilise the oases. A slightly higher proportion of the people inhabit the High Sierras which form three ranges of extremely steep mountains towering to enormous heights, and consequently the land available for crops between the tree-line and the snow-line is very poor. Many of the canyons take nearly a day to ascend the 6,000 feet from tropical jungle to permafrost páramo, offering a bare grazing of Puna vegetation. The population here is mainly one of illiterate Indians (though three quarters of all Peruvians are basically literate); these Indians live on subsistence diets, speak in Quechua and live virtually without money or knowledge of any modern conveniences, even running water. In the towns too the majority forgo basic amenities. It is only these people who can live and work under such abject conditions. The remainder of the country, 62%, forms the Selva and occupies the eastern slopes of the Andes right down into Amazonia. Only 900,000 of the 19,000,000 Peruvians live here along the rivers, including the Amazon, which rises in the high mountains west of Lake Titicaca far to the south. Gradually the jungle is being opened up and is already a rich source of oil, timber, and a variety of forest plant products. The west coast of South America and the Andes, particularly Peru, was inhabited by Man before 8,500 B.C.. Some of these cultures adopted their place names, e.g. Chavín, Paracas, Mochica, Tiahuanaco, Chimú, and High Nazca. The Incas became established late in the eleventh century and lasted 500 years before the Spanish colonials predominated. Apart from the official languages, Spanish and Quechua, other Indian tongues are spoken, particularly Aymará among the Indians in the vicinity of Lake Titicaca. Lima was capital of all Spanish South America from the date of its foundation in 1535 for nearly three centuries. The break with Spain began as a result of the Creoles (nationals of Spanish descent) bearing resentment against their secondary status as taxpayers to, — and subjects of -, their cousins in Europe.

Ann and I sat in front for the border crossing, but the scenery all day was of arid desert and squalid humanity. Until we reached the border at midday the desert supported only scrub. The boundary is defined by a river with Huaquillas on the Ecuadorean side and Aguas Verdes on the Peruvian side, and connecting the two ramshackle towns across the bridge is a bustling market with various military, police, and custom-posts. The locals wandered backwards and forwards, effectively across the international border, without let, although the Peruvian officials checked for contraband entering their country, either visually or with a long needle probe pierced indiscriminately into backpacks and bundles. They were on the lookout for luxury goods such as foreign radios, cameras, and electronic equipment which are forbidden imports. Even so the search is just token, since the products are smuggled into the country across the mountains by night anyway, following a brisk overt trade in these same articles by day. Ann and I browsed around in the market and discovered we had accidentally crossed into Peru, so walked smartly back over the bridge without hindrance.

The Huaquillas banks only change money at a poor rate owing to very high inflation of the Peruvian sol, which provides for a healthy black market. The money-changers all carried little black attaché cases, and it was not necessary to approach one since they gathered around the truck touting for business. We had to watch very carefully while they counted out the soles because they had a reputation as expert swindlers, and by some sleight of hand the 250,000 soles they were counting out might easily add up to only 25,000 soles when they had gone. Coming the other way was a coach tour, and Paul and Lou, the driver of the coach, were old friends. The

Ecuadorean authorities closed the border against us all, ostensibly 'for lunch'. On this occasion when the passport officer asked for a bribe, he spied the cassette player and asked for 30 dollars and a few cassettes to let us through 'before lunch'. Luckily Paul had prepared for this eventuality by carefully hiding all but one of the cassettes, and declared it to be his only one. We had a three-hour delay, whilst Lou paid the bribe and came through. Since the authorities were not letting us pass, Paul blocked the bridge so that no traffic could flow, and took a walk with Lou who had bad news from Paraguay where terrorism had resulted in the borders being closed against them for a fortnight. Across the bridge in Aguas Verdes, the Peruvian authorities apparently had a 'late lunch' because we were delayed another three hours, which we spent in a car lot. While the others explored the market, Maria and I stayed behind to guard the truck, and I found myself in the centre of a bevy of little children. I love children, and for those hours I was lost in their world, and we told each other about our backgrounds. Our group soon returned from the colourful market for it was largely filled with such kitsch as religious models in plaister of Paris, or plastic pails and shovels, ceramic tourist trash, tearful tots painted on velvet, and the usual food displays.

Throughout Southern Ecuador and again in Peru we saw that nearly all the dwellings had crucifixes with little ladders, animal figurines, and other iron models arranged on the rooftrees. Within two miles of the border we were on the northern outskirts of the flat barren Sechura Desert, named after a town 150 miles further south. Virtually nothing can survive in the Sechura Desert, though there are areas of specialised bird and plantlife. Near the tiny town of Sechura only occasional condors or red-shouldered hawks make their nests, while on the northern edge of the desert there were just low flat-topped bushes and the occasional flock of goats. Gradually xerophytes became more common, particularly a cactus like the Joshua tree of Arizona, and everywhere these stark ligneous plants bore curious masses of fruit similar to beige furry plums. Out of this dry dust in the rain shadow of the Andes, we would occasionally find the beds of rivers which had changed their courses during times when they were raging torrents, and we saw streams supporting oases of bananas and long-staple Pima cotton and other luscious green vegetation, but within a mile the water and greenery would end again in the lifeless desert. The Russians and West Germans have committed financial and technological aid to this region and are piping water via tunnels (one over ten miles long) and aqueducts from the other side of the Andes within the Amazon watershed, and are gradually reclaiming 1,550 square miles of useless desert. We passed through some low-lying sandstone hills, so worn and aged that we probably saw the same views as the earliest Indians to settle this coast over 10,000 years ago. The desert here is bleak and impressive in its vast emptiness, just glaring distances shaped into hills. It used to be the ocean floor millions of years ago and is visibly strewn with fossil sharks' teeth and other hints in the form of mineral deposits.

The Pan-American Highway took us onto the shore-line past a few small fishing villages, where the huts were cuboid of flimsy woven bamboo matting, and the tiny odd churches were mere barns in effect. The only change was from sandy to stony desert, with rocks as big as cars. In good time we made camp on the beach and all plunged into the sea, which was warm and refreshing, but with a persistent north-bound current, the very edge of the freezing Humboldt, rich in micro-organisms which fed the great shoals of anchovetas, themselves the food of the guano birds. Until 1972 anchovetas were so superabundant that they were being fished at a rate of 180,000 tons a day by upwards of 1,600 seiners. In this way Man has practically eliminated the anchoveta and the guano birds, the two main pillars of the Peruvian economy. There are three major species of guano birds, the guanay cormorant, the Peruvian booby, and the brown pelican which we have been seeing since the beginning of the expedition in California. The guanay shags, referred to as 'billion dollar birds' because of the extreme fertility of guano (Quechua for droppings), go out to feed at all hours of the day in long lines in search of the shoals, and sit in close proximity until they have digested their enormous meals of anchoveta, and then fly home together. The boobies are actually gannets and feed in a most spectacular way: when a line of boobies spot a shoal they turn in unison and spear straight into the sea from a height 60 or 70 feet drawing in their wings at the last possible moment, all splashing out of sight together and leaving the sky empty. Then they surface and return to bombard the shoal, a veritable waterfall of birds all hitting the water at great speed. Pelicans are fascinatingly graceful in the air, but because of their enormous bills and gullet pouches they have perfected a different method of fishing: they also fly in lines but along the face of a breaking wave which they crash into when they spot their prey, and upon emerging they lift their bills to drain the seawater. In a vague seven-year cycle a warm current, El Niño de Navidad (the Christmas Child), brings equatorial waters as far south as Chile and heats the ocean surface more than the ecology can tolerate and so the food chain breaks down entirely with catastrophic results locally and in the worldwide weather patterns. Every time it has come El Niño has wrought havoc on the Peruvian economy and caused the starvation of tens of thousands of sea-birds by driving the huge anchoveta shoals into Chilean waters, though the latest visitations by the Christmas Child have virtually obliterated the entire food chain already weakened by exploitation.

During our dip in the sea we were tossed helplessly by powerful breakers and cast ashore in a sandy mess. Poor Maria, the kindest and gentlest one among us, started to squeal when she was badly stung by a jelly-fish. Armin built a big driftwood bonfire, and Sam and Chantal, and Ann and I sat around it, while Rolf, looking like a satyr, played his pipes of Pan beautifully on the crest of an immense sand-dune, and the stars came out really bright. Ann and I strolled along the darkened beach, and in the gloom we blundered down

CHAPTER ELEVEN   PERU

an embankment making a fascinating discovery in the moist sand. At every footfall a spray of phosphorescent sparkles glittered green instantaneously. We kicked and scuffed and stamped, and sure enough the tiny lights winked back at us. It was warm enough to sleep out that night to a lullaby of pounding surf and scraping sand.

Ann and others began a regular programme of walking on ahead of the truck, and thus it was next morning that she discovered some vultures guarding the fresh carcass of a giant sea-turtle, also the sun-bleached skull of a bottlenosed dolphin, so we thought, but we could not discern any eye sockets in it. There was little to see as we drove down the coast. Inland was sandy desert, and out to sea a few fishermen were punting or sailing flat reed rafts, and guano birds flew in line along the surf, occasionally banking like a jet fighter squadron and plummeting straight into the brine to emerge at surprisingly great distances with their catches. The sand itself was fairly interesting as it changed colours in layers from a pale yellow to a deep russet, and black grains under the yellow showed through like a dusting of soot. The village of Santa came and went in a minute. It was a conurbation of mobile homes for the oilmen, whose untidy pipelines criss-cross everywhere from the dozens of oil-wells in the desert and lead off overland to the Talara seaport. The first oil-well went into production in 1850 and was dug, not drilled. Now an infinite variety of donkey-engines slowly nod the days away and each year more will fall still as the wells are exhausted. Going through the oilfields we climbed to a high vantage point in the Amotape Mountains. On one side we could see the continental divide of the Andes through a yellow heat haze, and on the other the ribbon of surf along the sea-shore and the indistinct boundary 'twixt sea and sky. The lifelessness of the place gave it a timeless quality.

We came upon a freshwater pumping station for the oilfields, and our need was great. This was our first supply since we left Quito and in addition to filling the tanks Paul arranged for a rough and ready shower to be rigged up, just a hose in a tree. While at the oasis

I spotted a dark grey desert fox and I tracked it for a quarter-mile when it disappeared. We were equally surprised when I flushed it out of a conduit and it sped off into the desert. Many of the people living along this coast depend on the anchoveta catch which is converted into fertiliser, fishmeal, and urea, plus a dense peach-coloured smoke which leaves the stench of fish and a misty pink haze about 100 feet up in the air. This haze gives rise to a peculiar colourful effect with blue sky above and below it to the west. We relentlessly clocked up the miles as we sped down the coast. From time to time the road ran a little way inland as the desert yielded to the barren rock of the Amotape Mountains where the road climbed over 1,000 feet. One spot in particular was in the midst of wild and desolate eroded canyons, whose sharp serrated slopes contained neither a blade of grass nor a single insect. There were only ranges of crags one behind another in glorious enduring colours.

Wherever there was any water, oasis communities irrigated the land and formed co-operative settlements. We saw asses so laden with grass that it swayed like seductive Hawaiian skirts as the animals tripped along, and motorcycles were also similarly loaded. As we drove further into the Sechura Desert we came upon their most infamous feature, the relentless shifting sands. The whole coast is in a rain shadow, but the Sechura Desert in particular had not experienced rain since a week-long torrential deluge in 1925 (an El Niño year), and normally has only a little rainfall once or twice per century. Great crescent-shaped dunes up to 100 feet high have been formed by the constant sou'-westerly blowing the yellow sand up the convex side to settle on the concave side, moving the sand-hills 50 feet a year. The whole time we passed through the desert sand was whisked across the road and was launched in visible plums from the crests of the dunes. Wherever the horns of a dune encroached on the road itself, bulldozers moved the sand over the road and had enough work to keep busy in perpetuity. Any vegetation which managed to take hold gave rise to a dune in its lee and gradually the sand-dune would grow to choke the bush or (more often) the succulent which would have to grow taller to avoid becoming interred, and thus high dunes have been created covered with vegetation to windward. As far as the eye could see in all directions the desert floor was dead flat with these queer crescents trailing wakes, and the Pan-American Highway cut across it straight as a die, elevated about four feet above the plain.

We found a little hamlet and some trees huddled out of the wind protected by some stupendous 60-foot high dunes. There were a few domestic animals and shy girls peering at us around doorways. I could not understand why there should be people living in the desert, but soon thereafter we reached an oasis with tall bowed palms, planted as a wind-break, whose leaves were all straining like windsocks. In the flat oases irrigation has resulted in square fields of crops of marigolds and toast-coloured rice and oats; and bulrushes (themselves most ornamental) grew along the ditches, and maize and bananas grew in quantity. New paddies were being levelled and flooded for more rice and Tangüis cotton. Along the verges in the irrigated areas were tens of thousands of the gorgeous red bougainvillaea flowers. And where, but in Peru, would one find a horse-drawn oil tanker? There it was, a 1,000-gallon tank on a solid wooden cart! Since leaving Amazonia most of us had been quite feeble with the 'Inca Quickstep', and here in the Sechura Desert we were stopped by the police, who climbed into the truck and singled out Alice for questioning. Twice she was beckoned out of the truck, but then the police were satisfied with her and allowed us to go on. The police were usually content with an international driving licence, as they like to write down a serial number. That Paul had expediently forged one did not seem to bother them.

We arrived at Puerto Agustin for shopping, but the village had nothing to commend it save the absence of streets, i.e. the houses were spaced out directly on the sand. All afternoon we drove through this unending desert and for miles before reaching Lambayeque the land was littered with garbage. As it never rains the municipal garbage is just dumped here whence it is blown about the desert by the constant prevailing wind, present for posterity. We passed quaint old Lambayeque, a town of narrow streets and adobe houses, many preserved with their singular carved balconies and wrought iron filigree decorating the window lintels. We drove on to Chiclayo, a fairly large oasis town, but excepting the parks and gardens it was entirely nondescript, and after one circuit we drove straight out again to camp on the beach in a high gale. Putting our tent up was a very worrying business as nearly all the peg loops snapped and the wind constantly threatened to carry all before it. We stuffed the tent full of luggage to hold it down and piled a quarter-ton of sand on the edge of the canvas, and so it held with a very dark restricted interior and the powerful gusts vibrated the fabric causing it to sing and reverberate like a drumskin all night. There was only half the usual amount of space inside, warm and still, while outside sand was flying everywhere in the noisy wind storm. Abalone shells and succulents with pink flowers littered the strand, but the wind made it too cool to hang around outside, so we crowded into the truck where Paul livened us up by playing the water hose like a bugle.

In the morning we returned to Chiclayo to reprovision, and this meant that Ann and I had to buy food which would keep 24 to 48 hours in the heat of the desert. The market was the best in Peru, very crowded and certainly the largest we had seen, serving a regional population of 400,000. Probably 20,000 people were thronged into its many alleys and large plaza. We had time only to buy food, but everything under the sun could be found. As usual we gave Sam 10% of our money for basic foods and went off to hunt for fresh meat first. For 15 minutes I was handling live ducks, guinea pigs, turkeys, kid goats, and chickens, but Ann prevailed against the idea saying that none of the others would tolerate my butchering them when the time came. Luckily she discovered that fish were really cheap here and we bought a number of very large fish which looked like sea-bream to make a 'ceviche' supper. We deliberately bought unfamiliar vegetables: tambote, a red-skinned tuber akin to yams with a sweet delicate pink flesh, which was edible raw (though we did boil it), and our greens were gehua, like oversized okra in appearance but capsicums to taste, fresh or boiled. We haggled over prices and we thought we did quite well until we saw identical items going much cheaper to the local Mestizos, demonstrating the price differentiation between them and us. To finish up we bought gooey yuca cake which looked like a sticky brown stodge but was very nice to eat.

All day long we drove south through the flat sands of the Sechura Desert which joins the coastal ribbon of desert no more than ten miles wide extending into Chile. There was no relief from the strong hot wind, a prominent feature of the Sechura, which blew such a gale that the canvas roof began bursting at the seams and the air was thick with dust, choking especially the people in the back seats. Whenever we drove through dusty terrain we had the problem of dust being sucked into the rear of the vehicle. The wind whisked sand continuously from the dunes and shrieked and whined past the windows. At our lunch stop Ann and I found all kinds of coloured rocks: basalt, rotting granite, quartz, ferrite, porphyry, silica, marble, and many others. Paul managed to bog the truck down in the desert and we had to dig it out, before pressing on all afternoon through the oasis of Guadalupe and past occasional roadsteads to Trujillo by evening, Peru's second city, set in the middle of irrigated greenery against a back-drop of brown Andean foot-hills. Frances was so ill that she was admitted to hospital as an emergency case, semi-comatose, and Maria stayed with her. We went back a little way up the coast to camp and since it was quite warm Ann and I just put up our camp-cots in the lee of someone else's tent. This compromise worked fairly well but for the constantly blowing sand low to the ground.

In the morning we were running short of fresh water, and to make a saving Armin took the big frying pan into the surf to wash it. Alas the tide snatched it away from him and the poor fellow waded into the sea with all his clothes on including his shoes and anorak. He searched for ten minutes wading in up to his chin, and to everyone's surprise he found the pan with his feet. As the sun began to warm us up we saw lines of grey pelicans with white heads and black wings skimming through the spume on their way south, to the fishing port of Salaverry no doubt. At the same time we watched a couple of porpoises following in their wake, leaping clear of the water as they swam only 20 feet or so offshore. We drove back into Trujillo to check on Frances, and Bill stayed behind with his girlfriend to relieve Maria much against his will. Although it has a population of nearly 500,000, we found little of architectural merit in Trujillo. Most buildings have just one storey, erected of concrete strengthened with steel cables which poke out crookedly a couple of feet or more above the concrete. The roofs are either flat or absent, there being no rain in the desert. The city does have a walled old quarter founded by Pizarro in 1536 containing churches, monasteries, and colonial mansions with graceful balconies, spacious patios, and grandiose portals.

From Trujillo we went to the crumbling ruins of Chan-Chan, the imperial capital of the Chimú realm which extended along the coast from Lima to Guayaquil. The Chimú culture reached its apogee a century before the Conquistadores of Pizarro and de Almagro arrived, and had co-existed with the Incas until the Incas besieged Chan-Chan in 1450 and reduced the Chimú people to feudal bondage. We were shewn around the Ciudadela de Tschudi by Professor Pedro Puerta whose life's work it has been to make an archaeological and anthropological study of the Chimú and other ancient cultures in this region of Peru. Tschudi is one of 17 very strange citadels making up a city of 11 square miles with a probable population of 300,000. These citadels were built to a common plan and were originally surrounded by triple town walls 50 feet high, each with only one narrow entrance, arranged in a defensive maze against invaders. Some of the clay brickwork has been reconstructed or grouted to preserve the revealing bas-relief sculptures. The entire city was built of lava clay which makes extremely hard adobe, but the greatest enemy of the ruins is rain which last fell in 1925, when it teemed for a week, washing down thousands of tons of adobe and obliterating most of the details for all time. Tschudi was divided into three basic sectors: ceremonial, funerary, and administrative, and had a sunken garden to reach the water-table. It had two large open squares, serried rows of storerooms and granaries, and a memorial platform mound, where the king's numerous concubines were sacrificed and buried with him and his treasures. A huge looters' pit cuts right through the burial mound, testimony to the colonial Spaniards' quest for treasure. Palaces and places of worship and business can still be discerned, even the narrow streets and houses, and what remains of the lava clay walls is still fantastic, though they are nowhere any higher than 20 feet. Everywhere we saw the repetitive symbols of pelicans, anchovetas, cormorants, fish-nets, sea-otters, waves, and the sun, on which things the Chimú culture and religion depended. Some friezes depict 'cinematographic art', Professor Puerta's discovery, such that, e.g., pelicans in a row would each be successively slightly different from the last and actions of moving and feeding can be read into the row. At least six centuries ago the Chimú people had already conducted water via channels and tunnels from the far side of the Andes to irrigate the bare Puno territory and used a style of architecture which has defied all the earthquakes since. One of the strengths of the citadel at Tschudi was its 125 wells in the sunken garden, but the Chimú never discovered the wheel, nor the use of pack-animals, not did they eat meat, but used their llamas and alpacas only for wool and leather.

From here we went on to see the restored Temple of the Dragon (Huaca El Dragón), or the Rainbow Temple (Huaca Arco Iris) after the depictions on the friezes. This was a small, solid, flat-topped pyramid enclosed by a single high wall, dating back over 2,000 years to the culture of the Mochica domain. As we walked along the temple wall, the professor explained the story being told in symbols. Two dragons (the thirsty desert) were under a rainbow (rain), and as they received rain their tongues fused (germination), and they began rising in the air (growth), and their tails fused (fertility). The temple has been well-restored since the 1970 earthquake by Professor Puerta who has a little museum next to it of ancient art, nearly all ceramic. There was a small charge to pay covering these and other fascinating nearby ruins. We returned to the professor's studio where he displayed numerous original prints he has made, his interpretation of pre-Inca art, which were quite fantastic. They were for sale in various colours, sizes, and materials.

After lunching there we crossed the River Moche through an irrigated agricultural valley with trees and pigs and all the other trappings of smallholdings which seem so strange after the desert. Paul stopped by a most peculiar set of ruins, the huge Moche Pyramids of the Sun and Moon, the Huaca del Sol and the Huaca de la Luna, which were solid and built of adobe bricks, tens of billions of them, basically in steps about 20 feet high. The bricks were ten inches by eight by six and the pyramids over 1,100 yards square, and apart from being enormously eroded were over 100 feet high, the largest pre-Columban structures in South America. They contained several dark tunnels excavated by fortune-hunters and on the plateau between them was an infinite number of shards of pottery just lying around, and Bernie found a very fine jar with a wide collar, a narrow neck, and a handle, but no bottom. All the while a strong wind blew and even threatened to dislodge us from the nearer pyramid. Late at night I went back around the pyramid and looked north over the plateau's edge onto the night lights of Trujillo, a sterile white pointillist map of the city, while the breeze tugged strongly at my clothes and hair.

Overnight the incredible happened: it rained. We burst out laughing. By now nearly all of us were suffering from an acute form of dysentery, and latest to succumb were Tobin and Maria, so Paul decided to make for Lima in the morning, a distance of 400 road miles.

CHAPTER ELEVEN   PERU

Rolf and Paul had a duel at dawn, battling out their differences musically, Rolf on his ukelele and Paul on his brand-new trombone. What a hoot! Since Paul bought his trombone at Trujillo (where they are made) we did not have an evening's quiet until somebody judiciously put a kink in the slide. Once on the road we drove all day long through totally empty desert, across the valleys of Chao and Virú and River Santa to Chimbote, a natural harbour and a large town. We did not stop; there was nothing to see but flocks of brown pelicans and islands studding the bay. The pervasive smell of fishmeal reached us though. For the next 180 miles the Andes virtually came down to meet the sea. The dunes became quite large like a frozen rolling ocean. Rolf and Armin went cavorting and sliding down the slopes of hot dry sand, slithering 40 feet at a time. For lunch we pulled off the road onto an apparent track but rapidly sank in the soft sand, which meant using the sandmats and a good bit of heaving on the part of the men while the girls took our pictures. In the desert the sunbathing was supreme; Tobin, Rolf, and I would just flake out and bake. It felt so good. After eating, Ann, Armin, and I went on ahead and the desert had a quality of utter tranquility, and we felt so much at peace with it, only our footsteps making a crunchy sound, and the zephyr breeze made the climate delightful. All afternoon we tracked through the endless bright yellow desert with occasional hazy blue glimpses of the rocky outcrops of high land. Most people dozed a little, for there was no variation in the beauty of the clean desert with its classic crescent Barkhan dunes, some covered with poor acacia thorn scrub, but irrigated patches of oasis greenery were very small and far between. All day long Ann and I noticed a distinct layer of pink haze about 100 feet above the ground, but we could not identify it until we came unexpectedly upon Huacho, a fishing roadstead 82 miles from Lima, on the very rim of the desert. Standing at anchor was a fleet of anchoveta boats and their factory ship, and onshore were the beginnings of an agricultural commune dominated by a colossal fishmeal factory complex from which poured billows of pink smoke, gushing and expanding as it rose, great swells of shrimp-coloured pollution. A level prevailing breeze caught it and drew it evenly along, giving rise to the phenomenon Ann and I had seen above the desert up to 100 miles away. As the sun fell we pulled onto a track through the desert three hours' drive north of Lima and found ourselves amid an area strewn with garbage despite many notices forbidding dumping. The wind was constant at only ten miles per hour and considering the warmth and that rain was as likely on the moon, half of us slept out, but we had not reckoned with the blowing sand.

During Bill's absence we all had a good lie in without his regular grating falsetto shout to shatter our repose. Packing the trailer, Manfred discovered a sizeable scorpion with a granular colouring which disguised it perfectly against the sand. Earlier I had seen a nimble long-legged spider, shewing that even in this forlorn and arid desert there is still an ecosystem. The journey into Lima was all through desert, gradually becoming more populated the nearer we approached, and we snaked along the base of the Pasamayo sand-dune, the biggest in the world, virtually a hill 13 miles long abutting on the shore north of Ancón. It towered over the road and all along its length sand-slips had left scars and the sand had been bulldozed into the sea. Roads here are commonly only notches in sand-dunes and drivers expect to be delayed by the hundreds of daily sand-slides, which may cover half the road or carry it away altogether. In this desert are the most unlikely woodlands in the world, the lomas, dependent on an equally unlikely water supply, fog. From May to November a thick freezing mist, the garúa, condenses as a result of the cold Humboldt Current sweeping against the baking Peruvian desert. The lomas are scattered and have mainly endemic life-forms, and after a century of logging and the advent of goats the lomas are now only a tiny fraction of their former size with a corresponding reduction in their fauna. The guanacos and pumas have now disappeared of their own accord while game species such as the white-tailed deer have been hunted to extinction. Wraiths of water vapour caress the plants and rocks, condensing and trickling down to support succulents and yellow calceolarias, and twisted lichen-shrouded tara trees lend the loma the claustrophobic feeling of a horror movie. The damp shadows are home to foxes, red-backed hawks, humming-birds, and the delightfully bright vermillion flycatcher.

From the loma at Lachay we reached Lima about noon, and Paul drove us around the old historical area playing a cassette-recorded account of the scenes we were passing and the glorious squares and statues. He drove on out to the posh suburbs of San Isidro and Miraflores which had beautiful homes and villas. How the other half lives! We passed an old olive grove, El Olivar, now a beautiful park, and the Pan de Azúcar (Sugar Loaf), an adobe pyramid probably built 18 centuries ago by the Maranga Civilisation. Other ancient settlements within a mile or so date back 12,000 years. Miraflores is the largest and richest suburb of Lima, and a coastal resort in its own right with another delightful park, Parque de las Leyendas, which contains a zoo and a handicrafts fair. The park is so arranged as to represent the regional topography of Peru.

Lima is the capital of Peru and together with Callao, its port, contains half the townspeople in the country. It was founded by Pizarro in 1535 as the capital of the Spanish Vice-Regency of South America, straddling the green valley of the River Rímac within 100 miles of the crests of the Andes whose foot-hills, Cerro San Cristóbal, came right down to the town walls, long since demolished. In terms of population, Lima, with 5,000,000 inhabitants, ranks third in South America after São Paulo (10,000,000) and Rio de Janeiro (9,000,000). A great many of these Limeños have migrated to the bright lights from the Sierra, or Peruvian Andes, with peaks like Nevado Huascarán, Peru's highest mountain at 22,205 feet. The result is a circle of 'pueblos jovenes' or squatters' shanty towns surrounding the capital. The city's heyday was in the eighteenth century, when it reached the zenith of its power and glory and was invincible against attack and richer than any city in Europe. Nowadays things are quite different; e.g. red traffic lights mean absolutely nothing to the locals except perhaps that an extra fast burst of speed is required to cross the danger area, but in any case the traffic light bulbs are quite likely to have been stolen or long since blown, nullifying the whole point of having traffic lights at all, and drivers and pedestrians alike take their lives in their hands when out in the streets. There is a flourishing black market in car parts in Lima (well, all over Latin America really), and anything removable is likely to disappear. In our case we lost some gas fittings here despite leaving the truck in a guarded walled compound, though Paul told us of a previous expedition he had led which was held up for a week while he negotiated to buy back a clutch assembly which just happened to resemble the one stolen from his truck.

We took our lunch break on the beach at Miraflores where Ann and I were watching a scuba diver carefully preparing to go spearfishing when a wave caught his goggles, and to stop them being washed away he jumped on them. Alas, he broke the visor and had to call off his sport of skewering little fishes, poor man! We joined the others at a beach shack where an ornamental type of popcorn was being sold. The mostly purple ears of corn were very large and fried without bursting. By evening we made our way back to our 'residencial', past the luxuriant wild calandrina flowers carpeting the base of the Mariscal Necochea cliff in a delectable soft pink, and the jet set playing raquetball in the country clubs. Lima does not possess a laundromat despite what the guidebooks say. I set out walking at great speed for three hours with several people's washing in search of one, but I should have known better, however I did see miles of the city in this way. In the morning I had a terse argument with the sour old Dueña of the hotel who tried to charge me ten dollars for washing my clothes myself since she would have charged me that if she had done it, as she monopolised the laundry for the clientele. She also demanded three dollars for the water, but I paid her nothing and hung my laundry to dry on the roof. She repeatedly confiscated it during the day, but each time I searched for it and recovered it all.

Ann, Tobin, Rolf, Frank, and I spent much of the day wandering through the crowded street markets full of Christmas shoppers shoulder to shoulder. Everything imaginable was for sale, but the best bargains were to be had at the Indian's stalls; toys, stationery, Indian artefacts, hand-spun and hand-woven textiles in the wool of llamas and alpacas in unusual or traditional Peruvian designs. There were fine leather goods and an infinite variety of fascinating postcards. The greengrocery markets were especially interesting and many unusual fruits were displayed, including guava, eggfruit, custard apple, passionfruit, soursop, quiche, papaya, and mango. Most of these made great drinks. Little kiosks, generally capable of seating a couple of patrons at a time sold every kind of comestible. At each an Indian woman with a charcoal or spirit burner kept a hotpot and percolator ready, and would prepare fresh rolls with a variety of fillings. Ann and I found this a very cheap and delicious way to eat and befriended a particular Indian woman near our residencial close by the Plaza de Armas, not far from a colossal equestrian bronze of Pizarro. All day and night we had suffered some acute variety of the Inca Quickstep, and Paul made arrangements for us to have medical treatment. Peru has the worst record and reputation in the world regarding hygiene arrangements and the doctors grow rich. It is the only remaining country where typhus is endemic and commonplace.

We discovered a delightful and very popular little café, Chez Giselle, run by an old lady from Belgium, formely a beautiful and famous ballet dancer. It was a great meeting place, especially for French-speakers and served the best breakfasts. Most of us would start off the day there with thick rye toast and milo, and came upon Al Townsend, and erstwhile companion of Annette, Rein, and Paul, who became stranded in the country years before over some bureaucratic bungle, and turned to organising Whitewater rafting and trekking over the Andes to the Selva beyond in the Amazon Basin. I joined Maria, Annette, and Bernie who had discovered the 'best' cake shop in town. Lima, in common with most South American cities, has a preponderance of fine cake shops which will sometimes serve nothing else but the most mouth-watering and richest cakes of every kind. This one faced south onto the Plaza San Martín, and was set back from it by a covered pillared arcade which lent it a colonial appearance. It certainly lived up to its reputation. With my chestnut cake I ordered café con leche which, as is the Limeño wont, was a sundae glass of leche con muy poco de café. The portions were huge and the prices cheap. On our way through the streets we had to be very careful not to tread on the wares laid out, not just on the pavements, but right across the whole width of major streets so that, ipso facto, they were turned into pedestrian precincts.

During the evening Rolf and I set off into the busy Old City and found an impromptu picture exhibition. The oil-paintings were all the work of one old man and captured the essence of Peru and the hardship of the Indians. It was a pity they were all painted on wood, which we could not wrap up and take away, but I have no doubt he had a good pitch because his display was set up outside the Crillón Hotel, which Rolf and I presently entered. We found ourselves in the domain of the ultra-rich, where even the flunkeys and bell boys were better dressed than us. There is an interesting mineralogical exhibition in the foyer, but we had come to enjoy cocktails in the Sky Room, Lima's most sophisticated restaurant 20 storeys up complete with a cocktail lounge and boîte. From the Sky Room the whole of Lima could be seen, and the night lights shone and blinked around and below us. We sat at the high bar and watched the cabaret and slowly drank our Pisco sours, a great Peruvian cocktail of Pisco brandy from the Ica Valley. The best sweet Peruvian cocktail is algorrobina made from carob bark. Later we were joined by Ann, Annette, and Al for the remainder of the Peruvian folklore show.

Ann and I spent a day exploring Lima's very notable churches, and incidentaly took in the markets and shops. The Quito churches may be the more heavily decorated with every inch dripping with baroque effects, but the churches of Lima are just as old and huge and are the better for being more simply adorned, with the artistry being concentrated in the numerous altars and the exteriors. The local beer is known as chicha and was invented by the Incas. Chicha de joja, or red chicha, is brewed in the time-honoured way from sprouting barley, beans, chicken, and a leg of beef, and is renowned as a fertility potion. I tried a pint with my supper at a working-man's café and it tasted like a rather passé sweet scrumpy and was over 100% proof and still fermenting, but I declined a second glass of this moonshine which would have rendered me insensibly inebriate. A couple more varieties exist, chicha de jora brewed from maize, and chicha morada which is a soft drink. The churches are quite different and well worth seeing lit up by night. After this, Tobin, Frank, and I repaired to the local restaurant, one of many which just prepared chicken dishes, but had an excellent pianist who knew only rhapsodies from the turn of the century, as though I was not maudlin enough already from the heat and the chicha.

The verdict of everybody's illness was officially returned as salmonella poisoning and most of us were on the mend after a week in Lima. Frank and I explored the baroque San Francisco church, monastery, museum, and catacombs. The church is famous for its bejewelled gold monstrance and the monastery for its Sevillian tiling, shewing pictures of holy men around the cloisters. In the museum the costumes of silver and gold thread were fabulously rich but could never be cleaned. The catacombs in the crypt under the church contained dozens of very deep pits with the remains of over half a million dead, some over four centuries old, carefully packed according to type, with skulls together, and femurs, ribs, etc., all sorted out. The main catacomb is a 50-foot well 12 feet in diameter with the bones radially symmetrically arranged. The musty vaults were gloomy and low making everyone stoop as he passed the pits and the coffins of a few luminaries. Scorpions reside among the skulls, impassionate guardians of these tidy relics. After that we visited the Court of Inquisition, which was created in 1570 and abolished 243 years later. The building includes a constitutional library of documents, flags, and seals, and the ceilings are of closely set parallel Nicaraguan mahogany beams, each carved in deep ornate patterns on the three exposed sides. The court house has been left in its original state, and the torture chambers themselves were gruesome and explicit; with the rack and water tortures self-evident in their application, and mannequins demonstrating the use of various stocks, whips, blocks and tackle, balls and chains, and torture chairs. Along a low secret subterranean passage were tiny dark cells, and more than one oubliette, and the stench of sewage must have been awful. In those times more secret passages existed connecting the court house with other mansions around the city, but most have collapsed due to neglect or earthquakes.

The modern day Lima rises out of the old, and skyscrapers stand in the major plazas alongside the palaces and fine colonial houses. There are also enormous wooden portals and huge elaborately carved balconies which jut out from the windows of the fine buildings and are from 12 to 20 feet high, and anything up to 60 feet long: the more inspiring the building, the more ornately carved the frontage, but even down the back streets all the old buildings have similar balconied windows, though in the poorest cases the window panes are absent so that there is still a fine long balcony of carved wood or wrought ironwork. In contrast to the sheer opulence of former times, beggars abound now. During the evening the stall-holders pack up and go home, while the scroungers pick the gutters clean. Twice during the day Rolf and I saw totally nude men, beggars who owned not a stitch of clothing, holding plastic bags to hide their genitals, filthy with tousled hair and sores on their bottoms. Once the stalls are closed up, the homeless fall asleep in the streets. Ann had spent the day touring the city and returned to the residencial at three in the morning with several slits in her clothes skin-deep from crotch to belt, along her money-belt, and through all the compartments in her rucksack, where an expert thief on a crowded bus had applied his razor, but she herself was unharmed and nothing of value had been stolen. Such thieves frequent trains and buses, in fact anywhere there are crowds in South America.

In the morning all that remained to be done was for me to take a taxi to refill the gas bottles, a trip which took me through the industrial sector of the town, an area containing most of the industry in the whole country. Paul gave us a final slow tour of the city on our way out into the desert once more, through Pachacámac and the Lurín Valley. We passed a few oases, each isolated in the dry hilly desert, growing a large variety of crops for the capital district in huge, flat, irrigated fields, Pima cotton and sugar-cane in particular. The houses were all like slums being of the grey clay brick walls or wooden poles and adobe about ten feet square with flat adobe roofs. Nevertheless those near enough to Lima to have electricity all sprouted television aerials. Many of the communities had huge poultry farms, rearing hundreds of thousands of chickens and turkeys in long roofed sheds. Water was obtained from artesian bores and was drawn up by mini-windmills. The sand was no longer drifting and the ground formed hillocks of gravelly moraine, but it was still barren desert. For half the year the mountain slopes turn green with the garúa mists coming in off the Humboldt Current, and the Sierra Indians herd their livestock to pasture on the temporary lomas.

At times the road swept south along the shore, where we were amazed by the fantastically energetic surf. Huge Pacific rollers higher than a man broke continuously immediately one upon another. We kept returning to the shore, sometimes at sea-level, and at other times overlooking the shore from the edge of a cliff. In places the beach reached back to the shale hillocks at the base of the Andes, and where we stopped for lunch near Pucusana, an attractive fishing village, the hills were of a stratified grass green rock, though yellow sand had covered up all but a few outcrops. During the afternoon we stopped in Asia, just a fishing village, despite its name. Later we arrived at the double town and port of Pisco at the mouth of a river of the same name, which flows down a valley effulgent with green vineyards. Pisco is the largest port in 400 miles of coast, and as such is the centre of local agriculture (particularly cotton) and fishing, notably whaling, and has an enormous fig tree in the town square, the Plaza de Armas. It is a pretty quiet place, and we stopped there near a market where Pisco brandy was very cheap. Pisco has a flavour all its own and a slightly bitter after-taste. We had planned to hold a beach party after Lima, and this was a good place to buy drinks. Paul also had the good fortune to locate a sawmill and we filled every square foot of the truck with offcuts for the barbecue.

From there we drove on through a landscape so bleak and utterly devoid of any solid feature that even a pebble or blade of grass would have altered the entire panorama. We were traversing the pink desert at a point where the garúa had encrusted the high rolling dunes, effectually preserving the visual image of frozen waves. For half an hour we passed along Las Lagunitas, protected little bays with the Chincha Islands off the coast, while the incandescent sun set over the hardened hillocks of sand and the sea mist sighed past us on a soft breeze inland. We passed a famous candelabrum 115 feet tall outlined high on a hill facing out to sea, an ancient landmark carved ages before any Europeans ever set foot on the New World. Quite a few such sketches have been traced out on the hillsides above towns in Peru since then, as often as not depicting the local coats-of-arms. Setting up camp we found the sandy appearance of the desert was deceptive, as it only formed a thin mantle covering solid rock into which we attempted to pound our tentpegs. We stayed a couple of days at the same spot on the Paracas Peninsula, a mere 100 yards from the ocean. Paracas means wind, the most notable thing about the town and peninsula of this name, rarely severe but unrelenting nonetheless. The beach was a great place to promenade, although

CHAPTER ELEVEN   PERU

it held the faint smell of death and dereliction, a testimony to the lethal power of the pounding Pacific surf. Decaying lengths of seaweed, jelly-fish of all sizes, and crab-shells were stranded high and dry in the sun, and the whole beach was littered with millions of shells, pink and mauve striped ones of little clams and mussels and other bivalves, abalones and sea-urchins, and a variety of coral. The prevalence of shell-fish in this area attracted the attention of businessmen in the 1960's and canneries were set up resulting in the near extinction of shell-fish here and that has affected the rest of the food chain, so that the birdlife has largely died out or migrated and also the Chilean marine otter (Lutra felina) and the fur seal (Lobo fino) have practically disappeared from this newly hostile region, partially from lack of food supplies but mainly because they have been hunted to the point where they are classified as endangered, never a deterrent to the dirt-poor hungry Peruvian fishermen who still eat them and sell their pelts. The marine otters seldom leave the ocean except to enter their holes or else to eat large red crabs which form the basis of their diets, and they and the fur seals are now gradually recovering their numbers in Chileans waters.

Walking along the grit beach of finely ground sea-shells brought into view the cliffs across the deep azure of the bay, with the lumpy hills shewing in geological bands of carmine, yellow, and grey under a perfectly clear sky. We paid a visit to a colony of sea-lions (Otaria byronia) on the southern edge of the peninsula which we could hear singing before we saw them. They were basking on stack rocks and swimming 100 feet below us at the foot of laval cliffs studded with plugs and knobs and bubbles of pumice. Hundreds of dark grey southern sea-lions were living on little rock islets which were frequently awash under the huge Pacific breakers. Time after time sea-lions were carried clean away by the billows into the dangerous channels between the rocks, and had to try quite hard to clamber back on their inadequate flippers, relying on a fortuitous wave to deposit them favourably. They called out with their plaintive siren cries and barks which we could easily discern mingled with the constant crash of the surf. The sea was permanently whitened and foamed for 30 yards around the rocks due to the frenetic energy of the surging water. Waves 20 feet high sent cascades of spray over all but the highest placed sea-lion harems, and as the seawater rushed back into the ocean the sea-lions could be seen to brace themselves with their noses up, distinct and grey against the white torrent. Swimming in the water they were so agile and graceful, some playing on their backs, and others leaping like dolphins. All the time a great many sea-birds were flying past, ugly red-headed grey-black terns, long-necked black cormorants, flamingoes and other migratory waders, in their unrelenting search for food. The Ballestis Islands group is just offshore to the north, west, and south of the peninsula and they are a natural bird sanctuary. They stink with the sourness of ammonia in the guano which has formed plinths like stalactites proving continuous occupation for decades by these birds, but altogether more unlikely are the Humboldt penguins (Spheniscus humboldti) which form colonies in the tidal caverns here and on the shore of the mainland amidst the cacti of the Atacama Desert. When the sea-lions come ashore to drop their pups the local population of turkey vultures and condors swells to feast on the sudden rich food supply of placentas and dead animals, though condors are opportunists and are not above killing a lost pup by pecking out its eyes first if pickings are not so good otherwise.

    There are more varieties of bats in South America than of any other mammal but the most infamous of all is the vampire bat (Desmodus rotundus) whose range extends from Patagonia to Central America. They carry a rabies virus to which they are resistant, but are susceptible to catching and hence spreading the disease when they are subjected to stress as occurs during the breeding period. They live anywhere that is handy, and not necessarily in remote out of the way caves: they are common in the cities under bridges and in similar spots. Naturally a lot of folk-lore has built up around them, but they really do not much like our taste, preferring farm animals though they will take whatever is available, even bird blood or, here at Paracas, sea-lion's. There are very few spots on a sea-lion which have thin enough skin for the bat to make a success of his attempted meal, only the nose and the flippers, and the impish bat has to scuttle backwards and forwards on all fours to avoid being flattened by the disturbed beast in order to finish its meal.

By the time we returned to the camp-site the sun had disappeared behind the dense veil of the Humboldt garúa and with the desert wind it became quite cool as we all prepared for our fancy dress party. I wore only a loin-cloth and painted myself all over as a savage, and several of the others also had bizarre outfits, for instance, Gaby was a big baby with a bonnet and bottle. Paul barbecued a whole sheep over the fire but it ended up so tough that it nearly defied eating, so he attempted to regale us on his trombone which was purgatory. But even so it was a great party with the alcohol flowing freely, particularly down female throats and all the while there was the sound of a heavy surf breaking and smashing on the shingly sand. Ann and I ended up talking with Maria who was the youngest as well as the prettiest member of the expedition. She was a most rewarding person to spend time with, whose generosity and warm personality pervaded her conversation and attitude towards everyone. During the night a red fox came through the desert scavenging for scraps of mutton and left a criss-cross trail of footsteps leading off into oblivion.

In the morning light, from our vantage point in the cab, Ann, Paul, and I were struck quite forcefully by the awesome beauty of this totally bare rock and sand desert with its feminine contours and distant ranges of rocky hills, some appearing rufous, some a russet yellow, and some almost invisible with a blue remoteness. We passed the little town of Paracas and stopped at a one-roomed archaeological museum nearby in the desert where there was an excellent display of local finds dating back more than 9,000 years covering the civilisations of the Chavín fisherfolk, the Nazca cavemen, and the Nazca city dwellers. The exhibition included mummies shewing that the Ancients were just as short of stature as the Indians of today. The bone-dry hot climate of the rain shadows west of the Peruvian Andes is perfect for mummification, and many cultures have carried it out over the aeons, knowing it would preserve their dead indefinitely. Numerous skulls were displayed illustrating how babies' heads were bound at birth to vastly elongate the skulls like bananas. Others were trepanned with quite large holes sawn out. There was a reconstruction of a hut of whale's ribs and vertebrae and straw thatch, with the inside hollowed out a foot at least into the ground to give more living space. The heat and dryness which have preserved Paracas' mummies also preserved their shrouds which were of amazingly fine quality, design, and colouring, resulting in a major macabre trade for grave robbers. The robbers dump the mortal by-products of their criminal pursuits in the desert, but nowadays the bodies are mostly fresh.

Thereafter we drove inland towards Ica, passing several large oases on the way, each about two miles square raising cotton and potatoes, and large vineyards with gnarled grape-vines trained over bowers in arches. The water for these oases in the valley of the Ica River is diverted through a tunnel nearly six miles long through the Andes from the Choclacocha and Oracocha Lakes at 15,000 feet in the Amazonian Basin. Wherever there is life there are fascinating birds and resplendent trees. There were a lot of little trees with an expanse of rich purple blossom, sometimes lighting up the sun-kissed crowns of thick foliage but often it would be a dense mosaic of red petals. There were many lesser varieties of flowering trees and plants, including crops of orange marigolds, with flowers the size of burdocks. We drove through one oasis specialising in hundreds of acres of neat orange groves.

By noon we had reached Ica, our shopping stop, but the large town did not endear itself to us. It was dirty and smelly with equally grotty snotty children, and very evident sewage and garbage disposal problems. We had our lunch a little way downwind, a wind like the breath of a dragon, while waiting in vain under the beating sun for the museum to open. Whenever, like this, our plans went awry, or we bogged down in soft ground, or Paul made a faux pas, he would utter, "What an incredible stroke of bad luck!" This expletive soon became the expedition motto. So we took off again and quickly reached the oasis of El Alemein, not surprisingly really after Guadelupe and Asia. The road to Nazca passed through flat stony desert for mile after identical mile with only small areas of dunes and curious tufts of grass in half-arches which had retained their distinct wave-crest shapes even after the sand had long since been blown away by dust-devils whirling across the desert floor in unpredictable dances. There were only a couple of very small oases in dips in the landscape, whose fields of cotton had desiccated and were being cut down, although there were other crops and a whole new range of wispy and spindle-leaved plants, including asparagus which had bolted to 12 feet. The whole region is memorable for its fabulous opulence of flowers and blossoms and blooms everywhere, all colours and sizes. Even the curious and desolate attractiveness of the fantastic contortions of the strange trees, twisted by the heat and the prevailing sou'westerly, was obscured by the sheer radiance of the floriculture. The desert oases surprised us with their delicate wildflowers, guanaco's paw (Calandrina discolor) and malvilla (Cristaria) both had fleshy succulent leaves and blooms of a gentle lilac colour, and the añañuca lily (Hippeastrum añañuca) was sudden on the eye with a golden fanfare of trumpets raised to the sky in all directions. So extensively do the oasis co-operatives irrigate their land that the rivers no longer reach the sea, and as a consequence towns such as Ica have dry river-beds most of the year, which means no sewage disposal and solving one problem has created another. All the oases we passed through sell their entire produce in Lima and Callao, which explains why they do not grow just staples but include such epicurean cash crops as asparagus and the luxury of floriculture.

From here on the desert grew increasingly arid with much thinner ribbons of arable land along the few occupied watercourses, and in places the sand-drifts encroached right over the road, which entered the craggy mountains of rich barren browns and red tinges presenting razor-back ridges and deep rifts and sharp gullies. The way lay straight as a die across the desert and then wound around the cliffs, and faced with a mountain plunged steeply through an unlined tunnel for half a mile. Going down the precipitous and tortuous road overlooking sheer cliffs covered in the debris of annual landslides, as was the road itself, we kept turning back on ourselves, hither and yon until we overlooked the Rio Grande oasis and passed at length through a majestic natural rock archway on the crest of a ridge and surveyed miles of the country to come. As we were on a mountainside looking down onto the valley hundreds of feet below, we could clearly see how the greenery was dependent on the river, just like overlooking the oasis from a plane. By late afternoon we arrived at the Nazca Plateau, a flat stony desert containing a very few rocky outcrops covered with line drawings on such an enormous scale that they can only be recognised from fairly high in the sky. That alone presents a quandary since there is nowhere to look down on the plain from. We stopped by the high observation tower that Maria Reiche, the German expert, has had put up near a couple of enigmatic stylised markings, a pair of hands and a tree. We could also see enormously long parallel lines like runaways going clear to the horizon of the plain. The drawings on the desert floor have been extensively vandalised mainly with tyre tracks by people who have deliberately gone joy-riding along the lines and driven in loops and whirls desecrating 3,000 years of history in three minutes. Apart from straight lines and geometric shapes sometimes miles in dimension, various objects are depicted: a humming-bird with a wingspan greater than 100 yards, a monkey, a dog, a spider, and many more besides. We camped 14 miles further south at the private Aero Condor airfield on the edge of the plateau with dry mountains raising the horizon. A piebald llama not yet full-grown was tethered there, and when I approached, it tipped back its haughty head and, looking me straight in the eye, pursed its lips and spat in my face to everyone's amusement. That is the only defensive gesture llamas seem to make, but normally they take to their heels at the first hint of an enemy. Llamas have a big harelip revealing stained teeth, but this one calmed down and made friends. The reason why llamas and the other camelids can live in the Puna and Altiplano regions of the Andes is due to their high blood corpuscle count. The Indians too have adapted in this way, but we had to endure the unpleasantness of altitude sickness if we over-exerted ourselves. Llamas and alpacas share their wilderness habitat with their forebears, guanacos, and the fourth member of the South American camelids, vicuñas. The major differences betwixt the llama and the alpaca is that the llama has a squarer outline due to the way its fleece grows over its chest and its tail is held away from its body. Although both animals are wholly domesticated, alpacas are of lower financial interest to the Indians since they will not accept a burden, are generally temperamental, and have a poor breeding rate, leaving them fit only for shearing and meat. Pack-llamas are thus the South American beast of burden, and are often to be seen with their ears pierced to take red tassles, paganistic protection against the evil eye. All the camel family have cloven feet with horny pads rather than hard hooves, and over the last four centuries the introduced hoofed animals have destroyed the fragile mountain ecosystem, with the loss of whole forests of polylepis trees and most of the native grasses, which cannot survive the destructive onslaught of teeth and hooves, and then the loss of the thin mountain soils. In this way the Altiplano has been denuded and Patagonia is even now the frontier for this exploitation.

The Nazca Culture peaked a millennium ago and a lot remains besides the lines to demonstrate how highly developed their engineering and civilisation was, most conspicuously their underground aqueducts leading from the Bisambra Reservoir are still used to this day to irrigate the land. In fact Maria Reiche considers the Nazca Lines to have been etched by a much earlier people to form an astronomical calendar. Ann learned from an American at the airfield that the Mojave Indians of North America have carved far huger and more numerous lines and drawings along the flood plains of the Colorado River. Half of us went up in small planes in the early morning, the best time because of the more horizontal light, and raved about the grandeur and the extent of the lines over the whole plateau. Ann bartered for her flight, paying in film, and when she returned she waxed eloquent about the view. She told me there are far more lines and patterns than are mapped out in the guidebooks, and the straight lines, some over six miles long, are all in a massive jumble. Other such as the 'astronaut' are drawn on hillsides.

From Nazca we returned to Pisco back the way we had come, through Ica. We had one nasty moment in the mountains; coming downhill round a narrow hair-pin Paul slammed on the brakes to avoid a herd of cows and we skidded to within inches of the sheer cliff. The whole purpose of our return was to visit the archaeological museum at Ica, but true to our usual ill-fortune it was still closed. So we camped in the soft flat sands, just out of sight of Pisco to avoid the usual retinue of curious inhabitants. This time we took no chances and smoothly manoeuvred the truck onto sandmats for the night. As often as we could Ann and I dispensed with erecting a tent, and here in the desert the stars shone with a clarity and brilliance which seemed to bring them much closer. All the while my condition continued to deteriorate. I had never been so sick and in such pain and cursed the terrible hygiene record of South America, a continent in which over two thirds of the population live with chronic dysentery and simply get used to it, and most people do not survive to their fortieth birthday.

The next day it fell to Ann and me to go shopping in the excellent market. Here we bought a new fruit, pepinos, which look like melons the size of a grapefruit and have a delicious, sweet, yellow flesh and yellow rinds with irregular streaks of purplish brown. Avocados, locally grown, were dirt-cheap here, and too late I discovered that sea-turtle steak, a delicacy worldwide, was the cheapest meat available at a dollar per pound. Raw it looked like jugged hare, i.e., a rich dark brown with no fat, but flippers and heads and other parts were also for sale at the fish stalls. I bought some for Ann and me and simmered it, and it was as tender as Châteaubriand but tasted much better.

From Pisco we launched ourselves into the extreme altitudes of the Peruvian Sierra and the Great Altiplano of Peru and Bolivia. We were to spend nearly a month among massive chains of soaring mountains, the Land of the Incas. Particularly in Bolivia and southern Peru the Indians are self-sufficient, entirely outside the monetary economy and have their own languages, mainly Quechua, the tongue of the Inca Empire.

We started out through very slowly rising desert terrain, which gradually showed more agriculture the higher we went. We were following the bed of the River Pisco which meandered through such a dust-bowl that we were stifled all day with dirt pouring in the windows. There were very few houses but many herds of cattle and flocks of sheep, even a few goats and horses, all tended together by a shepherd boy or girl on the band of greenery so arduously won on both sides of the river. We passed dozens of low stone rings each with a single entrance, before we found one in use. They were pigsties and corrals of dry-stone walling. At high noon we stopped at Tambo Colorado 30 miles up the valley, pre-Inca ruins, unique in that they were built of adobe bricks on stone foundations. The whole complex was used by all the co-existing ancient cultures as a trading centre, and had features of Chimú architecture, such as being built in a maze pattern all enclosed within a high city wall. Every couple of feet along each wall were double niches, i.e. a smaller one set back from a larger one. In olden times each one had a little idol of gold or silver or platinum, a total of thousands of idols. The main palace complex was for nobility, women, and guests, and contained a big ceremonial courtyard. Since rain was rarely encountered the roofs of palm thatch were primarily for shade. There was also, over the road, a barracks for the men and other ancillary buildings. In due course the Incas dominated the city and their wall paintings survive faintly. Looking south over the next mountain we could make out the original Inca Highway climbing over it towards the Inca heartlands of Vilcabamba. Until the arrival of the Incas the Indians of this region never discovered the use of wool or dairy products or pack-animals, and kept llamas and alpacas for slaughter only, and fished, tilled the land, and traded.

As we drove on, basically following the Pisco in the dale far below, we noticed irrigation ditches hugging the lip of the road, diverting water from much further up the valley. The dust was terrible but the clear view of the high, brown, rugged mountainsides showed us clearly the convolutions of rock strata going in loops and ripples for miles, and sometimes climbing vertically. Attempts to utilise this land were mind-bending to behold. Rock-fields had been cleared and either the hillsides were terraced with the stones or cairns were built with them just to get them out of the way. Where irrigation had been managed, crops survived, together with trees such as Lombardy poplars and eucalypts and scrub and scattered xerophytes. Wherever the herds and flocks grazed there was always a woman or a child in attendance snugly wrapped up. As we drove along the single-lane ledge, backwards and forwards, gaining height slowly all the time, we passed along crude burrows cut straight through the mountain, barely the width of the truck; such a tight squeeze that in one we lost a wing mirror. As the road crept even higher towards the pass at 15,500 feet so the land became more verdant with pastures of grass and mosses and lichen, and there were more grazing flocks.

We reached the only possible camping-spot in the mountain

wilderness at 8,500 feet in mid-afternoon allowing plenty of daylight to go rambling. Close on either side of us were steep ridged escarpments and on the third side of the triangle about a mile away was a mountain wall across which the road traversed many times. When a truck approached we heard it first and then pinpointed the tiny object as it crossed the mountain a number of times, successively lower until it turned towards us and went right around completing the triangle, taking 20 minutes to advance a mile as the condor flies. Our camp-site was covered with scrub brush and scattered irregular boulders, just the same as the rest of the arid land we had covered, but now we became aware of a dusk chorus of birdsong. Armin set about building a bonfire of dead cactus boughs which burnt fiercely with high flames, just the thing to keep out the chill of the fresh breeze which blew up during the evening. In the darkling twilight, a silent gaucho made a perfect vignette, wrapped in his poncho and soft hat, as he rode by on horseback, clip-clopping all the way round the camp along the road high above our heads.

From our location we climbed into increasingly pretty country of painted mountains and left behind the arid desert. There was more and more water available, visibly oozing from the rock faces and tumbling along in rills and streams. Every surface was covered in vegetation except the vertical precipices and the mountain summits. As we gained altitude all morning we scanned increasingly beautiful panoramas, and at 13,000 feet we reached the shoulder of the mountain, where the gradient diminished to a mere ten degrees for quite a broad expanse. We stopped there at Castrovirreyna and were immediately surrounded by over 100 children all uniformly dressed in grey or black which seemed to be the traditional colours for these mountain folk. Ann discovered that there were an average of eight children in each family, mainly illegitimate to deliberately mix the genetic make-up. Breathing was already difficult here, but we had to make the pass at 15,500 feet through grassland, waterlogged in large patches. There were a great many llamas with red tassles fastened to their ears. Their fur was piebald or skewbald, and very few were of only one colour. One of the advantages of the streams and waterfalls was the chance to wash off the dust from the desert, although the brown floodwater was numbing.

It was all downhill for the rest of the day through a wonderland of colour. Ann and I were really curious to see how the landscape developed as rounding every corner presented a new marvel. The mountains and volcanoes were rich in minerals of many kinds and the rocks were soft pinks and deep mauves and pastel yellows with tinges of blue and green and multicoloured whorls fingerprinted on small rocks and cliffs alike. The highest peaks were snowcapped and others were decorated or veined in an off-white scree. The wildlife and plantlife added their colours to the layers of mineral-rich geological structures. There were few trees allowing views for great distances over the close-cropped rolling curves of grass and mosses. Now and again we passed trees in bloom and solitary or grouped dwellings decorated with gardens full of flowers. These mountain folk wore very dark clothes except for some of the women who had on layers of petticoats and very colourful strips of woven cloth in which they carry their loads or babies on their backs, and the babies wore delightful knitted Inca balaclavas. The head-gear in Peru was varied in the extreme: the nation is universally hatted, excepting the most macho young men, but throughout Bolivia and Peru the Indians always removed their hats in church. Trilbies and pork pie hats were ubiquitous and a few imported designs were sometimes worn by small boys, such as baseball caps and berets. Most common of all were the traditional styles in patterns peculiar to the various tribes and villages, in natural dyes or in undyed black, brown, and off-white wool. Caps risible in Western eyes were everywhere, like imaginative wide-brimmed bath caps, along with Panama hats, stiff woollen hats on wire frames with simple adornments, and straw toppers or morning hats sported by the Indian women. A variation in the colour indicated the valley where the wearer lived.

CHAPTER ELEVEN PERU

Suddenly, in a mining area called El Milagro (The Miracle) we came upon a huge mineral formation which looked just like the nose of a miniature glacier. It was as though a gigantic gush of soapy white foam had been frozen instantaneously, capturing forever a tidal wave front, and on closer inspection the effect of fluidity was even more intriguing as the whole thing clearly issued from a hole in the mountainside about ten feet in diameter and must have flowed down the slope about 100 feet spreading out just like a lava-flow. In the white crystalline mass fanned out streaks of black and grey. Wherever we looked, huge areas of the mountain slopes were barren of flora but beautifully coloured, being rich in mineral ores too poisonous to support life. There was quite a lot of water draining down into the muddy brown river, which even at these altitudes was quite a torrent. We never quite left behind the copper-rich rocks which had so many greens and blues in them, nor the fragmented and crumbling basal stone in shades of red from shrimp pink to the colour of brick, but by and by we descended through the zones of bunch-grass and brake undergrowth which manage to survive high up, into a region of good grazing and agriculture once more. Once again we had no choice but to take the first suitable camp-site, rocky flat shelves of turf by a fast stream, a lovely spot at 11,500 feet, but overnight the temperature dropped to a mere five degrees.

In the morning we continued to wend through these green mountains, driving for the most part across sloping plateaux used as pasture for llamas, alpacas, and cattle with dewlaps like soft curtains. Pigs and hens also roamed freely scratching out a diet. For hours the one-lane road descended, and in places was reinforced where the land had slipped into the abyss, giving us distant views over the gently rolling hills. Families along the way were few and far between, and their homes were perched in the most inaccessible nooks and crannies since there was not a level acre up here. After the bleak desolation of the snow-covered pass, it was most welcome to see so many flowers again, and such a selection: little, tiny, blue 'eyes' hugging the ground, and sprays of white and cream and yellow blossom on the trees, and red and yellow cactus flowers, and tall royal blue lupins, and roses, pelargoniums, and many others which Ann and I had never seen before. We could see Ayacucho for hours before we reached it nestled in its prosperous valley at 8,010 feet. As we dropped down the mountain towards the town, we twisted from side to side, losing sight of it for minutes a time. Ayacucho was founded in 1539 and is steeped in history and this is reflected in the old stone architecture of the Cathedral, City Hall, and Government Palace around Parque Sucre, the central plaza. Some of the buildings were entered through square arches, achieved by cleverly shaped cap-stones. After a spell guarding the truck wrapped in conversation with interested locals I joined the others in a stroll through the cloisters surrounding the square. Rolf and I came upon a cameraman taking portrait pictures with an extremely primitive home-made box and bellows camera by the simple expedient of momentarily removing the lens cap, and then he developed the print on the spot by working inside the camera with one hand, using a long black sleeve to keep out the sunlight. There were lots of arts and crafts shops selling a profusion of alpaca woollen and fur products, rugs and tapestries, and the city's specialty,- miniature figurines in familiar settings such as the manger scene, milliners' or bakers' shops, all from carved and painted wood in tiny cupboards the size of matchboxes. Its other specialties are the manufacture of harps, and mates burilados (carved gourds), a traditional folk art going back to pre-Inca times. Paul took us on a long slow tour of this old colonial city with its 33 churches and numerous colonial mansions before striking deeper into the high mountains once again.

 40 miles further east we could still look back on Ayacucho from our lunch spot, a bare outcrop, strewn with rocks and thorn bushes and lots of little wild flowers. Between Ayacucho and the next town, Abancay, are three mountain ranges and some of the most appalling and roughest dirt-roads Peru has to offer. Even the bus-drivers refuse

to drive on them at night: the word 'bus' is a misnomer as here a bus is more likely to be a cattle truck or a pick-up full of standing people than a Pullman coach. For the whole afternoon, the drive became more and more impressive as we rose high into another pass and the gorges were correspondingly deep beneath us with more of the colourful mineral-stained rock, and ever changing wealth of flowers. A couple of times we saw lop-sided yoked oxen drawing ploughs across the slopes, and at other times saw groups of villagers preparing a potato field with dibbles, or working near their homes. Several times we confronted traffic coming the other way, and considering the great distance a casualty would fall if forced off the road, Paul always hugged the high cliff wall forcing the oncomer to take the precarious outside of the ledge to get by. The sheer heights we negotiated were breath-taking, and to climb or descend the mountains the way zigzagged a dozen times. We stopped, once beyond a creaky sagging bridge to collect pails of water for our tanks. Thereafter the road seemed to descend endlessly without the slightest chance of our pulling off it, and at the first opportunity, likely to be the only one, we crossed a tricky ditch into a rocky depression, but to do so we all had to pitch in and heave hundreds of rocks aside to allow the truck to pass and to clear spaces for our tents. The thunderstorm which had threatened for an hour arrived slowly and the lightning lit the tents up very well. Since it was my birthday Gaby and Chantal made a caramel and banana pudding for me to dish out. It was quite the best birthday I ever had.

We moved on in the morning through more high steep mountains with cultivated river valleys. The mountain Indians, herdsmen and gauchos, are clean and proud but in the villages the people are much more squalid or just plain dirty. We started out down the amazingly steep mountainsides until we came to a tributary of the River Apurímac which we crossed and climbed thereafter. The whole valley basin was agricultural and extremely fertile, and time and again we saw unusual plants and crops and always beautiful flowers, heretofore unknown to us. For instance we came upon a tree the shape of a yew with enormous leaves and hundreds of white trumpets fluttering limply about nine inches long. Just as in Colombia the landscape changed rapidly with each new locality. We stopped awhile in Uripa, a village high above the clouds, yet still in the midst of an enormous agricultural valley. The village people did not smile, but simply stared at us with blank limpid eyes and virtually none lifted a hand in greeting. In this village we saw a very old man, naturally composed and heedless of his grimy rags, reclining against an adobe wall with an equally mangy mongrel curled up beside him asleep in the crook of his arm. His wrinkled weather-beaten face of leather contained the sagacity of the whole community coupled with their lethargy which belied the necessity for hard work.

We ascended high out of the maize fields to the second pass at 14,000 feet for lunch. There was not a soul in sight, only the birds and the wind whispering through the hard grassy páramo, host to a plague of caterpillars with long red and brown fur. The birds were having a field-day, even eagles were gobbling up the insects. The eagles were in two colours, the cock birds being black and white and the hens brown and tawny. Driving along the pass we began a descent through the clouds, later climbing again over an eastern lip at 14,000 feet. All afternoon we continued through this high scenery which offered staggering views, but I missed most of it as I was too weak to sit up until we made camp on a mountain-top in a cold lumpy area where, within minutes, we were noticed by locals who looked so cold and hungry that Maria fed them. These ragamuffin Indians were brazen-faced about approaching us, and were not beggars at all, rather, inquisitive opportunists. Every evening Tobin would set up his bar outside the truck, and the Indians really coveted the empty bottles, but since they had no money Tobin hung on to them. These herders were accompanied, as usual, by several very shaggy dogs, and just the same as their dogs they presented themselves silently close at hand and watched and waited for something to come their way. They were disgustingly filthy with the dirt of weeks ingrained in their naked feet and sore faces.

At the crack of dawn the sun started to illuminate the highest pinnacles, and in this early dawn lighting I was out marvelling at the unrivalled view we had from our perch 13,000 feet high. To our backs was the lumpy pasture of our mountain-top with a few scattered adobe huts and corrals of dry-stone walling, and mere inches beyond the road the land dropped away 1,000 feet to a tumultuous rush of water, fast crashing its way down the ravine. The other side of the gully was even higher and more sheer and my eye was drawn by drifting smoke to several primitive thatched hovels nestled against the grim slope, invisible but for the curls of dung smoke filtering through the grass roofs. There was neither a square yard of flat ground nor the vestige of any foot-path passing near the huts. Turning my gaze south-east over the third pass there was a range of snowy summits about 60 miles distant, and the low angle of the rising sun threw back dazzling highlights. The impression of brilliance lessened every second as the lower slopes also caught the harsh light. Unfortunately a mantle of clouds below the pass blew across and obscured the view in that direction.

For breakfast we had curious local buns baked in clay ovens, made from flat discs of dough which had turned out quite uneven and were sprinkled with tasty seeds, not unlike caraway, and lots of bits of black carbon from the rustic oven-shelf. Reorganising my kit in search of more Flagyl tablets I found some bars of soap which I gave to one of the peasant women. We started down the mountain bundled up against the crisp cold air and, whenever the cloud allowed, enjoyed wide views extending easily ten miles over a moist green landscape with fields wherever humanly possible, sometimes on gradients of more than 60 degrees. Occasionally homes or hamlets were visible, tiny in the remote, rich, green valleys. Abancay was spotted from a distance of 35 miles, and made a wonderful sight as it sprawled high up a glacial valley with a crown of mountains all round, and a deep gorge in front of it, and puffs of white cloud above and below it. The countryside we passed was enormously fertile with a rich red soil and plantations of eucalyptus and ever more flowering plants. There was only one drawback, the hordes of tiny, red, blood-sucking flies.

As we hugged the cliff along the dirt-road, there was always a long drop from the other side and the view of mountains opposite with their inspirational beauty. But the cliff face, inches from the window, allowed us a close study of the plants Ann and I were so inquisitive about. We carefully scrutinised the exotic plants in the erosion scars and growing from the curious adobe walls and brickwork. The Indians were immaculately dressed in gaudy clothes. The women wore such gay pinks and greens and yellows but no-one had a brighter costume than her neighbour. We stopped on the outskirts of Abancay after shopping there, and while we ate we looked back over the perfect little dell, a patchwork of neat fields hedged with tall trees. The furry pigs, poultry, cattle, hobbled horses and donkeys, and sheep and goats all ranged freely, excepting those few tied to stakes. There was one mutant variety of black sheep which quite distinctly had three horns. Later on we saw a much higher snow-capped range, rendered unforgettable by a large rainbow against the clouds and plain hovels in the foreground nearly hidden by cacti and flowering shrubs.

The afternoon brought more picturesque scenery as we gradually sank lower into the Apurímac Valley, through much more of this wild and rich land, with its landslides and colourful Indian peasants working the fields by hand in the traditional way or with yokes of oxen in hand drawn wooden ploughs. The larger clusters of population tended to be in the valleys in pretty little homes spread out among vegetable gardens and pocket handkerchief fields. Late in the afternoon we stopped at a swift rivulet which crossed the dirt-road at a hair-pin bend to refill the water tanks. With true opportunism some of us took advantage of the rare chance to have a bath. As usual

Ann set off walking ahead and when Paul caught her up he drove straight to past everyone's alarm for several miles. In fact he knew the region and we shortly arrived at one of the most idyllic camp-sites of the whole expedition, set among ridges and peaks visible all around with curious cloud formations adding a timelessness and a serenity to our isolated location. There was not a moving thing in sight and the roar of the Apurímac River could be heard distantly. Paul was a natural entertainer and had no trouble getting everyone to laugh and have a good time. He used to lead us in singsongs, admittedly a trifle bawdy and once we had got going he accompanied us on his trombone, and now and again introduced a 'new talented star on the harmonica' such as Alice, knowing full well that Alice could not play a note, but equally would not be embarrassed as it was all in jest.

Sandra, our nurse, kindly attempted to treat my illness, but it was beyond control and I had been in continual pain for weeks.

The next day we entered the heart of the Inca Empire, and descended from our camp-site slowly down into Limatambo. Ann and I had the cab seat again which meant the best views of the Upper Apurímac Valley, immense beyond imagining, despite a rainy start. More than ever we were impressed by the millions of flowers everywhere we looked as we drove into the cattle-raising Anta Valley. All the domestic animals had young scampering around them. It was so amusing to watch the dear little baby donkeys or tiny, furry black piglets which kept overtaking their own legs, and the chicks and ducklings which were all startled into fleeing from our approaching truck. For a short distance we followed the river which crashed headlong in a fury full of yellow-brown silt, augmented by clean brooks of wild water. The wet season was now nearly over and most of the fields were ploughed with crops already sprouting, but today and every day we observed gangs of men, sometimes dozens-strong, labouring in the fields, either all digging trenches, or ploughing furrows, or spraying, or gleaning. The arable land is worked as a communal venture. The colours around us were so clear and beautiful, and the clouds receded and the early light on the cliffs and mountain faces was very subtle bringing out delicate tints in the amazing ever changing florid vegetation and the natural variation in the colours of the rock strata, pushed together in a huge twisting pattern of reds and light blues blending into white. The texture of the verdant mountains opposite resembled a velvet carpet due to the close cropping of the moss and grasses. Even though the slopes were almost vertical, the mountain goats and sheep and loose cattle graze them with complete disregard for the stupendous drop into the hollows below.

Thus, all the way into Limatambo we passed through rich cultivated fields with lots of trees, large plantations of eucalyptus which are blue-leaved when small and clumps of cheery yellow Scottish broom trees. Cactus plants of several kinds stood out aggressively. Saguaros pointed their prickly fingers at the sky and gnarled pepper trees and curious spindly and spiky shrubs found purchases on the bare rock sides and were often used as hedgerows, and agave cacti were favoured to cap country walls, since their falchion leaves were saw-edged as well as protection from erosion. Limatambo itself was a resting-place for the Incas and their couriers. These couriers were a very important aspect of the Inca administration and ran on a network of roads built to accommodate the military intentions of the empire. There at Limatambo we saw our first Inca temple, with walls constructed of big polygonal masonry, smooth at the front and fitted together perfectly. Limatambo is 48 miles from Cuzco and is the main town in the valley and for over an hour we drove away from it through an extremely fertile region covered in fields, not just to the edges of the mountains, but right to their very summits beyond the clouds by means of a system of terracing, a spectacular legacy of Incaic times. These terraces give the Andes their name, the Spanish for steps being 'andenes'.

We pulled out of the valley over a low pass into quite new rolling countryside with short grass and fields of furrowed red tilth, given over to maize for the most part, and on the other side of the road was a long thin lake beside which we stopped for lunch in lovely warm sunshine. Descending a short way the little town of Anta appeared before us all of a sudden. It looked quite modern, and was served by the Machu-Pijchu Railroad and the wandering River Urubamba. The railroad was built by the British long ago using Chinese labour which accounts for the numerous chifas, or Chinese restaurants, in the towns of this region. In the south of the country a railway starts at Mollendo and Matarani, roadsteads serving southern Peru and makes its way to Puno on the shore of Lake Titicaca, the highest navigable lake in the world more than two miles above sea-level, before turning north along the River Vilcanota, which becomes the Urubamba north of Cuzco. The river, Machu-Pijchu Railway, and main road continue north-west from Cuzco through the Gorge of Torontoi as far as Anta, where the river and railway switch along the Urubamba Valley, 'The Sacred Valley of the Incas', to Machu-Pijchu and Quillabamba, currently the end of the line. The Sacred River continues northwards and along with the Apurímac becomes the great Ucayali, one of the main tributaries draining into the Amazon. A road will eventually be built along the Sacred Valley, bringing 'development', which in these intermontane valleys means settlement and certain destruction of the habitat by shifting agriculture. The pattern is one of slash and burn and plant on the ashes, and within a few years the land is exhausted and merely testament to the millions of acres of ruin where previously stood tropical rain forest.

We reached the main tourist road, a good tarred high road at last and made good time to Ollantaytambo in the densely populated Sacred Valley. This small town was unique in our experience as it was built on two levels by the Incas with the residential level at 9,200 feet at the bottom of the Y-Junction where the narrow Yucay Valley from the north runs into the Urubamba Valley. First we explored the flights of terraces, the fortress, and the unfinished temple built right on the sharp spur of the junction where Manco Inca's warriors successfully guarded the narrow valley necks against Pizarro's brother Hernando in 1536. Unfortunately the ticket to the ruins cost 3,000 soles, which also covered ten other sites in Cuzco and along the Gorge of Torontoi. We went up a high staircase passing 17 terraces about eight to ten feet high, which apart from their coincidental defensive purpose, were actually constructed to provide flat grazing within the garrison walls for llamas, alpacas, and vicuñas. The fortified walls went virtually all the way round the base of the stronghold and were well-plaistered with a straw adobe, built by Manco Inca, who also built fortifications to close off the Yucay Valley from the south, though the temple and terracing had been started before his birth.

At the top of the steps the ruins to the left, on the point of the promontory with the most commanding view, belonged to the temple commenced by the Inca Pachacutec, using the Colla Indians of Lake Titicaca for labour, who abandoned the project for some unknown reason. Some of the blocks of stone used to make the temple weigh more than ten tons, and measure up to twelve feet by six by five with the seams so perfectly matched that a knife blade cannot be winkled between them. Not all the rocks were carved into rectangles, but included a variety of square-cut polyhedrons with seats or steps set into or protruding from a single block. It really came home to me how amazing it was that the Incas manipulated stones with wedges and levers, some weighing as much as 30 tons, all without pulleys as they never knew the wheel; and that just their terracework so far discovered would extend over 80,000 miles if put end to end. The temple surfaces had been highly polished, and there was a variation in the quality of finished Incaic masonry according to its purpose. The Sapa Inca himself had the most perfect stonework in his apartments in whichever town he visited, and temples and fountains were of slightly inferior quality, and so on down the scale of nobility, artisans, and townspeople, to garrisons, agricultural and enslaved

CHAPTER ELEVEN   PERU

labourers' terrace houses, to the terraces themselves, constructed of scarcely shaped rocks, but nonetheless all were well matched.

Elsewhere in the ruins, which extended hundreds of feet up the nose of the cliff, the stonework demonstrated variations in walling: the thicker walls and squared off corners were strengthened with an adobe or mortar infill. Restoration work to an arch of large blocks was in progress involving original Incaic techniques, using ropes, a wooden battering ram, and a lot of manpower. Facing us at an equal height on the other side of the neck of the Yucay Valley was the large tiered and castellated Temple of the Virgins of the Sun, which was entirely inaccessible and the erstwhile home of virgins selected for sacrifice or possibly to join the Sapa Inca's harem, for the absolute Sapa Inca was the Descendant of the Sun, and his vice-regent here on Earth. There were a couple more smaller similar constructions built into the very face of the cliff without any possible access by foot. From on high we had an excellent view along the Urubamba Valley and the curving flights of terraces delineating the contours of the valley. Little boys followed us about and offered to whistle tunes for money, and pestered us all in turn without success.

Next we went on to explore the town built on Inca walls so durable that the streets still contain diverted stream water, and the layout of houses and corrals is Incaic. The town is extremely beautiful and the stonework amazing. Ann and I walked into a courtyard under an old wooden verandah. We went into a dark room containing curious relics, antique carved clog-shaped stirrups, a very old harp with a sound-box, and an equally ancient heavy ox-yoke. The walls were massive and the ceilings constructed of low beams. Dirty little beggar girls with mucky noses followed us around through the rooms. The next room was very large, 40 feet by 20 at least, and was patently a victualler's shop with a huge semi-spherical brick and adobe bread-oven as high as the ceiling dominating one corner of the room, and giving it a great sense of atmosphere, enhanced by the second-hand light from the courtyard (the only illumination), and aided by the cool ambient temperature. There were more relics and an old wooden counter across the middle of the room. The place was a gem, a haven of peace and quiet unchangeable by history.

We went down an outside street to look for the Baño de la Ñusta (the Bath of the Princess) of grey granite in a field outside the town, near tangled gardens of blooms and peach trees in the valley. The old streets were all covered in crazy paving and drain either centrally or down one edge into the finely engineered system of water channels such that every street in the town has cleverly arranged ducts flowing swiftly with clear water, which keeps the town clean besides having a delightful babbling brook outside every window. Actually a few gutters were dry as a result of roadworks since Inca times interfering with the waterworks. Sometimes the water was channelled under or through houses. Peeking in the open doorways, of trapezoidal Incaic construction, we viewed either a dim room, the home of a family, or else through an ante-room into a courtyard beyond used as a miniature farmyard complete with donkeys, chickens, contented little black pigs, ducklings, guinea pigs, straw, sacks of Indian corn, wood-piles, tools, manure, and hayloft junk.

At this time of day we met the men and boys on their way home from the fields, carrying heavy loads on their backs with the aid of slings around their shoulders. The local women were out and about too, making use of the sunshine to spin their thread by hand. Ann and I had been fascinated for days as we watched the herders tending their flocks up in the mountains, unanimously carrying spindles and assiduously spinning their threads all day long. At last we were able to watch the mechanics of the operation close up, and spoke with the woman awhile. Her hands were stained with the purple dye from the wool, which was for her own clothing. Every so often she stopped the revolving spindle, hooked the worked thread over a catch and gathered in what she had spun. Strolling around the back streets with pigs wandering loose, the Indians seated in their doorways respectfully saluted us, and the adolescents were a bit giggly, but the grubby toddlers always begged. Most of us wound up at the Alcazar Café where the padron spoke English and served generous melt-in-the-mouth banana and caramel soufflés for a mere 100 soles.

Leaving Ollantaytambo, we merely went down the road past a eucalyptus grove to a sloping quarry right at the foot of the cliff to camp. We watched the evening trains steaming up the valley from Machu-Pijchu to Cuzco, first the expensive but supposedly safe, policed, tourist train and a quarter of an hour later the infamous, crowded, local train, renowned for its professional gangs of thieves who victimise the Gringos so successfully that the majority of them lose valuables despite foreknowledge of the gangs. The gangs specialise in razor-slashing at the chief times of jostling at the ticket barrier and when the train passes through unlit tunnels. Frank, Ann, and I decided to simulate the conditions we would undergo on the Inca Trail over four days without proper tents. My arrangement of a poncho, fly-sheet, and numerous rocks looked odd but stood up to a severe test of freezing rain all night. It was Stephanie's birthday and we honoured it with another late night party.

Our next objective was to arrive early in Cuzco to allow those of us intent on hiking the Inca Trail to organise our provisions. We drove high up along one side of the Gorge of Torontoi allowing ourselves spectacular views of the Inca (and pre-Inca) agricultural terracing, which goes all the way up to the very top of the defile in places. We stopped halfway at a point opposite the three superb hill fortifications of Pisaq, almost hidden towards the summit of the mountain, one above the other with excellently preserved masonry. The little town itself sits in the bottom of the Sacred Valley and, like Ollantaytambo, is near enough square with streets intersecting at right angles. The Inca engineers not only diverted water from the eastern side of the Andes via tunnels and aqueducts to irrigate the desert, they also remodelled whole rivers. Here at Pisaq the Urubamba used to meander in ox-bows down the valley, but in order to obtain the maximum acreage of arable land, they levelled the flood plain and canalised the river straight along the foot of the western cliff. We continued along the ridge, and soon passed the village of Urubamba itself and a few miles short of Cuzco we saw a couple more of the huge hill engravings, one reading 'VIVA EL PERU' and the other shewing the national coat of arms, a llama, an orange tree, and a cornucopia on a shield, surrounded by corn and mare's-tail, above 'B89' which is the number of the battallion based at Cuzco. The valleys roundabout are chequered with manifold plots of cultivated land, and a profusion of trees and yellow gorse add their colours to the flecks of wild flowers. Some of the vales are heavily forested and contain hundreds of tobacco trees (Nicotiana tormentosa), growing on nearly perpendicular slopes.

Cuzco (11,500 feet) was the capital city of the Incas whose empire-building gained them dominion over 700,000 square miles from Colombia to Argentina. The Incas incorporated the skills of the civilisations they conquered, particularly construction engineering, carving, weaving, pottery, metalwork, and farming. To maintain complete control the Sapa Inca had four lieutenants, each in charge of a region in the directions of the cardinal points of the compass. Under them was a strictly tiered hierarchical political organisation based on numbers of families, or ayllus, as the smallest units. The worship of the Sun preceded the Incas, and had been developed by the fundamental Tiahuanaco Culture, but the Sapa Inca was revered as a deity with unquestionable autocratic spiritual and secular domination. Both these fields of prowess had no fixed élite; recruitment to priesthood and the administrative and military hierarchies went according to merit, and extended to the defeated tribes. The Inca's absolute power depended greatly on a fast communications system, which necessitated the construction of the finest road network of its day in the world, much of which yet survives 700 years after it was built. The couriers delivered messages by running in relays, and could not slow down or walk along any part of their sections on pain of death. The roads also allowed the efficient movement of armies and so furthered the expansion of the realm. The Inca Highway had two basic arteries; the coastal road, 2,520 miles long and up to 26 feet broad, from Tumbes on the Gulf of Guayaquil to Talca in South-Central Chile, and the 1,250-mile long royal road from Quito to Cuzco which was extended another 2,000 miles as the borders of the kingdom were rolled back into Columbia and Argentina. The royal road varied in width due to mountain conditions, but averaged 16 to 20 feet. These major routes were interconnected with a web of lesser lateral roads to form a largely unpaved network, though the paved sections across water and in the mountains involved laying extremely deep foundations, so that the road effectively ran along the top of a wide wall or up flights of stone steps. Every 12 to 20 miles there were official rest-houses and stores in which the agricultural wealth of the nation was stored against times of need. The upkeep of each tampu (corrupted to Tambo in modern place names) was the responsibility of the local ayllu.

In Cuzco we put in at a hotel in the still relatively unspoilt old area. The Old City has a style and charm of its own, incorporating as it does the Inca stonework and layout. It is full of narrow, old, cobbled streets of which one, Gringo Alley, gets this nickname from the patrons frequenting its cheap cafés. There are so many ancient structures, and Incaic stonework is found in the Plaza de Armas, with the Cathedral to one side and the University to another, and everywhere throughout the city. Indian peasants sit on the pavements selling their wares, sometimes fruit, or colourful woven bands (a very popular buy), or sweets and bars of chocolate. In many streets we saw workers in wood and found earthenware statuettes and biblical figurines, and carved Indian subjects and other authentic local crafts, such as knitted and woven items and antiques and soapstone curios. Some of us had little time for sight-seeing as we had to arrange our backpacks for the assault on the Inca Trail. The essential point was to pack lightly as we would have to climb steeply to almost 14,000 feet with the load. Together we made our way across town to the

San Pedro rail terminal in Ccasparo Street, where we bought tickets to Kilometro 88, the usual access point to the Inca Trail, whence it is a tiring 30 miles to Machu-Pijchu. It is impossible to buy tickets for the morning local train on the day as it leaves before the ticket office opens. We bought single tickets on this train at a twentieth of the cost of the tourist train which departs hours later. Our hotel only had freezing cold water although the sun was boiling hot and dried our laundry in a matter of minutes.

Ann and I went out late into the night and came back laden with food for the trek, the best foods being naturally dry like home-grown Brazil nuts, the local fresh corn baps, milk powder, chocolate, oatmeal, crackers, and juice crystals. Fruit, cheese, and tins of fish were nice but heavy, and we kept these down to a minimum. We decided against carrying cooking equipment as water would have taken ages to boil in any case at the great altitudes. While shopping we managed to haggle the prices right down, particularly in Ccasparo Street market which did not close at night for the greengrocery, food, and drink stalls, some of which were not stalls at all but a cluster of seats for the clientéle around a spirit-burner over which a basic beef risotto was being prepared. Wandering back slowly we saw many tea shops which served mate de coca, mate yierbaluisa, and other brews. They looked cheap and were full of locals. We entered one on the corner of the plaza opposite the San Francisco Convent and tried mate coca, a mild brew of coca leaves, and were enormously relaxed, whether more from the cocaine or the welcome rest I Cannot say. We found a guild-hall for Peruvian artisans in the Plaza de Armas, and inside was a collection of arts and crafts for sale in all kinds of materials, including jewellery, alpaca and llama fur and wool, and ceramics, especially wall decorations. The guild-hall itself was fascinating study, and at its farther end looked like a baronial hall raised on a platform upon which stood a long trestle table, and around this a cultural meeting was in progress over a late meal On the walls were heraldic bearings and other antique hangings which gave the place a venerable mood, full of the dignity and prowess of handicraftsmen.

We woke at 4:30, and once we were ready gathered in the cloistered quadrangle of our hotel, eight in all. Maria (who was going direct to Machu-Pijchu), Ann, Dee, Stephanie, Frank, Rolf, Tobin, and I set off through the ancient corridors of Cuzco, dimly lit with decorative old street lamps. At the half-dark station we were full of apprehension about the numerous bold gangs of thieves, and we were caught up in the terrific crush of people against the platform barriers and suffered the impersonal animalistic hustle for nearly an hour. When the gates Opened the mass of humanity burst forth onto the pavement and sprinted for the insufficient seats in the second-class carriages. Rolf and Tobin had tickets in these carriages and were the first people to reach their carriage but found nearly all the places already taken by locals who had bribed their way on board before the rush. The rest of us sat together in a first-class carriage ignorant of the seating system which guaranteed us specific places, and we took others, so a big argument arose when the ticket-holders tried to claim their seats, which they succeeded in doing only after fetching the guard who explained all to us. We need not have undergone the indignity at the barrier, but finally took our allocated seats.

The journey started on time at 5:30 north out of Cuzco in a succession of slow shunts backwards and forwards up the side of the valley, giving us a commanding view of the city. As we chugged along, passing the Gorge of Torontoi, Pisaq, Ollantaytambo, the beginnings of the Anta Canyon, and abruptly right into the Urubamba Canyon, we were enthralled by the sheer beauty of the Sacred Valley of the Incas. The train ran between snowcapped mountains along the banks of the rushing brown waters of the Urubamba, the Sacred River of the Incas. Both sides of the valley were terraced up the flanks of high cliffs, and the sheer mountain walls of this deep valley lifted out of sight beyond the top edges of the train windows, and were beautiful in themselves in red and brown rock, sometimes forested or covered in grass and cacti, and all the curious local flowering plants, not least of which is Calceolaria tormentosum whose flowers reach 20 feet. Vendors passed both ways along the aisle selling anything and everything from hot coffee in well-wrapped corked bottles to live pigs. The train was jam-packed with passengers as it was, with Indians sitting on sacks of maize and other purchases in the corridors and toilets, in fact anywhere there was a space. Some of the hundreds of hawkers were mere children, often specialising in chewing-gum or cigarettes or chocolates. I tried a cup of coffee which was very hot and sweet, but the Indian did not want payment until she came back half an hour later to collect her cups, which goes to show how trusting are the Quechua Indians. Other passengers around us were mostly day-trippers, holidaying Limeños who took a great interest in Ann and myself, and plied us with plums and wild cherries while we conversed in Spanish.

We alighted at Kilometro 88, Pampaccahua, immediately after a tunnel 54 miles from Cuzco, with great alacrity and agility, since the engineer was notorious for his disdain for Gringos and stopped for less than ten seconds, and pulled away with Ann still aboard, so she leapt for her life. Elsewhere Frank, Rolf, and Tobin jumped from windows. This station is at the Inca ruins of Koriwayrachina which incorporate part of the tunnel since put to service by the railway, and also some steps leading away out of sight up the cliff above the station. Our first task was to cross the river by means of a curious mid-air ferry, consisting of a platform and a pulley system 30 feet above the torrent. We were accosted by a man selling tickets for the Inca Trail against whom we had been warned, but there was no way out and without such a ticket the ferryman would not countenance taking us across, and he charged us yet more money too. This then was our starting point at 8,200 feet. Back on dry land we set off through beautiful eucalyptus woods, while the air was filled with the scents of a hot summer's day, pregnant with the smells of eucalyptus gum, spearmint, and of course the thousands of flowers turned out to be a feature of the Camino Incaico, not just the yellow cactus and shrub florets, but flowers in all hues and sizes, especially lupins the colour of lapis lazuli, and bright scarlet stalks with hanging, crimson, tulip-shaped heads with yellow stamens, growing out of a sleeve formed by a thick, hairy, crinkled leaf, dark green edged in blood red — these were begonias.

We passed through woods and saw more Inca ruins up the hill, basically a set of agricultural terraces and a small very ruined fort, Llactapata, which served to guard the confluence of the Urubamba River and the lesser, but crystal clear Cusichaca River. Crossing the tributary we settled down to a leisurely lunch on the flat greensward along the bank and took it in turns to bathe and change into our lightest clothes, as the sun was at its zenith and poured down a drowsy warmth. Towering on the other side of the Urubamba was La Veronica, the highest peak in view at 19,042 feet, at least the top of 2,000 of which was under a blanket of dazzling white snow. All afternoon we trudged along the Cusichaca Canyon and climbed 1,000 feet, but sometimes descended a bit. The trail has changed over the years owing to erosion and landslides and reforestation obliterating sections of it. The going was terribly slow, no more than one mile per hour as Dee and Ann were in need of frequent rests at this altitude, and were fighting losing battles with their packs which made them both very sore.

Most of the way up was through dense forest and all day long we kept meeting local Indians, maybe a dozen or so, some on horseback and some carrying loads much greater than ours, but they overtook us nevertheless despite their lack of shoes. Whenever the view permitted we caught glimpses of a little horticulture around the very few dwellings, but for the most part the mountainsides were far too steep and only the tough red epiphytes, hardy cacti, and mosses gripped the cliff faces. There were many bluffs and overhangs, and the immensity of the heights all round us was fascinating in its primordial energy, captivating to observe, such sheer vastnesses of rock skirted with jungle for half their height, and echoing with the constant accompaniment of the muffled boom and splash of dozens of streams and waterfalls which filled the Cusichaca River. The past few months had witnessed the heaviest rainfalls here for six years, and all the rivers in southern Peru were high or in flood, which was good for agriculture but also brought numerous subsidences and they closed roads and disrupted commerce. Various paths criss-crossed through the woods and every junction was a cue (or an excuse) for a rest-stop to discuss the way up.

By early afternoon we reached a simple bridge of half a dozen logs over a river, but it was perfectly safe as the Indians ride over it on horseback and lead cattle across it. On the far side a shaggy dog was guarding the half-decomposed corpse of a horse, most of whose ribs had been laid bare by condors or bears. It must have broken a shank crossing the bridge and died on the bank. In the heat we were all drenched with sweat and were amazed to come upon a coca-cola bar, a sideline for some entrepreneurial Quechua, who must have brought the coca-cola in himself over the mountains. From then on the climb became steeper and the forest thinned out to sunny woodland until we came to the Llulluchayoc River where it emptied into the Cusichaca. We crossed back by another log bridge and climbed sharply up the track, losing it on a grassy ledge. Looking around we saw the tiny village of Huayllabamba (at 9,000 feet) with a simple thatched schoolroom. Ann went to ask directions and led us out again upstream through the woods, all panting due to the altitude. With so many paths and streams we could easily have got lost, particularly where a stream-bed formed the path. We were all pretty tired and tetchy since we realised we would never make it to the first of several passes by nightfall.

By five o'clock, with many stops along the way, we arrived at a major landmark, the Forks and the Three White Stones, at a point where the Llulluchayoc is joined by the Huararo River which involved another precarious log bridge. We reached a major landslide with a very loose surface across which a narrow foot-path had been pioneered by previous hikers, at which point we turned back along the bridle-path to camp on a ten-degree slope a few minutes walk away. Rolf and Frank discovered a cave, but the rest of us erected shelters. Taking off our packs we felt as light as birds and revelled in the sensation, but not for long; nightfall and mosquitoes, were closing in on us. Ann, Stephanie, and I (on advice from Frank, unusually enraptured by his surroundings) went to fetch water from the Llulluchayoc. We negotiated an extremely tricky 100-foot bank and entered into another world. Here was jungle so thick that the light only filtered through a few chinks in narrow shafts. Flowers proliferated, the likes of which I had never seen before, in this strange ecosystem where the clear cascades cooled the air right down, and moistened it so much that in the semi-dark environment the Spanish moss hung in thick beards from each twisting bough. Every square inch of bark was furry with growths and glistened with beads of moisture. As the glade was so sheltered from air currents, extremely delicate flowers survived on etiolated stalks with fragile beige-pink petals, and there were tropical insects, hard-cased like the dung beetles of the desert, but now metallic turquoise with bright green heads and Morocco red legs kicking in protest at being turned upside-down. Another insect there was a wasp over two inches long with a thin body, glistening blue-black, and hard, shiny, steely blue legs and narrow, incongruous, orange wings an inch and a half long. The wasp had come to drink, and did not fly so much as hop in disquieting diagonals with the aid of its wings. There was also a brown millipede there of unbelievable dimensions that I unwittingly startled into a rippling run. The constant tinkle and swish of the water falling over the rocks was muffled by foliage so thick only specks of sky were visible.

Still deep in the woods, we passed a cold night on the mountain and were woken before dawn by the pattering rain. Stephanie, Frank, Rolf, and Tobin set off nearly an hour before us. The path steadily grew steeper but Ann and I managed to catch up with

Stephanie and we decided to wait for Dee; a very long time. She and Ann realised they would never make it: backpacking up mountains at these altitudes is a very serious business, and they turned back so disappointed. Stephanie went on, but I was now encumbered with both six-foot tent-poles. One on its own made an excellent hiking aid, particularly as the sharp tip was steady on any surface, a real boon going downhill. I caught up with the others just as they reached the end of the woods. Rolf relieved me of a tent-pole and went on ahead with Stephanie and Tobin for the hardest slog of all, a climb of 3,000 feet in under three miles up to the first pass. I left with Frank, climbing up one side of the valley with a clear view of the pass at 13,800 feet to the north-west and the glorious snow-clad tip of Mount Salccantay, standing 20,550 feet high to the south over our left shoulders. We just stuck one foot in front of another and bent to our task along the stony path up the everlasting hillside which was strewn with huge broken rocks, mostly granite. There were cattle and horses grazing freely all around which Clearly used the path a good deal judging by the mess they made of it.

We all travelled individually at different paces, with Tobin way in the lead chewing coca leaves for all he was worth, with Stephanie and Rolf close behind. Frank was half an hour behind me but the hard work gave me such a healthy appetite that I stopped for a meal every hour and he kept catching me Up. A few other hikers overtook us, including two Peruvians who were running the trail, high on cocaine and wearing just singlets, shorts, and pumps. An hour before I reached the pass I saw the first three there, tiny on the horizon, and could hear the bewitching sound of Rolf playing his bamboo flute which came haunting and lilting down the mountainside and encouraged me to move on. Arriving at last at the pass, I allowed Frank to catch up with a new-found American companion, talking 19 to the dozen on Frank's favourite subject, anthropology. At this height the sun's radiation really warmed us but the cooling influence of the wind up the pass was even stronger especially since we were soaked in sweats Thus the top of my head was cooking while the rest of me was shivering.

We walked together down into the next huge valley and entered a quite different terrain, changing slowly to woodland again, and dense jungle spread out below us in the basin of the Pacamayo River. We went around the side of the valley and crossed the first stream fairly high up. As we descended to meet the river the going was fast but treacherous with mud and slippery rocks which skittered away underfoot. From this side of the pass I could see why it was so wet here compared to the rocky side. The pass formed a bottleneck for the clouds, which were funnelled through it and dispersed on the other side. One minute the vale would be hidden under a rolling fog and the next the fog would be lifted and swept straight up and through the gap leaving the forest bathed in sunlight. As we descended we became aware of the dominating tumult of the Pacamayo cascading down in large waterfalls 600 yards to our left, filling the valley With its resonance and cutting a white gash in the clumpy bottle green panoply of jungle. Crossing the river by the mandatory rough-hewn logs we staggered through a gooey marsh, and with sucking sounds began to ascend the 2,000-foot climb to the second pass with took us high over the gorge with a pretty abrupt drop below us. A few trees grew as high as the track away from the jungle proper and mountain lupins, gentians, and other flowers were everywhere spaced out among the perennial tussock-grass. All of a sudden we were mobbed by a big male black-chested buzzard eagle (Geranoaetus melanoleucus) Uttering its alarm cry, taken up by a couple of fully fledged young females in a tree close by us. The male had white underwings, and the females were brown with tawny breasts and underwings, and the latter took off in pursuit of the adult down the valley. Not expecting to see them again we were stopped in our tracks a few minutes later by the plaintive call of one of the eaglets, Weak and apathetic to hear, just beyond arm's reach. There was not even time to photograph the disobliging fledgling which capered along the path, and spreading its wings, launched itself into the void to join its sister on their nesting rock a little higher up the mountain. The nests of black-chested buzzard eagles are quite casual tangles of twigs set upon rocky vantage points, and these carrion-eaters rival but do not threaten the condors.

As the going got tougher I left the others behind and noticed for the first time I was actually treading a built granite path, the Inca Trail proper, in an acute state of disrepair due to the disturbances of frosts and roots and animal hooves during centuries of abandon. The trail was very crooked and stepped in places, following the contours of the mountain up to a high ledge, a position of natural advantage over all the valley where I caught up with Stephanie, Rolf, and Tobin, while they had lunch. While I climbed the irregular man-made stairway up the ledge, they advanced on round the mountain on their way to the second pass, but did not stop to study the Inca ruins along the way as I did. I sat on the ledge to wait for Frank and his new-found chum and looked around at the prolific and varied flowers. Thus it was I who made the discovery that the whole ledge was not. natural at all but actually a built-up fortification such as a sentry-post overlooking the L-shaped valley. Within sight of the guardhouse ledge, about half an hour higher up the valley, was Runkuraqay, an Inca waystation, with a door at the back opening into two concentric circular walls, between which were rooms ten feet wide and long. Here (as everywhere that people camp) was a lot of garbage, the one unpleasant feature of the hike. This ruin is at 12,500 feet and I explored it until Frank caught up. The second pass was only a mile further on and 600 feet higher, but the climb up to it was almost all in one flight of extremely steep broken steps. The Runkuraqay Pass is marked by pools on either side of the trail, one about 40 feet higher than the other.

Looking back from from the pass, apart from deep in the gorge, the terrain is mainly high grassland, but looking forward it is dense, wet, tropical jungle, The descent was easy, initially very steep down the Inca Trail, carved out of the mountain in places, and paved up to six feet wide in others, and later if ran almost level high along a mountainside above the jungle. In places cliffs overhung the road, and at other sections the drop off the edge of the trail was a precipice going down 100 feet. About midway betwixt the second and third passes is the major Inca ruin of Sayajmarca, just at the point where the Inca Trail crosses the Yanachoca River. A high flight of stairs leads from a coincidental cave up to a promontory at 11,750 feet with a view over the surrounding land for 290 degrees. Unfortunately the fort is overgrown with grass and weeds, but it is very big and could have housed 150 people. The back wall is amazing as it was built flush with the very edge of the mountain which drops vertically for hundreds of feet to thick jungle in the abyss. I explored the ruins thoroughly in the heat of the lowering sun and discovered terraces. The ruins were built on a standing finger of rock with a sheer drop on three sides, and backs against a cliff on the fourth side, virtually impregnable, but every drop of water had to be carried up from the river 400 feet below, where I went next. Before I crossed the log bridge I stopped to fill my canteen in a burgeoning waterfall set amidst a naturally beautiful bower of big rocks, trees, Spanish moss, and all sorts of tropical jungle plants. To the side was a thatched open-sided shelter for campers. The evening sun angled along the gorge and penetrated the bower perfectly to light up the waterfall and make it sparkle like diamonds.

From there to the third pass the Inca. Trail climbed slowly and steadily through firstly jungle and later grassy swamp. In the jungle the Inca Trail revealed one of its secrets; it is actually a road running along the top of a very high wall built on the sheer side of the forested mountain, and to avoid the stonework offering moisture to questing tree roots which would tear it down, the entire wall is built to allow an air gap between it and the cliff, and only the road surface reaches across to the cliff. Some of the roadstones had fallen through into the gap. In places the foundations are 100 feet high and walking along it made me distinctly uneasy, the more so when the trail was under inches of mud and water and was downright slippery. The jungle environment here was in complete contrast to that at Misahuallí. Here it was denser, darker, and with huge twisting tree roots, dank mouldy smells, dripping foliage, stands of bamboo and tree-ferns and palms, home to hummingbirds with polished metallic sheens. After a few miles this gave way at a higher altitude to somewhat flatter swamp which entirely submerged lengths of the trail or else a rill would flow right along it. At these places my tent-pole came in very handy for feeling out hidden rocks as stepping-stones and I gradually climbed out of the marsh onto the side of the mountain, and although the fall was vertical it was hidden by tall grasses, bushes, and bamboos which had at last managed to take root in the very wet foundations below the road.

There was only half an hour of daylight left and I knew I would have to accept the next possible sleeping-place, when I heard the very welcome sound of Rolf's Inca pipes from just around the corner. He had set up a bivouac in a large cave which overlooked the Yanachoca jungle valley and allowed us an unequalled view of the snow-clad Andes Mountains all around us. The night was clear and crisp and cold, even in our down sleeping-bags, and the nearly full moon shone on the white peaks which twinkled like bright stars. At the back of the cave was a constant drip of water oozing from an outsize rock slab which formed the roof, but Rolf and I were quite dry. We were up before sunrise, and from the cave-mouth the snowy summit of Mount Salccantay was gradually being lit up by the pre-dawn light. I kept looking out to see the sunshine encroaching on the peaks as the horizontal light made them glow like Bessemers, a whole range of dazzling mountain-tops with dark forests below.

Then we were off and soon came upon a tunnel down which steps were carved. It was very high inside, the result of a natural deviation of two rock strata, but only 20 yards in length followed by an equivalent flight of exposed stone stairs. A couple of minutes later we came to a freshwater rivulet, but it was underground and solely accessible by clambering awkwardly through a narrow gap and then reaching as far as possible between a couple of boulders to fill our canteens. The water was freezing cold. After this the trail curved around to the right and into a saddle between two summits. Without realising it we had reached the third pass at 11,700 feet. The view all round was one of the best so far and snow-covered mountains were before and behind us, shining in all their glory. Two sets of ruins were visible from here; behind us Sayajmarca was in view and immediately ahead of us on the very apex of the levelled summit was a watch-tower belonging to the ruins of Phuyupatamarca immediately beyond the pass. We climbed up to a high vantage point and enjoyed the spectacular view in all directions. There was a bit of everything in it: rivers and waterfalls clearly audible for miles, cloud- and snow-covered peaks, ruins, forests, lakes, and pastures, the chirring of insects, and the sounds of wind in the grass. Birds flashed past, and butterflies rose up where our footsteps disturbed them, and to cap it all the sun's warmth began to win over the chill of the dawn.

I set off ahead of Rolf down to Phuyupatamarca which is approached past a couple of working Inca fountains one above the other which drain away along stone grooves under the Inca Trail to irrigate some terraces. These waterworks have been abandoned for many centuries and still they work perfectly with not a stone out of place. The ruins of Phuyupatamarca themselves form a small fortress guarding the valleys on both sides of the mountain, nestled on ledges about 400 feet below the watch-tower on the table pinnacle. From the major upper part of the ruins, a staircase of extremely short steps wound its way 50 feet down through the lower levels whence the Inca Trail carried on hugging the side of the mountain by means of ingenious stonework. The ruins and trail were again considerably overgrown with masses of thick weeds and bushes, but most impressive is the way the ruins were tucked into the shoulder of the mountain hugging it smoothly, not built up. The very lowest portion of the ruins were thatched as it had been in Incaic times to give shelter to wayfarers. For several miles hence the Inca Trail was in pretty good condition, particularly while it stayed above the jungle. In patches it was almost as good as new, six-foot wide lumpy crazy paving, and where the slope became too steep, stone stairwells were either built or carved out of rock. In many places the granite blocks had been rotted to a fine grit by acidic rainfall, but this made for an improved crunchy surface most satisfying to walk on. Between the third and fourth passes there was no water fit to drink though in places the trail was submersed inches-deep under the water-table in mud, or formed the bed of a trickling stream.

Rounding the mountain the track entered light woodland and dense bamboo thickets which hid the valley but were interesting in themselves. The bamboo shoot's grow like red and green spears to a height of five feet or so before the first leaves turn out. Emerging from the woods in a venial mood I saw way down the hill on my right the Urubamba River paralleling the Cuzco-Santa Ana Railroad and from my condor's perch thousands of feet above the river I sat down to Wait for a train and attended to the gargantuan appetite I had worked up. While I watched the Clouds below whisked past me and sailed thinly over the woods behind me and the valley was clear for a few minutes more, though a distance to the north a thick blanket of cloud sat all morning considerably lower than I. I heard the two-tone klaxon of the steam-engine but I could not see the train for some time, until I noticed a tiny thread of orange so minute that it came home to me just how high up I was. In the moorland clearings between the woods there were so many wild flowers, including many exquisite little ones altogether new to me, some like moon daisies, others erupting flush with the ground from hardy compact high-altitude plants, and geraniums and many others, but everywhere the beautiful blue lupins and the curious red-stalked begonias dominated.

CHAPTER ELEVEN   PERU

The path descended very little, passing woodland and grassland by turns but always with a very steep drop on my right. Every time I exited a section of forest I looked down at the perceptibly closer Urubamba, whose roar welled right up to the high trail sounding strangely like a steam-engine to my wishful ear. All of a sudden after an hour gently promenading pleasantly downhill, the ridge came to a very abrupt end and from its extremity I saw my goal, Huayna-Pijchu, or Young Peak, the higher twin of Machu-Pijchu, or Old Peak. Now the fun began as the path plummeted with extreme suddenness over the nose of the ridge. I was glad indeed of the tent-pole down this treacherous slippery track which dropped 500 feet in 100 yards. The Incaic stones had all been moved out of place as the trail was a brook in the wet season, and extreme caution was called for, but even so it was as hard a task descending as it had been climbing the first day. At last I made it to the bottom where pylons carried crackling and buzzing power cables from a nearby hydro-electric power station across country to Cuzco.

At a pylon the path forks, but there are no signs giving directions. The path straight ahead in the direction of Machu-Pijchu was well-defined, but Paul had advised us to take the lesser path to the right. This I did, and for Rolf and Frank I scratched a huge arrow-head indicating my choice which I signed. This dirt-path plunged steeply into the jungle and there were frequent, confusing, criss-crossing tracks and foot-paths with practically nothing to aid me in my choosing the right way, so every time the direction was in question I left more signed arrow-heads, yet another use for my tent-pole. The initial descent through the forest was down a really steep, well-worn, zigzag path under the power lines and when I saw nothing ahead but the hydro-electric plant I felt sure I had indeed gone astray, so that all my arrow-heads would lead Rolf and Frank and who knows how many countless others on a wild goose chase. The path I had taken committed me to the most perilous journey of my life, additionally the most scary, challenging, rewarding, and interesting. Here and there I saw faint skulls and cross-bones and 'PELIGRO' (DANGER) painted on rocks along the way.

As I rushed 2,000 feet down in crazy irregular zigzags and sometimes climbed a little way, fears of getting lost in this thick jungle were briefly entertained, but I pressed on following the faintest hint of a path with occasional footprints in either direction. The jungle was so dense that I was walking quite clear of the ground on tree roots and plants and ferns for yards at a time, through dark dripping tunnels of Spanish moss and aerial roots draped from ugly trees like mangroves, with lianas and huge roots and branches blocking my path and I had to wriggle over or under them. Sometimes I went through ankle-deep squishy mud and sullage and past tree tobacco and other tropical rain forest plants. The arches of trees and mare's-tails were host to many smaller creepers, climbers, and epiphytes, including gigantic spider plants. Algae and slime grew over all the rocks and bark, and bedewed spiderwebs told their own tale of the primaeval struggle for survival, and curious beetles with metallic tints bathed in the warmth of the occasional sunbeams. My tent-pole was nearly my undoing snagging everywhere on the close undergrowth and several times it sent me sprawling. For over a mile not a yard was level. Having clambered, stumbled, jumped, and fought my way through the deepest, most claustral jungle I could imagine, bashing my head, elbows, shins, and ankles on hidden obstacles, and getting whipped in the eyes and ears by spindly branches and leaves, I came upon a clearing in this humid mini-world and could see closely now the hydro-electric plant and dam and hear plainly the rustle of the Urubamba as its brown waters gushed and swished over and round the huge fallen rocks in their course.

Machu-Pijchu was out of sight and I was guessing the trail, gradually making my sweat-soaked thirsty way round the skirt of the mountain. Grimly I followed a climbing path and found a flight of extremely steep stone steps, evidently the handiwork of the Incas. Heartened by this I pursued the tiny track, attacked by mosquitoes and huge hairy deer-flies and annoying midges and emerged onto a slope so steep that I doubted it could be climbed or descended. I noticed on a tree the old, scarcely legible, painted letters 'M P' with an arrow clarifying the way to Machu-Pijchu — up! The path wound tortuously up a scree path held together only by the roots of the bushes beside it. With every footfall I sent scoops of loose soil and gravel clattering down the mountain, but by judicious scrabbling and grabbing plants I made it up and along the path. Had I slipped I would have fallen over 1,000 feet to a certain death, but my troubles were not over by a long chalk. The path curled round the top edge of the jungle and then traversed an enormous landslide, the largest of several spanning 300 yards. The unstable rocks and earth had not yet settled and I pioneered a way, treading as lightly as a cat across each one.

Once past this section, I reached a former mule-path littered with discarded underground piping, remnants of a recent endeavour to tap all the springs on this mountainside to provide potable water for a luxury tourist hotel, a scheme which had fortunately proved too much of a white elephant to finish. I came upon an odd concrete house and peering through a frosted window saw it was the abandoned water-pumping station. From here the trail became extremely narrow, less than a hand's width owing to landslides (probably as a result of blasting which I had heard several times during the day), but the long fall into the abyss whetted my concentration and I crossed the 100 feet of lesser slides onto the safety of a large flat ledge where a development company had gouged out a squared off platform 200 feet long from this saddle between two mountains to put in the hotel. A trough of stagnant water here was very tempting. I had long since drained my canteen but I knew better than to drink any — although I dearly wished to soak my burning feet. Any hazards I had hitherto encountered paled beside the next one. To get off this shelf I had to negotiate (with a backpack and tent-pole) an awful, crumbly, three-inch ledge of rock jutting from the vertical cliff and dropping clean away to the Sacred River, a distance of 3,000 feet. This was technical mountaineering at its most foolhardy. The ledge widened to about a foot after a few yards and 20 yards further ended in a steep flight of short granite stairs, in themselves almost as scary as the ledge but at least they confirmed I was on AN Inca trail which I stuck to, descending steeply back into jungle again.

Then I came to The Rock, a 20-foot long, sloping, rounded boulder, green with algae, so slimy and slippery that it was quite impossible to walk down it. Fortunately several stout bamboos had fallen across the impediment and grabbing hold of these was the only way to save myself from sliding down out of control, and fortuitously they were strongly rooted as I lost my balance and my tent-pole in the manoeuvre. The path now descended extremely quickly with long steps down, but signs of old Incaic stonemasonry gave me encouragement, and coming up to a large bare tree which had fallen blocking the path, I wrote a sign indicating the way to fellow travellers who might follow me thus far, and I signed and dated it (as did Rolf also, for Frank's benefit). Quite by surprise this torturous, steamy, jungle track deposited me on a major paved path — at last I had found the real Inca Trail, and following this I made much quicker time. Rounding a corner I arrived at the ruin of Intipata, a remote jungle guard-post. Henceforward the trail climbed and went over more log bridges but was a much more enjoyable walk. The bridges though were amazing; they spanned sheer chasms, and the ends were at different levels, so the logs formed shaky ramps, sometimes with a crude banister.

Although I was still in the jungle the road was in good repair and as it ascended it sometimes went up long flights of stairs, the last one climbing about 130 feet to a guardhouse at a natural look-out bearing more Incaic ruins. This was less than half an hour's walk away from the fourth pass, but I did not know it then; besides climbing thousands of feet had done a number on my knee-joints, so I took a long rest to let my sweat-drenched clothes air while I filled up on gorp. I was a little worried at seeing neither hide nor hair of the others, but when I was good and ready I set out again and quickly reached Intipunku at the fourth pass where I met Stephanie taking her ease, barefoot, to relieve angry blisters. She told me that Tobin had gone down the mountain to fetch water. Intipunku is a substantial fortified outpost guarding access to Machu-Pijchu via the pass and is within sight of the last ruin I stopped at. I also set off, packless, for water from the ultra-modern hotel built for American tourists beside the ruins of Machu-Pijchu, but better than water was the opportunity to have the first decent wash in days.

At the ruins I met Dee and Ann and escorted them for the hour-long walk back to Intipunku where we all set up our tents, while low over the ruined city a condor circled. During the afternoon Rolf, then Frank, caught us up and other couples also camped at the Intipunku Pass. I set up a tent for Ann and me on a tiny terrace smaller than the tent itself, using displaced stones to hold it in place. Since the night brought a brilliant nearly full moon, Ann, Tobin, and I descended the trail by moonlight for a drink at the State Tourist Hotel, which involved clambering around the ticket gate overhanging a terrace, a tricky manoeuvre to say the least. Everything on the tariff was so expensive that we settled for soft drinks, but we looked that scruffy compared to the rich tourists that we came to believe they were staying out of the bar on our account. On our way back up to Intipunku a game little terrier frightened the life out of us, but only chased us to go for a walk and slept in my tent. I hope it slept, it certainly shivered a good deal.

When the sun rose, people hastily emerged from their tents to enjoy the legendary view of Machu-Rijchu captured in the magical effect of the dawn rays. The sun beamed weakly from directly behind us and lit up the ruins with the precision of a spotlight while all else was yet enshrouded in shadow. The mist rose from the city leaving cotton boll clouds behind. In the background the high snowy ranges of the Sierra glistened brilliantly against a clear pale sky. Dee and Ann had to catch the early local train back up the valley, so we traipsed the mile down the Inca Trail to Machu-Pijchu. In this morning light the turbulent Urubamba and the rugged mountains beyond and around the last bastion of the Incas looked quite different. The slopes sheered up from the depths below us to pinnacles high above us like so many green-clad cones crushed together thousands upon thousands of feet high. From the modern State Tourist Hotel Ann opted to take the arduous foot-path down to the station, making it in the nick of time, hopping on board the train just as it was pulling away. Dee took the bus which plies the dusty road with 13 hair-pin bends descending the 1,000 feet to the river, but then she came back up again as she had forgotten her tent at Intipunku.

At this early hour there is practically nobody about, and escorting Dee wearily back up the trail to the pass in the blazing heat of the sun, much hotter at these altitudes, I met the first of the 1% of tourists who attempt this walk, taking a couple of hours over it. The majority of tourists who visit Machu-Pijchu are overweight brash North-Americans who fly into Cuzco, take the very expensive tourist special to Kilometro 112, and then the bus up the hill to the modern restaurant where lunch is part of the package deal. After a couple of hours at the hotel they 'do' the ruins of this unspoilt paragon of Incaic architecture, with few shewing any comprehension of the stupendous amount of work needed to build it, before retreating to the shade of the hotel until it is time for the bus to catch the train to catch the plane to another tourist resort Ann saw an American prying a carved rock out of a wall to take home as a souvenir, and heard another arrogantly and ignorantly remark, upon seeing flag-stones carved to represent a condor, the Incas' sacred bird, "Well, I guess they had fried chicken even in them days!" A mere handful of the hundreds of tourists who visit Machu-Pijchu make the effort to climb the trail as far as. Intipunku, whence the best views of the ruins can be had; and virtually none take the Inca Trail any further back than that, so they never do see the swamps and jungles, mountain passes and tampus, waterfalls and pools, and Inca Trail and its bridges.

CHAPTER ELEVEN PERU

Hiram Bingham, the great American archaeologist and explorer, discovered Machu-Pijchu in 1911 when all but a few terraces were preserved in virgin jungle. The two Indians working the terraces aroused his curiosity and when he began to dig he discovered the site had simply been abandoned three centuries ago, and female skeletons outnumbered male skeletons by a ratio of ten to one. Perhaps this was a sanctuary for the Virgins of the Sun. It is estimated that 1,000,000 Incas were involved in building this city for 800 inhabitants, which is still not all reclaimed from the jungle. The ruins are laid out in distinct areas, agricultural quarters, a quarry, wide open grass courts, a 'street' of fountains, temples, palaces, towers, a jail, a sundial, and craftshops, all connected by staircases and tracks.

Back at the hotel I found my friends from Rein's expedition had arrived and I teamed up with them to climb to the top of Huayna-Pijchu which overlooks Machu-Pijchu by 1,000 feet. The Temple of the Moon is visible on the side of this mountain, 'the Young Peak', but it was too difficult to get at and was in times of yore a refuge for the anchoritesses destined for sacrifice. The climb was almost straight up on slippery badly worn down steps, and it took an hour to get to the ruins and terraces at the very top, but it was well worth all the effort, for the bird's eye view of Machu-Pijchu is quite superlative and unequalled from Intipunku. At the same time the whole saddle of the mountain and all the paths leading hither and thither through the forest were visible all the way down to the Urubamba hastening right around the base of the mountain in a sweeping ox-bow. It took us as long again to return to Machu-Pijchu and as I crossed the neck of the pass connecting the Old and Young Peaks I spied a two-foot viper sunning itself on the path, a real beauty with patterns in brown and cream all down its length. I attempted to pick it up with my flannel but it curled up and shook its tail like a rattler, then darted forward striking the flannel with its fangs. The snake tried its best to flee from me, but side-winding in the dirt-track, its belly could not manage a grip and its efforts to climb the path became frenetic.

Perchance it touched a tuft of coarse grass and within three seconds slid out of sight under a ledge.

I studied the ruins as thoroughly as possible starting from the terrace watchman's hut, next to which is a carved sacrificial rock about seven feet long and four feet high with three steps cut into it. There is a dry moat defending the city wall, down which round boulders could be rolled on invaders. Most of the scores of terraces about five feet high are still unclaimed from the tropical jungle and this can best be seen from Intipunku. On the main part of the ruin I was amazed to find a lovely woolly alpaca which investigated me without the slightest fear; it was more endearing than its slightly larger cousin, the llama, sharing in common the twisted hairlip but with more wool of a different texture particularly on its breast, and a differently shaped tail. This one was pure white. I just wandered about, lost in the ruins, aimlessly exploring them all, particularly the temples, mausoleum, and mortar room. As in Ollantaytambo the quality of stonework varied according to use, e.g. the Inca's bath (the third fountain) and the tower had perfectly matched polished blocks, and the terraces had selected stones merely well-placed. I noticed how the temples had been rendered earthquake-proof by grooving the interfacing block surfaces in jigsawing arches, invisibly pressed together once the blocks were in place, but there for all to see, if they cared to, in the Temple of the Three Windows which had a wall with a crack in caused by a seismic tremor. There were, too, more examples of building with massive rocks weighing many tons each, matched to perfection. Corner-stones, jambs, and lintels were usually very big, and very often the stones were smaller and the walls narrower higher up, inclining to the centre or 'battered' in the idiom of stonemasons. Several of the houses had thatched roofs which gave a truer impression of what the city once looked like.

All too soon it was time to leave and disdaining the bus, I set off down the foot-path to the railway station: the path had many short cuts, sane newly made, and as I thought it would take me all of the half-hour before my train departed, I took every short cut I saw. I really cooked shoe-leather down that mountain but took a wrong turn early on, and entirely missed the windy road which I should have crossed eight times, and I plunged through treacherous jungle, as dense and humid as the last section of the Inca Trail. I had to duck under, climb over, and slide across obstacles. I realised I had gone wrong and hearing the train's klaxon I fairly tumbled down the boulder-strewn track and emerged in the vicinity of the Museo de Sitio. I lost no time in crossing the Urubamba foot-bridge and climbed onto the station platform dripping with sweat. I need not have rushed as it took me little over ten minutes to descend the path and the train at the platform was the tourist special. On the platform was the thrust and bustle of a busy Indian market selling everything from woven goods to food and drink, even coca leaves. The local train pulled in as soon as the tourist special moved off, and was already so crowded that nobody found a seat and none of the doors would close. The entire market was packed onto that train. People hung onto the handrails outside, standing and sitting on the steps, while more rode on the roof and on the ladders and foot-plates between the carriages. Every square inch of the train was jammed with people, even the toilets. Frank, Tobin, Rolf, and I, and my friends from Rein's expedition piled our luggage in the toilet, wary of thieves.

 The overcrowding was so great that Rolf and I had to hang from the outside of the train, in common with hundreds of others. At last he made himself comfortable on the roof and I on a ladder, but for our pains we had the best possible view of the Sacred Valley of the Incas. The journey back to Cuzco took five hours, and followed the Urubamba upstream all the way. The river was in stupendous flood and raged along with such violence that it formed a set of continuous rapids swollen and brown with alluvium. From place to place clean water poured into it from maddened mountain streams causing eddies and whirlpools. The buildings of the Incas were all along the valley, sometimes other villages or ruins, and a lot of terracing and aqueducts. Sometimes the ruins were situated in astonishing positions on the rim of the cliffs above the dizzy chasm, seen as dominating silhouettes, castellated and militaristic, each menacingly guarding some vital watercourse or section of the canyon. The Whole valley is beautiful, but the evocative views of the high snowy Sierra were dazzling in the afternoon sun, even the crests 30 miles off. The ticket inspector and guard, both strong stout men, managed to force their way down the train very slowly, and when they reached the hinge where Rolf and I were riding I was able to buy a ticket from them. The blockage of vendors trying to pass each other and the stationary crush of passengers entirely prevented anyone from moving even a few inches in any direction. The officials took charge and helped the vendors clamber out one end window and in another, passing their baskets of provender after them. I saw the guard's watch neatly removed from his wrist by a thief riding on the roof while the guard was vulnerably reaching out to help a fat girl through the window. The watch then passed to an accomplice inside the carriage. The vendors queued on the plates between the carriages until the bottle-neck of passengers gradually let them through, but it took an hour for each to make the transition. Eventually I discovered the most comfortable place to sit was on the step running-board with the fresh air rushing past me and the sleepers speeding by within reach. When we reached the tunnels, the knots of people hanging from the outside grips on doors and windows hugged the train as tightly as they could, all decorum forgotten.

 When night fell I moved in at last but was far less comfortable as there was no room to sit, even on the floor, and my ear was jammed against the ceiling. Most of the locals only reached my chest, so to them I must have been a giant. Just as the train approached Cuzco the guard muscled his way unceremoniously down the train warning us to shut the doors and windows tight and let no-one in. I had such a cramp that I had to go outside again and ride on the foot-plates just as the train was about to start shunting to and fro down the zigzags into the city. As the train slowed to a halt the first time, a swarm of boys rushed onto the outside appurtenances of the train, hundreds of them, climbing onto the ladders, steps, running-boards, and roofs. They were brazen thieves. One heaved my foot out from under me and tried to slash my boot off with a cut-throat razor, and for his efforts I kicked him away as hard as I could clean off the mountain. Another with a bright flashlight grabbed my stetson, but it was held on by plaited leather thongs. Others undisguisedly plunged their hands in all my pockets, and flailing my fists I plunged back into the carriage and other passengers quickly slammed the door on their clutching fingers. The boy-thieves tried their best to find a way in, without success, and rapped on the windows and shone lights in our faces.

At the pitch dark San Pedro terminus we stuck together in the crowds but were not molested and set off for the hotel, but Frank knew of an extremely cheap restaurant along the way, and our hunger had the better of us, so Rolf, Tobin, and I joined him for a steak dinner at under a dollar a head. I found Ann at the hotel, and we went out again with Dee and Stephanie but I was dog-tired and left them to enjoy the Cuzco night-life without me.

The next day was scheduled for a visit to Pisaq Sunday market and the Pisaq Ruins, far better preserved and more extensive than Machu-Pijchu. The group also visited Sacsahuamán, renowned as the largest Inca fortress of all with huge stones impeccably fitted together, some weighing 30 tons. At Sacsahuamán three enormous walls run parallel along the edge of the flood plain for nearly a quarter of a mile with 21 bastions. Sacsahuamán is on the northern outskirts of Cuzco, a fine parade-ground where the Inca could review his troops while seated on his throne, carved out of the solid rock. Zigzag grooves have been cut into the ground around the throne, supposedly channels down which chicha beer flowed during festivals. Wide stairs approach both sides of the throne and a little way uphill there is an Incaic slide, the Rodadero, presumably for children, in the vicinity of a great many flawless seats sculpted out of the bare rock. Cuzco seemed grey and empty; all the shops were shut and only a few Indians remained in the streets huddled against the cold, selling fruit and chocolate.

As soon as the banks opened I joined the crowd, but with true Mestizo efficiency the hour-long queue at one window was only for a form to hand in at a second window after queuing for another hour. One man jumped the queue exclaiming he had a plane to catch, but even if it was a hoax, who can blame him? He changed his money in under a minute, and good luck to him! Fortunately I spotted Jeanette, Rein's friend, and sold her the ticket I bought at Ollantaytambo which admitted her to all the local ruins. The Plaza de Armas has been the heart of Old Cuzco since its foundation, and the town is uniquely beautiful with Inca stonework forming the bottom half of many buildings blending in well with colonial balconies, arches, and cloisters. Many streets in particular are perfect Inca originals and there is one famous stone with 12 angles immaculately fitted into a wall in Hatun Rumioc Street beside the Cathedral. The very names of the main Inca sites are evocative, Palace of the Serpents (Amaru-cancha), and facing it across Loreto Street is the House of the Women of the Sun, and the Temples of the Stars and Moon which are almost intact

That afternoon we packed our gear on board the truck while members of Rein's expedition looked it over enviously. Their truck was much older than ours and their arrangements were quite different. We drove south climbing fast out of Cuzco for just an hour to a beautiful valley in the mountain wilderness, and had to clear aside rocks and prickly plants and stunted cacti to make camp. In the morning the weather was surprisingly warm and balmy considering we were above 10,000 feet. Paul was the most recent one to fall ill and still felt under the weather and only drove for a few hours, basically following the course of the River Vilcanota to Urcos whence a road has been cut eastwards into the heart of the Amazon Jungle through the Hualla-Hualla Pass. There were Inca ruins along our itinerary, particularly at Raqchi, the site of the magnificent Templo de Viracocha curiously dotted with enormous cairns of black boulders. We passed Sicuani, a centre for the local agriculture and Indian produce, and Maranganí amid green fields and eucalyptus groves before stopping at the foot of a cliff behind the railway station at Aguas Calientes, the sole building at that location.

We selected a camp-site at 13,000 feet 100 yards away from the startling phenomenon which gave the place its name, steaming mineral springs which burble and boil in an acre of grassland, giving rise to a hot water stream which makes an excellent bath, particularly at its junction with a cold stream. It was in a high plateau and, in view of the wind and an impending thunderstorm, we hurriedly put up our tents. There were some truly amazing pink flowers nodding in the breeze whose properties I learned when I bared my bottom behind a rock. The gorgeous pink flower with a yellow centre looked as though it was made by origami but its entire surface was protected by minute hairs which delivered a poison more potent than any dead-nettle. Every day we came upon new flora and fauna if we looked for them. As a naturalist and conservationist my interest was drawn equally by the sharp, spiky, Altiplano bunch-grass as it was by the mixed flocks of alpacas, llamas, and sheep which crop the plateau alongside cattle, horses, donkeys, and mules, nearly always tended by Quechua women or girls. The natural rock formations and terrain held a beauty of their own at Aguas Calientes. Close to hand the stark jagged boulders around our camp-site had evidently been split off the crags overhead by frost. Even in summer here temperatures plummet 15 degrees below freezing overnight due to the extreme altitude, and average only three degrees above by day

Once our tents were up, several of us went off to explore the hot streams. It was beyond imagining. There was one perpetual geyser boiling furiously in the middle of a cone of red earth caused by ferruginous deposits from the water. The seething puddle was about two feet across but the water was leaping and splashing just as high in the air, as big bubbles of vapour raced up to the surface. Surprisingly the water was not especially hot, just a comfortable 104 degrees Fahrenheit. Surrounding this natural fountain were smaller ones, agitating and effervescing in the short prickly grass. Wherever there was any of this activity the ground was just a mudpan with strange surface colours or else bore a fine carpet of crisp grass. There were hundreds, possibly thousands of the hot fizzy springs, but the majority were tiny and just served to convert the ground into a steaming swamp which did not appear marshy until one trod on it and sank into the squelchy goo. The hot stream where it was joined by the cold one had a current of at least 100 gallons per second, and tracing it back along its length I saw it rose in the main from a dozen gushing springs. The most outstanding feature of the site was its unworldly colour scheme full of silica and chlorides. The mudpans were a pale yellowy ochre, but the bed of the brook was tinted a screaming orange by heat-resistant algae, locally verging on red with frequent patches of black deposits which I assumed to be dead organic matter. Frequent traces of other colours could be discerned along stones, notably thin streaks of royal blue where the stream surfaced against particular kinds of rocks.

The landscape all round was of a flat plateau for several miles across and bore neither a single tree nor bush, only sharp-tipped festuca grass and small evergreen shrubs right up to the mountains which were smothered in snow a little higher up. The most Spectacular Puna plants must be the bromeliads, and different sorts of these grow in different climates, e.g. the pineapple plant is a tropical bromeliad, and here is found the strangest bromeliad of all, the giant puya. It grows for 100 years as a gigantic tough pincushion extremely slowly, and then suddenly produces a tower another 40 feet high composed of 20,000 flowers rather like a round file a yard in diameter. The flowers bloom progressively from the bottom and are pollinated by humming-birds, and when the 12,000,000 seeds are set the plant dies. The Indians destroy the puyas wherever they herd their animals for they claim the inward curving spikes trap lambs and even children, and certainly the birds which nest in the spines are commonly caught and so the fate of the remaining Puya raimondii is sealed.

The only moving thing was rising steam drifting silently across the Altiplano, and occasionally a not so silent train or truck. The opportunity of a mineral bath with unlimited lashings of hot water was too good to miss, especially as Frank, Armin, and Bernie had taken the plunge before me; so braving the freezing Andean wind (El Friaje) I took a luxurious hot bath at the confluence of the streams. Most of the time the hot water was a relaxing tonic, but just now and again a curl of icy water eddied around me, rudely shattering my spell of reverie. After half an hour I had to work out how to get out without instantly freezing solid, and just made it back to the truck before the thunder clouds. They had been threatening us since we arrived, creeping along the valley with a visible veil of grey hanging in tatters where snow was falling from a bleak and dismal sky. In cold or wet weather the truck quickly filled up with people, and we used to sit squashed together elbow to elbow. To keep in the warmth we fastened the windows, trapping a real fog of cigarette smoke and steam from the cooking. We kept up a trivial polyglot chatter, and some of the girls kept clattering away at their knitting, and taped music added to the background noise. I usually called it a day early on account of the unresolved battle with my debilitating infection.

The next day was Christmas Eve and we woke to a perfect summer's day after an overnight temperature three degrees above freezing. Within minutes of rising the sun shone brilliantly and it was already hot. I returned across the railroad to the hot springs and the effect of the water vapour was all the greater as it rose 25 feet before dissipating into thin air. I moved a fiery red rock and discovered a miniature toad which had adapted to suit the warm water conditions. Its skin was so thin and delicate that the redness of its blood (or maybe it was a skin pigment) clearly showed up. It had miniature webs 'twixt its tenth of an inch long claws, and when it sat still it was as little and round as an alley marble, with tiny creamy warts all over its back. When we left we climbed still further eventually reaching a pass at 14,200 feet in the permanent snow zone, where the villagers at La Raya were engaged in a fiesta which included a snowman competition with at least one buxom snow-woman of imaginative proportions. There was snow everywhere as far as the eye could see, covering the ground, the roofs, the railway carriages in their sidings, and hiding the tracks, though it was not particularly thick. Even so it was timely for Christmas.

As we drove on we passed huge droves of llamas and alpacas tended by colourful herdswomen who always wore the regional costume even though it became quite dirty. All the Indian women-folk wore lots of petticoats which made them appear pregnant, but must have made their lot easier in the bitter breezes and the freezing nights and mornings. We had to endure the bumpiest and dustiest road imaginable and went south past Santa Rosa, renowned only for its llama and alpaca goods. Varying the speed did nothing to alleviate the conditions so Paul charged ahead at a good lick, with the result that a couple of times the truck bounced so high that not only we but the luggage, trailer, and crates of drink (Tobin's bar) bounced in the air and some of the bottles broke. Our morning shopping stop was at Ayavari, a small unfriendly town, which was quite unattractive though it had all the usual Peruvian characteristics:- a central plaza dominated by a large church with belfries in square towers, squalid dirty streets, adobe buildings with curved, red, clay tiles or corrugated iron roofs, which caught the sun and dazzled the eye with the brilliance of a welder's arc. In Ayavari Bernie was robbed for the third time this trip and the worst, and had his purse slashed from a leather thong around his neck. Alice lost her second camera satchel, also slashed. Back street robbery is a common way of life in South America and the footpads are usually nimble child-dips or razor specialists.

Once we had cleared the town we pulled into a wide open tableland and edged off the road to have lunch beside a field, obviously ploughed by draught-oxen as the furrows were particularly crooked. The weather was gorgeous and the sun baked us from a cloudless cyan canopy. I went on one of my customary botanical rambles checking out the new plants to be seen. Here there was an unusual cactus, the size and shape of a banana, covered thickly in vicious white spines radiating an extra couple of inches. Oftentime we had noticed agave leaves laid atop the adobe walls, and had wondered why, and here we realised these were used not just to deter intruding animals or people that could easily walk around, but to prevent the dew freezing and cracking the soft clay. The fauna of the Puna is very limited by its harsh Arctic climate, and in many instances is restricted to tiny localities, such as certain rare humming-birds not found outside their few canyons. We saw virtually no small animals and only a few birds, though we kept our eyes open for Darwin's rheas and were unsuccessful here but did see plenty in Patagonia. Guinea-pigs are wild in this region though we only saw them for sale as meat in the markets; and as for reptiles, only two species are found at these heights above 12,000 feet, one a very ordinary harmless snake and the other an iguanoid (Liolaemus multiformis) which is adept at making the most of the available shelter and sunlight and altering the pigmentation of its skin to stay up to 30°C warmer than its environment. From here we went on past Pucará, renowned for its pottery bulls, as far as Juliaca (12,600 feet), an Indian town known as a centre for wool and hides, particularly its alpaca goods, hand-knitted pullovers, waistcoats, gloves, hats, sashes, and skirts. The alpaca fur rugs and clothes were beautifully soft with exquisitely tender leather, sewn together to make pictures in variously coloured fur and bordered in the same way, all sizes and shapes, and with cleverly cropped fleeces to vary the texture in different areas of the scene. Ann, Gaby, Paul, and I went off to do the Christmas shopping, and halfway back to the truck we stopped at a café in the plaza for a cup of coffee, when Paul was struck with the idea of buying the Peruvian equivalent of our Christmas pud. They do not have anything like plum duff but a special kind of saffron bread baked with chopped up dried fruit, called pannetone. I suggested we buy custard to go with it, to Gaby's perplexity as in Italy custard is rarely eaten, but the nearest equivalent Paul subsequently found was créme caramelle. Also sitting there partaking coffee were Annette, Maria, Sandra, and Bernie, laden with a variety of alpaca knitwear, waxing eloquent about how they bargained the prices right down. Beggars came into the café which doubled as a bakery, but the act they put on and the specially affected pathos in their whine and the way they grovelled for the food on our plates did not make me the least bit sympathetic. All the child-beggars and many of the adults were disgustingly filthy with repulsive habits and snotty noses. The destitutes were followed in by a bevy of Indian women rug vendors, who started exhibiting their wares, charming silky smooth wraps, wall hangings, and coverlets, every one different, displaying dancers, pipers, hunters, llamas, and alpacas, Indians in national costume, men lassoing a horse, musical instruments, pottery, and all sorts of vignettes. I was caught up in the mood and was delighted with a rug about a yard in diameter depicting a haughty piebald alpaca against a representation of a flaring sun. I bargained the Indian down to 2,500 soles (a little over seven dollars), a real snap. When Ann saw it she wanted one too and returned with me to the market in the plaza, but she was not satisfied and saw nothing as pretty as my rug. Paul joined us still shopping and soon a blustery wind sprang up and big drops of rain lanced at us from a fast occluding sky, sending us scurrying back to the truck carrying big sacks of shopping — Paul, had a 20-pound turkey and I had 18 loaves of bread. All these Peruvian towns have characteristic licensed tricycles with the single wheel at the back, a very strong double frame, and a big cargo platform as much as three square yards, the back edge of which forms the handle-bars. Many are used as street stalls, others as cargo haulers, and on numerous occasions we saw Indians peddling their families along the street. Tobin, sensing that his time sight-seeing was up, hired a trike to carry him back to the truck, to everyone's amusement. The operator charged him 15 cents and hied him hither and thither at great speed even though the tricycles are not taxis.

We escaped from Juliaca just in time as a tremendous storm moving in from the north-west lashed the trees and poured down freezing sleet and hail in such quantities and so suddenly that people went scuttling through the streets and every surface was submerged under a layer of white. The cloud cover was so dense and dark and the sun so near to setting that the sickly glum light was an evil yellowish grey and looked even more ominous through the windows caked and spattered with dribbling sleet and ice mush. The rear window was clear, and showed a view back to Juliaca of an utterly black sky with the ground sidelit by the wan sun already dipping behind the mountains on the horizon, which made a mobile silhouette, the more so since the travelling grey veil of rain gave a midway contrast between the brightness of the yellow sun and the blackness of the jagged silhouette. Yet looking out of the other window to the east the weather was fine and sunny and one could never have guessed that a gigantic storm covered half the horizon. Within a few minutes we had passed out of the tempest so abruptly it was as though someone had turned off a faucet. We drove to a remote pasture outside Puno, the local capital at 12,660 feet on the shore of Lake Titicaca, and hurriedly put up our tents in the cold breeze expecting the foul weather to catch us up. In fact it passed by over Juliaca providing us with a vivid display of lightning, the wind dropped almost to nothing, and a large moon and stars came out clearly.

Gaby and Joan and most of the girls shooed us males out of the truck while they put up Christmas decorations everywhere and we all sang carols, conducted by Paul, inevitably our M.C.. We had our first vegetarian meal since the expedition started, not a bad record. It was due to the measures taken in Peru to ration retail meat, only available for the first half of each month. The festivities continued after supper, and we all sang carols from our different countries, Dee and I sang a duet, and Rolf, Paul, and Tobin hammed their way through a creditable musical performance. The highlight of the Christmas party was a visit from Santa Claus, of course. With a lot of piratical chuckles and shoulder shrugging, Santa (who else but Paul) came in with his sack of presents. He tried to explain away his blue drag outfit and gaucho boots, but at least he had a full set of flowing white whiskers. Everyone was called up to sit on his knee in turn and he ribbed us all and gave presents to each of us. The singsong went on very late aided by liberal draughts of wine.

This Christmas Day began for us in complete contrast to previous ones with the sun already blazing from a clear blue sky, and the scene was set for a long idle day spent sunbathing with a book or walking in the hills. We were camped on the edge of a mesa which stretched northwards as far as the eye could see and behind us were a row of low worn down hills. Little Aymará shepherdesses stood watching us from the safety of some rocks until after lunch, not attempting to communicate, but allowing us to approach them with sweets. They led their donkeys and flocks of sheep to graze within yards of us. Dee and Stephanie made so much banana pancake batter that breakfast lasted right up to lunch time. At about that time Armin and Bernie returned from exploring in the hills above us declaring that Lake Titicaca was visible from the top. All in all it was a decadent lazy day, a complete change of pace. After massive preparations for our Christmas dinner Ann and I took a stroll towards the ruins of the pre-Columban funeral towers of Sillustani nearby, known as chullpas, on a peninsula in Lake Umano, the local part of Lake Titicaca which is really an inland sea, but the sun was close to setting and within minutes the temperature had dropped unbearably and we never made it to the ruins. We returned by supper time to learn that Sandra and Paul had prepared a huge feast with a menu and wine list. It was a traditional four-course Christmas dinner, and though the turkey was no butterball we polished off the lot, washed down with another crate of wine. Once again we had a grand singsong by candlelight, mainly carols and folk-songs, and we drifted off in ones and twos as lassitude befell us. Armin and Bernie could be heard loud and clear happily singing German carols (at least I hope they were carols) from the sanctuary of their tent, indubitably inspired by alcohol.

There was so much food left over from Christmas dinner that Ann and I had only to buy enough for supper and breakfast. Paul dropped us all off in Puno and most people went to see the fascinating waterfront quarter where the Peruvian navy has a number of small warships, but Ann, Maria, and I went off to explore the huge market zone for food, and trying to buy meat was a real hassle, since the Aymará woman really did not want to sell us the better quality beef which she displayed to draw custom. She could sell that easy as winking, and kept on including a llama's jaw or a sheep's tail when weighing the piece of beef. Invariably the prime cuts contain a large bone as the butchers do not want to be left with pounds of bone when they can sell it as meat. The Indian cut our meat with an axe, wielding it overarm several times, but at least we obtained the beef we wanted. The market had a wide display of hide goods but more interesting were the little reed boats, carved stone amulets and other charms, and Ekekos which are household talismans from Bolivia.

Since Puno is set amid a semi-desert the recent fast growth of the city has taxed its water and power supplies beyond the limit. While Paul negotiated with a luxury hotel to buy water for the tanks, Ann and I prepared the lunch right there on the shore, of Lake Umano, a pinched off section of Lake Titicaca which was a truly intense aquamarine, and we could see the Bolivian snowcaps 40 miles and more across the water. We progressed some way around the lake through the village of Chucuito with its many sculpted stone entrances to the houses. Along the shores and shallows are the typical beds of reeds the Uru Indians use to build their floating islands out on the lake. We had decided on a boat-trip from the Bolivian shore since the Peruvian guides had formed a trade union and had a monopoly on group tours which were consequently more expensive. The road around the lake was exceptionally poor and was made of choking dust, and crossed a wide river at a ford marked by rocks. Several of us walked ahead of the truck knee-deep in the freezing water. The road soon led away from the deep blue lake into the bone dry Altiplano and the typically meagre plainstown of Ilave.

Ann and I wondered how come this dust-bowl was ploughed since it seemed incapable of supporting crops, and despite the furrows only low-level prickly scrub and bunch-grass seemed to grow, and the whole plateau was strewn with large pebbles anyway. As if to give the lie to our doubts about the land's fecundity, quite a lot of Indians live on this mesa in single-room stone and adobe houses, some roofed with red brick tiles or reed thatch, but mostly with shiny corrugated iron, off which the sun's reflection pierces the eye like a dagger. Near the Mestizo town of Juli were more of the abundant reed beds all along the shallows. The curious tortora reed boats, made famous by Thor Heyerdahl in his Ra and Tigris expeditions, floated at anchor or else bore just one standing fisherman punting through the rushes. The craft were about ten feet long, constructed of four long faggots stressed and bound to leave a concave space in the middle, and I also saw some made from a single bundle about six feet long which were ridden astride.

Our camping-spot was in the even Altiplano Desert, and we stopped in time to witness a very colourful sunset, for which the Lake Titicaca region is well-known. The ragged rain clouds had an internal fiery crimson luminosity and the sky turned a daffodil yellow. Ann and I made a pretty good cookery team and she always enjoyed producing visually memorable meals and now came up with a rum-butter trifle. Nevertheless we were always glad when our turn was over as by the time all the clearing up was finished in the evenings we were just about done in, and I at least would sit soporifically, drained of sensibility, waiting patiently for the group to leave the truck, since the cooks had the option of sleeping in it to prepare breakfast by the time the others had their tents packed away. Consequently I woke up and stepped outside into the freezing desert. There was no moon nor the slightest puff of wind and looking up through the perfectly clear air, I saw the zodiac as never before. From horizon to horizon the constellations were so bright and distinct that for the first time I saw the Magellanic Clouds. To find them follow the line of Orion's sword a quarter of the way across the night-sky and they show up as two faint, diaphanous, vertical lenses; complete galaxies.

I was still awake to see a hazy sunrise shift through bands of pastel colours in a clear sky. As ever a cluster of filthy children found us and stood in a group dumbly incomprehensive whilst their mangy dogs more boldly scouted out the crumbs we dropped. Sandra and Maria gave them what was left of the pannetone and biscuits. Back on the road we noticed that nearly all the available space was given over to cultivating potatoes, which were no doubt predestined to be freeze dried becoming chuño to be sold at market. Ann and I saw some such when we shopped in Puno, extraordinary tiny grey-brown nodules when desiccated, or slippery, leathery, and half-skinless when reconstituted. Only an inch or so long, they were reputed to be a delicacy. Oca, another vegetable tuber, is also sold in a freeze dried form called tunta, considered equally delicious. The answer to yesterday's enigma regarding the fertility of this powdery plain was solved when we saw numerous pools. The water-table is within inches of the ground surface, while the porosity of the tilth, the merciless arid heat by day, and no dew by night all combined to deceive the casual eye. The small towns and villages along this littoral were all quite unprepossessing except for their outstanding Mestizo churches which dominated the communities. One pueblo consisted of simple one-roomed adobe houses built in the sides of ash grey cliffs on either side of the road and, if space permitted, adobe walls enclosed tiny backyards. The roofs were of reed thatch and as the dwellings were exactly the same colour as the cliffs and irregularly spaced, they blended harmoniously into the background.

We made a brief stop at Pomata, a very small town in the usual vein, too insignificant to even boast a market, though it did have an amazing church with a tiled dome and exquisite stone carving inside and out. From there we progressed to the border through a monotonous landscape with a very few small hills the only diversification. The crossing from Yunguyo on the Peruvian side to Kasani went through very smoothly with no hitches. On both sides of the border friendly customs men in plain clothes came aboard to search the truck, and Tobin, concerned lest his cache of coca leaves would be discovered, hurled them from the window in the broad expanse of no man's land between the custom-sheds. He really did not want them for his own use anyhow, as they had done nothing for him except give him an aching jaw, a dry mouth, and caused him to bite his tongue.

ENCOUNTER OVERLAND

LONG-RANGE EXPEDITIONS ACROSS SOUTH AMERICA, ASIA & AFRICA

Indian with his treasured turquoise beads from the Mojave Desert, Southern California

*Supine Toltec holding a sacrificial bowl on his stomach.
It is an altar at Chichén Itzá, Yucatan.*

*These ancient carvings overlook the Magdalena River Canyon,
and we hired horses for a day to reach them.*

Amazonian Indians often keep pet parrots, retiles, & coatimundis.

The author's catch of a piranha & 2 lorons. The piranhas' jaws are in my palm. A memorable dinner

The adobe ruins of the Citadel of Tschudi, once the capital of the Chimu Kingdom, destroyed by the great rains of 1925. The depictions represent the way of life of the Chimu people. Chan-Chan, Trujillo, Peru.

This is Reinkamer's truck. Camping on the permanent snows of Cotopaxi Volcano, Ecuador.

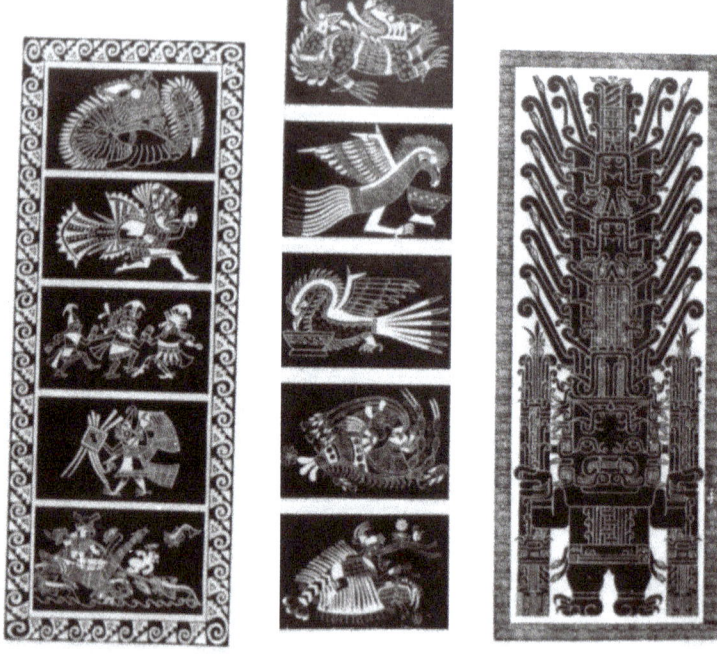

The Chimu used art to give a message. Dragon men, bird men, mermen, & a seal catching a fish. The totem pole represents growth

Chimu cultural art at Chan-Chan, one of 17 defensive citadels built of adobe in Peru.

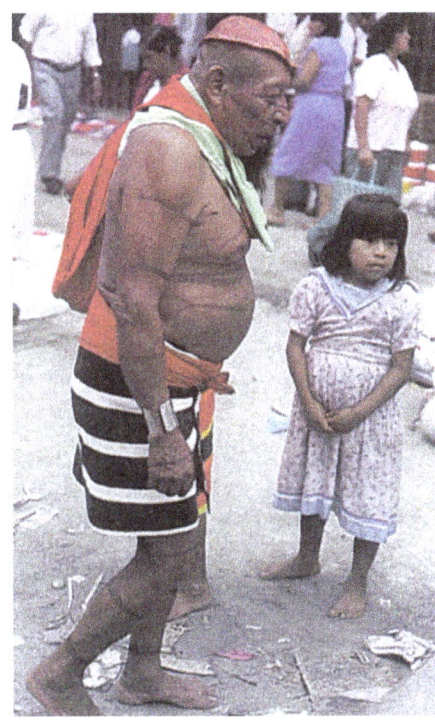

The man is a beggar. We saw several like him.

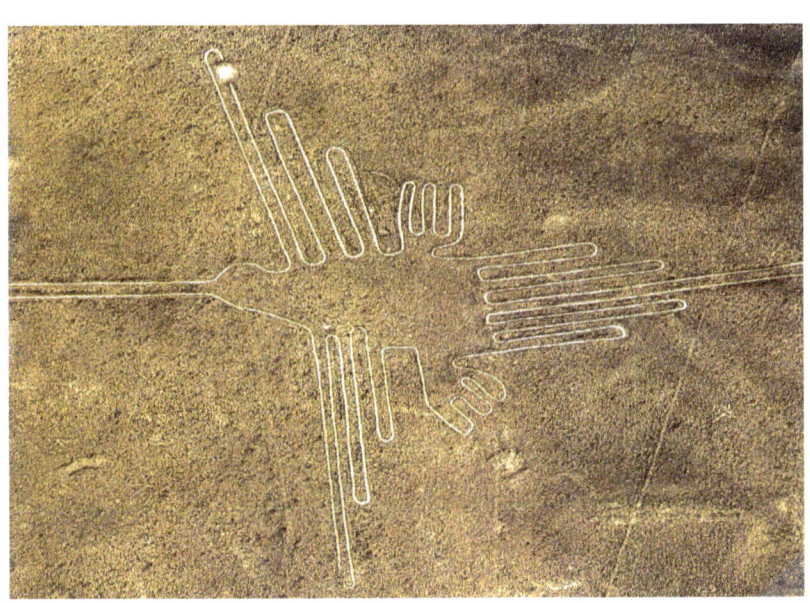

A hummingbird etched onto the Nasca Plateau spoiled by car tracks.

Incaic oil lamps depicting syphilis

This well dressed girl is wearing modern clothes.

In the Valley of the Incas llamas are shepherded past Incaic fortifications. Statues of Christ stood on many peaks.

The Incas matched stones perfectly without mortar. The alcoves held statuettes. The bath fountain has flowed for centuries despite earthquakes.

Pisaq street market. Hats identify the village, but Western hats are common.

3 women in traditional dress take their llama to market. Red tassles ward off evil spirits. Each village has its own traditional hat & dress designs

Indian girl from the Sacred Valley, Peru, in mixed traditional and modern attire.

A young mother and babe at Pisaq market. Always shoeless. Red is a protective colour.

Barefoot Peruvian shepherdess in traditional attire with her young alpaca

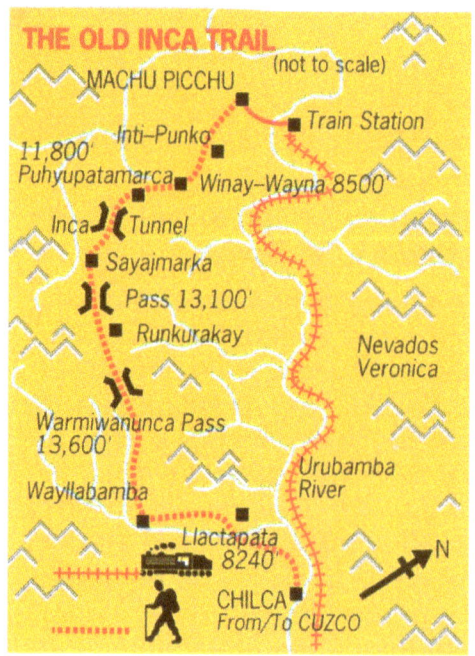

Inca Trail 3-day walk. I started at Chilca and ended at Machu-Pijchu.

On the Inca Trail. Very little remains in this condition.

A condor with its collar of feathers carved on the ground.

Cracks due to earthquakes have shifted stones. The new thatch shows how Machu-Pijchu once looked. The central staircase goes right up the mountain.

The single rounded building in Machu-Pijchu was an observatory.

Rethatched houses and some terraces at Machu-Pijchu. Walls are inclined inwards to survive earthquakes, i.e. they are thicker at the bottom than the top.

Machu-Pijchu today

The infamous Machu-Pijchu–Santa Ana narrow-gauge railroad. The steam-train averages 14 m.p.h. through spectacular gorges but the train is always packed out and is known for its thieves.

The parade-ground of the Inca's army at Sacsahuaman.

Aztecs, Incas and Armadillos

Christmas card with all our signatures.

*A peasant gathering reeds on Lake Titicaca.
The canoe is made of 4 reed faggots.*

Southern Peru. The Colca Canyon near Arequipa drops 2000 metres.

Some llamas wear red tassles on their ears.

Setting of camp in a gravel pit in windswept Argentine Patagonia. Rolf is perched atop the gravel mound playing his flute.

Humboldt penguins have a huge colony on islands just west of Callao. See p188.

Near Colonia Sarmieuto Argentina, the wind has dried the clay, splitting it into huge lozenges.

*The author with a Patagonian armadillo.
Others are racing to fetch their cameras.*

The author standing on the Perita Moreno Glacier at Lake Argentino.

Kaiapalo Indian in Xingu Reserve, from the Koluene River district of Brazil. We saw toads bigger than this in Argentine Gran Chaco.

Amazonian Indians with blowpipes in a ceremonial dance

Village scenes, Upper Amazon. Full or near nudity is normal.

Views of Iguassu Falls. With astonishing walkways out to vertical escalators. Expect 130 decibels.

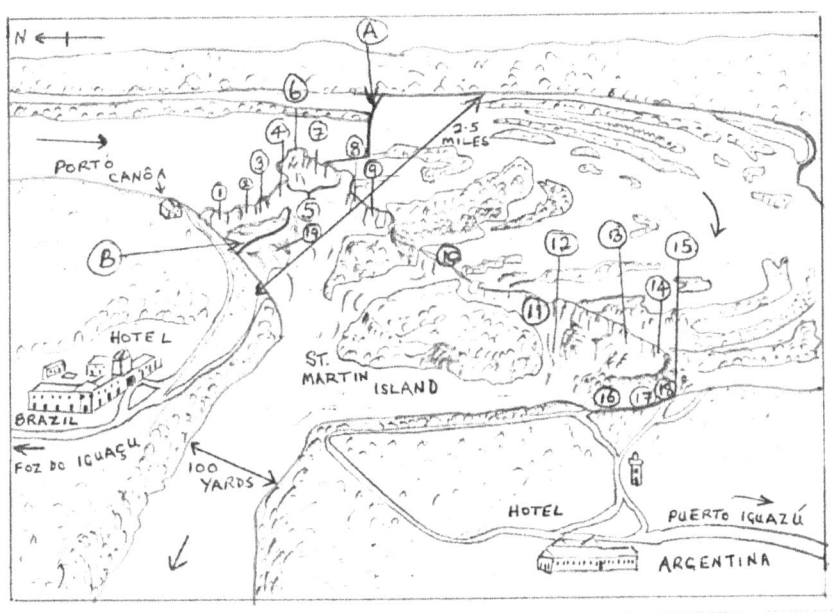

The Iguazú Falls, on the River Iguazú 14 miles upstream of its junction with the Paraná River. A and B are catwalks and the major cascades are:-

1. Florian,
2. Deodoro,
3. Benjamin,
4. Union,
5. Devil's Throat,
6. False Throat,
7. Mitre,
8. Rocky Mountain,
9. Belgrano,
10. Rivadavia,
11. False St. Martin,
12. St. Martin,
13. Adam and Eve,
14. Boseti,
15. Bejaruna,
16. Cow's Head,
17. Two Sisters,
18. Raminez,
19. St. Mary.

The noise was defeaningly loud.

Opposite page: The Iguazu Falls are set in virgin jungle on the border of Brazil and Argentina, and are split into 275 cascades, many with names of their own. Seen here from an observation tower on the Brazilian side are Florian and Deodora Falls, with Mitre Falls opposite. The river is normally an orange colour.

Guanabara Bay with Sugarloaf Mountain & Christ the Redeemer on Hunchback Mountain

CHAPTER TWELVE

BOLIVIA

Bolivia is a large land-locked country and since it was founded last century numerous wars have whittled away its borders to the gain of all its neighbours. The south-western third of the country is tawny desert in the permanent rain shadow which stretches half the length of the continent. Most of the country is between 12,000 and 22,000 feet high, namely the Western Cordillera of the Altiplano and east of it the higher Puna, itself the pediment for the gaunt Eastern Cordillera. To the north and east is the Oriente in the Amazon Basin, and the enormous valleys of the Yungas. Well over two thirds of the population is Indian, speaking their own languages; near Lake Titicaca it is guttural Aymará, elsewhere largely Quechua, the language of the Incas, while Uru is almost extinct on the lake and in the southern Altiplano. Most of the Collas or highland

Indians speak Spanish. The Bolivians are one of the poorest nations on Earth with a mean per capita income of $14 per week. Throughout its colonial rule the Spanish raped the country for silver and only in recent decades has an embryonic industry begun to tap the mineral wealth of the country and build cotton gins and roads and drill for oil and gas. Infant mortality is 40% under two years of age and life expectancy a mere 46 years, with the Indians still outside the economy, largely because there is no way as yet to bring their produce across the mountains to the few cities.

Once over the border we came upon the first trees since Puno, cedars and eucalypts, and it made all the difference to see the lake through a frieze of trees. The huge Altiplano is treeless except in the inhabited river valleys, so with these trees in view we stopped there for lunch and were soon joined by a German couple who did an emergency brake when they came round the bend and saw us sitting or standing in the sun. On top of their Volkswagon van were three big aluminum trunks marked in Spanish, 'Danger, Poisonous Snakes'. The couple worked in Bolivia collecting snakes for research: at least that was what they told the officials, none of whom ever opened the trunks. Early in the afternoon we reached Copacabana where we embarked on a hour-long motor cruise on Lake Titicaca to visit the Islands of the Sun and Moon. Going the time passed quickly as there was so much to look at, little islands, big islands, distant shore-lines with yellow and russet hills. The water itself was a fascinating colour, like diluted blue ink, and quite choppy, slap-slapping against the hull and rolling the boat in quite a therapeutic way.

We passed one particular small island populated by sheep. It is just as well they do not know boredom, since they had only 200 acres of poor pasture to live on. As the Island of the Sun came in view we saw that the entire island was cultivated in terraces, except for a small area near the tourist jetty, containing a glade of some of the hugest trees I saw in South America. There were enormous oaks and gums and cedars and others like overgrown yucas, and through the middle of the grove ran an enormous old Inca staircase straight up the side of the island which was very steep, and underneath the steps was a channelled stream. The island was quite substantial being at least a mile long, and climbing up to an abandoned estancia on a promontory, it was evident why it had been built just there — the view was of dozens of islands, some no more than barren rocks, others green or brown, studding the limpid blueness of the lake with the shore and clouds beyond. After wandering around for half an hour we returned to the motor-boat and sped off to a second bay, where we found the same terracing covered in peas, potatoes, and maize. We picked our way between the plants to some unique Inca ruins. I noticed that some of the terraces contained five-foot high niches as did the ruins which constituted a building of small separate cells on two levels. The unique feature was that the lower set of rooms had high vaulted ceilings made of step-arched stone blocks, capped in each case with four coping slabs completing the centre of the ceiling and incidentally forming the middle of the floor above. There was but a solitary tiny window set high up like a peep-hole overlooking the lake. Returning, time really dragged as it became quite cool. The lake once covered 3,500 square miles but is steadily shrinking and may go the way of many others which have become salars — enormous expanses of salts and borax — and it now covers 3,140 square miles. By virtue of its enormous volume, it is 1,214 feet deep, the lake stays at a constant 50 degrees Fahrenheit year round and this moderates the weather on the shore. I had heard of the giant toad of Lake Titicaca which has reverted to an aquatic existence to escape the cold dry air. Its lungs are vestigial and it breathes through very loose skin and its eyes and limbs are similarly specialised. The Indians catch them when they are fishing. Once again we had another artistic, sunset but Frank was unimpressed; as a Viet-Nam veteran he declared he had seen much finer sunsets. The shadows lengthening on the islands illustrated them like a relief map in black and brown. By the time we came ashore the sun had set, and we were in trouble for a camp-site.

Paul drove along the shore a little way when, all of sudden, the back of the truck dropped two feet as the wheels burst through into a culvert, and we had no choice but to camp right there on a ploughed incline. The clocks in Bolivia run an hour ahead, of those in Peru, and so we lost an hour but decided on a late reveille to make up for it. Gaby and I both saw showers of meteorites, one of which crashed into the Andes and burst in an explosion of sparks more brilliant than lightning. Just because it was there I stood with Manfred and watched a silver glow turn into a moonrise with a wide halo of pearly aura.

The morning sun was really warm and revealed a wide valley ploughed in vain, since nothing but perennial bunch-grasses vied with millions of pebbles for space on the slopes. We had arrived right at the beginning of the ten-week rainy season which accounts for three quarters of the annual rainfall. We made our way along the peninsula which pinches off Lake Huinamanca from the rest of Lake Titicaca, and marvelled that such parched, featureless, Altiplano peaks could support anything on their grey dirt, while suffering high winds, frequent dust-storms, and extremes of temperature by night and day. Even so vicuñas, alpacas, llamas, chinchillas, viscachas, and other animals seem to manage. There were some pools near a house where several beeves were taking a drink, which looked all wrong, given that the ground was as dry as a bone. At the end of the spur were the Straits of Tiquina, named after the ferry town on both sides, and descending to it we had a good view of the lake and islands and the Bolivian navy. The water on either side of the promontory was different colours and the whole was stilled in a flat calm.

We alighted at Tiquina so that Paul could drive the truck onto one of the dozen-odd ferries. While Paul accompanied his truck over the straits we all took a motor-boat for the five-minute crossing. The vehicle ferries were the most amazing, primitive, wooden vessels without bows. A truck or one or two cars drove onto the forward end, and a shallow wooden railing ran along both sides and around the stern. The outboard motor was in fact inboard down a hole in between the vehicle platform and the stern. To start and stop the ferries men heaved on punts while there was insufficient draught to lower the motors. Once across we drove along the southern edge of the lake, much closer now to the titanic snowcaps that we could all see in a row. Ann and I were greatly interested to see how the rushes were harvested and worked to make the balsas, as the traditional, boats are called, and although we watched the reeds being cut and gathered, and observed a good many balsas, we never saw any being made.

On this side of the lake large numbers of eucalypts and some spruce have been planted in rows along the kerbs and around the tiny little fields growing all sorts of vegetables, including cereal crops such as barley, quinoa millet, and cañava which has small dark grains. All in all there was a lot more greenery taking advantage of this shade. Pigs and cattle were fettered by the roadside, and half a dozen sheep were tethered in one spot which ensured that the rest of the flock, being gregarious, would not leave them. We drove for a few hours across the unredeeming, dusty, brown Altiplano with its few llamas and adobe huts and stacked stone walls. Here and throughout the Andes, the efforts of previous generations to farm the unyielding hills have left their marks in the form of colour contrasts, with decaying pebble or adobe walls enclosing squares of yellow clay dust surrounded by darker areas where the lichens and cacti and scrub brush have never been disturbed by mankind. Here men have tried to eke out agriculture on the impossible slopes beyond the highest successful fields.

Before La Paz is the little industrial town of El Alto, and it appeared most disappointing with every vehicle raising a choking cloud of dust and for a while we passed nothing but factories, but this impression was nearly reversed by the town's several charming characteristics. The Indian womenfolk were dressed, in the most beautiful and imaginative way. The traditional, woven, patterned shawls and carrying cloths used as slings around their shoulders to carry infants or heavy loads were still here, and every woman wore a bowler hat perched atop, or slightly askance of, her head, always in too small a size, with half the women preferring to turn down the brim. The bowlers were only in a dun tan or black, and either bore a buckled hatband or a cord whose ends dangled in smart knots over the left ear. But the skirts and petticoats, the shawls and dresses and aprons were of velvets and brocades and had plaids and patterns in Creole styles. Admittedly the textiles were factory-made and the dyes synthetic but the colours were so rich and attractive, and the panels of beige and brilliant Vermillion so eye-catching. The shawls often had tassled fringes up to a foot long, but the greatest difference of all was that everybody was clean, and their clothes were also of clean new materials. Quite a few vendors wore cloth of gold or patterned lurex fabrics, evidently quite the thing.

There was a huge hardware market spilling beyond the town square and filling several streets. Vendors specialised in selling empty cans or bottles with lids. Others sold second-hand screws and tools, or just cheap hammers, sheet metal, corrugated iron, planks of wood, even dismantled orange boxes. A very few shack kiosks were interspersed among the other stalls, and there were Indians with sheep and pigs for sale, or bolts of cloth, some homespun. We wandered into the main square and saw there a number office cream carts unique to the environs of La Paz, like miniature kiosks with sets of photographs filling the windows, all stills from old black and white Hollywood films. There was a food market there as well as the bric-á-brac and junk stalls, and nearly every one was run by an Indian woman or a boy. We made one of our democratic decisions and voted to visit the Moon Valley, reputed to contain 'the weirdest rock formations on Earth'. Coming onto the autopista, the main road down from El Alto, we were suddenly confronted with the amazing sight of La Paz spread out along the steep-sided Choqueyapu River Valley, 1,210 feet deep, out of the bitter wind and sandstorms of the

Altiplano. The whole city was a riot of paint colours and pinkish adobe, and since it was built up the walls of the rift, virtually every home of the majority Indian population on the higher slopes had a panoramic view.

    La Paz is not, in fact, the highest capital in the world. True it is at 11,820 feet, but it is not the capital. Sucre is the capital of Bolivia, although La Paz, with 700,000 inhabitants, is the seat of government, and the foreign and domestic national representatives reside here. Mount Illimani, the highest in the Altiplano, rises 9,370 feet above the city. We had such trouble trying to pick our way through La Paz that eventually I took a taxi and Paul followed it to the Moon Valley. The taxi ride led us through the archaic business centre with its courtly charm, down, down, through the wealthier residential suburbs of Calacoto and La Florida, past the Presidential mansion with armed guards outside and the national police headquarters across the road. Within a few miles we came across curious erosion effects caused by the rain in the soft base-rock cliffs on both sides of the road. The rock was tierra de creda, fine dry clay with particles like talcum powder. The clay stood out in chimneys and deep clefts in weird formations and canyoned dry stream-beds. Often stones lodged on the very tips of the multi-stepped pinnacles, and acted as protection against the erosive rain. We descended to the River Abajo which we crossed. Dozens of women were on their knees washing laundry, heedless of the clouds of choking dust from the road. We began to wind our way past the lovely picnic spots up the mountain of clay and stopped at the famous Ancillo Arce Cactus Gardens, where a display of the various xerophytes from the Bolivian Altiplano fill a natural dip encircled by the road in a most bizarre terrain. Where the road threaded along above the garden it went through a few soft clay tunnels, and in addition to the curious variation in the colours of cacti, succulents, and thin flowering plants, the distant side of the naked, mountainous valley was arranged in three distinct bands of colour; red, blue-grey, and a dull Paris green.

As we drove along this phenomenal valley the ground became more and more lunar, with fantastic oddly shaped pillars of solidified cream-coloured dust, like a series of statues in butter, molten under a searing sun. So far the crumbling stacks of clay were under ten feet tall. Passing through a village we reached a region where the clay stood in pillared shapes over 40 feet high (actually deep, since the columns are all which remains of a previously flat area), and a plantation of 20-year old eucalypts spreads right up to the edge of the canyons and gulleys, planted in an effort to control the rapid erosion. The tops of the clay formations were razor-back ridges which crumbled under my weight, sending mini-landslides of stones and powdered clay to the bottom of the fantastic crevices. Walking on these columns and pinnacles was a foolhardy and uncertain enterprise, as, quite apart from the concentration required to keep my balance, saddles of clay collapsed without warning. The sun shone for us during the evening, even though thunder clouds had threatened all day long, and the coppery lighting in the coppice set a tranquil mood. The rainy season at La Paz extends from December to February, and owing to the altitude snow is also known.

During the evening or before we left in the morning, most of us went across the road to the actual Valle de la Luna, an altogether alien environment. The crude towers of clay etched out by the rain appeared entirely vulnerable to the slightest touch, and I was captivated by its appeal. At the very bottom of the valley 90 feet below, a muddy stream meandered in ox-bows carrying as much silt as the current could bear and its continual sussuration could be heard at the top whence I gazed along the jagged melting chasm, with its tens of thousands of small lateral canyons in which virtually nothing could survive, save one or two etiolated bushes which had had the mishap to germinate in the never-never alveolar regions of eternal shadow at the base of these thin cracks. The truck's horns summoned us and within an hour we had driven to our hotel, the Panamericano, in La Paz. Cold and rain set in for the day and in addition to my interminable dysentery, I felt the effects of soroche (altitude sickness), and had no strength or breath left after carrying baggage up to the top floor. Ann, by contrast, always had a restless energy and sped through the streets at a pace I could never match, particularly intent on seeing the museums and fine churches. The focal point in the hotel was its refectory, and half the group put in an appearance there during the afternoon. While Frances, Kathy, Dee, and I sat down to supper Paul returned with a huge pile of mail to distribute, and Stephanie came back from the 'Mercado Camacho', the central market, with an Inca queña, a yard-long cane flute of a peculiar double-barrelled construction, somewhat akin to a saxophone, with a beautiful tone, decorated with Indian engravings on green paint, and woollen pom-poms (for less than five dollars).

The morning developed in complete contrast to our first day in La Paz, and the sun blazed from a clear sky bathing the whole city amid its circle of snowcaps. Ann, Dee, Frances, Stephanie, Bill, and I set off to obtain immigration permit stamps in our passports, but partway there met Kathy at the Argentine Embassy in the Prado, the main street and a popular siesta promenade, with strips of grass, flower beds, and shrubberies laid out along it, and a band on Sunday to play to the crowds. We walked halfway across the city, descending into wealthier residential zones and the actual business at the immigration office only took a minute, and then we went our separate ways. I returned along the Prado, a great place for window-shopping; one of the displays included a scaled down replica of Thor Heyerdahl's Ra II tortora reed raft. I also looked in on the foyers of the grandest hotels, and shops selling live fish; boga, white pejerrey, and salmon trout from the river. Down back alleys little cafés sold a strictly limited range, just coffee, the hot maize beverage known as api, and salteñas (little chicken and vegetable pasties) which were delicious, hot, and sweet, and so full of juice that it was impossible to avoid getting a sticky chin and fingers. Most of these cafés were mere counters set up in sheltered corners in stairwells or crannies under the eaves, and all sold local fruits and little wedges of unpasteurised cheese against which Paul had warned us.

The post office was a focal point, and in its vicinity were dozens of card vendors with little portable cabinets stocked with seasonal and birthday cards, but only a few postcards behind glass which were numbered. Round the corner from the post office were the formal gardens of the Plaza Murillo, the heart of the city, the address of several of the most impressive public buildings, including the Government Palace (a hive of military activity) and the graceful Cathedral. Guards in red uniforms stood on crude pedestals (genuine soap-boxes) on either side of the palatial portals, but they were flanked in their turn by several military police in grey uniforms, and neither stood to attention, but shuffled and lounged about. Making my way through the back streets I found a number of tiny cafés which sold fresh bread rolls, delicious on their own due to some herbs mixed in with the dough. As usual the water was not safe to drink, but milk, sometimes flavoured, was very cheap in plastic sachets. Coming upon Rolf quite by chance, we shared a plateful of the juicy hot salteñas before wandering around in the fine Indian market, so huge that it incorporates a dozen blocks of the city, and everything conceivable was for sale. Rolf and I were searching in particular for musical instruments up and down the steep cobbled streets. A fiesta must have been in the offing, possibly the New Year celebrations, as some of the stall-keepers specialised in fireworks and multicoloured confetti. Typical of La Paz were the vendors of sacks, which cost only a few cents apiece and were usually white painted with bright logos such as the Red Hand of the Inca, and the name of the mill and the product, such as flour, and the town and country of the mill. We saw cordwainers at work in the streets with Singer sewing-machines and primitive lasts, and Indian women installed wherever there was shade, even under parked trucks with their merchandise spread out on cloths on the pavement. Looking into small courtyards through ancient, sagging, stone arches we could see more of these stalls and chickens and pigs investigating the ground for fallen fruit. One patio was entirely filled with Indian women selling plums, all competing with one another yet charging the same price. We wandered up and down for several hours just musing among the stalls, examining the silverware from Potosí and other areas, which was a particularly good buy, especially the large Napoleonic coins which were selling for less than the European silver premium. Many stalls sold nothing but coca leaves and resin: the coca leaves were displayed in four-foot diameter wheels, packed thus to avoid desiccation, or else in large plastic bags. There were local instruments like ukuleles made from armadillo armour, including the heads, known as charangos. When we looked out over the steep streets the roof-tops sagged crazily in valleys of red tiles, and looked to be in imminent danger of collapse.

In the late afternoon the daily downpour materialised and we took refuge in the high doorway of the modern Cathedral and as we arrived the sacristan simultaneously unlocked the doors from within and let us in. The dark interior was in complete contrast to the rich colonial churches of Quito and Lima, and was very plain and graceful with an imposing crucifix silhouetted against tall stained glass windows, so that the enormous black cross and the arms of Christ could be made out against a colourful picture of militiamen paying fealty, and the window was arranged rather like a totem-pole with scenes one above another. The rain had set in for the night, so we spent a few hours at the cinema, costing only a dime to watch 'Star Wars'. We emerged into the rain among the smells of the traditional bargain-priced hot dog and hamburger stalls which appear in the streets every evening. In the morning, Rolf and I continued our exploration of the city, starting with some local delicacies. I tried api, the fortified maize beer, which is renowned as a tonic and source of vitamins. We returned to the market which was fairly empty owing to the early hour, the only time of day when the newspaper vendors are found there before the papers are redistributed throughout the city. Many of the few Indians were still asleep in their stalls, and we found two products in particular which are unique to Bolivia: beautiful carvings in guayacán and jacaranda wood, and a selection of local fruit which had survived the long journey to the city; amboiba which looks like a glove and is eaten by sucking the 'fingers', guayparu which are similar to wild cherries, ocoro and achachayru which are tangerines with spiky protective rinds, and pitón, literally sour grapes. Rolf rummaged around in a music shop for a long time before selecting a complementary pair of reed pipes with a very sibillant airy timbre.

By the time we had returned to the hotel Rein's group had arrived and was moving into our rooms. We drove out the way we had entered on the surrounding road which climbed up around La Paz, giving us our last all-embracing vista of the city basking in brilliant sunlight. Once we had left La Paz behind, we were back on the Altiplano where the scenery scarcely changed for mile after mile. There was not a solitary tree to be seen and very few Indians indeed outside the occasional, tiny, adobe villages, with adobe or dry-stone walls enclosing backyards and partitioning the fields. We climbed gradually all day, and stopped at lunch time in strong heat and light but there is a perpetual breeze in the Altiplano which blows in gusts and never quite dies to nothing. During the afternoon we passed a new type of housing. The adobe structures had thatched roofs of reeds or possibly very tough bunch-grass, but about a third of the buildings were circular, approximately 15 feet in diameter, and they and most of the regular rooms were windowless against the dust-storms and freezing cold of night. There were oval ovens at nearly every hamlet, sometimes backing onto a hut to provide warmth for the peasants living therein. These ovens are about the height of a man, some with a little chimney-stack, otherwise a simple hole in the adobe serves the same purpose.

All morning there were large flocks of alpacas feeding on fine grass, but this only occurred in the natural basins, enclosed by much

CHAPTER TWELVE BOLIVIA

larger areas which bore only the tough couch-grass and little prickly shrubs about two feet high. The landscape looked green, but it was really only this hardy stuff which thrived. Occasionally sheep or llamas or cud-chewing cattle could be seen in the countryside, and in the farmyards a very few chickens and pigs, though every family seemed to have a dog which considered itself honour-bound to see us off, and furiously chased the truck, barking its head off for half a mile or so. Gradually the landscape changed, becoming more broken with hard-rock strata in white and cream standing out jaggedly from the flat Altiplano plateau. Elsewhere in utter contrast were more of the Moon Valley formations, crevices cleaving the main plateau, and some clefts threatening to slice wedges from the road itself. It was as though there was another level to the Altiplano and the weather was eroding the clay from the upper level and allowing it to settle in a new flood plain 20 feet lower. Streams and puddles became more frequent, many of which we had to ford, and snowcaps could be seen ahead to the south-west while the Altiplano stretched grey-green as far as the eye could see to the rest of the horizon. The distant mountains were beige and yellow and subtle shades from orange to white, or even hues of blue if they were far enough off.

Towards evening the ground became very broken with distinct rifts, dry lakes, and river-beds, and the soil was drier than ever and stained white with mineral deposits leached from below by evaporation. We reached a military garrison at dusk, where a fine was imposed on us as Bill was wearing his U.S.A.F. uniform. (Before entering Bolivia, a military dictatorship, Paul had instructed us all not to wear any khakis, but throughout the trip Bill had ignored the warnings, and even in La Paz he wore his fatigues — despite the military curfew.) Soon after, the sun already having set, we camped in the bleak exposed Altiplano in a stony area full of mountain viscacha burrows. Viscachas look like rabbits but for their long fluffy tails and are likewise rodents, and they live in colonies of several dozen creatures. They come out to sun themselves shortly after dawn in their favourite nooks, with their eyelids drooping sleepily and their long black whiskers atwitch shewing that they are really alert to any trespasser or worse, a predatory bird or fox. Usually one viscacha keeps guard while the rest graze and on its sounding the alarm, a high drawn out trill, the colony disperses in an instant to the security of the burrows. Viscacha flesh is highly favoured by the Indians but they do not breed in captivity and their fur is useless, so instead the Indians keep the familiar guinea-pigs (Galea musteloides) much as Europeans keep backyard chickens, except the guinea-pigs are kept under the bed. Closely related to the viscacha is the chinchilla, not much larger than a dormouse, and now on the verge of extinction in the wild: one species seems to have been wiped out 70 years ago in the rush to turn them into fur coats, and another (Chinchilla laniger) survives only in one colony near Santiago under strict protection. It seems ludicrous to me that the reason for their scarcity, when they used to be found in their millions, is that their pelts fetched 40 dollars each during the First World War. Quite a variety of small rodents have adapted to this high Andean environment, and sharing our campsite with the viscachas were some entertaining little mice (Aulisomys boliviensis) with great round ears, a specialisation to make the most of the warming sunshine. All these animals feed on the various cacti, acacia, bromeliads, and cushion plants: there are many sorts of cushion plants as the hummock shape is a natural one for the conservation of heat and moisture. There was nowhere suitable to erect the tents as the curious brilliant lime green moss formed into rock hard pillows. This moss is yaretal, an Ice Age relic which grows terribly slowly, about six inches per century to lumps up to 20 feet in diameter and four feet high, and it is a prized fuel in Chile with the result that it is rapidly disappearing. It is covered with a tacky resinous insulation over thousands of rosettes of tiny leaves arranged in tightly packed whorls. It was too cold to see in the New Year in style forcing most of us early to our beds, but the Australians never let slip any chance for a party, and we all heard Kathy loud and clear when she proposed a toast and raised three cheers for the New Year right on midnight.

Once again Ann and I rode up front for the border crossing. The dawn augured well with a gorgeous pink sunrise, and by the time we had thawed out, we were well on our way towards a vast, conical, snowcapped peak, the Payachatas Volcano, 20,250 feet high. We passed several pathetic little villages, each a handful of adobe huts with a peculiar adobe church, whose belfry turret, also of adobe, was separate and usually empty. Around them were stone walls and corrals, and probably a dozen or so lived in each tiny village together with their dogs and domestic animals, existing, I assumed, in abject poverty, though one of the larger of these communities boasted a country schoolroom. The scale of the cliffs and hills became more grandiose and swelled them into valleys and mountains, some with streams or standing water which we had to ford. The stratified rock was an even cream colour with streaks of brick red or even white, and wherever small scrub and tola bushes grew the surface of the land was speckled with drab brownish green.

And so by mid-morning we arrived at Tambo Quemado (quite literally 'The Scorched Place') the Bolivian frontier post, and had to wait a few minutes for any signs of life. The customs men and immigration officials turned up in a mixture of mufti and uniform, drunk as newts, which made Paul's task the easier since he merely pointed out the spot in each passport where the official obligingly applied his rubber stamp. We passed through there in about ten minutes, a record, due to the beneficial and liberalising efforts of the New Year celebrations. The frontier itself is a 16,000-foot high pass, but it is a virtual no man's land since the customs and immigration offices are at lower levels on either side of the pass. In this intermediate zone we stopped for lunch, and this was the last time we had to endure such altitudes as the remainder of the expedition took us no higher than 8,000 feet. Every hour or so throughout the day we met a high-sided wooden truck coming the other way carrying two new cars, one tied up on a flimsy platform above the other. Here it was we spotted four vicuñas in the road, which bear a superficial likeness to deer but are in fact cameloid and are a rare protected species. They are smaller, just, than alpacas and extremely graceful with short coats of very fine wool in golden brown and white: the wool measures ten microns, a third the width of the best merino wool. It was the extremely high value of the wool mainly taken from the throat and chest, and of the skins which caused the vicuña to be hunted till no more than 500 survived by 1970. Blanket protection, especially where we were now, has allowed the vicuña to multiply 15-fold even though their fertility is very low and their environment and food sources enormously depleted by introduced grazing animals with destructive hard hooves: cameloids have padded feet. Luckily the adaptations of the vicuña, such as continuously growing lower incisors to cope with the hard grasses and others, aid in its survival; for example, they were so wary of us that no-one could approach within a quarter-mile.

CHAPTER THIRTEEN

CHILE

Chile turned out to be a complete change from the previous countries. Straightaway we noticed that there were no indigenous Indians, in fact the Araucarian Indians were only defeated late in the nineteenth century after being contained for centuries in the far south, and now number about 150,000. The rest of the population contains distinctive groups of settlers who have retained the characteristics of their fatherlands. It is not surprising that Chile's 2,700 miles of coastline span a range of climates. In the north are some of the driest deserts on Earth, the heartland is a beautiful, balmy, and fertile region, and the south has huge tracts of cold and stormy forests extending to Tierra del Fuego, itself given over to prodigious flocks of sheep. Historically Chile has depended on big landowners producing its food using very cheap labour, but since the peóns were emancipated the system has failed, and for this and other reasons inflation figures in the hundreds have occurred in recent years. Over the last decade the cost of living has risen two thousandfold. The Andes extend the length of the country in two parallel ranges. The country's main industry is mining, particularly copper, and fortunately through diversification and the discovery of oil in the Straights of Magellan, the economy is recovering.

Coming down from the pass we reached the Chilean frontier-post of Visviri, at 14,300 feet, where the Chileños were so friendly, that it took us over an hour to end the social chit-chat and break free with our passports stamped and our regulation tourist cards in hand. Directly opposite the outpost is the picturesque Chungurá Lake, a system of permanent water cushion bogs, or bofedales, at the foot of the large snowy Payachatas Volcano for which we had aimed all morning. The lake held plumps of waterfowl including pink and white Chilean flamingoes with black wings, buff-necked and black ibises, all sorts of ducks and geese, and waders like nimble oyster-catchers, plovers, gulls, and herds of curlews. There were many light-footed smaller birds, notably the legendary Andean flicker woodpecker which is said to carry a special plant to dissolve nest holes in cliffs. The edges of the lake were white with mineral deposits, very likely gypsum and guano. The lake is about three miles wide by several long and is green with duckweed and frozen hummocky vegetation along the shore, which stays prettily covered with kaleidoscopic patterns of ice most of every day. The hummocks resembling green brain coral withstand being regularly frozen solid due to their high sap content. Known as yaretal, this plant is an enigma as it may survive for thousands of years with only imperceptibly slow growth. The whole area is known as the Parque Nacional Lauca, and contains Altiplano peaks including the stupendous Guallatire Volcano and more cold blue lakes. The park is inhabited by condors and contains a Chilean government experimental breeding station which we passed later. Rabbit-sized vizcachas (closely related to the chinchilla) thrive in the park in colonies of several dozens, and graze on the cushion bogs side by side with Bolivian mice, recognisable by their huge round ears.

A couple of policemen cadged a lift with us from the border to Poconchile, i.e. to within ten miles of Arica, a major coastal oasis town of 160,000 people. As we descended from the frontier the outcrops of rock along the heights appeared castellated like ancient ruins. We spied a second flock of the fleet vicuñas, but Bill, unthinking in his haste for a close-up photograph, loped up to them and scattered them before anyone else had time to dismount, which was a shame as it was the only time we saw them at close quarters, and we were all becoming peeved at Bill's lack of altruism. The vicuñas inhabited a terrain that was virtually barren rock desert. There was a narrow strip where a brook of crystal clear water maintained a few bushes and a bare minimum of rough grazing. From the pass at 16,000 feet we dropped to 800 feet at Poconchile in little over 60 miles, but the terrain we went through marked the commencement of the great Atacama Desert, which is perpetually dry and extends southwards for 700 miles. The first signs came when the mountains grew gradually devoid of life save for a few varieties of cacti, laying bare the straw-coloured rocks which showed all the usual pretty signs of having been eroded by water, runnels and grooves coming down symmetrically from the tops of the rock hills and peaks, while the only verdure in sight was a ribbon along the rill, but once again it was just enough for the wild herds where the fertile patches broadened into an enclosed pasture less than a square mile in extent, the last grass for many miles and the habitat of about 200 alpacas and llamas and a dozen vicuñas. A modern building showed this to be the experimental farm.

As we left the Altiplano behind we came upon new patches of tarmac and really flew down the hill occasionally hitting dips in the road which bounced us clean out of our seats. To both sides of us and as far as we could see were smooth rocks of such a beautiful, soft, salmon pink forming uninterrupted towering cliffs, rising hundreds of feet from the valley below, and sometimes the road ran along a widening shelf on the side of the valley. It was along this shelf for a couple of miles that we saw sparsely scattered cactus plants exactly like dead Joshua trees, with nutbrown thorns so dense up the first eight feet of trunk that they resembled thick brown fur. All of a sudden rounding a bend in late afternoon, a distant, green, valley bottom came into view, flanked on both sides by the high, barren, pink cliffs. After 30 minutes of immaculate, and inspiring, clean, rock desert with pure bright colours, from white to pale sepia, and latterly the pastel pink and tangerine cliffs, the vivid slash of greenery, which spelt wealth to the valley folk, etched its way jaggedly along the half-mile wide flats whose edges were sharply defined by the gorgeous steeply rising mountainsides.

The road wound in hair-pins and long, fast, smooth stretches down the side of the valley, with the impelling colours drawing one's gaze to the rock strata. Not all were the pale lobster pink, some were pure white and others consisted of packed scree like pebble-dash on a grand scale to incorporate boulders which protruded like bulging pop-eyes and overhung the road. For considerable distances the strata descended parallel with the road, sheltering the verge with wide natural eaves of rock, underneath which the softer material had been cleared or blown away. At last we reached the dense, agricultural, oasis hinterland which supports Arica, 20 miles ahead, a free port and trade outlet for land-locked Bolivia. Here were ploughed fields, good roads, big copses, and a clear tumbling brook with irrigation channels leading off it. We passed a smithy built of bamboos which grow in huge beds. The reeds and bulrushes closely mark the wandering watercourse. The sun had already set by the time we dropped the policemen off at Poconchile, but we carried on in search of a camp-site. Ten miles further we found a perfect location just off the road on a flat powdery field with the beck passing only yards away.

We all felt mysteriously revived at returning to sea-level again after a month in the highlands of the Incas. The Chileans have a weird time system, such that we lost a couple of hours upon entering the country, and it makes more use of the dawn light so that it did not feel like the wee hours when most of us retired. By a democratic decree we decided that the morrow would be New Year's Eve again in order that we could celebrate it properly in warm congenial surroundings. Paul kept us regaled relating how his bachelor friends back in London conspired to send him a typically English Christmas package, which included a cassette of their machinations, a clockwork frog, an adulterated packet of dried peas, a stick of that most British epicurean confection — Yarmouth rock, a pack of titillating playing cards, a tin of finest black pudding, and last but not least important, luxury toilet tissue. The weather was too warm to miss the chance of sleeping out, but we were woken by a plague of mosquitoes and sandflies which gave no quarter and galvanised me into getting up hurriedly.

Within minutes of being on the road we left the conch pink rock hills behind and entered Arica at the foot of the Morro Headland along a wide beach fringed by sand-dunes looking out onto a major port. The city had absolutely nothing in common with any of the towns we had seen hitherto. Firstly prices jumped tenfold over those in Bolivia, and there were no Indians here, no markets, and none of the simplistic naïve and unsophisticated imagery or creativity that exists further north. The people here are Mestizo with a predominant European strain, and the city is modern and developed, looking like an up-and-coming new boom town without any historical buildings and a sprawl of single-storey cheaply erected homes, undecorated, or else bearing a mass of unrelated kitsch ornamentation and the usual cobwebs of electric cables and bristling with television antennae. We stopped there a few hours but the place offers little for the tourist, though the Cathedral was constructed in iron by Eiffel. As we returned to the truck horror stories rebounded about, the prices in the shops, higher by far than in America or Europe. We pulled out of Arica into the Atacama Desert for lunch in a temperature of 105 degrees Fahrenheit in the sun.

The desert here consists of rainless hot plains and brown hills perfectly devoid of vegetation. The Pan-American Highway, too, contrasted completely with the earlier surfaces we had driven on, being smooth, first-class, dual carriage-way with good maintenance and traffic markings, the first we had seen in all of rural Latin America. All afternoon we made fast progress across the vast tabletop with nothing but shades of brown going into the distance. Ranges of mountains at the edge of the desert appeared as barely perceptible blue sawteeth blending into the sky. Now and then we came upon thin strips of vegetation following a subterranean trace of moisture, and at one oasis we endured another police check. Here there were row upon row of stunted small evergreens, possibly firs, and more tropical trees. Hours passed with not the slightest change in the level scenery except the length of our own shadow. It was amazing to count how many cars could be fitted on the passing car transporters; one had 21 new cars stacked sideways. At about eight p.m. with the sun low in the sky we branched aside from the road onto a fascinating dried up lake-bed. The surface was in solid cakes of mud with such a high nitrate or other mineral content that they were studded with pearly knobbly nuggets as big as tennis balls all over the ground, which was split and cracked into small tectonic plates, not flat but with an undulating flowing surface. Along the edges of the cracks, too, were traces of white salts which had been leached from the lake-bed over hundreds or even thousands of years, since no rainfall has ever been recorded in the Atacama Desert. Walking on the inches-thick crust of plates caused thin metallic sounds to ping and creak from their grating rims as the strain of bearing my weight was transmitted evenly throughout the crystalline platform.

The deposits were really abrasive on my boots, and chafed into the leather uppers like shagreen. Everywhere the mud had dried and the surface cakes had baked as hard as concrete with four-inch splits between them, which had a partial infill of loose silt dust.

Climbing down from the truck we were assaulted by a powerful wind from the direction of the Pacific, and had the double task of finding flat spots to sleep as well as escaping the strong wind. Luckily there were a couple of buildings in ruins, mere tumbledown walls, but adequate. Clearing the ground we found the brick fragments sealed to the ground with encrusting crystalline salts, and some of the pieces we moved were chunks of tola heath peat and blocks of yaretal, the resinous moss with its thousands of tiny leaves arranged in rosettes. It is found in rock hard pillows as much as six yards in diameter along the Bolivian frontier in the Altiplano, and is mined with dynamite by the Chilean army for use on manoeuvres as a fuel, since it burns like bituminous coal, with the result that it is rapidly becoming extinct. The New Year was again celebrated, properly now with bottles of wine and spontaneous carousing. Frank was finally impressed by a South American sunset, but it was truly spectacular. The reflection of the vivid sheet of tangerine filling the west lent a bizarre imagery to the broken shards of the dried lake-bed turning them to a burnished copper colour, a carpet of flames licking over the whole parched desert. The night sky which followed was particularly clear and brightly starlit, and cold as iron.

Our well-intentioned plans to make an early start were scotched by the need to sleep off the previous night's wine, but once on our way we went through miles and miles of relentless desert, unchanging, wickedly hot, yellow, and flat as a pancake. The smooth macadamised road stretched our fore and aft straight as a die to the edges of our world. The sun blazed so strongly that the heat haze caused mirages with the most distant humps on the horizon turned into islands in limpid blue lakes. We saw a few oases during the day, all artificial, where miners lived, dependent on water pumped from the

Andes. The miners extract nitrates, metal ores, and other minerals from the desert, and the mining camps were connected by rail to Antofagasta, the major port and city of Northern Chile. We stopped for lunch at a very interesting location, notwithstanding we had been unable to shop anywhere. We pulled up at an old disused railway station miles from anywhere in the middle of the desert. It had been built in the Steam Era, and the old water-horse was still standing there, patiently waiting to be pulled across by its chain to fill up the water tank on the next steam-engine. The station building looked just like a southern United States colonial, mansion with verandahs, multilevel roofing, and tired old paint. The heat was blistering, and the still air utterly silent. Ann and I wandered around and found some shade beside the track near a couple of curious trees with tiny leaves and a bird's nest. That amazed me, because I would never have supposed that the birds could find any food in this unlikely inhospitable habitat, let alone the trees find water.

After an hour's siesta we carried on as before, past the mining communities and their strange cemeteries in which the graves were topped with crumbling adobe bricks, gradually baking to dust, and marked with simple crosses of wooden slats, looking very poor and drear. Owing to the paucity of fresh flowers there is a tendency to place plastic ones on graves, church altars, shrines, and on spots where there have been road fatalities. Soon after this a pipeline joined up with the road and ran alongside, mostly buried, all the way to Antofagasta. We missed our chance to visit the largest open cast mine in the world, a copper mine, though Rein's expedition diverted to take in a visit there and were staggered by the sheer size of the hole, which is the source of income for a township of 30,000 people. The whole Atacama Desert has cakes of white salt, but we passed one large area under a daffodil yellow deposit, which I took to be flowers of sulphur. For the lead up into Antofagasta we passed through increasingly high cliffs of brown rock, a small coastal range of hills, and once through them we saw the city of a quarter of a million individuals spread out at our feet with a fine port, Puerto Artificial, where large ships,, tankers for the most part, hung at anchor.

Driving in, we were on the look-out for grocery shops but saw only the shanty suburbs which gave way to a better central area, with all varieties of garden flowers, especially pinks and white roses. Paul did a customary brief tour before parking in the main plaza, embellished with ornamental masonry and tilework, tall shady trees, and a public garden, one of the city's many good parks and leisure areas. Our primary aim was to reprovision the truck for a couple of days, and I went shopping with Gaby and Chantal, but everywhere the shops were closed for the weekend, until fortunately and quite unexpectedly we chanced upon a large covered market in the Old English style, built by the British settlers and kept scrupulously clean, a far cry from the unhygienic, smelly, jam-packed, Indian markets heretofore. We found all we needed but everything was expensive, very, very expensive, even by Western standards owing to a decade of wild inflation up to 400% per annum, started by Dr. Salvador Allende's Marxist regime, which had turned the old order on its head with an agrarian reform and other sweeping changes which all failed.

In early evening we left Antofagasta behind with its beckoning beach and huge, crashing, roller-coaster surf, without even the chance to dabble our toes in the reputedly warm Pacific backwash. We camped an hour out of town on perfectly smooth grit, overlooked by low rounded hills of rock half a mile away. So featureless was the desolation that for those of us who ran up the hills to photograph the desert sunset, from a mile away the truck appeared as a dot on a billiard table. The climate here is perpetually fine, varying no more than a degree from a steady 67 degrees Fahrenheit, so that most of us slept out. Oversleeping again, we arose to find a thin sea mist had settled over the entire plain, so that we were engulfed in a 20-foot high blanket of haze, tinged pink in the dawn light. We pressed on through the Atacama on the dead flat road. The relentless pale beige sand panned out to both sides, although we were within a few miles of ranges of rock hills. The only changes were that the ranges receded from the road over the eastern-horizon and nearly as far to the west, and the desert turned to very gentle slopes strewn with rocks and pebbles.

There were few well scattered mining concerns along the Taltal Railway, but they were the only population centres. At one of them, Catalina, we were fortunate enough to refuel the truck and take a break, before returning to the everlasting desert. So smooth was the road that nearly everybody fell asleep, even Paul had to rouse himself from a stupor by blasts on the horn and turning S's down the straight road. The stop for lunch was just a hiccough in the day, a mere acquaintance with the nearly flat gravelly plain, under the searing heat of the sun in a vast unbroken azure sky, but afterwards the views perked up a little bit and there were more mining camps. Veins of coal black rock became visible in the increasingly rugged hills once more and the road began to descend in wide loops but we could more easily have driven straight down the hill. After 600 miles of these rough black and brown rock hills we came upon the first desert flora, cacti and lichens, succeeded barely perceptibly by other plant life, prickly scrub and flowers on the lead up to the roadstead of Chañaral. As we entered the town there were rows of little, box-shaped, wooden dwellings surrounded by small yards. A line, of cafés vied for patronage at the inter-city bus stop, where we parked within walking distance of the beach, but Ann and others who made for the sea had to brace up to a cool, stiff, sea breeze. Out to sea jagged rocks protruded above the surface, forcing shipping to anchor offshore. Now that we were covering hundreds of miles a day on the well-metalled Camino Longitudinal, Paul's policy was to introduce a couple of lengthy coffee-breaks into the day which meant starting off at first light, and driving till dusk. Thus we had half an hour to explore the mining port, but it was not worth the candle.

A large conveyor belt system has been built where the cliffs overhung deep water to load copper or gold ore onto freighters, and indeed there was a steamer in position. The town depends entirely on the export of ores for its existence. Starting off we followed the coastal road along beaches and cliffs eroded into weird shapes. A feature of the particular kind of weathering the length of this coast was the fragmentation of colossal blocks of granite, as though moisture had frozen, and expanded in fissures, cleaving off slabs here, there, and everywhere. The entire region of cliffs appeared so broken and peculiarly mis-shapen that in parts it simulated steps in black and brown stone. After an hour hugging, the shore-line with deep aquamarine water fringed with white foam to one side, and. the tedious, low, rounded hills to the other, we turned inland for a spell through the dull expanse of evenly dispersed rocks which must, have been moraine left behind after the Ice Age, since all round them the desert was entirely flat and smooth and bounded by regular rounded eminences along both sides of the very wide valley.

Just before we camped (early) the environment changed utterly with a literal blanket of green covering the land, all of one species, a low dense bush. At our beach camp-site near the oasis and iron ore port of Caldera, amid the gigantic boulders, was a large variety of colourful plants tossing their flowered heads in the light warm current of air coming up from the ocean. The colours were amazingly shiny and bright, crimsons and blush pinks, and one plant, a succulent, had fat leathery leaves of no particular shape but of the oddest rusty colouring. There were animals too, little perfectly speckled lizards, totally camouflaged against the granite rocks, where they sunbathe until they are disturbed and then give their positions away by scuttling a few inches to no obvious advantage. I trapped one with my hand and was astounded by the raucous vibrant hiss it emitted, more befitting a snake than an inch-long lizard. There were also crabs and dead starfish, baked as hard as shoe-soles with varying numbers of fingers up to 20. In patches the beach was composed almost exclusively of hundreds of thousands of limpet-and whelk-shells, and smashed sea-urchin carapaces — understandable considering how forcefully the Pacific rollers were impacting on the litter of rocks which extend into the sea. All this death recalled to mind the fish-eagles at Chañaral soaring among the cliff-tops and the much more dramatic vultures which we had passed stalking stiffly around the corpse of a large mongrel, a road casualty. There had been four of these strutting scavengers, a dark slate grey with gruesome red heads, bald and ugly and wrinkled, sporting smart white wingtips, which being folded nearly out of sight looked like chevrons. After K.P. Ann and I still had an hour before sunset to explore the beach and go for a paddle in the rock pools to clean the travel-dust off our feet. Right on the beach lived a lone fisherman in a driftwood hut 50 feet back from the pounding surf. In front of his curious shack half an acre of shingle was laid out with drying bull kelp seaweed, and parched bundles, a hundredweight each, were stacked up ready for transport. The man stood at his threshold contemplating us while smoke curled up from the chimney. We stopped to sit on a rock and watch the big red orb of the sun set and illuminate the underside of a thick grey rain cloud. By the time we had guessed our way back through the maze of high boulders, everyone was playing bingo. Paul was the caller and the whole session was endlessly hilarious and we all won prizes, before being lulled to sleep by the constancy of the surf.

Our journey continued inland the next day and the scenery changed frequently to contain increasing areas of flowering alstromerias and the little green bushes, but these patches were passed in a few minutes and the desert would be complete again. The significance of the plants was that we were close to the edge of the Atacama Desert, which is generally held to extend as far as the River Copiapó a few miles further on, the life-blood of the farms and orchards along a ribbon of land 100 miles long. For miles we passed more of the frail and transient malvilla (Cristaria) and guanaco's paw (Calandrina discolor), fat-leaved succulents with red stalks, leaves, and flowers, practically the only plants to have germinated here after years of

CHAPTER THIRTEEN CHILE

drought, but for a few narcissi, and which grew so thickly that the ground was carpeted in mauve right up to the edges of the hills which define the Copiapó Valley. Houses and plants were restricted in the main to a few oases, but after mid-morning we came to Copiapó itself, the very pleasant capital of the Atacama District, laid out along rectangular lines. The climate here was most equable, and the inhabitants appeared entirely European in origin and wore suits and western clothes. I went to examine some trees in the main square which were of monstrous proportions, and found the boles were hollow with enough space inside to incorporate telephone kiosks without any trouble. The shopping groups went out, including Ann and I, walking through typically European suburbs to the municipal market. Again it was surprisingly clean and spacious and airy with the produce carefully arranged and stacked, but expensive, as the exchange rate against the dollar was rising daily. We had far more than we could carry, and a lot of it was soft, such as nectarines; so Paul drove by and picked us up, and then lost his way leaving town, accidentally taking the road for the San Francisco Pass through the Andes. South of the pass is the Ojos del Salado Mountain whose height is controversial, being estimated at from 22,560 to 23,320 feet, but it does make the difference between being the second tallest and the tallest summit in the Western Hemisphere, a statistic long since held by the Aconcagua Mountain further south, a titanic 23,040 feet high. The third highest is the Llullaillaco Volcano, south-east of Antofagasta, which is 22,060 feet high. The Copiapó Volcano itself is a mere 19,950 feet by comparison.

Paul's diversion took us up the fecund valley along the river, or rather, the fast stream, whence irrigation channels were led off to water the crops of barley, alfalfa, fruit orchards, bushes and trees, and bulrushes and flowers. An hour out of town Paul realised his error and we stopped for lunch, where, as ever, the sun blazed overhead in a cloudless sky irradiating us with its pleasant warmth. The swift little brook was a most welcome change, presenting our first opportunity to wash since leaving La Paz. Bernie, Bill, and I went through the high beds of bulrushes and took a shampoo and bath but the rest were more modest. Thereafter we returned to Copiapó and found the right road into the desert again on our way south. For hours we saw little other than more of the enormous yellow and brown desert. Every so often a truck-track led off across the bare sand, over a knoll and out of sight, raising the supposition that someone must live or work at an oficina or mine at the other end. We by-passed the city of Vallenar without seeing it. It is in the Huasco River Valley, renowned for its good wines. Very slowly hereafter came a transition from empty desert to the agricultural plenty of the heartlands of Central Chile. The change was marked by several rivers which traverse the semi-arid land to the Pacific Ocean, providing irrigation for grain crops, and alfalfa for the ruminating cattle.

At last we saw buildings perched on a hill, Cerro La Silla, east of the village of Tres Cruces, and they turned out to be the Australian-European Southern Astronomical Observatory about a mile aside from the road. It was well-situated since the desert skies are guaranteed to be almost permanently clear. Further south again, we were virtually out of the desert in semi-arid scrubland with moist lowland patches supporting tufts of tussock-grass and copiapó cacti, hummocky contesserations of low growths which give the town its name, when we were forced to a halt, engulfed by a seemingly limitless flock of goats pouring down a bank onto the road and beyond to fresh pastures. We saw many flocks of goats after this as the desert grew narrower, rockier, and greener until we pulled up fairly close to the regional capital, La Serena, founded by the Spaniard, Juan de Bohon, in 1544. La Serena is one of the loveliest colonial towns in Chile, and built on a hillside, the azulejos (coloured roof-tiles) and many gardens and churches make an attractive sight. The Spaniards had to contend with Daguita Indians who sacked the city two years after its foundation, and later on suffered the attention of the British men-o'-war. Descendants of the Daguitas can still be found, but not of the Molle tribe who also inhabited this region. La Serena is built at the mouth of the Elqui River, in whose pastoral valley we camped.

In the morning we left the Elquino valley folk behind and drove along the coast all day within sight of the amazingly blue sea, passing the modern port of Coquimbo early in the morning, with its fine harbour, mole, and pier. Inland on another peak, Cerro Tololo, is the largest observatory in the Southern Hemisphere run by the Americans. Out to sea a faintly orange cloud sat on the water until mid-morning; why it was such an odd colour I could not guess. Throughout the day we passed numerous small towns and villages and the land was given over to intense cultivation. Most of the little towns were merely erected on either side of the Pan-American Highway without any other streets. Rivers and streams flowed lazily through the vales. At first the fields were small, but gave way to large open expanses of wheat, maize, barley, peach and walnut orchards, and vineyards to support the local pisco distilleries, and grazing for sheep. All kinds of trees, not just varieties of fruit, were growing naturally in this pioneer land with its lack of sophistication and the air of being 20 years behind the times; Its Mestizo population has very little Indian blood and is mainly of Caucasian origin. The weather was as balmy and congenial as a late spring day in Europe, and the slight breeze blew aside the long flowing curtains of green dangling from the weeping willows like cows' tails. There were hedgerows of dogroses, fields full of red and yellow flowering crops, garden blooms and wild flowers to be seen everywhere. The crops were worked so neatly that it was completely in accordance that the settlers in this area were mainly Germanic, and at a gas station we looked down over a large field where black billows belched from the high smoke-stack of an old tractor as it chugged along the furrows. A few moments later we passed a ploughman with a team in hand drawing a tiny wooden plough, the last thing I expected in twentieth century Chile with its Western image.

The scene gradually became more urban after many endearing

coves as far as Papudo, where we dipped inland passing globe artichokes growing wild like weeds along the roadside, and then returned to the coast at Viña del Mar, a well off bathing resort, and rather more than just a suburb of Valparaíso, being a truly beautiful large town in its own right. Viña del Mar has been developed with sheltered commercial beaches and lovely architecture to give large numbers of people living on the rocks and cliffs commanding views of the seafront with its long wide strands. The houses were so beautiful and expensive with hanging gardens of flowers cascading in terraces. Many sizes and varieties of trees grew-naturally or in arbours everywhere, and just before the town we drove through mile after mile of peaceful countryside almost entirely given over to fruit orchards. Here in Chile we found all the top quality foods and goods we had not seen since California: the country is truly more cosmopolitan than Spanish in character, climate, and racially, but at a cost of higher prices than in Europe. Driving through Viña del Mar had us all craning our necks at the tall artistic buildings, the flashy cars and rich suburban Chileans wearing the latest fashions, the grass-thatched beach huts and imposing statues, the colours shining from enormous public flower beds and parks, and ships and dinghies at sea. Everywhere was a hive of activity, a splendid panorama of happy well-to-do citizens enjoying a naturally beautiful social resort.

 We drove on by as it was getting quite late in the day, and I struck a bet with Tobin that it would take us over half an hour to stop at a camp-site. Since Paul was going strong 25 minutes later in the suburbs on the road to Santiago, I thought my bet was safe. A minute later we did an abrupt about turn and pulled alongside a tall grove of eucalypts, and to my chagrin the engine was cut and I lost my money which everyone found very funny. It was still light at a quarter of nine and the air was gravid with the scent of the eucalyptus gum, a delicious refreshing perfume which hung very strong in the still, warm, evening air. As. was now our custom, Ann and I slept

CHAPTER THIRTEEN CHILE

out under the stars; not only much more convenient, it was also very pleasant, to fall asleep contemplating the panoply of heavenly bodies and to be woken gently by the dim dawn twilight. We returned the way we came to Valparaíso. Seemingly everyone grew lilacs, roses, hollyhocks, sweet peas, flowers and blooms of all kinds. Valparaíso is an enormous city with the principal port and a naval base, second only to Talcahuano (at, the mouth of the Bío-Bío), and is. in two parts, the lower commercial heart, resplendent with many commemorative statues and. buildings dating back over, hundreds of years, and the higher hillside crescent of tattered decaying homes and musty residential, quarters, poorly served by the municipal authorities and with a maze of haphazard roads. Pack-mules and funiculars ply the hillsides. The conjoint population of Valparaíso and Viña del Mar is half a million. What makes it different is the lingering aspect of its previous condition before big business corporations began to put up high-rise earthquake-proof blocks. Aside from the old colonial city area, El Puerto, founded in 1536, there are signs everywhere of its Hispanic heritage. Car tyres are used way beyond the stage at which chunks of tread fall off, and remain in use until they puncture. Old sit-up-and-beg cars with large shell head-lamps are still in operation. Horses and traps are seen together with reminders of poverty, and a complete and utter disregard for the problem of roadside litter except in the city centre, built on land reclaimed from the ocean.

Paul drove us slowly through the port works before returning to the main boulevard to park for the morning. In. the harbour we saw amphibious flying-boats similar to small Catalina seaplanes, one resting on the water and the other flying, remarkably slowly overhead like a big fat pelican. At noon we returned to Viña del Mar, past the richer suburbs of Barón and El Recreo, to a less crowded beach for the rest of the day. Ann and I walked along the sands watching a huge tanker manoeuvring a few hundred yards offshore while its great anchor chain clanked rhythmically as it was being weighed. Later Frank and I took a stroll towards the Naval

Academy 20 minutes along the promenade and spying a display of shipboard weaponry, we vaulted a chain fence and began to examine the arsenal in detail. Having prodded and pried out all the secrets of depth-charge delivery we were on our way to tickle the private parts of a torpedo-launching system when we were restrained by a sailor with a rifle and asked to leave. A few minutes later we reached 'La Red', the best of many good seafood restaurants in this area. The service was excellent and we tried a variety of platters, but the Caldillo de Congrio, or Conger Eel Stew, was the best of all along with Macha Clams. By the time we finished we were pretty soporific and returned for a spell of supine guard duty at the truck. I felt it would be a waste visiting the jet set beach resort of Central Chile without going for a dip and went for a walk in the surf with Ann. The beach was so steep and the waves rushed up it so energetically that they crashed against us with surprising force. It was great fun but impossible to swim in. As the sun was setting we retraced our route through the suburbs, where the red sun was reflected in all the windows setting the city on fire. We camped in the same eucalyptus grove as last night, and we all lost sleep by waking well before dawn to have a full day in Santiago.

After breakfast I set off running in the cold of the pre-dawn half-light, passing Alice and Ann who were walking, and I even overtook a cyclist commuting to work. Regularly Ann and others walked ahead of the truck while Bill and Bernie used to run, particularly at meal times. The smells of the beautiful wooded countryside and villages were very nostalgic, particularly the sweet aroma of barley and corn being milled which took me right back to my boyhood summer jobs. The truck caught me up within six miles, but Bill had usually gone twice as far before we reached him. Soon after we left the asphalted road and entered the coastal range of mountains and in a matter of 20 miles we climbed more than 4,000 feet. The terrain was really pretty and green again, lush with moisture but very hot under the direct rays of the summer sun. Towering cacti flourished alongside date palms and puyas and acacias and many types of conifers. No. particular use seemed to be made of the naturally thick vegetation and woodland in the mountains which was usually left as fallow grazing.

We descended swiftly into Santiago and debussed at our hotel, the Colonial, emptying into it the entire contents of our truck and trailer as usual. The hotel had absolutely no merits beyond hot water and a low tariff. Ann and I (presumably the others too) were given a squalid cell without, windows, but with collapsed creaking joists, badly torn and peeling faded wallpaper, and filthy stained paintwork. Four rank toilets served the entire hotel which had an additional bad nocturnal, reputation, so that all in all it was pretty average for Latin America. Ann and most of the others lost no time in exploring the capital, and returned waxing enthusiastic about the city. Santiago lies in the valley which spans the Mapocho River which is a tributary of the Maipó to the south. The metropolis is the largest in Chile, covering 40 square miles, and has now grown since its founding by Pedro de Valdivia in 1541 around the Santa Lucía Hill to contain over 4,000,000 inhabitants and half the national industry.

Ann and I spent the afternoon seeing the sights, starting with the Mapocho River, but with reliably dry summers the water fills only a fraction of the stone-lined channel 100 feet wide. We made a circuit of the public parks and gardens, full of grandiose statues and water used decoratively and imaginatively. Many of the buildings were quite spectacular, such as the 22-storey Diego Portales building, the temporary seat of government until the Palacio de la Moneda is restored, following the aerial bombardment in the coup of 1973. The plazas and avenues are equally as interesting; the beautified main artery, Almeda Bernardo O'Higgins is over 100 yards wide and is named after the first head of State, whose Sligo father, Ambrosio, became Viceroy of Peru. Andean peaks of nearly 20,000 feet are visible over 60 miles away to the east with their brilliant white snowcaps. Santiago's oldest church, dedicated to San Francisco is on the Alameda and is also a monastery, whose most renowned sacred treasure is a statuette of the Virgin Mary brought by Valdivia from Peru mounted on his saddlebow.

Ann and I followed up a lead on an alfresco student ballet which took us miles across the city, but discovered a café renowned for its folk-lore music. Ann determined to return later for this, and next we found ourselves at Santa Lucía, the smaller of two focal hills in Santiago. The other one is the conical San Cristóbal to the northeast of the city developed with many points of interest. We were at the former defensive citadel, the Hidalgo Castle, rising 230 feet above the Almeda on Santa Lucía Hill, now a fantasy of fountains, beautiful stone carvings and statues, including one of Caupolicán, the leader of the Araucanian Indians. There are benches and balconies all the way to the top, and an equestrian statue of Lieutenant Diego de Almagro, one of the original Conquistadores. Dusk was rapidly falling, but the whole place was subtly spotlit and being built of rough-hewn pink stone with look-out turrets jutting from the corners of the battlements, the whole setting had an Old World romanticism, enhanced by the concealing trees which overhung the ramps and fortifications, while vines and flowers provided a thick ground cover. From the top Wonderful views of the whole city could be seen. The night was warm and the heat rising from the city below made the thousands of lights twinkle and shimmer. Since Santiago is in a volatile earthquake zone there are few skyscrapers, and the view from the citadel with its quaint castellated ramparts and parapets was nearly unimpeded, and of the few extra tall buildings, most were architectural masterpieces, such as the post office tower which is entirely round with different diameters at various levels, all brightly adorned with red lights to warn off aircraft, and the well-illuminated dome of the Cathedral. As we wandered around the Hidalgo Castle, every dark nook and cranny, all the benches, alcoves, and, balconies were occupied by young lovers spooning, and at the top we came upon an eternal flame on a pedestal in the centre of a formal paved terrace with flag-poles. Beside the colonial fortress, the peak is shared by an observatory, and every day the report of a cannon marks the noon hour, while in the depths of the stronghold there is an historical Indian museum.

Back at street-level we wandered vaguely in the direction of our hotel, checking out the night-life. The cooler evening air had brought out crowds of strollers onto the pleasant broad streets, with their boutiques and Chilean handicraft stores specialising in the local black pottery, hand-wrought copper and bronze articles, and wooden carvings. The street vendors stay out late into the night, and I think some stall-holders never close for business, but ply an overnight trade by the light of hurricane and Tilley lanterns. Cafés and bars stay open as long as there is custom, and particular stalls appear only in the evenings to cater for the hungry. Typical of these is a common type in the shape of a Spanish galleon, the size of a perambulator and mobile in just the same way, generally full of confectionery and tobacco. There were also individuals selling fried eggs in bread rolls with a rich sauce, and men walking around with a couple of one-gallon flasks, harnessed in front of them, dispensing hot, sweet, black coffee by pressing, a pump button in the lid and holding a disposable cup under a tiny faucet. Ann went off to return to the folk-lore cabaret show, but I could not resist the appetising fumes rising from pots of meat and sausage being fried along the pavement, and sampled the streetside specialty served in a bap. It turned out to be tripe in a rich, piquant, tomato sauce.

Santiago is one of the loveliest cities in the world, with a perfectly healthy climate, and it compares favourably with any city in the Northern Hemisphere, and by light of day it was interesting just window-shopping in the carefully arranged pedestrian precincts and roofed, arcades. Every man's budget can be satisfied here, from the economy stalls of dairy products and bakeries to the most chic fashions and furniture, and the people too were very pleasant, and, are either Caucasian or barely Mestizo, and convey a strong sense of old-fashioned mores and ethical values. Almost to a man they wore suits, except the dapper shop assistants in fresh white overalls or uniforms, while all the women were stylishly dressed. All through the expedition Frank had been kicking himself for not buying a chessboard in Mexico City, where they are cheap and very well made in marble, onyx, jade, and fancy hardwoods. He found one here in walnut veneers and was quite gratified with his bargain. Aside from chess, Frank's other great interests were philosophy, cinema, and gourmet cuisine, and joining him for the remainder of the day, we indulged them all. Cinemas in Latin America generally show films in the original dialogue with Spanish sub-titles, and are priced at a tiny fraction of what we were used to paying, literally a cent or two to get in. Thereafter we went on to the large and extremely popular Chez Henry night-club just to one side of the Plaza de Armas. It had three large dining-halls with musicians in each and a soda-fountain. We went through the orchestra room where spruce waiters in white with serving cloths over one arm directed us to one of the best tables on the edge of the dance floor next to the band. There were 80 tables to choose from, but we were given unusual attention as we were obviously tourists. I took the house specialty, excellent conger eel and other seafood, and we enjoyed easily the most expensive meal of our lives, but well worth it. However the bill did not add up and we kept querying it until the figures at least tallied at the fifth attempt. It was the early hours of the morning by the time we rolled up at our hotel, but everybody on the expedition was having a late night as it was our last one in any town until the trip ended a busy six weeks later.

With no windows in our room it was pitch black at any time of day, and stifling hot. I much preferred the nights spent camping out to those in seedy noisy brothels, as often as not the only establishments we could afford. In the morning we made ready to depart, and to fill in the time I took my last stroll in a circuit of the parks and tree-lined streets such as Avenida Vicuña Mackenna, named after a former historian and governor of Santiago responsible for the embellishment of Santa Lucía Hill. We left Santiago on the Camino Longitudinal, the name the Chileans give to their stretch of the Pan-American Highway, and passed-through pleasant suburbs on the fast straight trunk-road. The landscape turned to farmland along the deadpan Central Valley, bordered by the Coastal Range to the west and the distant Andes to the east, with streaks and patches of snow which caught the sunlight. By and by numerous pointed hills erupted from flat ground and these and the blank mountains were studded with meagre clumps of rough grass, but were otherwise an arid sandy brown in total contrast to the strikingly vivid young greenery which filled the vale. The new maize crop was especially bright green, as the tender new corn shoots and leaves had not developed the tough dark foliage of mature plants. Flowers were thick on the ground and along hedges and banks; wild roses, tall bright red hollyhocks, brilliant mauve bougainvillea trees, and fruit blossom. Over large areas vines were trained up wires and along overhead traceries like bowers. These vineyards were huge and took up most of the valley, unmistakable with their unique shapes of cascading questing tendrils. It was a veritable sea of cloud in bubbly bursts of green.

Thousands upon thousands of trees of many species grew unchecked in the valley. The stately eucalypts were everywhere, and also rows of tall Lombardy poplars acted as neat hedges and wind-breaks. Large stands of spruce grew in plantations, and banks and thickets of bamboos waved gently in the southerly breeze along the river, peacefully nodding their feathery tips. Many other kinds of trees grew in copses all over the valley; beech trees, ilexes, large orchards of peaches, nectarines, apricots, and miniature papayas, much sweeter than the larger variety, and normally stewed or tinned to eat at their best. The regular small-leaved ceiba trees which grow commonly all over South America were here in large numbers with their gnarled trunks all tortured and deformed. But the valley is far and away most memorable for its beautiful weeping willows which grow in profusion; more common than any other type of tree here, with the fetching gracefulness of their curves and their soft greens and curtseying branches swaying provocatively like hula-hula skirts in the light wind. The strands of green dangle nearly to the ground, but around Curico in the country of the huasos, Chilean cowboys, the horses and cattle crop back the delicate leaves and soft green twigs so that the whole underside of these willows is an even height from the ground. A wide river cut a highly convoluted gravelly bed through the valley, but the stream itself filled only a narrow channel gouged in further loops through the gravel. In places stagnant pools of water a hectare or more in size formed the basis of some very exotic water gardens with wafting willow branches and stands of bulrushes. Children played in the water, some ferrying row-boats about between the little peninsulas and isthmuses of land with natural scenic clumps of trees and the snow mountain peaks in the background.

We all felt quite hungry by midday and pulled off the road into a service station at Buin, where we had over an hour for lunch while Paul repaired a couple of punctures. A lot had been said on the truck about the volatile military politics of Chile, notably about the recent violent purges. At this garage a man climbed off his tractor and started a conversation with me, which was at once very amicable, educational, and unbiased about his work and the state of the nation. His name was Juan and he explained how the standard of living has risen in recent years to encourage private enterprise in order to compete on world markets. He ran an experimental farm using hybrid seeds of melons, sunflowers, and other crops to be developed on his farm and then grown in the United States. We gathered quite an audience, who quizzed him on all aspects of education, progress, politics, and future national prospects, and he talked easily and casually giving us a picture of his country on the right track towards self-sufficiency and economic expansion. He ended by telling us about the natural beauty of Southern Chile, beyond Puerto Montt, and of the glaciers and lakes and organised cruises through the southern archipelagos, an extension of the coastal range. Juan was the son of a German

CHAPTER THIRTEEN   CHILE

migrant, clearly no politician, but demonstrated the independent entrepreneurial spirit which has been a strong motive force behind the Northern European emigrés to Chile for a century. His conversation provided us with heated discussions for days.

All afternoon we drove through the flat agricultural plain up to 100 miles broad, which continued just as before with its wealth of trees and waterways; a rich, warm, prosperous farmland, with broad fields of wheat and other cereals. We camped before dusk in the vicinity of Talca in a gravelly truck-siding well of the road. As the temperature was so equable Ann and I opted as usual to sleep flat out under the clear night sky. With the River Maule nearby it is not surprising that clouds of immature mosquitoes swarmed to the lights of the truck and made a tremendous nuisance of themselves all evening. The Chilean farmer's outlook was still prompting strong conversation among us. Tobin was a member of Amnesty International and had strong views in solidarity with the political prisoners and condemned the farmer as a stooge of the government, even though Tobin had not met Juan, while I defended Juan's stance on individual freedom of opportunity. To offset the negative aspects of the evening Nature pulled off a stunning sunset with pencil thin clouds lancing across the sky, crimson below them and Halloween yellow above. A needled frieze of spruce trees in the gaps between the coastal mountain peaks sliced the smouldering sky with its black silhouette, and later it turned out warm and starry.

The sun had long since risen by the time we woke to perfect weather. The chorus of birds twittering in the weeping willows accompanied us through breakfast. Ann and I rode up front and enjoyed a superb view during the trip through South-Central Chile, probably the prettiest market garden scenery in all America. Basically it was an extension of the long arable valley we passed through yesterday. We soon reached the large agricultural centre of Chillán where we shopped. The city has twice been razed to the ground by earthquakes and then rebuilt, and in consequence appears full of modern architecture and well-planned avenues lined with shady trees. We did not stop long, and drove out past a large innovative concrete church, basically constructed of arches with a large modernistic mural above the portals. There were a couple of external towers, and one of these was certainly a belfry. As ever we attracted ogling bystanders reckoning up the value of our amazing truck and trailer in millions of pesos. Thereafter the landscape became rather hilly with more grazing for the livestock, since there were too many trees for efficient cultivation. We passed huasos with greater frequency, and also yokes of oxen and horses drawing rugged carts or primitive ploughs.

We stopped very suddenly at the Salto del Laja at my request, which Paul missed in his haste to make headway, and we turned back to spend some time at Chile's most spectacular waterfalls, which cascade over 150 feet and are set back about a quarter-mile from the road bridge over the Laja River which runs another 50 miles into the Bío-Bío, the greatest river in the country. The waters of the Laja are green because the river rises as a glacier in the Andes, scraping through a bed of clay, and it is the suspended clay which lends the glassy hue to the river. From the bottom of the torrential waterchute (now at low water) the current has cut its way through deep narrow clefts in the rock so that odd effects of erosion have exposed many strata of bed-rock with lumps in the side wall where harder bits jut out like fins. Judging from the enormous volume of water crashing over the cliff, the eroded gulley must have been at least 100 feet deep as it was only 20 feet wide at the bridge. Ann and I decided to approach as close as possible to the main falls, and as we made our way along the river-bank we were assailed by the most horrific and persistent tabanid horse-flies as gigantic as cockchafers with mouth-paths the size of pen nibs. These monsters were black with furry orange abdomens, zooming extremely fast just like hornets, favouring elbows and shoulders. Blood-sucking insects are amongst the few things I cannot abide, and with these devils diving at me, I was slapping at them non-stop while Ann and I were trapped there in polite conversation with a couple of day-trippers from Santiago. Not before time we got away to the base of the waterfall where clouds of water vapour and droplets of spray rose high in the air splashing us 25 feet above. The water really shot down with an incredibly strong current over three long lips of rock 100 yards across in all. Big dragonflies darted about, and the sound of tons of water crashing into the basins it had cut was slightly muffled by the trees all around and an island betwixt us and the main body of falling water. I had had enough of running the gauntlet of giant flies, after getting a bite like a vaccination which startled me so badly that I was nearly precipitated into the falls, and so I returned, but Tobin and Ann ventured down into the spume as far as possible where each saw a complete circular rainbow around him (or her, respectively).

Soon after lunch we passed through 'The Region of the Seven Rivers', though I counted many more, the main one being the Bío-Bío, a natural landmark as it is huge and extremely wide, over a mile at its estuary, and until the end of the nineteenth century was as far as settlers could go owing to the ferocious wars waged against the Arauca Indians, who eventually lost by virtue of becoming nearly extinct after centuries of isolation and war. As we went south, so there were more and more trees until the terrain was clad in woodland with unused clearings in it. We had reached Forest Chile, and here the roads were bad over considerable distances since the cement is laid without a hard-core foundation and rather than repair the road the gollies put up road-signs warning of bad roads, though we did see several traction-engines and some ancient road repair equipment. By now we had passed out of the region of dry summers, and the Central Valley began to change tangibly. It was heavily forested especially with beech trees separating the little farms and vineyards. The abundance of trees resulted in our passing numerous lumber-mills and yards. Forestry has practically and permanently eliminated the once far-stretching forest of alerces (Fitzroya cupressoides), a species of evergreen larch related to the giant sequoia. It takes several centuries to attain maturity at about 130 feet and those that remain may easily have germinated in Biblical times. Due to its durability and attractiveness as a cabinet wood, protection for the remaining stands is ineffectual. The houses and little churches too were timber-framed and shingle-roofed, identical to those in the great forests of New England. The same high smoking snow-cone, Llaima, 9,974 feet, had been visible in the Andes 60 or more miles to the east all day, mainly because the plain had been wholly flat as far south as Temuco, but for the last couple of hours of the day we passed into high hills and had quite a change of scene.

    We camped right on the very brink of the wide Chol-Chol River (alias Gol-Gol) where there was scarcely enough room for our camp-cots as ploughing extended almost to the river-bank. During supper in the truck Frances told Ann and me she could see a water-rat on our bedding — how cheerful! Grey parakeets live along the banks of the river looking something akin to rather elongated pigeons with hooked bills. They were extremely noisy as they skimmed about just above the ripples catching insects. Within an hour of nightfall a heavy dew had already settled on everything, and lying listening to the burbling of the current the dominating images of the day went through my mind — the endless miles of mauve flowers like lupins which grew wild along verges and filled the fields of timothy grass and the borders of brewer's barley, so that a casual observer would think purple plants were the cash crop. They and the white cow parsley had been constantly visible from morning till night. Further north a mountain, Cerro Tomate, gets its name from, the blanket of reddish flowers that occasionally clothes it. The weather changed overnight, and we woke to a chilly dawn and a leaden sky — Forest Chile is a land of tempests at any time of year, for (at 40 degrees south) we were nearly into the Roaring Forties.

    We drove quickly as far south as Valdivia skirting the western edge of the Lake District which extends between parallels 38 and 42 south. It is one of the loveliest regions of Earth, with an agreeable climate, no bothersome insects, and a dozen great lakes with crystal clear water, ranging in colour from an intense blue through aquamarine to pure emerald. Additionally water is seen in all its forms, including snowcaps and glaciers on Andean volcanoes offering excellent skiing from 5,000 to 10,000 feet up. Large rivers traverse the forest feeding waterfalls and are full of fish, or alternatively one may enjoy the thermal baths throughout the Lake District. Despite the great tourism potential, the region has scarcely been touched except for its excellent roads and is little known outside Chile. We passed more huasos along the road, many of whom are descended from Arauca Indians now centred in this region. It was still early morning when we reached Valdivia, the capital of a province of the same name, founded by Pedro de Valdivia in 1552, but the greatest imprint has been made by the German colonists who arrived over a century ago. Evidence of German order can be seen in the shop names, and in the gabled Bavarian wooden architecture and clapperboard walls, also in the methods of agriculture, with steam-driven traction-engines still in use on the small family farms, in cleared gaps among the forest and small lakes, just like the potato counties in the hilly back country of northern Maine.

Wandering along the shopfronts everything appeared expensive with a typical provincial image, with broken pavements, peeling paint, the regular clip-clop of horses' hooves, and the rattle of little carts. There were scarcely any motor-vehicles and no particularly big buildings other than schools and hotels. Valdivia is in a highly active region and was partially devastated in 1960 by the permanent effects of an earthquake and tidal wave. I came upon the River Valdivia by chance as it flowed wide and serene within brick-lined embankments. As I was approaching a market on the wharf a chime tower on the opposite bank sounded for ten o'clock, and then played a medley of melodies in dulcet electronic tones and chords. Strolling among the open air fruit stalls my interest was suddenly quickened when I saw the market was mainly for fishmongers, selling long fat conger eels, both black and red varieties up to six feet long and 35 pounds in weight, and large marine corvinas, no lightweights either at 20 pounds, and little pejerreys which look like eight inch sardines, and merluza (or hake), and mussels, and 'tacas' which I took for clams. I thought I had made such a picturesque discovery that I rushed back and fetched Diane, Stephanie, and Frank to this unique wharfside market, where we picked up the eels to marvel at their size. The girls went on the river in a row-boat to pose with the colourful fishermen.

We stopped just outside the town for lunch and spread out our dew-saturated sleeping-bags to dry on the rocks, short work for the sun and pleasantly cool breeze. Of all the species of trees in Forest Chile a quite plain one was the source of power of the Mapucho Indians of Valdivia over other tribes. It is the sorcerer's tree (Latua publifora), and unsurprising for a member of the nightshade family its blooms, dangling purple bells, are used to concoct intoxicants. The native monkey-puzzles were superabundant, properly known as araucarian pines (Araucaria araucana) and exclusively associated with these trees are several dozen species of insects, also the slender-billed parakeet which has adapted to negotiate the spiky helices of hard leaves and cones. Striking inland without stopping at Osorno, the beauty of the heart of the Lake District was somewhat lost to us as we peered through gloomy shrouds of mist and rain. All we could see was a great variety of trees covering the immediate hills, and for a few miles drove in a ghostly forest of skeletal spruce, pine, and larch destroyed by bud-worm. We passed several tiny lakes, but the first named one, Lake Puyehue, was so grey and dismal in the mist and drizzle that the farther shore was lost to view. The roads were bad and bumpy all the way through Puyehue National Park and a couple of river bridges had been downed, but for the first time in Chile, workmen were on the job with massive road-building equipment.

By five o'clock we had reached the Chilean frontier and the Puyehue Pass through the Andes, in a region of impenetrable temperate rain forest with heavy foliage everywhere. Thick stands of climbing bamboo, dwarf beech, and dense trees hung with festoons of Spanish moss, and clumps of wild flowers were all about us, lining the road with berberis, fuchsias, poppies, and a host of others.

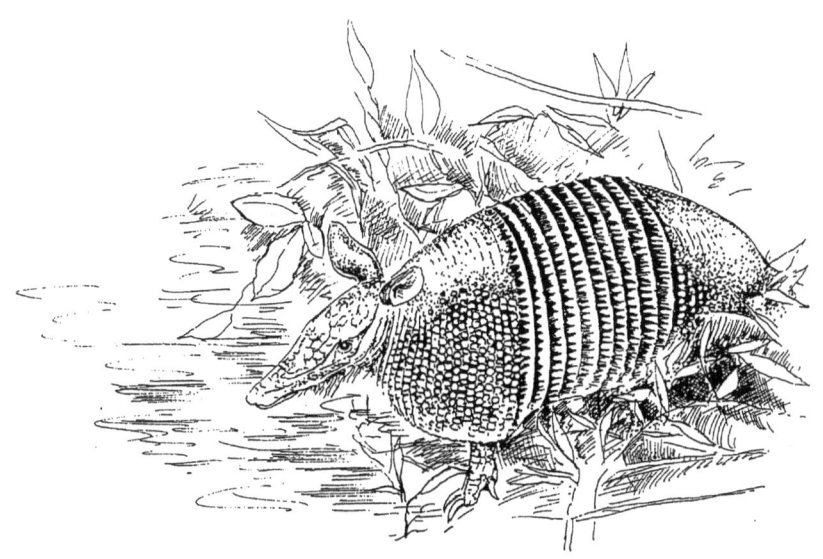

CHAPTER FOURTEEN

ARGENTINA (Southbound)

Argentina is the second largest country in South America and we were to travel the entire length and breadth of it, during which we traversed the enormous regions of the Lake District, Patagonia, Tierra del Fuego; and north bound, the Humid and Dry Pampas, Argentine Mesopotamia, and part of the Gran Chaco. Naturally we experienced changes in the climate, but not as much of a temperature change by day as by night when the chill wind of Southern Patagonia made us seek the shelter of the truck. A great deal of Argentina is semi-arid and even more is treeless and perfectly flat. Since we had deadlines to meet, we sped hundreds of miles a day across the relatively uninteresting regions, but by contrast some of the loveliest terrain in the world was along our route. Socially Argentina is much the same as Chile and Uruguay, a White country identifying strongly with Europe whose nationals are wooed as immigrants. Formerly it was the British who engineered the introduction of industry in all its forms, and founded most of the sporting clubs. In short the British controlled the social hierarchy for more than a century. There is an underlying and inevitable rivalry with the Chileños; after all, both countries lay claim to the mineralogically wealthy islands south of the Mitre Peninsula and to part of Antarctica. Firstly the Spanish and then the other settlers systematically wiped out the indigenous Indian populations, but in the earliest years it was as often as not a question of self-defence. The history of Argentine development reflects the growth of its railway network and the occupation of the Pampas by cattle barons, who brought in lucerne as a fodder crop, since supplanted by sorghums and other grains.

In crossing the Puyehue Pass through the Andes we went over numerous turbid mountain streams coming down to the Argentinian border-post of El Rincón, where it took a couple of hours to process us. On this side of the frontier the road wound along in virgin woodland which was incredibly eerie as so many of the centuries old gigantic trees had fallen over or been choked to death, and great timber trunks 150 feet and more in length lay smashed to tinder, rotting like so much matchwood. I surmised the reason for it to be the shallowness of the soil. There were a lot more beautiful ponds and lakes in the forest and extremely sturdy wooden chalets in hollows with painted tin roofs, or little small-holdings with endearing gatherings of farmyard livestock. At this time of year the lake waters are still as mirrors, and perfect reflections of the Cerro Tronador (Thunder Mountain), Cerro Otto, Cerro Colorado, and other bare or forested mountains and snow-clad peaks glinted up at us as we drove by. The deep blue lakes poke fjord-like arms (called brazos) deep into the Andes, and the lakes extend from Lake Nahuel Huapí National Park through 12 degrees of latitude to Los Glaciares National Park at latitude 51 degrees south.

CHAPTER FOURTEEN   ARGENTINA (Southbound)

Deep in the forest we suddenly came upon enough of a clearing for Paul to pull off the track next to a rushing glacial river. Quite a few other campers were in the woods or camping-grounds along the way there, some as close as a few yards from our final stop, as this was their midsummer and beautiful weather for camping. Ann and I went for a walk along the river just as the sun was sending its dying rays sloping through the trees. The woods were full of wildlife, particularly aquatic birds and woodland flowers, and when the light of dusk had quite gone we returned hoping that supper, or at least a cup of tea might be ready, but with Bill and Frances doing the cooking the long wait was best endured away from the truck, as past experience of waiting the two or three hours in the truck full of cooking smells always made me feel hungrier than ever. From our camp-site on the shore of Lake Nahuel Huapí near Villa La Angostura we carried on next day through more of this diverse temperate forest. All morning we drove along the shore of this same lake which is about 50 miles long. The road followed the shore-line faithfully, and we had the prettiest view over the lake to the tree-clad foot-hills and snowy peaks beyond it all the way along. It was very gratifying to note that several of the others were just as delighted by the unending banks of flowers and clumps of berry bushes. Everywhere were foxgloves, several colours of lupins often growing in masses together, fuchsias hung with little scarlet blossoms prevailed along the trails and roads, and all over the little fields we passed lilies and primulas and geraniums and a profusion of other wild flowers insinuated themselves among the pastoral plants. Along the way we passed a very few small wooden houses, shacks merely, from which smoke drifted lazily up through the branches of the towering aging trees; and around the houses down to the water's edge were the only strips of grass in the woods, cropped back so hard by the few animals the woodsmen owned that they appeared as perfectly mown as crown bowling-greens.

We entered (San Carlos de) Bariloche on the southern shore and stopped there for several hours. The town of 45,000 inhabitants is beautiful with Swiss architecture, wooden chalets, and a very attractive main square overlooking the lake, basking under the relaxing warmth of the sun. The mountain air was very clear, and the town is built on the steep moraine at the base of Cerro Otto. Wood and stone are used artistically everywhere to erect the most inspiring show-piece buildings with sweeping roofs evenly tiled in split cedar and natural stone worked into fancy foundations, colonnades, and archways. Chantal, Gaby, and I went off on a shopping foray for food, and went all the way round a supermarket agog at the Monopoly board prices. Postcards cost 1,000 pesos each, and a cup of coffee 6,000 pesos. Inflation had reached such proportions here with 2,000 pesos to the dollar, that provisioning the truck with food and fuel for a few days could cost up to 1,000,000 pesos from joint and personal funds. We found a fairly small but immaculate, tiled, covered market where we bought most of our greengroceries and handled big bills like millionaires, but the food was premium quality and better than anywhere hitherto.

Back at the car park on the shore a northbound expedition had parked their truck next to ours. Their journey had started in Rio de Janeiro and was basically the reverse of ours and so we stayed there into the afternoon swapping yarns about the places we had explored. We voted to camp together overnight on the shore of the amazingly blue Lake Nahuel Huapí, but before that we drove for an hour along the shore-line until we reached a huge rocky outcrop a couple of miles in circumference renowned for its caves with prehistoric paintings. We slogged uphill for 35 minutes through the prickly scrub on broken flat stones which tinkled like glass as we kicked them. We discovered several caves, the first of which were basically large holes in the side of the hill of rock with bushes hiding their mouths. Most people were satisfied with this,

CHAPTER FOURTEEN ARGENTINA (Southbound)

but a couple of Australians from the other expedition, Ann, Armin, and myself persevered over a difficult escarpment and found a huge cave where 100 people could easily have taken shelter. The roof was jagged in sawtooth ridges from five to ten feet up but the cave became narrower and lower until it was only 20 inches high about 90 feet back. The two Australians borrowed my flashlight to explore it, first one until his voice faded out of earshot and then the other. After half an hour they came back to relate that the tunnel soon opened into a cavern 60 feet long and 15 high which ended in a lagoon. In addition to the prehistoric pictures there was a great deal of graffito, most of it by two twentieth century lovers who had painted sweet nothings throughout their tryst. It was quicker for us to walk up and over the summit of the cliff than to walk back around, and as soon as we reached the trucks long after the others we set off again to the eastern end of the lake, where we found a joint camp-site which was extremely burry. The burs even stuck into skin, as well as bedding and clothes.

I chanced a dip in the lake even though it was startlingly cold, as opportunities to wash did not arise most days. The other group told us that 700 miles further south they had swum in Lake Argentino which contained icebergs newly calved from the Perito Moreno Glacier. We all helped to hump logs of sun-bleached driftwood to build a big camp-fire, and for the most part we spent the warm evening socialising. There was a lot of spoor and other evidence of wild animals in this region, as little river-martens or rock-coneys darted away through the undergrowth at the sound of our approaching footfalls. A wisp of snipe flew by in the early twilight, and Sam brought in a ten-pound salmon while looking for driftwood. Rainbow trout, red deer, and other new species, including vegetation, have been added to the indigenous ones in and around Lake Nahuel Huapí and its many islands, chiefly Victoria Island where a forest research station was established at the turn of the century. To add a lovely touch to the evening, anemones with delicate yellow petals began opening up all around us, to my mind some of the loveliest I had noticed all along, like poppies exactly. The only damper on the day was my eternal illness which made me feel rotten almost without a break for a week at a time.

The morning was really bracing, and after sunrise we had to endure an hour in the cold shadow of the Cordillera while we could see the borderline of sunlight creeping down the mountains facing us, mirrored perfectly in the glassy lake. Bill found a baby scorpion during breakfast and called me over. It was a dark ash grey and blended perfectly with the dusty grit. There were plenty of signs of life everywhere: birdsong filled the air, and Ann and I, walking on ahead, spotted a red-backed hawk perched in a dead tree-top eyeing us directly as we went by. It presented the magnificent image of a proud wide face with a neat hooked bill and boot black button eyes reprimanding us. We saw rabbit and plenty of tracks of red fox, deer, and wild dogs, and furthermore the air was pregnant with the fragrance of mauve lavender-shaped blossoms on tall bushes. The drive through the Lake District led on through very scenic mountain country with dense foliage provided in the main by Araucaria pine, larch, and poplar trees. There were many turquoise streams chattering alongside stretches of the rocky forest track which wound along, connecting mountain hamlets, many with police checkpoints. We gradually left the lakes behind and the trees thinned a little to be succeeded by high wild savannah grass growing in the clearings. The further south we went the thinner and squatter grew the tree cover until it became a great treeless and windswept plateau comprising the provinces of Chubut, Santa Cruz, and all but the south of Tierra del Fuego. There is a pioneer quality to the beauty of Patagonia which acquired its name from the nickname 'patacones', Spanish for big feet, a reference to the various Indian populations who inhabited the continent south of the River Plate until they were virtually exterminated during the genocidal Desert Campaign of

CHAPTER FOURTEEN   ARGENTINA (Southbound)

1879 to 1883. Tierra del Fuego translates as Land of Fire, alluding to the Indian system of firewood beacons which early sailors saw lit at night especially to warn of their approach.

All morning we ploughed along dusty dirt-roads through the hot woodland, only stopping at lunch time on a wide grassy bank betwixt the road and the River Chubut where most of us took the chance to wash off the road dust. It was high summer weather with just the vaguest breath of air fluttering the leaves. Patagonia has a mild climate year-round, though the very little rain it does experience turns the dust-bowl into a sea of mud, which we subsequently encountered. Along the Atlantic Coast there is a desert stretching well over 1,000 miles, except up the river canyons which provide grazing for most of the 15,000,000 sheep on the estancias, the traditional backbone of the local economy. All through lunch big gadflies droned through the air and made a great nuisance of themselves, alighting on shins, noses, and elbows in preference to other juicy areas. Shaking my head or swatting at them in mid-air did not deter them in the least; I had to let them settle and then kill them, several dozen before we moved on. As insects they were gorgeous to look at, an even, pale, olive green with eyes like shot silk, and where the light caught the eye facets just right they glimmered redly. Despite their attractive qualities they kept coming on and gave no quarter, and thousands of them were drawn to the truck by the smell of meat.

After lunch we passed more of the same terrain, only the trees and dwellings grew noticeably sparcer. The Andes were in view all day long: in the morning we drove along their slopes in loops and humps and dips, but by evening they passed into the background and dominated the horizons with shallow patches of snow nestled among the peaks all along the range. After several hours of this beautiful wild country, where few signs of man are visible beyond the straight lines of fencing and tall Lombardy poplars planted in avenues down the edges of the road, we rested an hour in mid-afternoon during our descent from the mountains in a grove of 100-foot poplar trees, pure bliss after the heat and jolting of the truck. Nearly the whole day we had driven along ungraded roads (to put it kindly) and had had to keep the windows shut and bake in the greenhouse effect or open them a little and eat dust. But now we lay on the warm dry turf and looked up at the branches with their ivy-shaped leaves dancing against the sky, and watched for an hour as the milkweed seeds and mare's-tail clouds floated by like gossamer webs.

When we went on we found ourselves in a new environment of gently rolling semi-arid scrubland at the mercy of the burning sun with seldom a tree in sight. Way off in the distance we discerned a gaucho on a white horse cantering across the wide foot-hills, but otherwise we had the whole of these badlands to ourselves, and drove and drove, startling into flight a bevy of small grey quails which were attracted to the roads to take dust baths. We also saw falcons half-hovering 20 feet above the brush and flowering shrubs as they scoured the ground for prey. Casts of small hawks were fairly common and their colouring was typically well-matched to the countryside as they had creamy buff breasts and brown and tawny chevronned back and wing feathers. Spotting an oasis of trees in this featureless void, we camped there early, and erected our tents under the spreading boughs of two large silver-barked trees with leaves like sycamores. There was a kaleidoscopic sunset lighting up the thin lenticular clouds all round, turning them through resplendent shades of crimsons, mauves, and fiery yellows. The banked up ridges of high wispy cloud kept their subtly changing magnificence for a long time, before dying into nocturnal greys. We were further south here than the tip of Africa and had yet to reach the Beagle Canal, south of Tierra del Fuego, with its fantastic long-lasting angry sunsets which endure for hours. Today we had 18 hours of clear daylight and another hour of half-light at both dawn and dusk and the further south we

CHAPTER FOURTEEN ARGENTINA (Southbound)

went the shorter still the nights became, and the smaller the arc of the sun from sun-up to sun-down, already reduced to approximately 120 degrees, quite a novelty to us who were brought up to believe that the sun rises in the east and sets in the west.

Since we were providing the only light for miles around, we drew clouds of flies of two species, both biters:- tiny weeny midges smaller than grains of salt, and narrow brown horse-flies of an evil appearance, each type in its hundreds. That was too much for me and I called it a day. Ann and I used not use our tent whenever we could avoid it, like tonight. Some hours later I was woken but I could not be sure by what. Insects were chirring softly in the nodding foliage all around, and as I lay ramrod still and straining my powers of perception I felt cautious paws very lightly walking over my feet and the weight of a small animal pressing on my shins, then my knees. I was quite pleased but in carefully lifting my head I scared it off so fast that I made out only something like a young agouti scooting away through the bushes. My guess is that it was a rock badger or hyrax which lived near this waterhole.

Bill woke us at five o'clock, an hour before the sun but even then it was twilit enough to get about with the brightest remaining stars scintillating like satellites, and Venus shining like a beacon unusually high to the northeast. About an hour after we set off we passed reed beds growing around an extensive shallow pond, and companies of grallatorial water birds moving about, representing just a handful of more than 150 species of birds in Patagonia. Set way back at the end of the marsh a ranch house snuggled under a bower of shady trees surrounded by a herd of cattle and horses at pasture. This estancia was the only settlement we saw for hundreds of miles and we took a break here, and within five minutes we were met by another expedition coming north a week behind the first one, just as Rein's group was following in our wake. It had the newest and best truck, basically the same make and chassis as ours but the interior was a foot higher and

309

four feet longer with more comfortable deeper seats and a larger three-ton trailer.

Fortuitously back along the road one of the small hawks was tearing strips of flesh off a rabbit, but it was wary of us and if approached flapped languidly off carrying a piece of its dismembered prey, only to alight on a stout fence-post and dispatch the morsel before returning to the rabbit in the midst of tufts of scattered fur. Ann and I noticed the strong perfume of pelargoniums which we traced to a type of plant with leaves like primroses and a two-foot poker of yellow blooms. Anyone who takes the opportunity to look at the desert plants of Patagonia will find a plethora of different flowers with exquisite scents. There are tall thistles, whose downy soft imperial purple flowers are laden with an elegant aroma. Most of the dry-climate flowers are quite tiny and have to be sought out, but are fascinatingly pretty. Even the bunch-grass, hard and sharp on the feet, produces lovely bushy white tufts of florets or seed-heads. Unseen grasshoppers rub their legs, sounding off like Morse code keys, and pretty butterflies, shiny black beetles with black carapaces, and coloured flies incessantly pass hither and thither.

I sat still for so long that one of the little hawks, about the size of a kestrel, flitted around me to satisfy its curiosity as to whether I was carrion and alighted on my foot for a few seconds, then looked me over before flying off with its mate to continue its quest for food. It was a really handsome bird, and I saw much more of its markings than hitherto: the leading edges of its wings were a slate grey, and its chest was mottled with dark chestnut spots in the very light fawn-grey down. Our two expeditionary groups sat around for a couple of hours over lunch, drinking wine and coffee, and interrogating each other about the trips so far to learn the best places to visit, or conversely, to avoid. An hour after we parted we arrived at a nondescript little town, José de San Martin, which had only a single bakery and one greengrocery from which

CHAPTER FOURTEEN   ARGENTINA (Southbound)

Ann and I had to select lunch at extortionate prices, and went out into the countryside nearby to eat it. The further we penetrated into Patagonia the higher became the cost of living.

For such an extreme latitude I was amazed that the sun should still beam down with extraordinary vigour, and most of us wore the minimum we could and soaked up the sunshine. All afternoon we droned on for mile after mile through a deadpan stony desert straight as an arrow along the gravel road, without so much as a rock to break the horizon or regularity of the desolation. Imperceptibly variations began to develop, and then little patches of grazing in among the scrub brush, until the ground was verdant and covered with sheep, but it did not last. Possibly we were travelling so far and so fast that we traversed enormous tracts of land without appreciating it. The landscape consisted for the most part of this unrelievedly poor pampa, not the Pampa of the geography books with high waving grass — that was far to the north of us, but a wind-blown, inhospitable, dusty wilderness. We came upon another small town, Facundo, hardly any larger than the latter, and had the good fortune to find a butcher's shop which opened for us. Mutton was the cheapest meat, but we could not believe the carcass we saw brought out of the cold store belonged to a sheep, thinking it must be a calf it was so big. The butcher called it 'capón', a new word to us all, and sliced it into cutlets with her bandsaw. The town had every kind of luxury, modern conveniences and equipment despite its utter isolation in the desert.

We still had more than five hours of continuous bumpy driving ahead of us across more of the Patagonian Plateau before we were to stop next, with the strong wind a constant factor and so much dust kicked up by the tyres that we were forced to keep the windows shut and the heat in. No matter: we again entered a new variation in the scenery, the swamplands of Lakes Musters and Colhué Huapí. Great areas provided grazing for sheep and horses and there was no defined edge to Lake Musters which was the one we could see. As we sped by a herd of horses, they broke into an incautious gallop scattering away from us fanwise through puddles up to their hocks, sending the spray flying. As the evening advanced the landscape grew more rugged yet and wind-swept domes of coloured rocks rose up around the plateau, some of them bearing the scars and runnels which typified water erosion in soft sandstone, such as we saw in the Moon Valley at La Paz, Bolivia, and on the Californian coastline south of San Francisco.

We had a set destination in mind, the petrified forest east of Colonia Sarmiento, and kept wondering whether we would arrive today and at nine p.m. we were still driving. Daylight endured another hour which took us to an unmanned road-block: at last we had arrived. A family lived here, 20 miles from their nearest neighbour, and the man came out to talk to us, explaining that he would give us a guided tour in the morning. Outside the truck the wind carried stinging sand whisking it chest-high and making it impossible to prepare food outside, so Ann and I saw to it in the cramped galley in a corner of the truck and pulled off our best culinary coup judging by the general eulogy. The high winds off the Andes kept battering us all through the night dropping the temperature to near freezing and waking us early.

By eight o'clock we were all ready to see the petrified forest. This was preceded by a visit to the museum which our guide, José Ormachea, had stocked from the site, named Bosque Petrificado José Ormachea after him since he has made maintaining it his life's work. Ormachea explained his various fossils and relics all of stone, including huge marine snail-shells perfectly preserved from millions of years ago, petrified dinosaur bones and wood. There were also ferns and leaves flawlessly outlined on flat stones both in shape and by discolouration. After this fascinating introduction to petrification we lurched back out into the high gale and made our way into the National Park where hundreds of fallen araucaria tree trunks lay scattered about. Some of the stone fossils are as much as 80,000,000 years old, though they date from distinct eras when the land was flooded and the trees petrified, so that some of the trees drowned a mere 70 millenia ago. Most were surprisingly big and intact and replicated in every detail, even to pores and phloem vessels and colour changes. Some of the trunks were 70 feet long and one I saw had a diameter of six feet at its base, and others had tunnels through the heartwood which had never petrified as they became buried in the diluvial sludge.

The great mass of what we saw had been evergreen araucarias, but at one location there were sections of a petrified palm tree which exhibited precisely the granular nature of the wood. Many trees were badly splintered and chips lay scattered by the wind in thousands all round the horizontal trunks. Ormachea explained that in wintertime the severe frosts cleave the stone along the annual rings and the hurricane force 'Roaring Forties' in winter and bone-dry summer alike and the searing heat on still days all combine to split chunks off the trees. For this reason the archaeologists who have studied the ancient logs have deliberately not exposed them in any large numbers, but in any case the ground is of great interest to them in itself. Over the eras at least a couple of hundred feet of loess and other material has been deposited, some it pebbly, slowly but completely burying the primordial forest. We could see these layers all around us in a variety of colours, standing among the pretty smoothed off hillocks and cliffs, grey, brown, black, red, yellow, and other dull shades under a duller sky studded with scudding leaden clouds, curiously fragmented and elongated by the high winds.

One tree trunk had been only partially petrified and its heartwood was still wooden, which Ormachea demonstrated by uncovering a buried portion of the tree and applying his thumbnail, nicking off splinters of preserved wood 65,000,000 years old. He had to bury it again carefully, for (as he explained) once it is exposed it will rot the same as any other wood. Since chasms have been etched into the ground by erosion, several chimneys and other beautiful formations have been left standing in distinct colours, like layer cakes; and one of these contains an unexpected natural phenomenon in the form of a 70-foot rock log jutting from both sides of a turret of clay which was once part of a wide ocean-bed composed during prehistoric times. Nearby another large mound had eroded in such a way as to show tons of leaves which had been turned to stone also, though being compressed in thick seams, individual leaves were indiscernible. What we saw was effectively a compressed compost heap with clearly coloured layers from the different geological epochs or periods of leaf-fail.

This petrified forest covers more than a square mile and it took us two or three hours to see the whole site. There are a couple of other sections of petrified forest 25 and 70 miles away further south. The guide's sheep-dog kept us company, running ahead of us whenever we began to move on again, and his friendly cat kept seeking attention by gambolling and rubbing up against the logs we were currently examining which lent a scale of reference for all of us taking photographs. In searching for the choicest souvenirs shewing the greatest detail and variegation, we walked all over the yellow pieces which tinkled like broken tiles. Ormachea led us up to a high steep ridge composed of the beautiful coloured layers, and as we walked on the friable virgin surface of wind-dried crazy paving lozenges, it crumbled crisply and softly giving an illicit pleasure, as every footprint forever spoiled the appearance of the pretty, crinkled, pushed up nodules of tinged soil. We climbed only the first 25 feet past a layer of carmine onto the black layer whence Ormachea pointed out a large lake in the distance, Colhué Huapí, where he was born.

The petrified logs were usually the colour of wood and bark, but some of them were stained in green or russet hues due to copper or iron in the original alluvial silt deposits, and when the logs were exposed to oxygen and rain once again the copper turned

CHAPTER FOURTEEN   ARGENTINA (Southbound)

the logs green as it oxidised, and as the iron rusted, so these logs turned a ruddy orange. One rusty log had a black section which was explained to us by Ormachea as carbon markings left by an Indian camp-fire over a century ago, when the four-foot thick log provided a wind-break. There are no Patagonian Indians left but we came upon one of their burial cairns. When the Indians buried their dead, they piled stones over the spot and this is just what we saw, demonstrating that the landscape has not changed in over a century. Before we returned to the truck, Ormachea bade us stop and leave behind any souvenirs we might have gleaned on our way round. We had taken up nearly the whole morning in the museum, petrified forest, and little souvenir shop afterwards so that we had no chance to buy food, and drove through the bleak estancia country until lunch time when Annette and Armin somehow managed to produce a meal out of nothing.

The wind and clouds did not fade away until late into the afternoon, and we spent the day making as much progress as possible through the eternal windswept estancia and hoping for a place of any sort to buy food. We broke our progress at El Bolsón, a little village which came after dozens of oil-wells, harbingers of civilisation and supplies. By dusk we were all very hungry and pulled into a gravel pit which had a level graded surface about 20 feet below the desert plain. Vast stretches of Patagonia are made of deep strata of porous gravel which accounts for the aridity. We did not pass a single tree all day long excepting those precious few imported and artificially nurtured in and around El Bolsón. Our bedding threatened to fly away in the cold night wind, so we held it down with big rocks.

Dressing a fraction before sunrise I suddenly saw in the toe-caps of my army boots such a reflection that I looked round at the light and exhorted Ann to wake up and look at the sky. It was that beautiful with such an intense pink picking out the jagged morning clouds that I had to show someone; but the brilliance of the dawn colours generally lasted only a minute. The Patagonian skyscapes are unique in their energetic beauty and in the extreme duration of the sunsets. There are constant banks of clouds being whisked across the sky and contorted into peculiar shapes which even appear penetratingly cold.

We made an early start and those of us who could stay awake only saw more of the wide flat expanses of grey-brown scrubland for yet another day. We churned on for tens of miles of uninspiring thorn bushes, when all of a sudden Bernie began to get quite excited about some birds! Everybody looked, but Ann and I, seeing nothing to gawk at, stuck our noses back in our books until we were told that the great attraction was 'ostriches'. We had more chances and often saw quite a few ostriches which I told them were rheas, about as big as fat turkeys with long legs and necks standing only a yard high, and possessing one more toe than the African species. They ran along in fast bounds and their ludicrous feather boa wings and tails bobbed up and down. We duly arrived at Perito Moreno, a township of only half a dozen streets each way, but prettily cared for with flowers here and there, and growing wild was a thin feathery desert plant which looks really soft and attractive to touch out on the mesa where it grows thickly. While the shoppers were gone Ann and I explored the town and noticed the menfolk wore berets and pleated baggy black leggings bloused at the ankles, somewhat akin to a combination of plus-fours and Dutch trousers, so designed to keep out the dust.

We pulled out into the countryside for lunch by the fast little River Deseado. It was a rare chance to fill our water tanks, and I saw it as a chance to get my laundry done as who could tell when we would next reach water in the desert. The sun and wind were both strong and I washed and dried everything in less than half an hour. While we were there we saw quite a lot of animals from chubby stubby lizards as broad as my hand to a graceful bounding pudu (Pudu pudu), a dark brown deer the size of a spring

CHAPTER FOURTEEN   ARGENTINA (Southbound)

lamb, which showed us a pair of nimble heels. We saw rheas and pudus quite often after this, and once I saw a herd of these tiny deer intermingled with a flock of sheep. Wild ponies were quite common, but I was quite surprised to see a seagull, or so I took it to be, in the desert hundreds of miles from either ocean. Hawks and small brown birds similar to orioles were quite plentiful, and from the cab Dee saw a puma eating a hare on the verge.

There was one major find for us: without warning, Paul slammed on the anchors, leapt down from his cab, and ran wildly off into the desert without any apparent aim, like a berserk ballet dancer persecuted by a swarm of bees. Actually he was chasing a delightful armadillo which darted about in whorls at his feet. We all took up the chase but the little mammal went to ground under a prickly bush and proceeded to flip the dusty soil up around it, rather like a crab taking refuge under sand, but it stopped when its eyes were covered and it could not have buried the greater part of its hump anyway, jammed up against the bush as it was. Everybody busily took pictures of this (to me, rather unsatisfying) scene. Hoping for a closer look at this curiosity, I took hold of its armour to heave the armadillo out, but I did not want to injure it so I was as gentle as possible. Its hide was in hinged bands and had the hardness and flexibility of tough melon rind and was surprisingly hirsuite, the hairs being long and soft. As I pulled so the little fellow scrabbled with its legs to stay down there, but it popped out just the same and took off, scurrying about at our feet which blockaded it in a ring. It was left to me to pick it up as everyone else was either scared of it or sympathetic. I stopped it with my hand on its dome a few times but this was insufficient to allow a good look at it, so I picked it up and it required a two-handed grip to restrain it from wriggling free. The top and side of its head were armoured with small solid plates, and it had a pointed, black, wiggly nose and little doll's eyes with long feminine lashes. All four legs were tough and muscular, strong out of proportion to its size, with big claws on big paddle-shaped paws just like a mole's, and as thick as a man's thumb. The whole animal weighed about five pounds and was 18 inches from end to end, its hump being about a foot long and six inches high and broad. Its lovely soft belly was a pale tangerine colour with the soft grey fur apparently completely inadequate to keep it warm. It had a curly black penis and waggled its legs furiously like an upturned turtle. In its fright the poor little armadillo made a mess all over my hands, but I bore it no ill will.

Other animals we saw as we went along were stupid jack-rabbits which tore along in front of the truck as hard as they could until it overtook them and then turned tail and zipped out of sight. At last we were lucky enough to see some large animals too, guanacos (Lama guanicoe) standing over five feet high at the shoulder. We saw a small herd of five or six individuals which had the elegance of gazelles, bright pale chestnut backs and pastel buttermilk yellow undersides, whose slimness was accentuated by their short coats. These encounters provided the highlights of our day, for there was really nothing else of interest to observed in the vast hostile tableland. Sometimes we were level with the landscape on all sides, though for a couple of hours Mount Zeballos in the Andes just pimpled the western horizon, but always there was the sweetness of sage-brush and bunch-grass in the air.

Paul had an eye for spotting gravel pits which occurred regularly since the gravel was used to build the road a foot above the general level of the desert. Once again he pulled into just such a pit to camp as much out of the wind as possible, early today since the sky was dark as thunder and a storm was bound to reach us shortly. The gale blustered around us with big drops of rain but fortunately the wind blew the storm clouds right over us in an hour and let the sun through immediately behind them which set at 10:45 with a yellowish gleam. It was one of our best social evenings in the truck, starting out with enormous Argentine

CHAPTER FOURTEEN   ARGENTINA (Southbound)

steaks for supper that everyone talks about who has been there. Paul made up another taped radio show and put on the tapes he made on previous occasions, including an expeditionary news bulletin giving us all a scandalous mention, also a selection of song requests, and 'Murder on the African Express' and other dramas by Paul Wood and Company. A flagon of wine added to: the general fervour, and we had a great time until there was only Kathy, Ann, Paul, and myself left. Kathy was quite tipsy, and often went to bed this way, pie-eyed and exaltant as a lark. It must have been the Tasmanian in her.

The morrow started out quite well. Ann and I had the cab seats and shared high expectations of reaching the beautiful Lake District of Santa Cruz Province on firm roads, and to start off the day I did the driving. Gradually the road became wetter and we left deeper ruts in the dirt, a bad augury for what was to come owing to the heavy rainfall during last night's storm. We were high enough here in the Great Central Patagonian Altiplano to see old snow by the sides of the road and in hollows under banks. The wind sighed mournfully past the windows and the clouds sailing overhead nearly filled the sky. We saw a fair selection of wildlife again throughout the morning, particularly fine horses, descendants from the draught-horses of the pioneers ambushed by the Onas and other Patagonian tribesmen in days of yore. There were lots more rabbits and hares, and flocks of sheep, which wobbled fatly as they broke their huddled ranks and cavorted to a safe distance as fast as they could. We also noticed more rheas and the proud erect guanacos which had much haughtier refined expressions than I had judged, yesterday.

Soon after Paul took over the wheel we approached an oil-drum in the road and road-signs warning of 'PELIGRO' and a diversion, but with true British grit and pertinacity (though some would not agree) Paul drove on another mile until he was stopped by a missing section of road. In turning the truck around, we encroached on the mud verge and instantly bogged down. We pushed and heaved and rocked the truck which only served to embed it even more deeply. Digging alone proved ineffective, so Paul crawled under the truck and jacked up the front axle to put sandmats under the wheels. This worked, with considerable elbow grease on our part, to extricate the truck from the sucking quagmire. Paul, wryly irrepressible, found the Simon and Garfunkel tape 'Slip Sliding Away' which became the theme tune for the day. We took the detour and it led us across country winding along a mushy track until we reached a solitary shepherd's house. The jovial barrel-chested peasant opened his gate with an expression of sage disbelief and let us through onto the pasture. His garden had the only trees we had seen for a couple of days and was set in a natural nook in the ground.

Back on the main road again Paul stole a glance at the map which nearly cost us all over lives, as he ran the truck right off the road and it tipped precariously on one side as it careered obliquely down the soft mud bank of the deep wide ditch and up the other side at just as scary an angle. With great acumen Paul wrestled the wheel and recrossed the ditch, pitching us first to one side and then the other as he regained the road. His whole countenance down to his collar flushed as red as a beetroot. We could easily have turned on our side as we left the road at 50 m.p.h.. We gradually climbed through a range of hills, and as we crested it there appeared for some time the biggest and best mirage I have ever seen, of a lake which stretched for miles across the forward horizon. We did soon reach the edge of the high part and looked down upon Lake Cardiel, a gorgeous sheet of turquoise water 25 miles long.

Shortly after we passed numbers of guanacos which are so nervous that it is impossible to approach them but we made the effort nevertheless and in doing so were sidetracked by ostriches, one of which was in great distress. The poor bird had a badly broken leg and had no hope of survival. I picked it up to examine it and found that gangrene had set in and fetched the axe to decapitate it. Bill did not wait until the wretched bird was dead before plucking a posy of its choicest plumes. I was revolted to see the headless body still attempting to get' to its feet and flapping its wings. I too brought back a lovely white quill feather, but I wished I had not pulled it and all afternoon I experienced quite a deep sensation of disgust about the whole morbid affair.

Anyhow something happened to occupy our full attention. All day long the road had been very soggy and we left deep tyre tracks behind us, and now we reached a fallen bridge which Paul attempted to by-pass. No such luck! The truck slewed down the bank and sank in a pool of mud in the ditch. This was the cue for i) much judicious swearing, ii) a loo stop, iii) lunch time, and iv) a rescue attempt with the steel sandmats which were getting pretty buckled and chewed up with so much use. Nothing daunted, Paul dug the sandmats in and we all strained to push the truck slowly out of the mud-bank. An hour later we ran out of fuel in the middle of this empty estancia territory with no chance of assistance coming to us. Providentially Paul had a few gallons of diesel in a jerrycan which gave us another 30 miles in which to find more. This problem solved pro tempore, we pressed ahead through the slurry in low gear, sometimes finding harder sections where we made up time and bounced along, and as luck would have it arrived at a permanent work-camp for the road-builders. The men here were very friendly and gave Paul several gallons of fuel at no cost and a warning that the road ahead had not been cut yet and was an almost impassable mudpan. Sure enough, ten slow miles further on the furrows we ploughed became so deep that we ground to a halt, but by now we were so used to pushing and our boots and shins were so caked in mud that we took it in our stride to manhandle the truck through the sticky clay for the third time. We struggled thus for half a mile until it finally broke free, with Manfred and Tobin riding on the trailer bumper and being swung from side to side as its wheels were too clogged to revolve. The truck kept sliding sideways alarmingly off the crown of the road and they loved it: I had felt distinctly uneasy when I was riding out the skids in the cab, but to them it was like a fair-ground entertainment. A mile down the road the truck again stuck fast in the morass, while we were still plodding along behind carrying pounds of clay stuck to each foot. When we reached it we toiled to free it for the fourth time and kept it moving until the truck's wheels had spun off their fetters of clay, splattering us, and managed to grip again. And so it went on all day long. Walking onto the gorse to clean my shoes off I made the discovery that the sweet smell which had been present for days came from the tiny sage-like leaves that were full of a wax or oil smelling strongly of eucalyptus when crushed, as did the bush's flowers also.

The main result of all this stick-in-the-mud hindrance was that we had to camp in another gravel pit instead of the beautiful Lake Argentino as planned. From the subterranean level of the quarry we could not appreciate the full splendour of the sunset. It began after nine o'clock full of colours as there was a lot of cloud moving across, and many of the amateur photographers left halfway through their supper to take pictures, but when I went to bed two hours later the north-western sky was still very strongly aglow in a Halloween yellow. We pulled out of the gravel pit in the morning into the dry brown plateau and made quick time towards the village of Tres Lagos. As we approached a remote outpost, probably an estancia, a large flock of goats darted away from the truck along a time-worn goat-track leading out of the tiny oasis onto the poor pasture. A high free-standing chimney of natural rock, part of a cliff face, threatened the oasis huddled against its base. Shortly afterwards we reached a second tiny oasis village with a similar stack formation and a stream and trees arranged exactly like the first — it was an uncanny coincidence.

CHAPTER FOURTEEN   ARGENTINA (Southbound)

In Tres Lagos our priority was to purchase fuel, but there was no diesel to be had, so Paul had to be content with kerosene which worked alright though it produced a lot of smoke. Now we reached a good dirt-road which we took to Lake Viedma, beautiful to behold, and was variously a pale turquoise or a darker shade of blue where the shadows of the clouds fell. Around the edges were arid hills of brown with spots of darkest green, almost black, where dense little bushes grew. It was quite a sizeable lake, about 50 miles in length and we drove along the edge for an hour until we reached La Leona River and we followed that for a while. There were a couple of netsmen at work waist-deep, quite likely fishing for trout or pejerrey which are common in these lakes. We reached Lake Argentino by midday, a very large and beautiful lake 60 miles long, one of the main attractions in the Parque Nacional de los Glaciares, which incorporates both the lakes and a section of the Andes as far north as Mount Fitzroy, not particularly high at 11,080 feet, but this far south the Andes are covered in glaciers, and the snow-line is very low. On the Cotopaxi Volcano at the Equator the snow-line is a little above 16,400 feet and rapidly falls from there on down the continent. At 38 degrees south the snows on the Llaima Volcano are permanent above 6,500 feet. A glacier on the side of Mount San Valentin comes all the way down to the sea, and that was 260 miles north of us, and later on along the Beagle Channel we observed the snow-line only a few hundred feet above sea-level.

Lake Argentino is surrounded at its eastern end by high brown hills and sends arms into the Andes with olive green skirts of vegetation and dimples of snow shewing a dazzling white. We had driven a long way without eating and not even the glorious colours in the scenery, most unusual milky turquoises, silver ripples, and streaks of much paler or sombre hues indicating wind disturbance or shadow could take our minds off reaching El Calafate, our next stop at the eastern end of the lake. Little by little the countryside we drove through became deeply forested and more interesting, though the road itself was simply appalling and we were riding in a fume of dust. Around us coloured plants formed a deep carpet of warm maroon red when seen as a whole, while soft fine green grasses and sphagnum mosses grew everywhere, and trees and bushes with thick foliage slowly limited our view to just the roadside. Flowers grew wild in and amongst the banks of prickly heath (Pernettya) and in clusters out in the open, and several varieties of plants grew knee-high pressing orange and red-green burs forward for the hapless sock or furry animal to rub up against and carry off.

The resemblance to Switzerland was augmented by a matching climate — hot in direct sunlight but refreshingly cool in the shade with a delightful zephyr breeze wafting down from the Andes over snow- and ice-fields. When sunbeams shone on the surface of the lake they made it glow with a filtered brilliance, not a murky turquoise any more but a livid slash of shining blue and aquamarine, with quicksilver ripples catching the light of the high midday sun. We pulled into El Calafate where the cooks lost no time buying something for lunch, and then we had a couple more hours to explore this tiny little town. Ann and I followed a river along to the lake. The banks were decked with drooping pale weeping willows, and as we emerged by the reed beds on the edge of the lake we found a charming chubby lamb, only a few months old, tethered in the shade. It had a cute young face, a soft clean regular fleece, and it was sad to consider its skin would very likely go to make a saddle blanket, as is the tradition here. We noticed a couple of gauchos or estancieros riding out over the high rushes along the shore-line. Each had a light riding saddle atop two entire sheepskins, skinside inside.

With supplies of food, water, and fuel we departed by five o'clock for the Peninsula Magellanes which is surrounded by Andean peaks up to 9,000 feet high, such as Mount Mayo to the

CHAPTER FOURTEEN ARGENTINA (Southbound)

west where huge glaciers rumble the year round. To the south of the peninsula is Lake Rico which is about five miles wide, and to the west it continues as the Channel of Icebergs (opening into Lake Argentino), and where they meet is the Ventisquero Perito Moreno, the Moreno Glacier, which seals the narrow gap in winter serving to dam Lake Rico, and bursts into icebergs with spectacular visual and sound effects during the New Year, when summer sets in warmly and evens out the levels of the lakes in a matter of hours. We arrived there a few days too late for this outstanding natural phenomenon, when the level of Lake Rico dropped nearly 20 feet. As we drove along the horribly dusty road in the shadow of the Sierra Buenos Aires, we craned our necks to see the amazing colours and beauty of the lake, when on rounding a corner, our breath was suddenly taken away by the sight of the dazzling white rough crystalline surface of the glacier still ten miles distant. We alighted for a look and could feel the ghostly cold emanating from the ice-fields, even at that distance.

Camping in the National Park is permitted in a couple of locations a few miles from the glacier and they were already chock-a-block with tents, but we pulled alongside an elderly couple, and within an hour they had disappeared. I wonder why! We erected our tents under the trees and descended to the beach where there where hundreds of silvery trunks of driftwood and acres of standing deadwood, where the winter ice had frozen their roots or the mossy marsh they stood in was too acid for them to tolerate. We fetched up about a ton of bone-dry wood, excellent for burning, and all the time we were at the camp we used it in lieu of gas for cooking, and used the steel sandmats as a hot-plate or barbecue grid. Before supper I took a load of laundry and a bucket down to the lake, but the water was not far off freezing and had icebergs floating in it. Even so I waded in and did my clothes, and decided since the fuel was free to heat up a bucket of water for myself, a luxury after weeks of dusty hair and only snatched cold water washes.

It was 11:30 by the time twilight was gone, and Ann saw the moon on the lake before she came back and told Bill and Tobin who made a big thing of capturing the scene on film. Tonight the moon was full and the air perfectly clear, with the pearly light thrown back from the snow on the mountains and from the ice and lake. The night was freezing as what little breeze there was came straight off the glacial Andes.

Waking before dawn, Ann and I determined on a brisk hike round the curve of the peninsula to see the glacier in the early morning light, thinking it but a 20-minute jaunt. We were away by seven in the gentle luminescence and not even a whisper of wind brushed our cheeks as we went down through the standing deadwood to the beach, and started to walk along the lakeside through squishy marsh, beach sand, and shingle, and over or round rocky outcrops. After a quarter of an hour we encountered Bill on a dark beach busy with his long range view-finder with which he could discern the tiniest remote details. He showed us the criss-cross crazing of the snow on the pinnacle of Cerro Mayo, and a bluish patch on the leading edge of the glacier whence a large berg had recently calved. It took us several hours walking and climbing up and down to reach the very nose of the iceberg, given that it had a convex cliff face two miles long. In that time we passed all kinds of plants: lengua trees, 'seven little beds' plants, blueberries, redberries, Calafate box-berries, (all sweet and good eating), enormous amounts of scented clover, and trees hung with white fruit from mistletoe-like mizodendron (Mizodendrum sp.) which later turn a reddish-orange. By the time we had clambered all the way round the convoluted shore-line the sun had raised the temperature from freezing to sweltering. Every time a large iceberg dropped into the lake the waves thus set up eventually travelled, the length of the 'brazo', accounting for the ripples slapping and washing the beach back at the camp-site.

There were a lot of ducks and gulls around the lake which rose up at our approach and settled on the water. As we grew closer to the massive wall of ice we began to get quite excited, appreciating for the first time just how huge it all is, dazzling, awesome, and noisy. When we reached it the lake-shore faced the glacier which climbed right up it along a quarter of a mile by means of a bridge of ice, though the main wedge of ice in the van of the glacier was about 200 feet high and the Channel of Icebergs was about 300 yards across. As it advanced imperceptibly in the vicinity of a yard per day, it emitted a constant utterance of cracks and groans and booms and the rustle of ice sliding down internal chutes and crevasses. We stood entranced, watching pieces fall off and crash into the lake with an explosive report which reached our ears seemingly too late when the iceberg had already plunged beneath the surface. Some of the best views of the glacier were through the trees which helped to put the wall of ice opposite us into some sort of perspective.

It always happened that the loudest booms made by the biggest icebergs occurred just out of sight around the corner, just like the fishermen's tales of the one that got away. The dam of ice formed betwixt the Channel of Icebergs and Lake Rico had become a tunnel which echoed with enormous crashes as the roof and sides gradually caved in, and great slabs of ice peeled off. At its extreme forward tip the glacier had pushed high onto dry land on our side: I went up to see if it contained any rock scrapings, but it was just a regular chunk of melting ice as big as a railway station. Some of the rocks that the ice rolls down the mountain are formed into very beautiful shapes and one I found was like a perfectly rounded and polished hourglass. We investigated an ice cave and there was a constant dripping inside as the hot sun was making short shrift of melting the roof. The corners of the cave were a limpid translucent cerulean I would not have believed possible of ice. Nearby a helical vent penetrated the glacier and served as a drain for all the melting ice. It went clear out of sight like a spiral staircase to the lake surface.

Making our way further round past the ice bridge we came to the Channel of Icebergs, where floes of pack-ice were being borne along by the current into Lake Argentino at its further end miles away. Ann and I explored the water's edge since we did not appreciate the danger of enormous waves washing us away or heavy blocks of ice swooshing onshore in the event of a stupendous iceberg calving. We went right down the rocky gradient and picked out little pieces of brash-ice to suck from the massed rustling chips, and just stood there awhile on the smooth rounded rock bank and admired the 'son et lumière' effects, and our exhilaration was increased by the powerful chill engulfing us from the bright wall of ice towering over 200 feet above us across the narrow neck of tinkling water. The ramped ledges we were walking on facing the glacier were smoothed into rounded shoulders, scarred with thousands of deep criss-crossing scratches made by stones rubbed and ploughed along by the glacier during the wintertime in its growing period. Climbing the cliff out of the ghostly cold the view improved the higher we went, and we continued on around the headland and saw past the point of the glacier that the leading edge reached the shore about a mile or more back, shedding icebergs along its length, but the roar and boom of these sounded muffled like distant thunder.

We met the 'guardeparque', the park ranger, dressed up in a khaki shirt and jodhpurs, high riding boots and a képi, talking to a couple of Porteños (natives of Buenos Aires), and we fell into a discussion with them, and looked way back along the top of the glacier seeking its origins, but it curled around a mountain in rugged formations of tip-tilted blocks of ice the size of office buildings. Vaguely a channel could be made out along the

CHAPTER FOURTEEN ARGENTINA (Southbound)

central portion where the movement was not as slow. The guardeparque declared that the Moreno Glacier is unique inasmuch as it descends further annually. It grows and recedes according to the seasons, so that in the blazing summer heat from January to April the front breaks up faster than it advances. One of the tourists, teachers both, lent us her binoculars and the beauty of the ice caves and tunnels brought into close-up capped everything we had previously seen. The recesses of the caverns revealed their secrets; the deep sapphire was incredible. We could see far into the crevices between the vast slabs, and as they widened so falls of crushed ice would fill them up. The most inspirational thing about the glacier was this strong inkiness, a fresh pale electric blue on the outside where frosting (due to condensation) on the surface served to lighten the blue even more, deepening to a strong cobalt blue at the back of the deepest fissures in the ice face where the light from above, slanting through the glacier, always permitted the deepest clefts to appear blue. As the powerful stresses and strains were transmitted through the ice, so it split into enormous upright slabs as it travelled down the mountain, anything greater than 15 feet thick and the height of the glacier. The fissures were quite obvious and the frozen monoliths of monumental proportions were surmounted by jagged cathedralic spires tipped on their sides. Often the panels would lean over so that if one should fall others would follow it like a row of dominoes.

    The long clamber round the inlets and coves and now the climb up the hill on empty stomachs prompted us to think of making our way back. At the top of the hill the view was down over the approaching glacier, a brilliant dazzling white under the noonday sun, never forgetting the high snow-fields and mountain-caps all round and the gorgeous lake with its changing shades of turquoise and aquamarine, and the dark verdancy of the forested slopes along the facing shore with an occasional dead bleached tree trunk still standing to give us an idea of the scale of all we surveyed. At the crest of the hill we found Maria, Gaby, Annette, and Bernie asleep on a grassy bank, for they had done the shore-line walk a little ahead of us and the beating sun was very soporific. Ann and I walked the five miles back to camp along the road, almost as beautiful in itself set amid shady woods, lakes, and mountain streams, and the constant sound of birdsong, suddenly magnified by a squawking flight of Austral parakeets passing through, but we could not help stealing glances back over our shoulders at the glacier. Almost home, we took a short cut across the tip of the last headland, where we met Frank making his way along with a determined air. We advised him the road was an hour shorter, and soon after we reached the camp-site laden with armsful of firewood.

    The truck was gone and in it our breakfast. Paul did not return till evening, and most of us enjoyed the holiday weather recumbent with a book or in conversation by the camp-fire. When Paul reappeared, he had a whole sheep on board and prepared to spit-roast it on a long branch rotating on a couple of crotched stakes. He skewered the lamb on the pole, then nailed it in position through its spine and wired its legs out straight fore and aft, and we took turns at keeping it revolving over the flames. From time to time Paul basted it all over with liberal applications of a greasy sage and onion sauce, while our biggest potatoes were put into the coals to bake. We had another foray for logs, and meanwhile the ranger came by on a high black horse with ugly oriental slit eyes and a pronounced Roman nose. He stopped to socialise and let Maria mount his horse which was really very docile despite its ferocious looks. We eventually had our lamb at midnight, but it was well worth the wait, a capacious feast for everyone, especially those who were prepared to get a little greasy with the bones. To dismember the carcass Paul had to apply the axe, and it was the biggest meal we had had, all seated somewhere in the flickering firelight to see what we were eating.

CHAPTER FOURTEEN   ARGENTINA (Southbound)

The next morning I think the whole camp had a lie in, sleeping off the banquet. Ann decided to spend the day at the glacier, but I took the opportunity to repair our tent, damaged in the Roaring Forties, and brought her lunch out to her in due course. There was not a hint of air stirring and once again the sun raised the drowsy camp-site to glass-house temperatures. Down at the lake I took a large brown trout by hand, which I gutted and scaled on the spot, skewered it, and set to cook in the smoke of the camp-fire for my breakfast. After lunch a number of others went by truck to the glacier, but I set off on foot and walked the road in two hours. It was most enjoyable apart from the road's being so deep in loose dry clay that passing cars raised a pall of choking dust. Along my way I came upon a large vole with a coat like black velvet, and it probably lived in a burrow along a stream nearby. As I arrived at the glacier I met the ranger riding the other way on his rounds, and Rolf and the others who directed me down the cliff to where Ann was sitting, right opposite the base of a very active section of the glacier.

Even before I found Ann I realised that a great deal of ice had fallen off as the Channel of Icebergs was jammed by huge grounded icebergs and all the ice-floes to have formed since had piled up behind them. Furthermore the roof of the ice tunnel had collapsed leaving just one enormous precarious arch, while to the left of it the large ice cavern was much larger than yesterday, and to the right a massive area, 200 feet high and broad, was as blue as yesterday's ice cave where an iceberg had just split off. Ann and I talked over the whole amazing phenomenon we bore witness to. The morning sun shines on the frosted ice and so dazzles with a hoary whiteness; but by mid-afternoon the heat of the sun and the glacier's own motion combine to make a number of pieces fall off, added to which the sun no longer shines on the front of the glacier but backlights it, and contributes to the unreal blueness, layered like rock formations so that clean deep hyacinth layers are interleaved with paler shades. The layers represent frozen rain and snowfalls, and look like stripey blue tooth-paste. Sometimes a layer of brown shews where at some stage the glacier scraped along the floor of the valley. The hyalescence of the turquoises and greens and browns in the pack-ice, lake water, and icebergs was amazing to behold and totally unexpected, and whenever the lake waters were stilled there were gently riffled reflections of the glacier.

Ann and I watched two main theatres of events; one was the ice arches which looked as though they should collapse at any moment, and the other was a system of deep rents and cracks which penetrated the tip of the glacier with a pattern of rhomboid shapes. All afternoon from both these locations there came a series of loud snaps and cracks like sporadic gunfire, and crunches and thunder, more so than from any other areas, but I kept scanning the whole face as bits fell off anywhere without warning, and plummeted into the lake with explosive reports, each kicking up a big splash with a plume which in turn set up a wash lifting up and down all the chunks of pack-ice, and depositing some on the natural rock ramp where Ann and I stood yesterday sucking icicles. Today hunks of ice up to five feet thick rested on that ledge, dripping prettily in the warm sunlight. When the water is set in up and down motion all the ice-floes including the massive icebergs wash backwards and forwards, and a crescendo of ice crashing and knocking against ice is matched by the glinting of sections of ice as they roll around catching the sunlight like stage jewellery, and take ages to settle down again in the sparkling aquamarine water.

Over to the right the Channel of Icebergs was bright with milky colours, and whence we watched we could see straight into the diamond shapes of the chasms taking hours to widen mere inches, and we were spellbound by the highlighting of the ice's natural blueness, which the sunlight penetrates as though it were a stained glass window. As the sun sank lower and lower onto the Andes the deep rifts in the glacier grew a darker amethyst blue, almost indigo or dense violet at the furthest recesses where the internal showers of crushed ice could just be perceived. The tension was mounting and although some splendid slabs of ice fell and all afternoon there was some activity, we sensed that something immense was in the offing. We dallied until eight o'clock and were amply rewarded. The great cavern and the archway of tens of thousands of tons of ice both calved some splendid icebergs but better by far was the series of icebergs which fell along the bottom of the rhomboid rifts which had been deeply undercut by the melting influence of the lake water. These were as much as 50 feet high and caused massive disturbances in amongst the pack-ice, some of which repeatedly ducked under and resurfaced lifting others on top of them. Once the underlying ice had gone, the whole upper edge of this cliff of ice yielded, little bits at first, then a cyclopean iceberg plummeted into the lake with a cataclysmic crash of startling loudness. It was 200 feet high by 300 wide, and about 3,000 tons in weight, and sent needles of ice and spray and a plume of water 100 yards up into the air, and set up wildly undulating concentric tidal waves. After the plume fell its thick mist drifted across on the faint breeze and wet us on the other side of the strait. The waves made all the pack-ice crunch and thrash around in the water; the biggest icebergs wallowed about like stiff dead whales, surfacing under lesser blocks of ice and bobbing down again, and more floes were stranded on the ledges below us where the hot rock dramatically turned the draining water to vapour.

Several times throughout the afternoon there had been sudden local disturbances in the crowded pack-ice, but it took a few seconds to locate the precise origins of the sounds. It was either an iceberg splitting or else rolling over in slow motion. The underside of an iceberg is quite bizarre; it is all clear, knobbly, wet ice and not even white but the colour of the impurities it contains, an earthy brown, or chlorophyl green, or bluish with fine clay silt.

At last we dragged ourselves away and set off back to camp well-pleased with our decision to outstay the departure of the truck. The weather was so comfortable and balmy, and the scenery so fertile and pleasant, that all seemed right with the world. Without warning a Magellanic woodpecker (Campephilus magellanicus) much more magnificent than the Chilean flicker, flashed out of the woods ahead of us, over our heads with a shrill squawk, and diving through foliage like a fire-arrow it alighted on the upright trunk of a hollow dead tree, which it proceeded to explore with staccato bursts of tapping here and there, interspersed with time enough to put its brilliant yellow eye to the holes. It was a resplendent bird with a scarlet head and crest, a 20-inch wingspan, a long yellow bill, bright button black eyes, and a fawn ruff. Its back was walnut brown and its breast an off-white, altogether an uplifting sight for me. A few minutes later Ann pointed out a couple of predatory birds stalking along on strong talons. They were a breeding pair of fish eagles, magnificent birds as big as roosters, with a haughty aquiline stare and cumbersome gait. As we approached they flapped resignedly out of our path, and one settled on a dead tree stump about 12 feet high nearby. Gingerly Ann went closer to it and the wary eagle stooped in the typical takeoff position a few times before soaring away to join its mate above the darkling lake in the shadow of the Andes, for the sun was setting now, and as we walked we discussed the great length of our shadows stretching out of sight ahead of us and other topics all the way back to the camp-site.

Supper was over, but ours was left — enormous T-bone steaks, one of the products for which the Argentine has such a reputation of excellence. We stayed around the camp-fire long after the gathering gloom of night, which was not fully dark till 11:15 and even then the snow-fields shed their wan ghostly illumination. For

CHAPTER FOURTEEN   ARGENTINA (Southbound)

the whole of our stay here the truck became a cold remote place, and stayed empty and virtually ignored while for the rest of the trip it was the very hub of vitality and action.

We made a late start next day, and gathered several cords of firewood which were loaded on the truck and we made El Calafate our first destination to shop ahead. Along the way I noticed several large hunting birds, possibly kites, standing on fence-posts, and despite the posts being only five feet high, they were the highest vantage points in the deadpan estancia landscape where only low-lying prickly scrub, coarse grasses, and reddish plants provided a meagre food supply for the grazing sheep. At Calafate Ann and I went shopping with Gaby and Chantal, and prepared an early lunch there by a stream before returning once again to the utter barrenness of the sheeplands, which we sped through in good time on hard dirt-roads. The hawks were visible all day, as for them this is a land of rich pickings, overflowing with insects, rabbits, and other small animals and birds in the golden plateaux and low hills. Apart from sheep, we spotted more families of rheas and loose horses, wild and free, and distant guanacos, great shaggy-coated males with thick necks as big as ponies, and delicate little baby ones. Guanacos are not deer at all, but are camelids just like their cousins, the vicuñas, llamas, and alpacas further north the length of the Andes. The whole day passed without any variation in the countryside — just miles of fencing-wire strung along posts under a searing sun, and we had to endure the heat in preference to the dust brought in with even the slightest ventilation.

We stopped short of Río Gallegos for fear of arousing police curiosity and turned back to camp in a gravel pit out of the wind. The police in Argentina and in particular the rural locations are wont to carrying out spot checks on campers in the middle of the night, fining them and moving them on quite brusquely on pain of arrest. Camping is still somewhat of a novelty and lacks the respectability of hotel accommodation, and thus is officially controlled by the unsympathetic police, and is permitted only at garages which are often equipped with showers for the purpose, a development of catering to the needs of truck-drivers. I decided it was warm enough to sleep out again as it seemed inconceivable it would rain. After supper the sunset provided a major and lasting spectacle. In part the streaming clouds seemed to radiate right out of the sun, and partly the colour changes themselves were so great, and contained every tone from cadmium to gold to copper to bronze to red lead. A number of us rushed up the ramp and watched it alter behind a silhouette of wooden fence-posts stabbing the sky. As usual the wind died to nothing during the night and there was no dew.

CHAPTER FIFTEEN

FUEGIAN PATAGONIA

Ownership of the 'Isla Grande Tierra del Fuego' is split between Chile and Argentina, and so are all the islands in the archipelago, though Chile retains the lion's share. It is a very important region on account of the oil and gas discoveries, but in addition it contains virtually unspoilt scenery simply teeming with wildlife; some I have mentioned, amongst which musk-rats and beaver have been introduced. There is a great variety of fauna found only here such as the Antarctic wild goose, or quequén, but the northern half of Tierra del Fuego is rolling prairie, giving way to lakes, rivers, and forests in the south and west where the Andean Range gradually drops away into the Drake Strait beyond Cape Horn. The land was once populated by the Ona, Haush, and Yahgan Indians: and Ushuaia is Yahgan for 'inlet from the east'. There is no real summer;

the winter weather is rarely severe and the sheep are left out year round. Outside the only three small towns, there are a few villages, estancias, oil-wells, and Armed Services outposts, and sometimes no traffic may pass for days on the few roads.

Over breakfast Paul explained his intention to attempt four border crossings and the Straits of Magellan in one day. Ann and I shared the cab with Paul, after winning a disagreement with Sandra who sat up front most days. We drove the few miles to Río Gallegos which is a windswept frontier town with all low buildings set in a perfectly rectangular grid of streets.

The deep-water port was the essential raison d'être for this provincial capital, as it provided an outlet for the wool trade and the crude oil, despite spring tides higher than 50 feet. We stopped there a few hours to take on sufficient provisions to cross Tierra del Fuego. This meant that Ann and I had to eke out 150,000 pesos ($73) for today's food. To put this in perspective, a cup of coffee cost four dollars, and in Chile the expedition was costing up to 1,000,000 pesos per day! We clearly could not buy our usual quantity but did get a bargain in two enormous robalos, large ocean fish like ling.

At the first border-post, Monte Aymond, the wind blew fiercely and we watched the butterflies fighting a losing battle to stay still; and the custom-shed, although only a single storey high, had need of tensioned steel guys to hold the roof on. As counterweights on all the booms at the border barriers, old worn out drill heads were used. I took a close look at one of them to see just how the drills work, and found three rotating multifaceted drill bits arranged at such an angle on the head as to be driven independently. Returning to Chilean soil we had a sense of déjà vu since the houses were brightly painted in fresh gay colours, with contrasts between the roofs and walls. Between the border outposts there was a substantial no man's land, an hour's drive. Beyond the first national boundary we had to cross a narrow strip of Chile to reach the Straits of Magellan at Monte Aymond where we tagged onto the queues of trucks and private saloons in line for the ferry.

There was nothing particular to see or do for several hours: a lighthouse and café provided the focal points. The mainland just comes gently down to the South Atlantic Ocean, and at this point the Straits of Magellan are only about eight miles across and are plied at high tide by a couple of W.W.II ex-British tank-landing craft which serve as ferries. They were bright blue with orange below the Plimsoll line, and the few rooms occupied the narrow sides of the craft on two decks. When we arrived a pilot boat was at anchor on our side but a big tanker (one of only 500 ships per year to steam by) came slowly along with the current, and quick as a flash the pilot was gone to escort the tanker out into the Atlantic. At ten p.m. Paul gave Ann and me the command to prepare supper, and just when we were ready to serve it out, we had to secure everything while Paul drove onto the ferry, so amid all the lurching we ate on the truck. I wonder if that qualifies us as seacooks. The Chileans certainly run an efficient ferry service with the minimum of dilatory bureaucracy. After the meal nearly all of us went up to the gunwales and we looked over the side where a school of black and white Commerson's dolphins were keeping abreast of us, swimming hard in the wash with their black dorsal fins breaking the surface from time to time. After watching a nondescript sunset it grew too cold to stay out and most of us returned to the truck. Apparently we had a very smooth crossing as Rein had led us to expect a storm-tossed passage with 30-foot waves sending spray over the whole ship, but as it was we disembarked in the black of night and suffered a puncture in the process and were all freezing cold. Paul could not take us anywhere, so we advanced up the beach and stopped for the night where we were, in a rubbish tip. I brewed up a warming pot of tea and waited for the others to drift off to bed so that I could sleep in the truck, the cooks' privilege. Ann strolled down to the waterfront and looking south saw coloured flashes like lightning shoot into the sky, and wondered if she was witnessing a southern counterpart to the Aurora Borealis; but in fact she saw the light of massive flare-offs at the oilfields nearby.

The black pudding we served for breakfast must have had some magical effect on Paul: we knew he liked it, but he drove like a maniac all day and we were bounced and thrown about in the back on bumpy dirt roads. We started the day on the wrong foot as we left Ann behind, who had set off ahead of us on foot — the wrong way — and we lost a good hour searching for her. All morning the view was of just the same bleak, flat, windy territory as on mainland Argentina, with a plethora of untended sheep. Whenever two vehicles pass, the drivers exchange what Ann called the 'Argentinian salute'. Palms are pressed onto the windscreens, but this is a prophylactic measure to prevent flying gravel from shattering the glass. It seemed amazing that cars should be driven without wire screens, which were not so much an extra, more a basic requirement.

We were held up a long time at the San Sebastian border crossing back into Argentine territory, but to our delight and amazement a baby guanaco walked out from behind the custom-shed, only 20 paces from us. I caught sight of it first and hushed the others who oohed and aahed at the infant not much beyond the stage of learning to walk, for it was still a fraction awkward and ungainly, yet poised and graceful with big, soft, dewy, doe's eyes and long lashes. Its fleece was a silky soft, pale chestnut brown on its back, and oyster grey underneath, and its legs were delicate wands with knobbly joints. It had come to drink and voices from the truck made it glance up at us a couple of times, and as sedately as it arrived it retreated from sight. Determined not to allow such a unique opportunity to slip helplessly away from me, I tiptoed around the building, aware of the group's stern disapproval of my having stepped outside the truck camera in hand at a custom-house, but by now I was accustomed to their disapproval of my initiative.

The baby animal allowed me to approach it and I was amazed by its very short fuzzy fleece, softer than kitten fur to the touch. It was absolutely tame and came towards me and gave me a kiss on the throat, and I realised that it had not yet got over weaning and was trying to suckle from me with soft, begging, baby grunts. I supposed its mother to be dead, for there was no sign of her. Enchanted and beaming from ear to ear I cradled it in my arms, all long legs and very warm, and I gently brought it round to the truck for the others to see while it emitted affectionate sounds. It was almost four feet tall but it only weighed half a stone, and as I set it down again it relaxed completely and lay down on its side. The others were out of the truck in a trice and photographing for all they were worth. It was a natural poser and stood or sat and necked with anyone, but Maria could not bear to leave it and stayed with it until the truck left half an hour later, laughing at its antics as it nuzzled her hair and jumper.

Several times during the day we saw estancieros, usually riding alone, with double sheepskins under their saddles (if they had one). All the usual animals were here also, plus cattle, especially where the terrain was wetter and greener. Ordinary cattle cannot cope with the climate down here for, though the seasonal extremes of temperatures are comparable to those in New York, in winter the wilderness is embattled by lashing gales and the herds are rounded up and yarded in cattle-pens at the estancias. The cattle we saw were a Charolais-cross, huge deep-chested beasts with lots of meat. We passed some huge flocks being, kept on the move by drovers with the aid of sheep-dogs reacting to whistled commands. One of these flocks was so vast that it took us a quarter of an hour to drive through it and the sheep looked odd and dirty as they had just been shorn. Once we spotted a proud adult guanaco with a shaggy coat, and hosts more species of birds, the most fascinating of these being arctic terns, generally flying in pairs. They travel halfway round the world to feed here and seemed quite at home in the scrublands though such birds normally inhabit wet marshy areas and estuarine mud-banks. According to the map there are quite a number of ponds in the vicinity since drainage is poor on this flat plain, and we were basically following the Atlantic Coast, out of sight for most of the time. We stopped in the unrelenting heat of the wastelands at lunch time, and to our misfortune, were preyed upon by a swarm of horse-flies with viridescent eyes, which pestered and bit us all. Before we camped we passed the port of Rio Grande, a cold windy town with an oil refinery and a Salesian Mission, but it marked a turning point in the terrain. The barren plain turned into more interesting contoured hills with forestation, mainly of different kinds of beech, and pools while we drove on towards Viamonte along the coast. The trees were amazingly twisted and contorted, some more dead than alive and none taller than any other as though some rough hand had crudely broken all the branches at a height of 20 feet. Vast quantities of smashed and broken timber lay in the forest but there was plenty of new growth, and young saplings grew in profusion and the land was verdant once again. We camped within 100 yards of the shore but could neither hear nor see the surf, as a dense sea mist, distinctly hoar and drizzly, blanked out our view and soaked the fly-sheets.

We woke to a still dull morning,, and the mist had lifted, allowing us to look over the Argentine Sea for what it was worth, an expanse of calm grey. We drove through thickening forest in increasingly mountainous countryside with occasionally enough of a gap, as at the Garibaldi Pass, to enjoy the panorama of waterways and forest spread out below us. Once more there were plenty of mosses, scurvy-grasses, and plants growing thickly enough to turn patches into natural flower beds in shades of apricot, russet, and lime with hosts of little flowers so miraculously intricate and miniature that it was easy to completely overlook them. The scenery was utterly different from anything else we had seen, especially as half the trees remaining alive were bent over at 45 degrees, i.e. perpendicular to the mountainsides, and all were snapped off short at the same height. We descended through the forest towards the Fagnano Mission at the eastern extremity of the long thin lake of the same name. There was a luxury hotel here, Hostería El Kaiken, where Paul pulled up to repair a puncture, but even a small cappuccino here cost a couple of dollars. Ann made some inquiries and discovered that the salaried class in Argentina earn about $50,000 per annum and up to double that in the remote regions such as Tierra del Fuego, where prices reflect the high cost of transporting absolutely everything the thousands of miles.

From the Kaiken Hotel we advanced only a couple of miles to a clearing in the forest where huge trees had been pushed over like so many ninepins when construction teams had quarried gravel to build the road. New trees were growing through them all round the edges of the pit. It was perfect picnicking weather, but long after we were ready to move on we were still waiting for the coffee to filter by which time it was tepid as well as insufficient. This may seem trivial, but in the context of our miniature social world being split into basically English and German camps it became a big social issue as somebody had to go without every time. Everybody but me used a messy archaic method which invariably took half an hour while the coffee filtered. My method completely side-stepped the problem as it involved making coffee as though it were tea, resulting in instant service, and freed the kettle for more coffee straight away. On the long hauls over the dusty plateaux since Lake Nahuel Huapí goodwill had distinctly flagged. The relative absence of anything particularly exciting to occupy our minds had affected our morale and social behaviour. The most obvious manifestation was the schism into language groups with the German-speaking girls forming a tight clique and assuming the right of authority all round, which was a great shame because the situation proved irreversible and progressive.

After lunch the curious forest grew thicker and the Andes thrust peaks up to 7,720 feet, the height of Mount Italia; in fact this one is in Chilean Fuegia which we did not enter. We drove by pockets of snow stuck up high, and passed whole zones where the stunted tilted trees had died, and the overall effect simulates the Oregon Vortex where everything grows at an angle. Lake Fagnano is connected to the Straits of Magellan via the Almirantazgo Strait and Useless Bay, and we could judge the snow-line to be less than 1,000 feet up. The road wound along the lakeside for many miles and passed a region of brown and orange mud patches rising above the general level of a bog which drained into the Olivia River. This ran a milky emerald green through such pretty open woodland that a number of parties were camped out under the trees along its turfed banks. Even here were eight-inch long beards of sphagnum mosses and fungi growing on the trees like bespoke fur coats, or thriving on the bogs in bold viridescence, sallow yellows, and rust reds. Pallid lichens and fungi were spread everywhere. One fungus (Cyttaria darwinii) was dried and eaten like bread by the Indians who merely had to pick the spongy orange puff balls off the beech trees. For the first time we noticed a ground cover of dockweeds.

At this point we were within nine miles of Ushuaia, the most southerly town on Earth, and travelling the mountain road above the lake (also known as Lake Kami) we were brought to a halt by a major landslide which revealed that the soil level is up to ten feet thick, and I knew the bogs to be virtually unfathomable in places. That amazed me, since the country is at the mercy of terrible weather for most of the year and ought by rights to have been subjected to high levels of erosion. For almost an hour we waited on Mount Olivia while a team of navvies and four bulldozers cleared a path for us. Within a few minutes we saw the outskirts of Ushuaia, home to 6,000 inhabitants, with its painted iron roofs and naval and military barracks and factories forming a neat little port nestled along the shore up a creek off the Beagle Channel, a natural haven of calm jade waters and brilliant warm sunshine under the brow of the cuspidate Martial Mountain, surrounded by dense woods and green rivers and waterfalls, wildlife sanctuaries, snow-covered mountains and impressive vistas in every direction. Our expedition had clocked up 12,000 road miles since leaving Barranquina in Colombia, and there were another 5,000 ahead of us to Rio de Janeiro in Brazil.

Years later I travelled in Antarctica, but here it gave me a curious feeling for it was just the same as Quebec Province in the summertime, full of autumnal colours and not at all the bitterly cold, blustery and tempestuous place of sailors' yarns. We camped early at Río Pipo, three miles east of Ushuaia on a lumpy heath by the fast little river Pipo, once again with water of a milky lime green. The heath was covered in tiny wild flowers of many charming shapes, and the commonest variety was cornflower blue. Of course there were still the plants with salmon red burs with long hooks and many prickly bushes, but also heaps of firewood just lying about, so we cooked on grills. Such a lot of dust was raised by passing vehicles on the camp road that it gave rise to whimsical lighting effects with bold bars of sunlight shafting through the branches where three boys were playing with a football and only their silhouettes were visible against the swirling airborne dust.

Ann was forever interested in the ways of life of the people we met throughout the expedition, and here she came back with the information that their warm season only lasts about four months, and that on their summer solstice, December 22nd, the sun is up for more than 20 hours and sets later than midnight, and by contrast rises at ten a.m. on the winter solstice when it shines a mere six and a half hours. It was midnight by the time we retired and a very heavy dew had come down on everything, but Ann and I had opted to do without a tent preferring to enjoy the starlight and wake up to the early glimmer of dawn and watch the great variety of birds already up and about. We rose well before the others to go bathing in the freezing rushing River Pipo and wash the cloying dust from our clothes. From the moment the sun peeped between the snowy cusps to the north-east it was immediately warming, and raised a column of steam off our bedding. We struck camp and returned to Ushuaia for most of the day.

We all went our separate ways, sight-seeing and shopping. There were here extremely good air-letter forms with five or six photographs grouped according to subjects, shewing the amazing midnight sun, penguins in Antarctica, and crisp wintry scenes. The postcards were just as good, and reflected the natural bounty of the area full of waterfalls, great opportunities for anglers, trappers, and ornithologists, or just holidaymakers who have come to enjoy the unspoiled pioneer mountain scenery or do some skiing. The naval barracks was originally built as a penitentiary and attracts the attention of knowing Porteños. Altogether tourists Outnumber the locals by five to one, and lodgings in Ushuaia reflected this in their tariffs; a basic room cost $60 for a night. One of the local attractions is centolla, or king crab, on the menu in most of the few restaurants. King crabs' legs routinely grow up to six feet long, and their first pair of legs can grow considerably larger than that.

It was another broiling day, leastaways it was so inside the truck, though the forecast temperature was 77 degrees Fahrenheit in the shade and ten degrees hotter in direct sunlight, which is about the extreme limit for Ushuaia. I went down by the shore-line and looked at the ships, including camouflaged warships, fishing smacks, and yachts in from faraway ports. Paul arranged for us to see some tourist films on Patagonia and Antarctica, unexpectedly some of the loveliest scenery on Earth, with such grandeur and majesty, stocks of animals, and skies which are unmatched in my experience. They also showed the best sequences of icebergs calving from the Perito Moreno Glacier, including the bursting of the ice dam formed by the glacier during its winter advance and the total collapse of the subsequent ice tunnel. Trout fishing also provides a big attraction, and anglers expect to reel in ten-pounders here in the lakes and particularly in the River Grande. Ushuaia is expanding rapidly, and a lot of colourful stylish houses were being built in timber with A-frame roofs and long overhanging eaves. A municipal attitude of embellishment has resulted in flower beds crowded with a riot of colours, and banks of tall black and orange poppies as big as sugar bowls, and dainty marigolds, buttercups, and other garden flowers. The police station set the best example.

Towards the end of our stay Ann and I went for a stroll along the promenade and fell into conversation with a fascinating man from Allen near Lake Nahuel Huapí who was drinking yerba mate the traditional gaucho way through a bombilla of ornately worked silver from a small enamel pot. He explained to us that gauchos do not have the opportunity to dismount and brew up, so each carries the drink on him in a sealed insulated pot (or gourd or horn) often of precious metal, even gold. Yerba mate is made very strong with a lot of sugar and no milk, and one pot may be passed around for each man to sip from through his own bombilla. A bombilla is a fancy decorated straw about eight inches long in any durable material, and the bottom tip is swelled out into a runcible bulb to strain out the leaves, and the bulb is also vaguely spoon-shaped to scoop the yerba mate leaves into the pot to start with. These pots and bombillas are often treasured possessions, even family heirlooms among the herdsmen from Tierra del Fuego to Brazil, and are worn on a cord around the neck. The man was delighted to talk volubly to us because we were English and made us a gift of a packet of yerba mate.

When we left him to rejoin the others we spotted some blackish Magellanic oystercatchers running in the surf which feed on razor-shell clams by the millions. Patagonia and especially Fuegian Patagonia is to naturalists an ideal resort for so many flora and fauna are found there, or (in the case of birds) migrate there, and many of them are very oddly marked or shaped or specialised. We jolted even further south-west past Mount Susana to a National Park at Lapataia on the shore of Lake Roca, an outstanding beauty-spot. The lake forms a basin surrounded by deciduous forest 100 feet high sheltered by cliffs and mountains all round. We entered a camp-ground with laundry facilities and hot showers, a rarity and a luxury in Latin America. Before we had parked we were aware of great numbers of rabbits and large birds of prey, called chimangos, which were everywhere and exceedingly noisy, uttering piercing calls like the wail of a new-born baby in staccato sobs, most of all during the dusk and dawn choruses. The hawks were the size of large barn owls and were a rich golden sapwood colour with buff undersides and long yellow hooked beaks. They were not afraid of us, and following one, I found its nest full of chirping young.

A high cliff rose up from the northern edge of the woods, 100 yards from us, while to the south was Lake Roca with calm water such a deceptively pale shade of turquoise as to be almost white, yet when I went right up to it the lake water was perfectly clear right down to the gravel bed, and the longer view was extremely picturesque of an extended stretch of water tossing around petals of sunlight, with forested foot-hills to either side, while beyond the far end of the lake lay high jagged Andean peaks under a mantle of snow. The woods were fairly open and the ground cover was of soft grasses and expanses of wide-eyed daisies, so profuse they looked like snow. Tiny crisp ferns added their delicate fiddle-heads to the plush carpet of surface vegetation and everywhere we looked massive tree trunks lay drying or rotting on the ground, and because the forest is so cold bacteria do not thrive and thousands of fallen trees make it a very untidy forest indeed while they are taking centuries to decompose. All the other forms of life of this region were to be found here: shrouds and tatters of Spanish moss fluttered soft as goats' beards, and parasitic fungi, tangles of Osnia, and other lichens and mosses decorated moist bark in colours gentle to the eye, oranges and whites and soft greens. The whole place smelled moistly of fertile dark leaf litter and wood-mould. There were so many good spots to set up our tents that for a change we all had privacy. Under the threat of grey clouds Ann and I compromised and set up just a fly-sheet, while we waited for the cooks to spit-roast the lamb. The rain did not tarry long and a tarpaulin had to be erected to keep the blaze going. Regardless of whether we took shelter under the fire tarpaulin, in our tents, or in the truck, the loud patter of raindrops on taut canvas drowned out other sounds and kept up all night, only diminishing very slowly.

When I awoke no-one else was astir but there was plenty of noise. The birds were all twittering and above all the chimangos were in good voice, screeching fit to bust. I just lay there taking it all in, looking at the park through the triangular entrance of our tent. The rabbits were up and about and the raindrops still softly drumming on the fly-sheet. The weather never really cleared and our strings of damp laundry hung listlessly. Visiting the shower block I came away without my hat before I realised it had been stolen in the few minutes my clothes had not been watched. It was a fine beaver fur felt stetson which I had worn all over the world and I really missed it. It was not its great expense which upset me, as I had lost nearly a third of my clothes and possessions to thieves along the way, but rather it had been part of my image. Theft is considered fair play by nearly all Latinos, not just the poor ones; to afford to reach this camp-ground the hat-thief must have been well-to-do. Apart from this morale-damper the day was a gloomy one with a totally occluded sky and a distinct nip in the air.

Another lamb was spitted and prepared for roasting. Frank invited me to join him in a walk, waxing enthusiastic about the chimangos, beavers, marine otters, and varied waterfowl, and complaining about the impossibility of such a pretty park existing in America where it would soon be 'developed', the wildlife depopulated, dispersed, and destroyed, and pollution and noisy people would replace the natural richness and variety of unique flora and fauna in tranquil harmony. Frank had lived his whole life in New York, and displayed a sense of wonder and great caring for Nature. We walked around the edge of Lake Roca whither it drained into a wide stream, on whose opposite bank the scenery was totally undisturbed by Man. Badelyngs of widgeon and red shoveller duck paddled hither and thither, the ducklings in line behind their mothers, and gradually working its way upstream in a tumbling brook was a male torrent duck (Merganetta armata) with an eye-catching black and white pinstripe head and a luminous crimson bill. I wondered how it managed to stay upright: after facing upstream for a few seconds it would tip up its stiff tapered tail and disappear, reappearing several yards further up. It was able to run on water at a sprint, and only seemed to rest from its day-long search for stonefly larvae to catch some sleep on a sun-warmed boulder. Wood martins and fat finches, the latter with bilious yellow bodies and chocolate wings, resplendent despite the poor light, flitted constantly over the ripples ,and skimmed at breakneck speed around the berry bushes, holly, and snowberries, which were further embellished by a parasitic plant with coppery orange leaves. There were plenty of wild flowers, especially daises and primroses. There were innumerate others unknown to me and ornamental sedges and grasses with curled fans of feathery fronds like heraldic fleur-de-lis. Even the dead tree stumps added their own charm, and some very tall marsh flowers like moon daises with multiple heads were growing scattered among the bulrushes along the river-bank. We followed the shrieking chimangos back into the woods as they actively established their territorial domains, flitting from bough to bough high in the canopy or occasionally coming down to settle on the ground. One sat patiently with its eyes rivetted on the rabbits but made no attempt to get any of the hundreds grazing all over the place. Frank and I watched several dozen together which lived in a warren under some spreading bushes and a hollow log.

By the time we returned to the camp-site, an English girl, now a teacher in Buenos Aires, had joined the group around the campfire and was recounting fascinating information about life there and in the Argentine as a whole. She told us how Argentinians identify strongly with Europeans and want more immigrants, and woo the English in particular, the traditional administrators of South America. She also warned us of their 100% dishonesty, and said that anything unguarded would be stolen as a matter of course without the slightest qualm of conscience. She made us all laugh when she described how women in pairs (professional thieves) operate to rob men on the beaches of Buenos Aires. Wearing skimpy bikinis they play up to the victim's machismo, and use their femininity and charms to divert his interest until one is in a position to grab a firm hold on his testicles suddenly and crush them together in her hands, while the other relieves the helpless man of all his valuables.

The evening was so cold that nearly all of us stood around the fire until the lamb was thoroughly roasted and ate our fill in a circle. The Swiss prepared for themselves a tureen of gluwein, spoken as 'glue vine', which is a hot wine punch with sliced oranges, cloves, cinnamon, and other spices; heady stuff, really warming and volatile enough to clear the sinuses. By the time everything was cleared away, night was falling, i.e., it was nearly midnight. Ann and I repeated Frank's walk to see the last tinges of twilight fading beyond a snowy mountain pass.

The bright morning sunshine augured well for a good trip back to the border, but we were in no hurry to leave and enjoyed our last hour by the lake. At Ushuaia we found that Rein's expedition had arrived, and that decided matters in favour of spending another night here, at Río Pipo rather than the much nicer Lapataia where Paul was stung for an admission fee of hundreds of dollars. On our arrival at the heath we busied ourselves collecting firewood to cook over. The afternoon became quite blustery and the rain fell just enough to keep us under cover. The cooks had the worst time of it as they had to contend with winds too high to light the fires and which blew the heat aside anyway. I helped to build up the fires and made us all some yerba mate. Two Germans, underwater photographers, approached and offered us some fish. They explained they had been out on a Polish trawler and when they disembarked they were given a slab of frozen fish fillets in excess of 40 pounds weight and they had no means of containing it or keeping it fresh enough to eat. It was an excellent gift and in return we invited them to supper. They had many interesting stories to tell us and were the hub of attention.

Rein's expedition returned from their day-trip to Lake Roca, and I went over to pass some time with Barry and others in Rein's group, and refreshing as it was to chew the fat, it was boring to learn that their disappointments were the same as ours, viz. that the German-speakers had formed an aloof clique and that the expedition funds could not provide sufficient victuals on the preplanned budget, in particular meat was too costly to buy in large enough amounts owing to the phenomenal rates of inflation in Latin America. Barry made damper, an Australian bushman's basic bread which most of us had never heard of before. He mixed flour, salt, and water, kneaded it together and put it in the embers in big balls. It was simple fare, good and filling, and he said that anything else can be added to taste, and to avoid charring it some people bake it in a pan. We were also joined by a Brazilian motorcyclist who gathered a knot of people around him to hear his account of the Carnival and how it is observed in the different cities.

It was very cold when we woke and a slight rain had set in. We said our farewells and our expedition set off north after months of travelling south, six months in my case. The wintry weather did dry out but the sun did not shine till midday and the scenery was not particularly satisfying, lacking sufficient light to draw out the colours. We recovered our tracks through the odd half-dead forests back to El Kaiken Hotel where we filled the water tanks. Several of us went down to the edge of Lake Fagnano, where Manfred discovered a bush bearing outsize burs, and started a hilarious bur fight, as they stuck harmlessly in our hair and clothing. The truck left without Ann and me for a siding with a lofty view over the lake for lunch, but following it we took a wrong turning and became a little alarmed when we did not find it for an hour. The afternoon scenery was increasingly open until the trees gave out altogether. We shopped in Río Grande, a nothing town, very windy and cool, where we eked out 150,000 pesos ($75) but it did not go very far to feeding 23 hungry people.

All through the afternoon we churned for mile after mile across drab estancia country, flat in all directions, wind-swept, and empty. The skies were pretty, with lenticular clouds driven before a high wind and spun out into fine white tails. There was no choice as to where we should camp as, quite early in the evening, we reached a spot near the frontier where we could drive off the road to the seafront. The high wind was fresh and invigorating after an unrewarding day and we hurried about putting up our tents. Sandra meanwhile found the skeleton of a ferocious flatfish with hundreds of teeth and two upper jaws, of which the front one was hinged and about six inches wide. Ann had been unwell all day and did not come to life until supper time. She was the latest to catch another tummy bug which was getting to us all. We went for a walk along the beach and saw her enigmatic 'Southern Lights' again, and definitely agreed upon gas flares. After the ugly drone of the truck, the rhythmic pounding and gentle sussuration of the waves on the fine shingle was music to our ears.

Strong winds and rain during the night continued to batter us so strongly that it was a strenuous manoeuvre just opening the door. The only thing to relieve the austerity of flat grassland was a massive flock of newly shorn sheep, many hundreds of them, being moved along by three gauchos, each with a second horse in hand to carry his pack, and 17 dogs which obeyed whistled commands. Watching the dogs work the flock was an amazing sight. They acted mostly without instructions, and when any sheep bolted, they rounded them up with great efficiency and alacrity. We did see some cattle and Ann caught sight of a couple of foxes, and South American terns and upland geese swooped by, but in the main the empty landscape appeared totally uninhabited. We caught up with Rein's expedition in an exposed shallow gravel quarry. Rein had to stop from time to time to let the passengers warm up as the canvas sides of his old truck were rolled up to allow them a view. Paul and Rein got talking about the ferry's schedule, and then Paul took off so suddenly that he left me behind. When I caught up I learned that we were making the effort to catch the two o'clock ferry rather than wait for the 8:30 one. There was not the slightest chance of our covering the 40-odd miles of dust and gravel roads in the half-hour remaining, but Paul charged on just the same as timetables are rarely adhered to in Latin America. We arrived in time to see the tank-landing craft coming in, but there was already a boatful of vehicles queuing ahead of us. That gave us an hour to wait in which the other group pulled up behind us and boarded the same ferry without having had to race all the way here. Also on the ferry was a three-tiered sheep transport truck, and the men in charge of it had a disappointing time trying to drag sheep back onto their feet after they had fallen down and possibly suffered broken legs or severe trampling. I say disappointing because many of the casualties never got up again. The weather had ameliorated quite a lot and the sun even shone for our crossing and made it quite cheerful.

CHAPTER SIXTEEN

ARGENTINA (Northbound)

When we disembarked Rein's expedition and ours went separate ways. We spent a lot of time waiting for clearance at the Chilean and Argentinian frontier-posts once again, and at the last post the cooks began supper to save a little time later on as the sun was already setting. The banks of cloud looked purple in the sunset, stacked up like pillows, blown flat by the Roaring Forties. The sunset was one of the loveliest we experienced and was quite unusual, developing in stages; and after the purple and grey period, the rain clouds developed brilliant glowing silver linings as though the sun was behind each one and the quicksilver edges made the sky appear a deep lavender by contrast. The stages each peaked in their glory and once past the zenith the kaleidoscope blossomed again with a burst of brilliant carmine with slight variations at the edges, but the undersides of the clouds were now illuminated casting shadows on themselves, giving the whole a bubbly effect in dark and light shades of crimson. Still later the sunset went through an orange and then a fiery yellow phase which was gradually pressed out of the sky by the mounting weight of clouds after midnight. Some of the galaxies shone including the Southern Cross and its pointers, but it had been a long day and I was too tired to star-gaze and reminisce as I liked to do.

When we woke we found we had slept in the most weird rockery of sharp grey clinkers of craggy igneous tuff a few feet high, unlike any formations we had seen elsewhere in Patagonia. We soon forgot this curiosity when we pulled away into the interminable bleakness. Everywhere the dry grass was just dusty yellow stalks. Low evergreen bushes akin to gorse and just as prickly grew plentifully, and when it was rubbed like quids of tobacco gave off a strong fresh scent as of ripe mangoes. The dirt-roads were deceptive: they appeared smooth and level and so we would get a move on and suddenly hit a bump and all be severely jolted from our seats. We arrived back in Río Gallegos late in the morning. I helped Paul fill the tanks at the gas station while the others explored the dusty streets. Then it was back into the deadpan plain for the whole afternoon driving in a perfectly straight line with almost no change other than drawing parallel to the sea for a time, and seeing heavy road-building equipment and enormous traction-engines with massive studded rollers for breaking up the hard-bated wheel ruts.

The only stops we made were for lunch, and later for coffee at a gas station at Piedrabuena, where we saw a pet black lamb and a soppy Dalmation puppy cavorting around in fun. This was a typical Argentine gas station, set up as a truck stop with a restaurant, shop, showers, and camping facilities; however if the proprietor

CHAPTER SIXTEEN   ARGENTINA (Northbound)

sees two dozen dishevelled campers making a bee-line for the hot showers, he is quite likely to turn off the water, which he buys by the tankerful. Paul stopped fairly early to check out a gravel pit but by 'an incredible stroke of bad luck' (to put it in his own oft-quoted vernacular) two of the rear wheels blew out simultaneously and we had no choice but to stay put. We had another splendid sunset, vibrant scarlet which took hours to fade into darkness. For the first time in half a year my dysentery felt under control, and since the night was really warm and clear and dry, Ann and I went for a walk just to get away from the group for a few minutes.

Paul's instructions were for a pre-dawn start to the day, and we were on the move by six a.m. for another day of unrelieved Patagonian scrubland in which nothing grows higher than 20 inches, and the only trees we saw were decorative or wind-breaks brought in to screen the very sparce estancias. For a quarter of an hour mid-morning we drove through low hills and small lakes and saw a lot of wildlife all at once, a line of guanacos in Indian file, some pink flamingoes sitting on the lake, and more sheep of course, and pudus, and a few rheas whose favourite nourishment is dandelions, inadvertently introduced by early Welsh settlers. That was our only diversion until we drew up at an isolated and very welcome truck stop for coffee, but Paul was so shattered by the long boring haul that he slept for hours and we made it our lunch stop as well, before moving on through the timeless wind-swept wastes of the Great Central Altiplano. The afternoon warmth was repressive and the strong winds carried dust through the gaps between the sliding windows, but there was no relief from it until we reached a tarmac road, and true to South American form it was riddled with pot-holes and had many diversions.

By late afternoon we reached Caleta Olivia, a small oil town, after travelling for some time along the coast of the Gulf of San Jorge. The townsfolk have erected a ghastly blue cement statue caricaturing a shirtless oilman opening a valve on a pipeline. The statue is at least 30 feet high, but its head and the nose most of all was so grotesquely out of proportion with the body that we supposed even the locals to dislike it. We stopped there half an hour and that was half an hour too long, mostly spent in seeking something cold to drink, but settled on ice cream with walnuts which turned out to be a cheap buy. Since we were only a short drive from the city of Comodoro Rivadavia we parked early on the beach to camp. The beach was crowded as it was a Sunday, despite the high wind. It was a pebble beach arranged in giant steps or shelves 10 to 20 feet high. Ann and I went for a stroll along the shingle and paddled in the water which we thought was warm but everyone else said was too cold to swim in. Gradually the day-trippers and fishermen packed up and left the whole strand to us. Ann came back flushed pink by her swim in the gulf waters, but the rest of us took refuge from the flying dust in the back of the truck where we gradually cooked like tomatoes, as the sun's rays were so strong. After supper I lay on my luggage talking with Frank while we watched and listened to the pounding rollers. The rustling of the pebbles lulled us to sleep and there we stayed all night getting sand blown into our hair.

   A bright rosy sunrise was trapped between a leaden bank of grey rain clouds and a navy blue ocean. The light woke me up but I was too chilled to move, so I just watched, and realised with a sinking heart that my old problem, Mexican tummy, was back with a vengeance. It took us little over an hour to reach the boom town of Comodoro Rivadavia. By boom town I mean it is growing very fast as it provides nearly a third of Argentina's crude oil, but by area, 90% is a shanty town of slums. We all rejoiced at finding somewhere with prices low enough to buy food in quantity again. Social relations took a real dive at this city. I did not go exploring during the couple of hours we spent there, but tried to get some relief from internal cramps by stretching out on the one long seat.

CHAPTER SIXTEEN   ARGENTINA (Northbound)

This earned me a haranguing from Bill, who gave me the full benefit of his military vocabulary. My crime was in not giving up the seat for him to do his exercises. Bill was a Playboy model and spent a good four hours solid every day on this seat doing his sit-ups, and expected it to be vacated for him by right every time the truck stopped when he would strip off everything but his briefs and work up a lather of sweat, counting sit-ups into the thousands instead of sight seeing. His life was non-stop physical jerks. This was the first time since leaving San Francisco that he did not have his way. Bill managed to get into heated arguments with every single member of the expedition, and this was the third time he had ranted at me. The other issue which came to a head was that we invariably had to wait for a straggler every time we were ready to move on, usually Bill and Tobin looking for subjects to photograph, thereby overrunning the rendezvous time. This time Paul drove off on time true to his word and left a couple of the girls behind. He only drove a quarter of a mile and then waited while Bernie ran back and fetched them. Paul had made his point and it provoked a lot of consternation, but it gave the group something to talk about on an otherwise perfectly dull day.

Leaving the town behind us we noted a great variety in the designs of donkey-engines, oil-rigs, and pipelines. The weather was very warm and would have been pleasantly moderated by the breezes if only they did not carry so much fine grit. At lunch time the mysterious bad smell we had all been very polite about turned out to be tonight's steak! After lunch the tedium of driving across the endless tableland, known in these parts as the Meseta de Montemayor, was broken by a sudden puncture which hissed dramatically. Paul repaired it on the spot but the patch did not hold, so we took a long break at the next service station, where a tame young guanaco was tethered. The ladies' room had a working shower, but a mere detail of gender did not stop Tobin or me from enjoying a sorely needed shampoo — let the girls wait! By twilight we reached the little town of Camarones where there is a colony of Magellanic penguins, the first time for any of us to see these comic birds. The word penguin derives from the Gaelic for 'white head', a nomenclature given by a Welsh seaman arriving at these shores in 1586. Raul drove down to the beach where we camped among great colonies of ants dotting the area. The ants had worn away a system of avenues interconnecting their nests; and a number of rabbit skins lay scattered about by trappers for whom the pelts were just so much rubbish, pulled off like gloves when they killed the rabbits, the easiest time to do it. I set my bed-roll out on the shingle beach, and despite the wind's attempts to rip the blankets away, it was actually quite warm once I bundled up.

We arrived early at the penguinery before the majority of the penguins had begun their daily trek down to the sea for fish; the adults relieve each other every couple of hours and in this way the chicks are fairly well protected. As soon as we left the truck we saw them in their thousands, with most of the colony out of sight in burrows or behind bushes in tussocks of dune-grass. A chorus of wailing filled the air as the males sounded off their territorial cries, piping out only a little less shrilly than the mobbing terns which flew low in ones and twos, seeking out weaklings to kill and scraps to eat. This braying sound gives these birds their other well deserved name of jackass penguins, but I was assured that the crescendo of hiccoughing noise is worse at night when all the males are competing their hardest for space. Apart from the strong wind the weather was kind to us for penguin-watching with nary a cloud in the sky. Within 20 yards of the truck in every direction was a sweeping expanse of the Patagonian scrubland, Cabo Dos Bahías (Two Bay Cape), covered with tough, low, yellow-flowered bushes. At the lower levels it gave way to a thicket of coarse high grass and away to our right (south of the cul-de-sac where the truck was parked) an area of approximately ten acres was stupidly fenced off with rusty barbed wire at knee-height to dissuade people from invading the most densely populated part of the colony, which it signally failed to do, but served instead to scratch out the penguins' eyes. (Typical Argentianian planning, that.)

The breeding-ground contained about 2,000 families, each with two young, and although the ground was fairly contoured to escape the constant stinging flying sand, the penguins had excavated thousands of shallow nests in the earth which was hard-packed shingle set in dusty clay sub-soil. Some nests were right out in the open but the best ones were in and under the bushes and clumps of couch-grass, and some burrows accidentally connected underground, so close were they together. They were very susceptible to being stove in by people walking on them, and a great many visitors have accidentally or purposefully destroyed many hundreds in this way. Those in the grass offered the best protection as the little fellows could slip invisibly away under the canopy of spiky grass. The Magellanic penguins had black backs and white bellies and underwings. Their faces were pink around the edges and had strong dark bills about four inches long, ending in preening hooks so that the tops overlapped the bottoms aquilinely. Their deep brown eyes displayed no fear, but to blink only the lower lid moved up and the nictitating membrane slid back and forward again quite frequently, as the wind irritated their eyes, which were situated in such a way on either side of the head that they could not be focused forwards on close objects together, and to look one over the birds rolled their heads to expose first one eye and then the other. A band of black down in a reversed horseshoe neatly outlined the breast and was in turn surmounted by a band of white, while the black plumage of the back contained as a strap under the chin, topped by more black and white stripes on the face. The chicks were getting on for three months old and were already almost as large as the hens which guarded them closely. The littlest chicks were a thunder cloud grey and all fluffy with long down which gradually receded as they matured, shed from the breast first and then the back and finally the tail, as the tight little permanent feathers grew through so smoothly as to appear glossy, partly the result of incessant preening and oiling which they did to each other in the places they could not primp themselves, i.e. the face and head, with a rapid castanet clashing of beaks like Eskimos rubbing roses.

Almost as soon as we left the truck we had the best views of the great numbers of penguins before they left in serried ranks and convoys en masse on their way down to the ocean. We saw a great many of them standing guard over their nests still as sentinels, and I got the strong impression of two-foot high chocolate biscuits with vanilla cream fillings. Some stood by themselves and others stood with their mates and offspring, always face into the wind for maximum warmth as they sunbathed. The few which stood the wrong way suffered feathers ruffled by the wind and squirmed and looked uneasy. They had such daisy little faces, full of bold expression. We went right up close to them in their bare nests under the bushes, and they did not flee but stayed put so long as we were gentle and restrained in our movements. The moment any of us stood up and walked about they waddled off upright, and the littlest ones, unable to keep up, continuously stumbled but kept their little legs paddling away and never stopped moving for an instant and regained their erect posture on the run.

All about us the piping of territorial cries and the other calls they make filled the air with sound, and mingled with the sighing of the wind and the clashing of the surf breaking among the rock pools. When a big male stakes a claim it sticks its beak high in the air, spreads its ridiculous vestigial wings out wide and emits a succession of shrill honks as long and loud as possible, so that its throat bulges with the effort and then sucks in when it draws breath. To reach the sea and hunt for the day's food, the mothers escorted their older chicks over the pebble dunes in convoys

CHAPTER SIXTEEN ARGENTINA (Northbound)

and they foregathered in little crowds for safety in numbers before negotiating the few paths through the sharp rocks to the ocean in Indian files, tripping and falling over the jags and into the rock pools along the way. The tide was out and I went to the end of a rock promontory entirely covered in black mussels and vivid slashes of lime green sea-lettuce (Ulva) and bubbly brown tresses of bull kelp (Macrocystis pyrifera) full of tough little air bladders which popped underfoot. In calmer waters this grows to 300 feet in length. The penguins would have to cross the reef and pass me to reach the open sea. I watched them approach, eyeing me uncertainly, but to my consternation they suddenly flashed past me underwater, using their wings as superb paddles just as Nature intended, and safely out of range they bobbed up and swam like ducks horizontally in the water, heads arched up and just paddling with their feet. To build up any speed they submerged entirely and used their flippers, coming up to breath for split seconds only.

Whenever there is guano there are flies — and here there were flies by the million, feasting on the foetid slippery seaweed and the corpses of a few unlucky penguins bashed to death on the reef by the wild waves. By sitting still watching the scenes unfold, Rolf had acquired a living suit of clothing — the flies had settled on him so thickly that he was nearly hidden. I found Ann walking near the main nursery and we looked for a likely friendly penguin for her to photograph, and in the dune-grass we found a lovely cuddly youngster which I picked up quite easily, though it did wriggle so. We found another one for her to hold but in picking it up it squealed and its mother came to the rescue, and bit me ferociously drawing blood from a razor gash across my knuckles. Ann was so apprehensive that she was just as glad as the penguin when she let it go. She was determined to get a close-up shot of downy chicks and adults in the open and spent ages kitten-crawling up to them until she obtained satisfaction.

I disturbed a buck jack-rabbit which bolted from the bushes at my passing, and only a mile away a large herd of guanacos, several dozen, were grazing, and other wildlife included several species of birds, in particular some like large chaffinches which hopped around in the penguin colony. Frank came back to tell me that he had seen a white rock shag sitting on the ocean, which would dive quick as a flash and dart sinuously about after a fish, and bring it to the surface and then juggle it the right way up to swallow in one gulp before carrying on as before. Teeming crabs also seethed along the shore; but out to sea are the enemies of the penguins, the predatory whales and seals and as soon as a black fin or hump should break the surface the penguins would make a bee-line for the shore and pour onto the beach in droves until the danger should pass. In the whole colony of an estimated 8,000 birds I spied two albino chicks which would colour up properly after moulting their nesting plumage. Penguins reach sexual maturity at 42 months, but even then competition is fierce as the cock birds fight for their mates, and some come off very badly indeed. We saw some penguins which had lost their battles or had had a rough time on the rocks, but at least they were luckier than those which succumbed to become carrion for the crabs and seagulls.

Down among the tussocks of grass penguins tugged out nesting materials, but most of the nests were mere holes in the ground with enough of an overhang to hide under. It is possible to sex them from their cheeks, since the males develop fat faces by sounding off so vigorously just like little heralds. The little chicks talked with their mothers in soft cheeps. When the young ones are left on their own they appear wholly vulnerable but they can give quite an effective nip with their sharply pointed egg-teeth, but warn the intruder first by hissing and corkscrewing their heads at him turning them round both ways by turns until their throats are

CHAPTER SIXTEEN   ARGENTINA (Northbound)

uppermost. Failing this bizarre display they give a sharp rebuke in the form of a feigned strike or a real one to draw blood.

We had to drag ourselves away at last and move on, but stopped at the exit of the Punta Tombo Reserve where we saw the most unlikely of animals, a Patagonian rock hyrax, alias a mara, which is a distant relation to the jack-rabbits which thrive here. When we saw it a man from the gate-house offered me breadcrusts which I held out for it. It chewed on them vigorously with its curved yellow teeth the size of fingers. The animal sat down to its meal which gave us little idea of its true proportions, but as soon as I stopped feeding it the rusks it stood up and moved away. It was about three feet tall at the tips of its hairy pointed ears with its head up and alert, and all four legs were absurdly thin with long narrow paws, the whole animal weighing about 30 pounds. It had a hare-shaped head the size of a labrador's and powerful wide hindquarters, and picked its way cautiously as it walked. The distribution and colouring of its fur looked most irregular because in part it gave rise to the mara's strange shape. The fur on its back and sides and around its rump as far down as the tail was short and sleek, a matt gun-metal grey, but was fringed with very narrow bands of marron brown over light grey which formed a regular skirt of longer hair. Its underside, throat, and chin were a tawny oyster shade, and it had long, quivering, soft, black whiskers and a habit of pricking up its feline ears which were lined with long hairs. It had the most derisory naked scut like a crooked little finger poking up through the fringe of long fur. The man told us he found it and nursed it as a baby and now it was perfectly at ease with people but lived wild and free, coming by at meal times, and spent most of the day with its own leverets which were not tame.

In this park there is also the only colony of an extremely rare species of sea-lion hunted almost to extinction for its velvety soft fur, but alas the group took a democratic vote to give it a miss. We returned to the little village of Camarones to buy meat to replace the rotten steak before setting off north again continuing across the Patagonian Meseta de Montemayor, bound for the Península Valdés. We passed a herd of fine horses apparently at liberty, and later as we drove through a dyke we startled a flock of Patagonian scarlet parrots into flight over the truck as one body and away into the wilderness, squawking in concert. They were pea green all over except for their red breasts, and it was good to see parrots in their natural environment rather than captive in some cage. Paul could not repair his puncture so we stopped early at another wonderful gravel pit out of the remorseless wind. There were times when even the shelter of a quarry was a very welcome idea.

Again the new day brought us a warm clear blue sky and another drive for hours along a perfectly straight road typical of the Patagonian plateaux. By lunch time we reached the seaside resort of Puerto Madryn settled by 150 Welshmen under the leadership of Parry Madryn, hoping to establish a utopian colony deep in Indian territory, a 'Little Wales beyond Wales'. That was in 1865, and the immigrants spread throughout the province of Chubut, today full of Welsh place names. Now, five generations later, less than 10% of the populace speak Gaelic, and there is no longer anything Welsh about Puerto Madryn. Ann and I went for a walk along the seafront promenade, until we came to a long pier used to provide anchorage for ships since the slope of the shore out into the Golfo Nuevo is so shallow. There is a pipeline and railway running the length of the pier, and men and boys sat fishing with their legs dangling over the side. To our amusement they fed their little tiddlers to a seal by the name of Pancho. When I tried to pet him I was bitten for my pains. Pancho was a light shoe polish brown and had big dull black eyes. He was about four feet long, and sleek and fat; and I noticed a really curious thing about his flippers, namely his toe-nails emerged halfway along the

CHAPTER SIXTEEN   ARGENTINA (Northbound)

upper edge of his toes, which were all floppy, black, and leathery at the ends.

Hidden by a trawler tied up at the end of the landing-stage was a yacht owned by Masa, a Japanese. Masa and Ann had a lot to talk about as they had both spent years sailing the oceans and discovered they had common acquaintances in the sea-faring community. Masa's arrival in Patagonia had been an accident since his intended destination when he left the Cape of Good Hope had been New England. That is quite an error, about 8,000 statute miles, but his yacht was diminutive and he had run before a severe tempest soon after his departure. He had taken on board a baby armadillo to keep him company, and to while away the hours he made silver filigree brooches which he sold to raise a little money, and insisted on giving us some.

Leaving town we drove through a huge complex of oil bunkers where tankers could pull up, and once they were out of sight we were back in the arid tableland on our way to Península Valdés.

We drove out to Punta Norte, the most north-easterly point of the peninsula where we had a couple of hours to spend at a colony of sea-lions and elephant seals, and once again as soon as we were within a quarter-mile of the colony we were assailed by a chorus of barking, yapping, and baaing sea-lions, and also by the pervasive musty odour of hundreds of enormous roly-poly bodies basking in the sun. There was a high chain-link fence to prevent the public from walking onto the shingle and disturbing the animals. Human disturbance has recently caused one penguin colony to be permanently abandoned on this peninsula. But the true function of the fence was to protect us from the sea-lions, not the other way about, as the big males guarded their patches of beach with ferocious onslaughts backed up by their huge bulk, which they could move with lightning speed when called upon to do so. As luck would have it, Ann and I made the acquaintance of an expert who was resident here to carry out a study of the aggressive behaviour of the males during the mating season.

Unfortunately the beach was layered with the usual high strata of pebbles dropping away from us, and the majority of the sea-lions where wholly or partially hidden from view. There were about 1,000 individuals in the colony which extended for 200 yards along the beach and has always been in the same place for more than half a century. The quarter-ton males had huge necks protected by a good 50 or 60 pounds of fat, necessary when acting aggressively during the gathering of a harem, since the bull males confront each other and seesaw backwards and forwards brazening it out. The weaker one backs off losing his harem to the other. Failing a bloodless settlement, the males clash quick as a flash striking mainly at the foreflippers which are covered in softer pliable skin and more vulnerable than the tough thick mane and blubber round the neck, shoulders, and upper torso. The teeth slice the opponent like a flensing blade and the fights last only a few seconds, but challenges against the male possessing the harem may occur as often as once every five or ten seconds for a quarter of an hour, and the family male must be ruthless against all comers. The young males up to four years old stand no chance against a bull male and therefore attack in packs, gaining females in this way, but subsequently lose them again when they in turn are challenged by another bull male.

The young males have dark grey fur just like the bulls but are only three quarters of their weight, and have no manes or collars of thick fat. The females, or cows, are a light brown like Jersey cattle with lighter coloured fur around their throats and muzzles, and have dark grey flippers in common with the pups and males. The cows weigh up to 20 stone (half as much as the bulls) and are very affectionate, nuzzling the males and giving them loving bites on the chin, and give birth to one pup per year. The colony is established for ten weeks each year, commencing in mid-December, when the males come ashore first and attract the females. Young males attempt to start their own colonies elsewhere along the beach but are unsuccessful as the cows are gregarious and will quickly leave to join the main colony. At high tide the greatest activity takes place as the water's edge forces the herd to relocate higher up the beach, and it is at this time that the bull males have their continual struggles to retain or gain cows, which are not loyal to one mate but may be served by a number of different bulls.

The great bull males are prepared before they leave the ocean in December for the ten weeks ahead, during which they cannot return to the sea for food, else they would lose their harems. They may lose 70 pounds in this time but start out in a special peak of condition, fighting fit. They can easily lunge and grab a 300-pound young male and fling him aside, or harmlessly whisk a female to a secure position by the scruff of the neck, but the pups are so slow and may still be blind, and are defenceless against trampling; and whereas the mothers take care of their young the males are less able to, being so long and huge, and having 'other things' on their minds. At the end of February the Patagonian sea-lions disperse from this and 50 other colonies around the shores of Chile and Argentina.

One bull with a single cow in his harem and her pup was much closer to the fence and we watched the behaviour of this family from a distance of 20 feet. Both adults had bloodied faces which the expert could not explain, but he told us that the bull was not very well and hence its remoteness from the herd and the ability to keep one sole cow. Most of the time they just sunbathed flat on the sand idly waving a flipper or whisking up a cascade of cool wet shingle onto their backs. From time to time they heaved their great bulks up on their foreflippers and stuck their noses high in the air and just basked like that awhile. Whenever they did move about, they kissed and the cow nibbled and tugged on the bull's lower lip, and they used their tough bristly whiskers to greet each other by prodding. To announce his territorial dominance the bull opened his orange mouth wide and emmitted a blood-curdling leonine roar followed by a series of gargantuan guttural bass hiccoughs. At other times it let out such sorrowful yawns like a tired old lion, full of pathos, before collapsing on the shingle again. The females also sang their long siren songs, plaintive and resonant, which helped to clarify for me the old sailors' myths about mermaids singing, back in the days of superstition.

The sea-lions moved along on all fours, taking their weight on the middle of the foreflippers (i.e. their palms) and on their heels which were only barely separated with their truncated leg bones within their torsos, and only the short fat tails protruding betwixt the heels. Walking seemed such an energetic task limited to about one mile an hour, as the rear feet were effectively hobbled by their morphology; but if the seals were in a hurry they ran three-legged, using both heels at once to bound like a frog at an easy ten miles an hour. When the pups are whelped they are charcoal grey, but by the time they go to sea in March they have undergone their first moult and are chestnut brown like the cows. In fact all the sea-lions gradually moult their winter coats in bits and pieces, starting on their bellies as they scrape them on the ground. I found a piece of moulted pelt and it was held together by tough epidermis. Despite our arrival at a relatively quiet period just after low tide, there was still constant activity along the beach: immature males were making sallies on large harems and were being rebuffed, pups were walking away and getting lost and being brought to heel by their mothers, and females and young males were making the diplomatically hazardous journey down to the sea for food. For them it was not just a matter of a stroll down the beach because it entailed crossing the territories of big bull sea-lions which defend their zones jealously and waylay the females for their harems while driving back the males which often ended up making a bolt for the water.

CHAPTER SIXTEEN ARGENTINA (Northbound)

There was a large jagged reef stretching 100 yards out to sea which had to be painstakingly negotiated by the hungry animals, clambering pensively and slothfully up and down the rocks before reaching the sea. Orcas (killer whales) breed in the Golfo Nuevo and just love eating sea-lions and penguins. Apart from them, elephant seals also share these waters and in fact share this very beach to breed on, but are completely ignored by the sea-lions as the two species in no way rival each other. There were a dozen of these monstrous seals resting on the beach looking just like light grey boulders, and one which had not yet entirely moulted was blotched with darker patches along its flanks. These flaccid beasts were massive and must easily have weighed a ton apiece. They measured 20 feet from snoozing heads to twitching heels, and their chests were about seven feet broad, and the huge flippers all of five feet long. Lying flat out on the shale they did not have distinct necks as they were so smothered in smooth flab, and their faces belonged more to expressionless flatfish than seals, with round, flat, black eyes peering up from flat faces, from which long wrinkled proboscides hung over their mouths bifurcating into distinct nostrils. There was one prognathous male, a freak, whose lower jaw stuck our further than its trunk displaying its white lower dentition. It was of particular interest to the expert as it was easily recognisable year after year and furthermore he wondered how it could eat with such a handicap. The females of the species were very similar to sea-lion cows but on a much larger scale, and watch as we might we only once saw an elephant seal change its position, and it just rolled over. These animals are without doubt the most lethargic in the world, and the only effort they made was to periodically flip a little more gravel onto their backs.

All the time we were there the tide was creeping in covering the reefs, changing the scene. We left in the evening and quickly found a camp-site on the beach facing several sand-bar islets used variously by penguins, sea-lions, and elephant seals. Ann and I slept out on the beach within sight and sound of the small colonies. The sea-lionesses serenaded all night long, accompanied by the gentle lapping of the waters of the gulf a few feet from us, and a brilliant canopy of stars came out. Other wildlife in this region includes foxes, skunks, and nandous (Rhea americana), but it all has to compete with the high population of sheep which graze Patagonia. Nowhere in the entire desert could we escape the windborne dust; it stang our cheeks and ruined out hair. I never had such unruly tousled hair as here, and gave up the daily fight with my comb since it was only pulling my hair out and the minute I was done the wind dishevelled it all again anyway. Diane had the right idea; she was always to be seen wearing a red scarf to protect her hair from the grit and sun.

We made for Punta Delgada at the south-east of the peninsula where it met the sea along a convoluted cliff, 60 to 80 feet high. At the bottom more sea-lions and elephant seals had colonised the narrow strand of beach and a large rock outcrop. It was very blustery on top of the cliffs and the air was full of insects. I captured a truly gigantic dung beetle as big as a plum. It had a cluster of pale pink eggs attached to its thorax between its legs, and serrated front legs to use as little saws when cutting up dung. I put it in my jeans pocket but within a minute it had sawn a hole and flown away. The weather was extremely hot and sultry, and even the gusty breeze coming up the cliffs was a thermal and afforded us no relief from the high humidity. From our vantage point we could see quite a variety of sea-birds, mostly different gulls and a larger dark grey species, but for the first time we had a great view of the sea-lions playing underwater, absolutely in their element. They smoothly manoeuvred through the clear water at their leisure, happy and carefree, and able to put on quite a turn of speed by undulating and flapping their powerful foreflippers. Elephant seals lay still, totally oblivious of the tide creeping over them, partially in the water, draped luxuriantly in shallow rock pools

CHAPTER SIXTEEN   ARGENTINA (Northbound)

and on smooth sand beside the shimmering silver sea. We drove inland awhile heading towards another renowned sea-lion colony at Punta Pirámides near the village of Puerto Pirámides, but on our way there we stopped a brief walk from take Manantiales, alias Salina Grande; the lowest point in South America at 130 feet below sea-level. The lake is a flamingo pink as the water evaporates leaving behind a dense salty residue. The approach to Punta Pirámides reminded me of the Paracas seal sanctuary in Peru; we again approached along bare cliff-tops. We descended as close as possible to the rim of the cliff which was fenced off and guarded by a ranger, because the cliffs are as soft and crumbly as chalk, and were worn away in scalloped inlets, and between these bays jutted out platforms of flat rock, colonised by the sea-lions, being only 15 feet or so above the water.

The nearest of the prismic ledges was home to four huge bulls sharing between them 25 cows and 32 pups, (which meant that at least another seven cows were away feeding). The swimming sea-lions could easily be followed by eye diving in the crystalline water or just lazing around and exploring the cliff edges. Farther out the intense aquamarine of the Golfo Nuevo was as bright as jewellery, brilliant and beautiful to behold. The little five-week old pups wobbled about and played like new kittens, bleating like lambs and sometimes wandering away from their mothers. Many of the pups were tumbling about together in a sprawling heap, being minded jointly by the females which lay without a care in the world, and seldom even shifted their positions, save to rest a friendly flipper comfortably on another sea-lion. The great bull males were just as indolent and sprawled out nearly all the time relaxing their colossal bulks, and wherever possible they dozed with hangdog expressions on their regal faces as they propped their chins up on the backs of their harems.

Since it was now low tide, few of the sea-lions showed any interest in going out to sea as it entailed flapping off the cliff in an awkward drive, but worse than that was the steep slippery return ascent, extremely difficult for their cumbersome restricted bodies. On another colony here several vagabond pups had crawled away from the herd and were making their innocent yet precarious way sightlessly along the rim of the shelf 20 feet above the waves. We could only watch while an obviously blind pup got into difficulties and bounced down the cliff face, just like falling downstairs, and started bleating for help in the sea. Almost everyone watching burst into hysterical peals of laughter at its misfortune, something I cannot understand. The mother, hearing the piteous cries of terror, sought out a way down the cliff face, jumped into the ocean, and went to its aid. Several other females were also near at hand in the water, more by accident than design, but only its mother showed any concern for the mewling pup, and by careful co-ordination with the waves she managed to deposit it high and dry, but the slope of the cliff was so sheer that it fell in again. The helpless baby was doomed, though we still had not seen the end of the drama when we left.

In the smaller colonies there was virtual amity among the bull males, and apart from uttering a few very aspirant screams like startled tuberculitic cart-horses, they contented themselves with repetitious, guttural, gravelly coughs to express their masculine message. Gulls ran or quickstepped around the sea-lions, right next to the sunbathing bodies, wary of the odd pup to show an interest. The best viewing was definitely through binoculars which brought into perspective the blotchiness of the moulting pelts and the big black eyes.

Paul found us a beautiful location on the shore of the Golfo Nuevo where the sound of crashing surf dominated everything else. Setting out my bed-roll I uncovered a very angry scorpion look-alike. Boy, did I jump out of my skin! Seeing that it was just a fat green insect mimicking a scorpion's appearance, even as regards a turned up tail, but an insect nevertheless, set us all at

CHAPTER SIXTEEN   ARGENTINA (Northbound)

ease again. The evening was one gorgeous long treat to very warm sunshine and some of us went for a swim, even though we had to walk out hundreds of yards through a revolting ankle-deep goo to reach a sufficient depth. The whole beach was strewn with the prettiest shells with delicate linear patterns and unusual colour schemes, and Ann found the skull of a monstrous fish, even more hideous than Sandra's, with four sets of needlelike teeth top and bottom. Sand beaches here shelve very slightly and tides are high and rush a long way very quickly, making a great deal of noise about it. Just after supper a young fisherman came up to us bearing a ten-pound fish which he called a 'false salmon' that he had caught offshore with a rod and line. Paul bought it after some haggling and the young man filleted it for us (very badly).

Though the night was very cold as usual, a sultry heat began to build the moment the sun slid up and extinguished the apricot sunrise. We returned to Puerto Madryn and parked on the promenade as before next to the shower block serving the beach, and as though of one accord we all did our laundry and draped it over the promenade balustrade quite shamelessly. We stayed all morning while the temperature soared into the nineties, and all afternoon we drove north, prey to a gathering oppressive humidity. At last the ground changed its appearance as we began to pass into the Mesa Volcánica de Somuncurá, the final stretch of dusty Patagonian veldt before reaching the wet grasslands of the Humid Pampa. The landscape still retained its billiard table flatness broken by gravel tips and the occasional oasis of trees. Towards evening we glimpsed the South Atlantic a few times, but ominous dark clouds over the Gulf of San Matías were harbingers, along with the portentous gusty wind, of a turnabout in the weather.

Paul drove right onto the beach to camp, but although the setting was perfect the weather was deteriorating rapidly. The hot wind whipped up the sand, but after a bit it would die down again and become more pleasant. The sea was half a mile out over a rocky reef, and after Ann and I had treble-pegged down every loop of our fly-sheet, she and Tobin made the effort to cross the reef for a swim. The rest of us took refuge from the sandstorm in the truck and watched a curious lengthy sunset made so by the thunder clouds which had set in and were flashing out their warning a mile or so out to sea. After supper when most people had drifted off to bed the first squalls of light rain reached us and pattered on the taut roof of the truck bringing in with it the braver ones amongst us who had decided against erecting tents because of the heat. From the haven of the cabin we watched the lightning effects splitting the murky rolling clouds repeatedly with brilliant flashes somewhere deep within them. The storm did not abate but within the hour the rainfall died almost to nothing and the company departed to fresh sites under the truck and trailer.

Frank came back with the news that our fly-sheet had blown down, and Ann and I went out to set things to rights but found all but one of the peg-loops rent from the canvas, and everything covered in wet sand and more coming in with every hot blast of wind. We packed away the tent in the pitch dark and used a table as a rudimentary wind-break, and had to lay on our bedding since we wanted to keep it. It was too hot for comfort and we lay there gritty all over, defenceless against the torrid gale. It was a thrill to enjoy the sandstorm once we became resigned to it, and we watched the angry sky for bolts of lightning, and listened to the peals of thunder boom and echo. The clear sound of a wild surf breaking on the shore made us wonder how far away it was, so we made the most of the occasion and went for a midnight dip. The surf had raced in to within 30 yards of us, and the water had been whisked to such a state of excitation as it pounded ashore that the phosphorescent plankton glittered like sparks. When we returned to our wind-break we were puzzled at a new sound like slowly tearing fabric, and rolling over to check my poncho I saw a few feet away what at first I took for two people carrying their

CHAPTER SIXTEEN   ARGENTINA (Northbound)

whole tent to a new location, but at second glance I realised it was only a couple of lost cows straying through with plodding hooves crisply crunching the sea-shells. Sleepily we braved the blustery weather but as we rested the tempest waxed and closed in around us. We woke to a tremendous cacophony and the rain was lashing down on us, the lightning was striking all around, and rolls of thunder roared on without a break. We spread the poncho over everything which seemed to keep out the elements temporarily, but not the noise nor the sand, and when our bedding filled up with water we admitted we were beaten and deployed to the truck where most of the seats had already been claimed.

We did not manage any sleep, though we did come close when at four in the morning Bill came in, slammed the door, turned on the light, and started cutting and scraping and making himself a very noisy breakfast omelette, using up the last of our gas and waking us all quite thoroughly. He rebuffed Kathy's earthy Australian request to let us sleep. When he had finished he turned out the light and slammed the door in a temper behind him, and left the six of us wondering at his selfishness. As soon as the first light tinged the ocean horizon I got up and cleared the havoc the sand and rain had wrought on our bedding. One blessing was that Ann had already arranged for us to ride in the cab as our itinerary veered eastwards towards Viedma. To start with we found ourselves on a flat green grassy plain with large tracts given over to growing maize, now pushing up in a leek green carpet of soft shoots, with murky rain-water flooding the ditches and forming pools along the roadside.

It was still raining when we drove into the port of Viedma on the River Negro. The streets were awash as all the storm-drains were blocked with sand and a sheet of brown water hid the pot-holes in the streets. The freshness of the countryside after the long, hot, dry spell added a rich vitality which even the rain could not dampen. It was still teeming hours later when Paul pulled off the road for lunch, so everyone stayed put which made it much easier for the cooks and me, they in the truck and I trudging about outside on six-inch clogs of clay, doing the 'helping'. All afternoon we drove north in this intermediate zone south of the Pampas through arable farmland, with hundreds of miles of taut wire-fencing enclosing enormous pastures, many with beeves or sheep grazing the saturated grass. There seemed to be two sorts of cattle, black ones of which we saw relatively few, and brown and white ones mixed, but we never saw the two types in the same herd. Once again trees grew in planted stands and coppices at frequent intervals; willows and other deciduous trees and the prettiest gum trees with multicoloured trunks. This type does not grow very high, only about 30 feet but the basically white bark was blotched with greens and browns and russets and beige in distinct camouflage patches. By the time the rain stopped it was late afternoon and we had reached the wide Colorado River, aptly named seeing it ran a mulberry colour. It was spanned by an amazing high geodetic bridge one lane wide serving both road and rail traffic. The river marks the boundary of Patagonia, now an indelible part of our histories. We were drawing nigh Bahía Blanca on the River Naposta at our usual camping time, so Paul carried on well past this large city before considering any likely spots.

Spying a grove of shady gum trees across the opposite verge, Paul investigated it on foot before cockily plunging the truck into a long alley of mud and water. Within 100 feet we were hopelessly bogged down and all jumped out to push, barefoot was best as we sank into the silty water. All our efforts availed the truck nought and only served to embed it more deeply. To add insult to injury the ignition solenoid suffered a burnt out wire and jammed the starter motor in the engaged position which set up the horrible scraping sound of metal gnashing against metal. Paul fairly flew out of the cab and amid a crackling shower of sparks finally managed to disconnect the battery. The first thing the English resort

CHAPTER SIXTEEN ARGENTINA (Northbound)

to in all such eventualities is to put the kettle on for a cuppa. While Gaby, Ann, and Chantal busied themselves with that and began to prepare supper in the galley in the back of the truck, a comedy was playing itself out on the road. Help was piling up. Truck after truck stopped; but after the first two had blocked the road no vehicles could pass anyway. All the macho Argentinian truckies thought they knew best what to do, and a traffic jam banked up for hundreds of yards in either direction.

Paul eventually took charge and commandeered two heavy goods trucks (the first one drawing two semi-trailers) to pull us out in tandem. Nobody could have guessed what was to happen, else we would have got the cooks out of the truck. The rescue team lurched forwards and no amount of steering on Paul's part made the slightest bit of difference; the truck and trailer ploughed helplessly through the mire straight along the bottom of the verge, listing heavily to one side at such a rakish angle that it was in constant danger of going over. Inside, Ann, drawing on her experience as a yachtswoman made everything shipshape with the cooking pots and kettles of boiling water on the floor. This feckless attempt pulled them 300 yards down the road while Paul's horn blared at the drivers to stop, but they had the bit between their teeth and hammered on. No advantage was gained and everybody got a fright. What a fiasco! The girls hurriedly leapt out of the truck; Gaby was sobbing in hysterics as the rest of us caught up carrying the sandmats and other bits and pieces.

After his débâcle there was an half-hour intermission while the Argentinians had another tête-à-tête and the traffic jam became four lanes wide, (the road itself was only two lanes wide) but Paul worked it out again such that one truck towed us forward and the other sideways; and thus he returned the truck to the safety of the kerb and we could all have supper, and the scores of spectators drove away. The long storm over La Pampa Province must have raised a lot of dust or pollen for the sunset was the most outstanding I ever saw. In the west the sky was lit up for hours in a single massive and brilliant wall of fiery rosiness merging with the real glory in the east where the bulging clouds shone in strong coral and crimson pinks, so that the entire dome of the sky was aglow with warmth. The sunset took an inordinately long time to dissolve into an incandescent tangerine orange and finally straw-coloured embers.

In the morning we set off on the longest single day's drive of the expedition, covering close on 500 miles and crossing almost the entire breadth of the Humid Pampa from Bahía Blanca to just short of Rosario, keeping right away from Buenos Aires. We set off through the drowned plain, sometimes seeing pools covering hundreds of acres broken only by stands of pine and other trees like islands, mirrored exactly in the sky-bright smooth expanse of water so that they appeared suspended in the sky. Out in the countryside we saw an old-fashioned covered wagon with an awning of black and white cowhide standing in a field as a memento of the pioneers. Needless to say we drove through the flood without stopping, past small clumps of trees and herds of cattle grazing in high savannah up to their backs, and watched the screeching grey parrots as they flashed by, piercing the air with their raucous calls. The plants and birdlife were a lot more varied now, but for miles the only perches were the fences or telegraph wires along the road, erected at great expense since wood for the poles has to be trucked in from Argentine Mesopotamia.

Despite summer storms like the one we had witnessed, the land being sandy and porous is prone to drought both here and further north in the eastern Gran Chaco. As usual we pulled into a service station for a long midday siesta and the first chance to dry out our kit properly since the sandstorm. All afternoon we just drove by the pastures, or fenced enclosures, some covering 5,000 acres. We saw none of the small agricultural towns which dot the Humid Pampa, and apart from the other traffic we did not see a soul, just grass, and maize and linseed crops, and cattle, sheep, and horses. We camped during another good sunset at yet another garage, and noticed what an enormous toll of beautiful butterflies had been taken by the radiator grill and stoneguard on the windshield. Dozens had been dashed to death and made a sorry sight of gorgeous wings in multicoloured patterns, broken and quivering in the soft warm breeze. We had now reached mosquito-infested territory again; fat ones like flies bothered us, and Kathy (whose tent was irreparably damaged by the storm) and I lit several mosquito coils to render the truck habitable for the night.

I got up in the dark to have breakfast ready at the pre-arranged time, but Paul learned that the garage had a steam-hose and spent half the morning cleaning off the mud and dust of weeks inside and out. As soon as we were on our way we made extremely good progress through the unchanging pampas in sweltering sunshine. The screeching dark grey parrots and long-tailed tits were ever present on the wires strung along the roadside, and sparrow-hawks sped over the tips of the crops. We drove through a waterlogged corn belt, but the countryside was still very lovely. There were blossoming agave cacti whose round white trumpet-shaped flowers grew on high spikes, and all sorts of trees, cedars, pines, gum trees, and occasional white quebrachos, or ironwood trees. There was a cornucopia of wild plants and insects which we appreciated during lunch in the shade of a natural bower of eucalypts. It was a fine spot full of different butterflies and big, fat, colourful dragonflies zipping everywhere, and in the tangled high chaparral beside the road were the prettiest locusts I had ever seen. They were a striped khaki and light turquoise along their bodies with transparent sky blue wings, hooped black and green legs, and red eyes; altogether very handsome. On the whole the group tolerated my collecting animals as they were very often interested as long as they did not have to touch anything. Ann, Bill, and I gathered some red and orange maize which grew as far as the eye could see, but when we tried boiling it, it remained as hard as bullets.

Time dragged while we drew closer to Santa Fe on the Salado River, a major tributary of the Paraná. The flooded countryside disguised the actual size of the Salado, which was patently not the 2,000-yard wide flow we crossed to reach the capital of Santa Fe Province. On the river we glimpsed elegant flamingoes, swans, egrets, and storks, all stock-still, oblivious of the traffic, hard put to spot their supper in the muddy water. In the damp gloomy weather the built-up areas offered nothing for us to see other than the high-walled cemetery with its glorified mediaeval styles of family mausoleums, highly decorated with religious statuary and ornate baroque embellishments. As in every Argentinian city there were squalid shanty slums, villas miserias, surrounding the urban zone in a wide sprawl, but even the city centre had unfinished (or unstarted) streets and public facilities. After Santa Fe our aim was find a camping-spot fairly early as we were far enough north now for night to fall by eight p.m., but we had a problem as the land to both sides of the road was awash and for hours we saw nothing suitable.

While it was yet light it was quite pretty with wide swaths of yellow sunflowers, and linseed, and barley and the other grain crops, but seen as a whole they formed a flat sea of farmland dulled by an obscured sky. Drying silos were a common sight and all were made of corrugated iron, often painted in bright slabs of primary colours, and frequently interconnected by their very pipes and scaffolds. It was after dark when Paul found a mowed lawn by an industrial power plant with a private tarred slip-road. To attract the least attention Paul asked us to set up our tents in a neat row on the squishy ground. It was too good to be true: just as I was going to bed last of all we were visited by five policemen pointing sub-machine guns, who behaved as nice as pie but nevertheless drove off with Paul in custody. The point was that it is illegal to

CHAPTER SIXTEEN   ARGENTINA (Northbound)

camp in Argentina anywhere other than at rare ultra-expensive registered camp-sites or service stations, of which the great majority are government owned. Paul's documents evidently satisfied the police as they brought him back, with orders for us to get out. So, in the middle of the night we broke camp and hit the road. The next thing we knew we were dozily aware of sliding down a muddy ditch, bashing into a tree and coming to a halt. Paul had done it again! Pushing proved no use, so we set up camp along the sloping verge amid garbage and gum trees, opposite the noise and bright lights of an all-night service station. Five minutes after we were all settled the heavens opened, and since most of us had not bothered with tents the second time around, we relinquished our new spots and slept in the truck. Every seat was taken.

Next morning we had the problem of extricating the truck from the quagmire, and pushed it inexorably deeper in. Eventually an oil tanker towed it out without trouble and into the service station where we stayed the morning. We entered the depot splattered like Turkish mud wrestlers and left it clean, even the truck was washed down inside and out with a high-pressure hose. The truck stop was full of repulsive flying beetles, cacalures, attracted by the bright night lights. They had powerful paddle-shaped legs and looked so gross by virtue of their similarity to cockroaches; their flattened dirty green bodies were over four inches long and had transparent sepia wings even longer and wider than that shewing a grotesque pattern of veins. They were there in hundreds, in the trees, and scuttling for the sanctuary of the drains with a lumbering repulsive creepy-crawly gait. In the yard of the restaurant the proprietor kept a number of different macaws and parakeets, quite at liberty to fly if they wished. One was a mere fledgling with a baby beak and its stubbly new feathers were just pushing through in bright red and blue and green and yellow.

We made a start in unpredictable weather, clear one minute and overcast the next. The lunch stop was at another service station where there were a number of vintage cars and trucks, old Chevrolets going back to the 1920's and the like, but they were not show-pieces but working vehicles in need of a lick of paint. A lot of the group slept the days away and came to life only when the truck stopped, for whatever reason. To pass some hours on the truck I settled down to the unwanted task of repairing the tears in my tent. All afternoon we travelled on through the pleasant Chaco which gradually improved scenically. New crops appeared, sorghum and cotton, but the flooding was very severe in many areas and a lot of waterfowl, particularly cranes and sords of ducks, were busy on the temporary ponds winkling out the frogs. We heard the frogs and toads wherever we stopped, piping out their bell-like tones in a dozen different sharps and flats, a constant almost musical accompaniment.

We were all afraid of leaving Argentina without a decent view of gauchos at work. We had seen quite a number in ones and twos, in prosperous little towns and along the roadsides and sometimes with a few cows; but in the late afternoon with the sun at its yellowest we stopped to see a fairly large herd being taken across country by four colourful gauchos, with the typical British pith helmets they mostly wear and sun-beaten weathered hands and faces. They were cheerful and friendly and willingly posed for their photographs, but they kept the herd moving and we had to keep running down the road to catch up to them. We drove until nearly sundown, arriving at Florencia for the night where we camped at another service station. The weather was sweltering hot and humid, and while the last rays of the sun shed a little light Ann and I went off to explore the village. It was just a small arrangement of squares with nothing special to commend it other than its favourable weather, but tonight that meant steamy heat. The gardens were lined with hedges of trees and bushes, and their damp smell and the sounds of nocturnal insects filled the air. It could have been a village in any hot climate.

CHAPTER SIXTEEN   ARGENTINA (Northbound)

Bill and Frances were cooking which inferred a very late supper, so when darkness fell we wandered into the shop at the service station. It proved to be an unexpected treasure-house of local curiosities, handicrafts, some souvenirs, and was in large part stacked like a warehouse with produce for sale. Yerba mate, first introduced by the Jesuit missionaries, and locally grown Assam tea, maize, rice, beans, and all sorts of dried foods were there in decorative painted calico sacks ranging in size from a pound upwards. There was the complete nest of an oven-bird, or hornero, on the fence-post it originally occupied carefully displayed in a natural setting in one corner of the room. This enormous nest was literally a baked mud oven a foot in diameter with the entrance low down leading to two internal chambers. The oven-bird is about a sixth the size of its nest which being as hard as concrete gives it absolute protection from marauders and inclement weather. Quite a few of the souvenirs, carved from chinaberry, eucalyptus, and other local hardwoods, represented local fauna such as the pink spoonbills and rheas and Mesopotamian wildlife such as water-hogs, tapirs, and jaguars. There was also a stuffed anteater with thick, wiry, coffee-coloured fur which had powerful forelegs with formidable claws. It was only 20 inches in length including its elongated snout and long thick pointed tail. Naturally there was a large selection of mate pots and drinking tubes, and folding three-legged camp-stools with cowhide seats.

One of the services this truck stop provided for its usual crowd of truck-drivers was a television, and I caught the news that the flooding we saw at Santa Fe had now reached 16 feet. This must be qualified by stating that the area to the north of Santa Fe is marshy anyway and the Salado and other major tributaries of the Paraná are prone to flooding as they are laden with so much silt off the Puno that they alter their courses every year. Watching the news bulletin I was distracted by the most gigantic toad I ever saw which had been attracted out of the marsh to feed on the bonanza of insects which dash themselves unconscious on the patio lights and fall to the ground. This giant weighed about ten pounds and was at least football-sized, and its bulging sides were knobbly with warts. I fetched Ann and Frank to share this phenomenon, and picked the creature up which croacked indignantly in a series of ludicrous falsetto squeaks. The proprietress saw us and came to warn us that the toad was poisonous and touching it could send me blind and mad, not altogether an old wives' tale as toads exude a milky poison and have venom sacs beside their eyes. This fellow was so big that it wobbled along on all fours like a soppy puppy with its belly barely clear of the ground. The women told us the species was common here and soon enough we saw an even larger one in her paddling pool.

Just by our tent, still releasing copious showers of grit onto our bedding, we found the oddest caterpillar with a luminous line of bright green lights glowing along each side, while its head glowed as brightly as a ruby in the sunshine, but this was the dark of night. The larva could not keep it up for long and gradually faded until it completely disappeared. At midnight the heat and humidity were still so close that sleep was impossible, and the rain suddenly began to soak the tent which we had only erected to dry out. The showers continued on into the morning and we set off before it was truly light. The sultry heat worsened as the sun rose higher and the only relief we had was from the breeze filling the truck as we bowled along the good high road. According to Frank's gauge we enjoyed our breakfast in 86% humidity and a temperature of 100 degrees Fahrenheit. From the soft conch pink sunrise until the weird orange setting of the moon at midnight the suffocating tropical blanket smothered us like the Lethe.

For the first time the wide fields to either side contained thousands of free-standing palm trees and other tropical vegetation, even tobacco, cotton, and rice crops. The roads were still lined with fences and telegraph wires, but as the region was marshy the poles regularly rotted off at ground-level and were replaced in the same holes a few feet shorter, so that the sight of cables bobbing up and down at random at any height from ground-level up to 30 feet appeared quite odd until we grew accustomed to it for mile after mile. We reached the provincial capital of Formosa where we stopped for an hour, but to me it was just a large river port in a hot climate, though I was favourably impressed by the Formosans. Lots of them rode bicycles and nobody thought of locking them up. A proportion of the population of the towns in the Chaco are migrant cotton-pickers from Paraguay, called golondrinas. Cotton is now a declining industry in the Chaco, going the way of the tannin industry before it, in the face of foreign competition. Both the red and white varieties of the tannin-bearing quebracho tree are logged in the mosquito-infested forests in the north of the province by hacheros, as the axemen are known.

From Formosa it was only a nine-mile drive to the Paraguayan border, but first we stopped at a picnic grove for lunch where at least we could shelter from the sun in a strong breeze and dry out our sweat-drenched clothes. At the back of the spot was a lily pond entirely covered in tender velvety lily cups and banks of reeds growing as high as a house. We saw a lot of wildlife during the day: a gleaming white heron egret flew by on wings like kites with its neck folded in a S, and black and white river-martins with long forked tails flitted about, and in the flooded verges storks stood like cricketers on the alert. Most of the girls, as well as Bill, avidly picked flowers to press and keep, along with butterfly wings, feathers, even shells and pebbles as mementos, and every day brought a fresh supply of floribund blooms of every description. On one of her forays down by the water-lilies Stephanie disturbed a snake. By day and night the chicharras, or crickets, cut the air with their shrill strident buzzing like a chainsaw. They vied with the caterwauling we sometimes heard and attributed to unseen birds in the thickets.

The border post, San Ignacio de Loyola, was only half an hour from the picnic grove, and we stopped there and settled down to wait for clearance in the battering heat, hot enough to melt the tar in the road. The wait dragged on interminably while we sucked on ice cubes and hid in the shade. We were next to another bank of reed-grass which ended in floppy seed tassles 14 feet up. At last, after six hours in limbo the situation was clarified; Latin bureaucracy had ensnared us. For the lack of Argentine insurance, road tax, and permission to enter Argentina, we had clearly never arrived and so we could not be let out. There is nothing more baffling to the golly mind than trying to cope with a direct paradox. So we had no option but to retreat to another service station and camp for the night where friendly bats twittered and swooped in the lamplight eating on the wing in the clouds of insects, mainly mosquitoes, which attacked us so unpleasantly.

CHAPTER SEVENTEEN

PARAGUAY

Geographically Paraguay is land-locked by its neighbours, Brazil, Bolivia, and the Argentine, and the country is broadly split by the Paraguay River. Westwards lies the Chaco which is drier and bleaker as one travels north-west to the Chaco Boreal, and only 150,000 people live here in 100,000 square miles, mostly Mennonites, the military, and nomadic Indians. East of the Paraguay River gentle hills give way to the Paraná Plateau, a single huge jungle. More than half of both regions is forested, and it is not surprising therefore that Paraguay is an extremely poor country with a history of disastrous wars and violence. Under the long and relatively calm rule of its current President, General Alfredo Stroessner, the economy is rapidly diversifying and improving. The main industries are cotton ginning, sugar cane (caña) distilleries, yerba mate, cattle products, forestry, citrus fruits, hearts of palm (palmitos), bananas, soy beans, coconuts, and tung oil. The Jesuits were the first serious settlers and left a considerable heritage (mainly architectural now) when they were expelled in 1767 after 158 years as top dogs. The Mestizo population is largely of Indian extraction and still speak Guaraní today. Only in the capital, Asunción, is Spanish the primary tongue.

Early in the morning we reported at the border-post where Paul agreed to settle the difficulties by giving the customs official $240. Even so we had a long wait, (the usual ploy to see if we would offer any more money) and sat around kicking our heels and listening to the lovely birdsong and chirring insects, while another blazing hot day developed under a hazy blue sky. We had built up a considerable library on the truck, everything from periodicals and Spanish textbooks to great classics and thick novels. I am sure that most of the group will remember Argentina for the chance to read that 1,000-page novel they had put at the bottom of their luggage. I think Frederick Forsyth is responsible for many of us missing a good deal of the scenery we drove through. We did eventually enter Paraguay at Puerto Falcon and drove through Asunción, the only city in Paraguay, without stopping. Since this is a military dictatorship, soldiers patrol the streets and direct the traffic at certain locations. We were all amazed at how young they were, mere pubescent boys handling automatic weapons and wearing Military Police steel helmets several sizes too large for them, giving the lie to their fresh-faced innocence. There is an apparent dirth of men in Paraguay, for whatever reason; certainly close to half the male work-force live outside the country where there is work. Horrendous bad health and frequent epidemics ravage the country, especially hookworm and tuberculosis, but these are not specific to the male population and do not explain why women outnumber men four to one.

CHAPTER SEVENTEEN   PARAGUAY

We stopped at the Botanical Gardens four miles out of the city at Trinidad. Camping is permitted free in these gardens, but their upkeep was rather haphazard. Near our location there were a dozen families in tents and a café and shower block. This was home for three days in the mottled shade among an enormous variety of trees and plants, many of them labelled, from all over the continent. Some had fronds, others serial roots or parasitic plants dangling from high up among weird fruiting bodies and pods. Just considering the bark along provided a fascinating study of textures and colours and growth specialisations. For example, one variety from the Chaco was the palo borracho (literally 'drunken pump-handle') which leaned heavily to one side and its bottle-shaped trunk was densely armoured with spines and its fruit pods resembled fat figs, but instead were full of large seeds and pith. In addition to the trees potted plants and shrubs added to the exotic effect, and insects of all sizes disturbed us: smoky-winged dragonflies hummed by, flies from a quarter-inch to an inch and a quarter came to feed on us, cicadas and all their cousins stridulated in the branches in 100 different pitches. Moths and butterflies of great beauty and extraordinary dimensions flitted about in the bright patches of sunlight. One handsome species of butterfly was velvet black except for the trailing edge of its wings which was a cherry red. Mean and menacing lean-bodied wasps, darting black horse-flies, and metallic green and steel blue flies and beetles investigated us. Inescapably the mosquitoes were there in every shape and size possible, with one thing held in common — they bit us. With all these insects about, plus fresh cohorts by night, there were plenty of bats and birds, and more of the mammoth toads, again lying in wait under the electric lights for dizzy bugs to hit the ground and then extent their grotesque tongues like sticky pizzles to swat their prey.

We added our tents to the others in the shade and discovering that the café sold ice cold McEwan's beer, repaired there for lunch, one of the few meals we did not cook ourselves on the whole expedition, as I recall. We were joined by a very friendly pretty lizard whose scales were shot with pinks and greens and other colours when it was in the sunlight. It was as bold as brass and passed from person to person but obviously took a fancy to Ann as it hid in her bosom. Its feet were particularly fascinating on account of their minuteness, with each digit smaller than an eyelash but as dexterous as a finger. Paul drove us into Asunción for the afternoon, but it really did not compare with any of the other major cities we had visited. Half a million people live in Asunción, but it was very largely built this century. The traditional villas were single-storied and demonstrated a strong Spanish-Moorish influence, archways, a private patio, and wrought iron grills on the windows. In the same direction as the Botanical Gardens is an Indian Reservation for the Maca tribe, forcefully removed from the Chaco, but the Macas now live off the tourist trade. One treat was the chance to cool off in the air-conditioned banks, but even so, by the time we returned to the gardens I was as lethargic as a zombie for the sultry heat was nearly boiling my brains. Frank gave us the readings at sunset; it was still 100 degrees Fahrenheit with a stewing 95% humidity, and whether we put on clothes against the voracious mosquitoes and sandflies, or took them off to cool down, we lost out either way. Throughout the evening all of us had beads of sweat starting from our brows and rivulets soaking into our shoes and waist-bands. There was no help for it but to force down more beer and endure it.

Torrential rain reached us at three in the morning, and the racket on the fly-sheet woke me up. Continuous lightning lit up the woods and showed an outright cloud-burst with rain falling straight down as from a waterfall. The ground was of sand, but the water level rose quickly over the lip of our tent (about three inches) nevertheless. I did some emergency bailing and took prudent precautions to keep the deluge out, then lay back and watched the red-hot tips of the burning mosquito coils, and hoped my repair jobs on the fly-sheet would hold out under the onslaught. When we awoke the downpour was still continuous but no longer hammering down. It eased further as the morning grew longer. Ann joined the shoppers just as Paul was driving them into town and she and most of the others were away for the day. My dysentery reached a new peak and I was in a fever all day, and no matter how I twisted myself I could not find a comfortable position. After supper I was transfixed with terror by an insect. I did not know it was an insect at the time since it took all my strength to hold it still before I could see what I had captured. Attracted by the lights of the cabin it clattered noisily as it shot in the window and latched onto my ear like a crab. I snatched it off and pinned it down under a towel before finding a glass to keep it in. I gazed in wonderment at its lance mouth-parts like a hypodermic needle three quarters of an inch long which it held out of the way between its legs. It had bulbous green eyes set an inch apart, and a strong shell with chevron markings alternatively puce and olive green, and a most complicated tail end. Its body was the size of my thumb and its rigid outsize fly's wings spanned seven inches. I had never seen a cicada before.

The weather cooled down somewhat overnight and was fairly promising by morning, and virtually everybody left except for Frank, and feeling a little recovered I used the opportunity to wander round the Botanical Gardens. Frank is memorable to us all for his conversations: they tended to be one-sided as once he got started he was pretty well set to continue for a record-breaking duration in the greatest unnecessary sesquipedalian detail, and no-one could claim his voice was exactly mellifluous. However he was a valuable friend and in common with Stephanie and Ann he was extremely observant, and there was always an unusually philosophic slant to his conjectures. It was great just to be able to relax and catch up for a day. As the heat built up it steamed the forest dry, for the gardens were almost entirely composed of thick woods. There were also unusual soft bamboos, all kinds of strange birds, and the gorgeous butterflies in every patch of sunlight. The heat ended very suddenly, as though it was switched off; an enormous tower of cumulo-nimbus snipped off the sun, and within moments the mantle closed off the sky, borne along on a chill wind. We rushed about getting our clothes off the line just seconds ahead of the deluge. And what a downpour; it tore leaves off the trees, and despite my precautions our tent was flooded again. After an hour the rain eased and was over by midnight, and Ann and I went off to the zoo to listen to the eerie sounds of animals by night. Ann had been here last night and it really was out of the ordinary to hear the sounds of unseen wild animals through the trees. In fact she had been jumped by a rapist and fled losing her glasses. We could not even be sure of where to look, but were due to leave at first light.

The new dawn was typically hot and bright as we drove north through Asunción. The contrasts there betwixt rich and poor, mansion and slum, stood out starkly. The upper crust live well in beautifully appointed villas amid private gardens, and the lowly exist in shanty towns, whole suburbs of cardboard, tin cans opened out, and plank shacks, without amenities or even streets. We turned onto Route 2 and made our way eastwards across country along the Mariscal Estigarribia Highway. Since proper roads in Paraguay are very few, each is named after a great national luminary. We made a halt after 20 miles at Itauguá, an artists' village renowned for its ñandutí, or spiderweb lace. Paul gave us an hour to explore the little town with its small shops, which are really private homes with the front room converted for trade with tourists. Their exquisite lacework was made into anything from little kerchiefs to edged hammocks and tapestries taking years to produce. Synthetic dyes allowed a proliferation of tints, and the designs were sometimes geometric patterns or motifs like cockerels which made it possible to work in a lot of colour. Many wall hangings contained a number of harmonious designs worked together. Other shops we explored sold all sorts of curious and local artefacts, including mate cups and bombillas in carved horn and silver. I bought a cup constructed from a decorated gourd and a bombilla of chrome and brass set with stage jewels. It was the most typical souvenir I could find in the gaucho tradition, though I nearly chose a carving in a Chaco hardwood, but the mate pots and straws are seen everywhere east of Chile wherever the cattlemen take their ease. Apart from the ñandutí-work displayed in the streets, the town is also renowned for its Guaraní-Jesuit architecture. The Jesuit missionaries persuaded the gentle Indians to build 'reductions' (or settlements) of stone, making good use of pillars, broad shady red-tiled eaves and stout airy churches to one side of a broad plaza in a central position among rectangular blocks of simple houses.

Moving east from Itauguá we drove through interesting countryside and into the Paraná Plateau. To start with we passed bush-forest, pastoral land, and flat fields of crops, but the emphasis was on the luxuriance and fecundity of the verdure everywhere. There were tropical trees and big plantations of palm trees for the hearts of palm canneries. Along the roadsides ferns and bamboos and high grasses nodded their heads in the breeze. Trees grew in all the gardens dripping with mangoes, guavas, coconuts, peaches, oranges, and a lot else, even little finger bananas which were very sweet. We passed a fair number of large estates with tree-lined driveways and private roads and large ranch house complexes behind screens of trees, all painted with a white chemical to a height of six feet to protect the leaves and fruit from hungry ants. Amid these woodlands were many lumber-yards, and all appeared shoddy and abandoned, with untidy wood-piles of greying planks, and not a soul was to be seen, since it was a Sunday.

From a high hill we noticed Lake Ypacaraí in the distance in rolling cattle country, composed of small-holdings and woodlands traversed by streams. This was the heart of Paraguay's agricultural wealth and it was red earth country. The strikingly red loam got into everything, not just shoes and tyres. It was visible along the dirt-roads and in the ploughed fields which looked quite the wrong colour. We passed many horses, donkeys, cattle, and fat little goats; and burly oxen drawing farm-carts along the road were a common sight; or else we saw them slowly plodding in harness turning millstones to crush sugar-cane while the peasants fed in one stick at a time between two cogged wooden rollers, and collected the juice underneath to turn into caña in their stills. The cattle here were Zebu or Dorset, or crossed breeds which look so superior and haughty with their slim muzzles. They walked along with graceful outlines and dewlaps swinging, and had grateful tick-birds perched on their backs.

We kept on passing tobacco hung out like washing to dry on racks: we saw this before in the oases of the Southern Sechura Desert, but this time the tobacco leaves were considerably bigger and very dark. For a stretch of 50 miles we noticed large cones of reddish earth, some of them higher than a man. These were termite nests and were regularly spaced a few feet apart, each looking like a stack of mud-pies slapped together and patted firm by hand. About eight inches from the summit on each one there was a vent an inch wide on the leeward side. I looked closely at a couple which had been knocked over. Their insides were layered with a dark grey in stark contrast to the lobster red-orange of the external crust. The Paraná Plateau had quite a sleepy Wild West atmosphere to it, and as we passed the many fine old ranches we saw the cowboys' horses tethered ready at the hitching-posts, and the ranch hands sitting about idly on the porches, hats askance and their knee-boots up on the balustrades as they passed the time of day in verbal camaraderie. Going by the bi-lingual road-signs (written in Guaraní and Spanish) we dug out our passports as we drew close to Puerto Presidente Stroessner, the newest and fastest growing town in the republic, on the bank of the Upper Paraná. When the truck stopped at the border, the Friendship Bridge, so did our cooling through draught and once again the back of the truck turned into a sauna. Luckily the border crossing went through very smoothly and just as we reached the Brazilian shore the tropical rains opened up once again and reduced our visibility to a matter of yards.

CHAPTER EIGHTEEN

BRAZIL

Brazil is the fifth largest country in the world and borders on all but two of the countries which form South America. It has half the land area and population of the continent and is split into five geographical zones. The Amazon Jungle covers half the country and is the greatest densest rain forest in the world with the greatest variety and concentration of wildlife, both flora and fauna, anywhere on Earth. The second zone is the River Plate Basin and between it and the Amazon Basin are the Brazilian Highlands with peaks up to 9,510 feet in the east of the country. The zone north of the Amazon is the Guiana Highland, which contains both forest and desert. The last area is the Coastal Atlantic Ocean where most of the population live. For a country which straddles the Equator the climate is very mild though the humidity is high, for instance, it averages 78% in Rio de Janeiro. The population of Brazil numbers about 120,000,000 and until the mid-nineteenth century it could largely be broken down into indigenous tribes (such as the Tamoyo, Capixaba, and Tupi-Guaraní) and Portuguese and Africans, the last brought as slave labour since the Indians have a tradition of leisure and made worthless slaves. Blood mixtures of Whites and Natives were known as Mestiços, Whites and Blacks as Mamelucos, and Indians and Blacks as Cafusos. The situation is now changed by the floods of immigrants, mostly Europeans, but also Moslems and Orientals (including 1,000,000 Japanese) who have come in waves during gold-rushes, or in search of high speculative profits from some boom crop requiring minimal capital outlay. Various European powers colonised or fought for chunks of Brazil, commencing in 1500 when the explorer Pedro Alvares Cabral discovered it for the Portuguese, and the borderlines have been redrawn oftentimes ever since.

Once in Brazil we had some difficulty appreciating the new culture. For a start the people are multiracial, and the new language, Portuguese, is not pronounced as it is written, and none of us could read Guaraní either. At our fuel stop Ann in particular was concerned that our pump attendant was a mere youngster of eight or nine. Education seems to by-pass the majority of children who make an early start at earning their livings, and one in every four children who do attend school stays beyond kindergarten level. We stopped at a proper camp-site five miles out of Foz do Iguaçu run by the Brazilian Camping Club, for whom camping is a luxury activity without the slightest hint of roughing it. The camp-site had ostentatious shower blocks, outdoor lighting, and the jet set patrons possessed the most modern camper vans and canvas houses, for they really were not tents at all.

On our first full day in Brazil, it was the turn of Ann and me to do the shopping and we did the lot for 4,000 cruzeiros which was comparatively cheap ($2.60 per head) after the horror story in Chile and the Argentine. We included a common local specialty, empanadas, which are piquant savoury puff pastries, and also bought fresh guavas, some pink and some yellow. We blamed them for the overpowering fruity odour that pervaded the truck until we discovered that some of Tobin's wine had fermented, blown its cork, and spilt all over the pan locker. We picked a scorching hot day to visit the Iguazú Falls, named by the Guaraní Indians: translated, iguazú means 'great waters'. National Parks embrace both sides of the waterfalls, both have catwalks and a 'Cataract Hotel' and boat trips above the falls, which are at a loop on the Iguazú River with Argentina possessing the much longer outer bank but Brazil having the better view.

To reach the Iguazú Falls we entered the National Park, where hundreds of particularly attractive flowering bushes and trees had been arranged along the well-kept verges, backing directly onto the dense verdancy of the subtropical jungle, alive with the sound of insects and the ever present rumble and burble of the River Iguazú, as yet unseen. After a mile we drove past the first-class Hotel das Cataratas, set amid attractive gardens and occupying a prime position overlooking several of the waterfalls. Another mile further on the driveway ended at Porto Canôa in a large car park with a bar, restaurant, and souvenir kiosks on the bank of the Iguazú Superior above the cataracts. The parks on both sides of the river are rich in wildlife which is protected from hunters, but most of the animals are too cautious to be seen. The first thing which struck us was the sheer size, quantity, and variety of butterflies simply everywhere. They were so gorgeous and clustered together slowly fanning their bright wings as they drank from recent rain puddles. The biggest ones had patterned buttercup yellow and black wings the size of dollar bills, and flew up in clouds whenever they were disturbed. Other particularly beautiful butterflies were a glossy royal blue trimmed in black, and whenever their wings, as big as playing cards with trailing streamers, caught the light the effect was dazzling. Out of all the other types my next favourite was the same as I saw in the Botanical Gardens at Trinidad, all black but for the blood red edge of the rear wings. I also spotted a pair of eagles winging their way the two and a half miles across the river, and many times throughout the afternoon we noticed lizards of every size, a dark olive green and often tailless, darting into view and out again after insects, or else sunning themselves, but always too wary to be caught napping.

The Angel Falls in Venezuela are the world's highest, tumbling over 3,210 feet; and the Guaíra Falls 81 miles north of us hold the world record for the greatest volume of falling water, though they will soon be drowned by a lake backing up from the Itaipu Dam, which will also claim a world record for having the largest hydro-electric power plant with the greatest output anywhere on Earth. When that happens the Iguazú Falls will succeed the Guaíra Falls as the largest in the world, but they are already the most grandiose, quite overwhelming, set in virgin jungle and studded with wooded islands. Ledges and tiny islets split the waterfalls into 275 cascades, some dropping 200 feet in one go, and others occurring along a crooked front for the next two miles of the river as it winds around in a loop. The Iguazú River normally floods from May to July, but it was in flood now and the current was a dirty orange-brown and was being dumped into mid-air at the rate of 60,000 tons per second. The major subsidiary cascades have their own names, and the most spectacular part at the bottom of the very tip of the horseshoe is called 'The Devil's Throat' (Garganta do Diabo), which we could not see from the riverside on account of the permanent dense pall of water vapour rising 100 feet above the rim hiding the cauldron of water pouring in on three sides.

At Porto Canôa we entered an observation tower with a ladder up to balconies at different heights and a lift down to the level of the main ledge in the cascades, where the enormous amount of spume from the Florian and Deodoro sections has created a perpetual mist enveloping the onlookers, who have the option of retreating behind glass screens where there is a little shop. The water poured down like thunder, and all around us the impenetrable forest was beset with orchids, parasitic plants, and serpentine lianas curling down from the branches, and was so thick that nothing was visible beyond a few feet. The waterfalls came crashing down onto basalt rocks providing an enduring cloud through which curved sun-bright rainbows. The tumbling water divided into hundreds of paths and presented a magnificent sight. All along the banks and on the islands flourished dripping begonias, orchids, ferns, and palms, and bright green grass under a constant haze which cooled us deliciously as we escaped the melting heat of the sun for a while.

We viewed the falls from the various levels of the observatory looking down on (and later upwards at) the vast body of falling water which separated and whitened as it frothed furiously in its descent. There was a background din of 'white noise', loud yet soothing in its constancy and uniformity.

Descending by lift to the foot of Florian Falls, we found ourselves on a metallic grid platform which trembled seismically with the energy of the inundation surging vertically by only inches from us, nearly blotting out the light and wetting us with its spray, pushed by a powerful current of cool air generated by the waterfall. From the platform a path ran along the edge of the river facing the falls and extended fingers out to especially panoramic viewing positions about every quarter mile. The first such extension snaked out like an S over the ledge. Everyone coming off the catwalk was soaked to the skin by the billowing spindrift, so I took off my shirt before going right out to the bottom of the Benjamin Falls. To take a picture of the rainbows descending into the nebulous chasm it was essential to prepare the camera inside a plastic bag, then whip it out and snap a shot before the whirling mist settled all over it. It was eerie to be right on top of a major waterfall, the Saltos Santa Maria, and watch thousands of tons of water disappear into the void right at our feet. From the end of the gangway we could see the Devil's Throat a lot better. It was a stupendous experience to admire the perpetual rainbows while the sound of it all around gave our ears a drubbing and we had to shout at the top of our lungs to be heard by our nearest neighbours. We had an excellent view of both sides of the falls and of the watch-tower but for the whirling drizzle. To colours in the water varied from an intense silty orange to lighter shades of frothy yellows and pale blues at the edge of the current and in the lesser falls. The whole amazing system was turbulent and angry and swollen with the recent extra floodwaters bludgeoning the bearded mossy rocks which jutted through the crashing torrents, splitting them into finer jets and torn curtains of white water.

From the catwalk we walked on downstream through the hot close jungle, vivid with its natural gems, the wild flowers and lustrous insects. On the one hand as we walked along the cliffs we were assaulted by the pounding reverberation of the churning curves of brown water, rolling over unseen precipices and resounding and booming up at us from the river below, and on the other we were aware of the chirrups and squeaks and rustles, small intimate sounds in themselves, enhanced by the nearness of the trees brushing our shoulders, and of the soil whence they originated. One viewing platform was placed to look back up at the Saltos Santa Maria, and others led out over the cliff to face particularly pretty cascades on the Argentine border, descending in brown and white plumes sometimes the whole 200 feet in one go. We stood spellbound and watched the water gushing over the steep broken slopes of the Saltos Santa Maria and leap and splash down at us, or else we revelled in the glory of the vast perspective of a curtain of water 1,500 yards long on the far side. The path came out a mile back at the bright pink luxury hotel which looked most inviting. Through its colonnades a courtyard and private swimming-pool were visible. Ann went in and discovered it boasted a natural history museum while I returned to Porto Canôa, going from kiosk to kiosk because the postcards were so good and affordable once again. The most amazing sand art is for sale in these kiosks, in bottles and phials and ashtrays. Miniature scenes of ranch houses, palm trees, cattle, and others are all clearly defined in coloured sands in glass containers sometimes as little as a thimble.

Back at the camp-site shortly after supper a Goways coach rolled in with 37 passengers on a 12-week tour of South America. Thay were of all ages but half were pensioners and this gave rise to endless possibilities for conversation. One thing the tour brought out in us was the need to talk to other people as our perspectives were narrowed by living in such an exclusive world of our own. Our expedition was scheduled to have finished by now: Manfred had to leave first thing in the morning to catch his flight home and Annette and Maria were also flying on ahead to Rio de Janeiro to arrange our hotel accommodation, not easy since the Carnival was less than a fortnight away. Therefore we made our thank you presentation to Paul that night for being such a good driver and leader, and gave him a thermos flask and a cassette recorder. Paul was duly overwhelmed and we all advanced to the bar to celebrate and listen with nostalgic amusement to the cassette with prepared messages from each of us. For a change the rain began gently, and gave us a chance to make it to our tents.

In the morning we returned to Foz do Iguaçu to buy food relatively cheaply but the town really had nothing else to offer, and looked as though every architect ran out of money and called it quits when the building or facility had reached a barely usable condition. Pavements were partially finished, dumps of sand lay in the gutters, all the buildings seemed to be in need of — or abandoned halfway through — maintenance programmes. Once we left Foz do Iguaçu we passed the whole day driving deeper and deeper inland through a beautiful plateau with low mountains and a semi-tropical covering of prairie, woods, and arable land. For a long time the soil was predominantly a purplish red, pinker than brick red, and as we were on a trunk road we drove smoothly through high cuttings where the sandstone contained layers of other unlikely shades from creamy yellow to peat black. Growing in the red soil was a profusion of beautiful flowering trees and bushes: blue Jacarandas, 'golden rain', white coffee florets, and blossoming plants in every colour, with especially thick banks of bloom on the sunny sides and crowns of the trees. We came upon a region in the south of the Serra dos Dourados mountain range where tail trees shaped like menora candlesticks jutted out on naked stems above the rest of the forest with a tight clump of branches only at their extreme tips curving up to achieve a flat top, not unlike monkey-puzzle trees. These trees are a national symbol which was often displayed.

The settlers in the State of Paraná through which we travelled for a day and a half are mostly refugees from the communist countries around the Baltic Sea, and have turned Paraná into the second most productive agricultural State in Brazil. Even earlier German settlers brought their knowledge of viticulture with them. The terrain was quite varied; like Colombia it had a bit of everything. Apart from the many unusual trees, we saw the ornamental pampas-grass growing up to 16 feet high bending in the breeze with enormous white plumes bowing sluggishly, and the sword-shaped leaves tip-tilted under their own weight. We just encroached on the northern end of the Serragerai Mountains as Paul squeezed the maximum driving time out of the daylight hours, since night falls in just a few minutes this far north. We pulled into a huge truck stop cum service station where we camped behind a large barricade of oil-drums. The truck-drivers in Brazil know better than to drive after dark, which is pure insanity, since the few night drivers like to belt along at top speed all the time and the roads are terrible anyway Throughout the evening a dry electric storm raged all around us, and sheet lightning flashed from cloud to cloud. We hardly heard the thunder against the din of the depôt's power generator.

CHAPTER EIGHTEEN   BRAZIL

We had not far to go to Ponta Grossa, a large agricultural town, renowned as the 'World Capital of Soya'. Portuguese was a new language to us but it is not so remote from Spanish that we could not be understood and I think it likely that Brazil has the most road-signs per mile of any country in the world, and for us they represented our blackboard. Diane, Ann, and I practised the pronunciation whenever we saw the signs. In the towns the styles of dress were very reactionary and respectable, with the locals wearing very clean well-pressed clothes, so that a lot of us attracted critical attention for wearing shorts. Everywhere we went in the streets of Ponta Grossa men ogled the girls, and were evidently not used to this degree of liberty of dress among their young women, despite the heat and humidity. Once again we saw for ourselves the disdain the children have for schooling as many of the street stalls were run by children down to a very young age.

As we drove along the red and occasionally yellow sandstone countryside, I noticed the novel, attractive, and economic way the cuttings were constructed in a form of landscape art. The sides of the road sloped down to the road in huge steps, with drainage conduits arranged fanwise to a single point at road-level. Amongst the banana palms and sugar-cane crops there were wild unused tracts of land full of bamboos, coppices of tall gum trees, beeches, pines of a sort, plane trees, and mature hardwoods to name but a few. With so many trees, there are plenty of timber-yards which were notable for their wood-drying kilns, large brick buildings pouring out smoke and water vapour. Where the land was not left to run riot in haphazard fecundity, it was arranged in small flat fields of neat crops, sometimes two being raised together, such as alternate rows of maize and coffee, as coffee benefits from the shade. The best of the grand ranch houses from a passing era are reached along driveways with thick borders of hydrangeas and bamboos. The typical cattlemen, here called gaúchos, at the northern end of their range, still wore bombachas (baggy trousers) and ponchos, while their horses fidgeted, irritated by flies. The gaúchos were quite relaxed in the drowsy heat of the day, drinking ximerão (unsweetened yerba mate) as has been their wont for generations.

Before we reached Curitiba, the State capital, we passed through a region memorable for its outstanding beauty: delicate mauve blossom crowded the trees above a carpet of pale orange florets and ornamental grasses. Curitiba itself did not strike me as a particularly attractive place, just another city full of traffic and pornographic magazines and sternly inhibited hair-styles and modes of dress. Frank and I strolled downtown on sidewalks made of grenade-sized blocks of white stone and black or dark green basalt. Most of the pavements we saw in the cities were constructed this way and were always worked into mosaic patterns sometimes including blue and brown and red rock. Often the picture would be a repetitive pattern but it was nice to come upon a pavement decorated in fleurs-de-lis, crowns, or other symbolic motifs. We made the happy discovery that basic foods were very cheap here, fruit at a penny apiece, and the coffee bars were full of people the whole time.

Paul drove all afternoon at great speed, and more than half the other vehicles were Mercedes-Benz trucks which are locally made. All the truck-drivers drove like maniacs and fancied themselves as racing drivers with devil-may-care attitudes and no tomorrows. A lot of them pay the penalty and we passed wrecked trucks all the time including a couple which had careered off the road that afternoon. The first left debris all over the place and its trailer blocked our lane, and the other, an oil tanker, had dropped 20 feet down a bank and lay in its side in a muddy corn-field. The countryside grew steadily prettier as we advanced north-east. Soon after we left Curitiba we were out of the hills of the Serra do Mar and into the more mountainous countryside of the Serra de Paranapiacaba in São Paulo State. This State has been extensively developed and half of its 22,000,000 inhabitants live in the Greater São Paulo metropolis from which roads and railways radiate to serve 70,000 factories statewide. This massive industrial development has not been at the expense of the more traditional rural pursuits, since there is so much land that there is room for all.

The mountains were full of small lakes and lots of rivers which all combined to make the road twist around more, and for the first time since leaving Patagonia we came upon new gravel quarries which will forever be associated with sheltering from tempestuous wind and dust-storms. During the late afternoon Paul and Tobin managed to patch live conversation through to us in the back and compéred another popular Radio BVST Show (named after the truck registration number). When it was time to camp Paul did not necessarily take the first truck stop he came to but picked out that with the best facilities, and most were unwilling to allow the expedition to stay. The one he chose at Juquia was huge, though the management cut off the hot water. As the heat of the day lessened a dew descended, but it did not stop Ann and me from sleeping out under the full moon. The still countryside was bathed in its strong silver light and shone right out to the horizons nearly as bright as day.

Overnight a standing mist rose up, and reduced our view of the hazy mountains several miles inland, but as the day grew hotter the Paranapiacaba Range gained definition. For the last time Ann and I shared the cab with Paul. The day turned into a scorcher and that and the smooth super-highway had a very drowsy effect on us until the weather broke in mid-afternoon. The attractive countryside was largely unused, and enormous areas, long since deforested, were left as bushy tracts with their own natural beauty and always more colours, flowers, and residual pools of rain-water, all for the benefit of grazing cattle and horses. Approaching São Paulo the villages became more frequent and blended right in with the ubiquitous banana plantations and all the different kinds of palms, from low fan-shaped cycadeous palm trees ten feet tall to enormous coconut and date palms higher than 80 feet which burst into leaf way above the burgeoning greenery. The houses were often constructed of bamboo with palm thatch roofs and walls, and the dirt streets were of the distinctive red or beige soil which is such a dominating aspect of the countryside. When it is wet it darkens almost to purple and is known locally as terra roxa, and is excellent for cultivating coffee.

Ann and I both remarked on the extraordinary amount of freight on the roads, long crocodiles of trucks nose to tail, going like demons. On steep inclines we almost ground to a halt whenever a heavily overloaded truck set a snail's pace. We crossed over some stretches of water, artificial lakes, and the swollen River Grande before we reached São Paulo. For an hour before arriving in the city itself we drove through a suburban sprawl chock-a-block with industry and small businesses. São Paulo was founded by Jesuit priests in 1554, and is now the biggest city in South America. It is truly cosmopolitan, and whether you meet Lithuanian, American, Arabic, or Japanese immigrants, they are all known as Paulistanos, as a distinct from Paulistas, the inhabitants of the State. The city is as large as New York, and skyscrapers filled our view from left to right topped by the Edificio Italía with 41 storeys above ground. We went in as far as the orbital by-pass which we took. It is 16 lanes wide, split into four carriage-ways, all full of macho truck-drivers proving their manhood by going hell for leather. It was part of the truckers' mentality that if we overtook one, he was honour-bound to re-overtake us immediately or else lose face. It did not matter a bit whether it was safe or not, and we often saw them double-overtaking on blind corners as a matter of no consequence rather than give way.

We arrived at the motorway to Rio de Janeiro, now only 270 miles away, and before committing ourselves to spending the whole afternoon on the road, we pulled into another truck stop.

These service stations are absolutely enormous and may cover 30 acres, mostly filled during overnight truck-parking. We all repaired to the transport café for the staple snack of spicy empanadas and tiny cups of sweet black coffee, the only way it is served in these places. The empanadas were just as small; tiny triangular envelopes of puff pastry containing half an ounce of mince. Paul intended to take the longer coastal route to Rio but never found it, and twice circled an unidentified town on the Tropic of Capricorn before we chanced upon a shopping complex with the odd name of Jumbo Electro. The modernity of the towns was very apparent in São Paulo, as there was very little in them of antiquity. The Paulistas definitely identify with progress and modern art which is evidenced by their statuary. Once we returned to the road we passed more wrecked trucks, but continued until poor light forced us into the hugest truck stop of them all. This one included a first-class restaurant and dance floor, the Ambassador Restaurant. It had hundreds of potted plants, an indoor barbecue grill, silver service at over 100 tables, and additionally there was a soda fountain and a third quick serve snack bar. Quite apart from this the building contained a supermarket, a gift store, an off-licence, and a police-post. The customers were not all truckers as coaches were constantly pulling in and out. As this was our last night camping we decided to throw a party and finish off Tobin's bar which had been augmented somewhat at our previous shopping stop. Our festivities attracted a number Negroes who were not averse to free food and drink, loud music, and the, ready company of our girls, especially as we were secluded from the main complex by a spinney of gum trees. The lilies and gardenias and other flowers released their strong fragrances to fill the still air of the tropics. It was an ideal night to sleep out for those of us who did much sleeping; Dee and Kathy partied with our guests into the small hours long after most of us had had retired.

It was a great pity that the latter half of the expedition was so marred by animosity on the part of the German-speakers towards the rest of its. It was certainly not reciprocated and was in fact practised by just a few of the girls who put themselves above us, kept to themselves, and cold-shouldered us. It was the same With Rein's expedition as a few supercilious Swiss formed a private and exclusive clique. Before we set off on the last leg we gave all the equipment a spring-cleaning. Soon after we started out, Alice suddenly called out to me for help — the most alarming insect had flown in the window whose mouth-parts were specialised as a forward-protruding stiletto half an inch long, and it was advancing with determination along the seat towards her bare thigh. I caught it in a jar as it was so attractive in its own gruesome way. It was a giant furry fly, and excluding its needlelike mouth it was black all over including its eyes and wings except for its head, which was purest white. All the way into Rio the countryside was full of things to see; the monkey-puzzles were draped in Spanish moss, and the bed-rock was still various shades of red marbled with yellow. At last I saw for myself an oven-bird's nest in the wild perched atop a telegraph pole. The cattle here were a mixture ranging from pure Zebu to the more familiar black and white English cows; and the differences betwixt one cow and the next were fascinating since the original breeds are so different. The hybrids were curious blends of demarara brown with blotches of black and white, and their shapes resembled neither of the crossed pure breeds.

It took us over an hour to enter Rio de Janeiro from the moment we first spotted the 131-foot high statue of Christ the Redeemer with arms outspread above the city on the Corcovado (Hunchback) Mountain. Rio is a beautiful city built along the shore of a natural harbour and straddles the end of a low range of mountains enveloping the Sugar Loaf (1,300 feet), Hunchback (2,330 feet), and Tijuca (3,321 feet). It was first settled by the French in 1502 and seesawed between them and the Portuguese who finally paid a ransom for it in 1710. It had a colourful history even after that as the First City of Brazil, which began as a scattered colony, became a regency, then an empire, and finally a republic. In 1960 Rio's title of Federal Capital went to Brasília, 600 miles inland near the source of the Paraná River. Rio has many splendid and palatial buildings. Straightaway we noticed the new Cathedral because it is an enormous cone with lots of windows shaded by concrete lintels and four huge outstanding stained glass windows cardinally placed.

We arrived at our hotel, the Mundo Novo in Avenida Mem de Sá, but were uncertain as to financial arrangements since the expeditionary funds had already been overspent. Most of us, too, were down to our last reserves and could not afford to stay there, so hunted for alternative accommodation. We were in the inner suburb of Lapa, a frowsy residential area with almost the cheapest hotels in Rio, though a great many are 'hot pillow' establishments. Ann and I hunted all afternoon but everything was taken in time for the Carnival. We were recommended the Hotel Riachuelo by two French girls at 200 cruzeiros per day but when we inquired there we learned it was exclusively a brothel. We did eventually find cheap lodgings at another hotel in Rua Riachuelo, the Alicante, which were ideal though the management seemed ashamed of letting the room out to us. We got word back to the others and a number of them moved in also. I do not think most people realise the level of street crime in Rio, but it is definitely not a safe place for a woman to walk out alone, or even a man carrying valuables. Indeed within minutes of arriving at the Mundo Novo, Alice had her necklace yanked off in the street by a gang of footpads.

By contrast Brazil has some of the loveliest girls in the world too. The city girls wear the latest fashions which complement their lovely skin tones and glamorous looks. Ann and I started our exploration of Rio in the Centro region, next to Lapa, which as its name implies is the business centre. Our priority was to make our departure arrangements to allow us time to see the Carnival. I only had to postpone my ticket out for a fortnight but Ann discovered she had insufficient money remaining to fly, which left only the option of taking a boat. The views of pedestrian precincts, imposing bronze statuary, fountains, and wide tree-lined avenues, and the open air way of life were very lively and refreshing. The Cariocas (inhabitants of Rio) have filled their city with greenery wherever possible. We bought a street directory which proved invaluable and set off for the docks to find Ann a passage. The dock zone was of dubious repute and frequented by drunks, and one accosted us, but he was only a lonely sea-farer being friendly. We made our way along the Praça Mauá to the Touring Club of Brazil where, hoping for information, we approached a milliner: she was a Caucasian and was thrilled to talk to us, and gave us all the details about the social structure of Brazil and Argentina, and how it has changed since she arrived on a British battleship, rescued from certain death during one of Stalin's purges. All the time we were in Rio we met and talked to fascinating people like this old lady.

In the Touring Club there was also a tourist kiosk with all the usual wares, but additionally it had a great many dead butterflies for sale, and pictures constructed from butterfly wings. I do not condone the trade, but I confess the scenes and patterns were stunningly colourful, some with reflective metallic sheens. Other grotesque souvenirs were bird-eating spiders captured forever in perspex. A side exit to the Touring Club opened onto the dockside where a luxury cruise liner, the Federico, hung at anchor. It was as good a ship as any for Ann to cross the Atlantic on, and so we went aboard and made inquiries. Five minutes later we found ourselves being hustled off the docks by customs men who could not understand how we slipped past them going in. Ann did not give up though, but tried all the likely ships and yachts she could find. Near our suburb, Lapa, are those of Glória and Flamengo, and along the waterfront is Flamengo Park, a beautiful playground to take a walk in. It was opened in 1965 on the Aterro, 250 acres of reclaimed land, and although its beaches are polluted the Cariocas do not seem to care, and whenever the rain holds off the beaches are too crowded to walk between the people. A miniature railway winds over the close-clipped grass and around the palms, and. sport's fever grips the visitors. Tennis, roller-skating, and football were all the rage, or else for the littler visitors it was kite-flying. Nearly at the southern end of Flamengo Park a couple of Negro families lived right among the boulders crawling with cockroaches. Their shanty homes were no more than cubby-holes sheltered by cardboard and plastic sheeting. They had no possessions and sat on the rocks fishing with simple canes and nylon lines for their supper which they cooked later in old coca-cola cans over driftwood and litter fires. Other Negroes squatted in the park with no homes at all, sleeping on the coarse grass by day; siesta-style, and mugging passers-by by night. I used to see them tearing down branches to feed the fires they had lit under the ornamental bridges, and following my first tangle with them after dark I avoided the park at night. Paupers are attracted to Rio de Janeiro and Sao Paulo like flies to a knackery, and in Rio the slums are a real public eyesore as they are built on the steepest slopes of the hills which have been left by the developers overlooking the more exclusive southern areas of the city.

Going down to the Botafogo district where there is another very popular beach of soft white sand, I arrived in the evening to find it left to the amateur beachcombers and a couple of netsmen, one astride two logs lashed together and the other a corpulent German with an enormous beer gut and a Bismarck crew cut, who despit his apparent 60 years, was energetically and fruitlessly casting a weighted net which spread in a wide circle, and then gathering it up again with a little shake of each armful to position it for the next throw. It grew dark early fairly often due to the low rain clouds, and when this happened the floodlit statue of Christ the Redeemer on the Hunchback Mountain was alternately in and out of view. The Sugar Loaf Mountain in the Urca district dominates the southern edge of Guanabara Bay, and the massive granite cone is too steep to walk up, so all day long the cable-cars ply slowly up and down, but I did not have enough money (seven dollars) to make the trip. There are a number of rocky islets jutting into the bay and huge freighters and tankers hooted as they moved out into the South Atlantic Ocean; and across the sheltered bay every half-hour or so would come the roar of the bandeirante air shuttles between Rio and São Paulo.

Rio has a lot of very lovely churches. In Botafogo is one of the most beautiful I have ever seen, named the College of the Immaculate Conception. I was passing just as evensong was being conducted and its open portals revealed a softly coloured candle-lit spectacle unchanged from a bygone age. The choir sang and the minister preached with outspread arms suspending his cassock and surplice attached at the wrists. The accoustics of the light green and gold interior were excellent. Three rows of marble columns supported a very high roof which made the edifice appear bigger inside than out. The lighting was all by candles concentrated on the simple altar. It is such a regular church on the outside that it is easy to miss. Whenever I returned along Rua Riachuelo after dusk to get to my hotel, I noticed so many prostitutes that I ventured to walk another way, but both sides of the street were full of them: after all this was the red light area. They made their intentions perfectly plain by slinking to intercept me and eyeing me seductively and pouting kisses. One, shaded from the sodium street lamp by a tree, practically ambushed me because I had not seen her. Her bodice was little more than a bikini top and her skirt was slit to the hip and pulled aside by a coyly bent knee. She addressed me in French, offering her services for four dollars which I good humouredly declined, also in French. Every time I passed these painted Jezebels they tried a little harder, for instance, sometimes two or more of them blocked my path and displayed their wares, exposing and wobbling a breast or attempting to press my hand to it, and even made token gestures when Ann and I passed that way together. They had probably only come to town for the Carnival season.

Bernie, a real ladies' man, told me of his good times at Ipanema beach with the beautiful ambitious girls who come there looking for rich husbands. Bernie made sure he was seen leaving the most expensive hotel in his new tennis wear, bought for the occasion. All he had to do was to take his pick of the girls who showed an interest, who were willing to fête him and pay for his every whim, in the belief that he was a rich, trendy European, and not just the handsome Swiss soldier that he was. Frank was one of several in our group who shared the Alicante Hotel with us and had made a most helpful Australian friend, Geoff, who knew Rio quite well and to some extent became our guide. The shower was communal and very primitive, and when we arrived it delivered cold water only. There was a heater built into the shower rose itself, and since the nights became quite cold, I decided to fix it. I had to do this whenever I used the shower and received an electric shock every time I twisted the bare wires together. This also electrified the water pipes to the steel toilet, and every day other people disconnected the cables to save themselves a rude zap with 220 volts somewhere unforgettable.

For most of our time in Rio, Ann was off trying to find a yacht to take her home, and so one morning I threw in my lot with Frank and went to the concrete canyons of the banking and big business area of the Centro. To get there we had to walk under the Arcos, now the only remaining route for trams, or 'bondes', in the city. This historical viaduct which crosses Lapa Square was built in the eighteenth century as an aqueduct to serve hilly Santa

Teresa, now the best preserved colonial and imperial suburb in Rio as well as the coolest. The city centre was no different from any other with all the usual multinational corporations, banks, and hamburger chains. Frank used to visit the bank to change his money almost on a daily basis because the cruzeiro was being devalued so fast and was halving in value every five months. The Brazilian hamburger chain is called 'Bob's', and in Brazilian cafés the money is taken first and there are often no seats, only counters, but portions are very big and the menus are based on beef, which is very cheap and hence the cafés are known as churrascarias (steak houses). I met Bernie again who was over the moon as one of his dates had taken the bait and was arranging to travel to Europe to be with him — he was a real charmer.

Meanwhile Rein's expedition had arrived at the Mundo Novo and everyone was full of stories and anecdotes. The Black Arts have a wide following in Brazil. There is umbanda which is a religious cult among descendants of African slaves, and there is macumba or black magic. One evening Alice, Dee, Kathy, and I had supper at a local churrascaria, where the silver service was amazingly good though we did not get the meals we had ordered, and Kathy and Dee, happy in the knowledge that spirits here were extremely cheap, drank gin and vodka by the rummer. On our way back to the Alicante we passed a macumba ritual being conducted by candlelight on the pavement. A very large number of candles are left behind to burn in the gutters or among the trees by the practitioners which usually blow out, but even the destitute squatters leave them alone, though they could be gathered up by the gross. Earlier I had witnessed another macumba ceremony being carried out under the Aqueduto de Carioca (the Arches) by a congregation of Blacks. It involved sticking white rag dolls with pins and an animal sacrifice, using a hen whose blood was collected in two earthenware pots and its feathers were strewn around. When the people left, the half-plucked hen, pots of blood, and gory mutilated rag dolls were on a crude altar of stones amid dozens of irregularly spaced candles guttering in the gusty breeze which soon extinguished them all. Another evening after a long day of sight seeing on foot, Ann and I sat down for a rest at a small shady intersection in the rather dingy Fátima district and a black magic spell was cast before our very eyes. A most sinister couple in their middle age came to the street corner where we sat, and while the very ugly man, a meagre wizened vulture with features twisted into a permanent sneer, held a big black mongrel in his arms, the equally unprepossessing crazy old hag who was afflicted with St. Vitus' dance took out of an old carrier bag several candles and lit them, placing some on each street corner. The man followed her about holding the dog's shaggy head so that it was forced to watch. Then quite deliberately the crazy woman went to each corner and smashed an egg in the gutter, and braving the unheeding traffic she jigged to the centre of the crossing and flung the rest of her eggs up in the air before leaving with the ugly man still carrying their heavy dog. Throughout the whole proceedings the old witch had muttered the words to a spell, but though Ann and I strained our ears the traffic drowned her chants.

Rio is so full of places of interest that our two weeks was not enough time. Some of the buildings have fine bas-relief carvings and frescoes and even mosaic scenes of Renaissance and Classical European cities. I discovered a Money Museum which was not mentioned in the tourist literature, as it was in the Bank of Brazil. The exhibits were priceless, literally, as most of the bank-notes were stamped 'specimen' in the appropriate language. There was a complete collection of Brazilian paper money, including draught vouchers, stock certificates, and coffee plantation shares right up to the present day cheques and credit cards. Paralleling it was a display of coins, and from earlier times, Indian cowrie shells, Chinese hatchet, key, and 'anka' money, and military campaign money to pay the soldiers which included diamonds, gold bullion bars, and silver plate. The history of Brazil is reflected in its currency; captured coin, pieces-of-eight, doubloons, and reis were often counterstamped. The international section was fascinating with paper money dating back to its earliest years, but as with the Brazilian notes most had a string of zeroes for the serial number, i.e., they were trials or proofs. The pièce de résistance was a salver stacked high with gold and silver coins, surmounted by the biggest of all, an enormous proof crown from Haiti depicting Sitting Bull, the famous Sioux warrior chief. The last section of the exhibition consisted of the Orders of Knighthood and the associated medalia and emblems. The beauty and complexity of the miniatures in particular depended on the most detailed and perfect jeweller's skill. Not surprisingly the exhibits were under the watchful eye of armed guards.

There were so many new drinks and traditional recipes that we never exhausted them. Rio is particularly renowned for the dozens of delicious tropical fruits which are puréed or squeezed or mixed with cold milk. My favourite was caju (cashew), and at least I knew what that looked like before it was juiced. Avenida Rio Branco in Centro has some fine public buildings such as the Opera House, an outstandingly affluent building. Every part of the patterned mosaic and tiled floors and walls was a work of art, wrought into scenes from famous plays in the most exact meticulous detail. Right across the street we visited the National Museum of Fine Art. It contained hundreds of paintings and sculptures, but the most remarkable exhibits were scenes from famous Brazilian battles, one against the Portuguese and the other against the Paraguayans. The canvasses were each greater than 1,000 square feet and could only be viewed from the other side of the gallery. There was also fine furniture, and a very moving statue of a nude girl with long hair lying drowned half submerged in the surf.

By the time we left it was getting dark, and we noticed the

precincts filling up with people. Each evening the Cariocas fill the streets which they have beautified with plants, mosaic pavements, and fine ornamental street lights. The taxicabs cut a bold dash and nearly all were yellow Volkswagon beetles with distinctive side stripes of black chequers. Near a statue of a woman hurling herself off a cliff we found a crowd clustered round a busker, a short hyperactive Negro boy who was swallowing the oddest objects, including various hunks of metal, petrol caps, a glass tumbler, keys on fob chains, watches, spectacles, even a coca-cola can. We actually witnessed him swallow three wrist-watches, and invite over a dozen bystanders to put their ears to his stomach and listen to the ticking and feel the watches. Then with much spitting and the sounds of retching and a drink of water he brought them up again. We saw him do the same with a bunch of keys and when they were returned the owner complained that one was missing, and the boy duly obliged by regurgitating it and spat it on the ground. The fellow kept the crowd at bay by spewing water at their feet and his habit of snatching for things to swallow, and a couple of times he grabbed my glasses but I never let go because the frame was gold and not worth the risk. We noticed Joan and Alice in the crowd and caught up with the news. Joan was living in luxury in the wealthy Leblon district with friends, while Rolf and Tobin had also struck it rich in Ipanema where contacts provided them with a luxury apartment, private servants at their beck and call, and everything money could buy.

    Another day's sight-seeing led us through the viaduct to a steep brick-paved street on Glória Hill with an inspirational view of Flamengo Park, the northern end of the city, the Santos Dumont Domestic Airport, and across Guanabara Bay to the city of Niteroi, formerly the State capital. The church we were at was simple and small on the outside, but it was the famous church of Our Lady of Glory on the Hill used by the late Imperial family. But for the caretakers locked in conversation we had it to ourselves. It contained a lot of intricate lacework and amazing window arches. The main wooden altar was brilliantly carved, and the room behind the altar was decorated in bluefaced Brazilian tiling, and the processional candlesticks had interesting brass crowns for the candles to prevent them from dripping or burning too quickly. In the rear vestibule there was a scalloped sink with a highly ornate lion's head faucet with water dripping from its tongue. Our next port of call was the Catete Palace, for 63 years the official residence of the President before the days of military dictatorship. It was one of the finest stately homes in the world and is now the Museum of the Republic. Every room had a highly ornate pattern in the parquet flooring using different coloured woods, and every ceiling was painted with scenes according to the style and theme adopted for that room. The sheer sumptuousness, expense, and excellence of the workmanship that had gone into the decoration, staircase, furniture, and even the gardens were on a magnificent scale. The displays included clothing, jewellery, plaques, ceremonial swords, and weaponry; and all sorts of items relating to the affairs of State were also on display. There was even a vintage presidential escalator on display built by Otis. Since the museum was staying open just for us we were treated to a ride down in a second ancient lift, not quite as gloriously furbished. One of the attractions of the museum is the bedroom where President Getúlio Vargas, the 'Father of the Poor', shot himself in 1954.

Back in the street we saw a curious machine the size of a fridge with a great basket full of yard-long sections of brown sugar-cane stacked on top. Cane juice is a favourite of the Brazilians and the operator was kept busy regularly pushing two sticks at a time into the maw of the machine, and down below there was an outlet and filter funnel for the creamy brown juice which he collected in a big jug. Inside its stainless steel cabinet the machine contained an electric mangle and another basket for the used canes. I returned home by metro, as it is very new and clean but it was a disappointment as it is almost clinically sterile and too spacious, almost cavernous. Back at the Mundo Novo Stephanie called in with the news that Gaby had been robbed of all her money, documents, camera equipment, and the other luggage she took to the beach. Visitors are strongly advised in the tourist brochures not to take any valuables to the beach as teams of boys make their livings as snatch-thieves while distracting their victims. In Gaby's case, she was joined by a group of young bucks who played on her vanity with glib smooth chit-chat and then sprinted off with everything she had.

Each day Ann and I had a comprehensive plan made out to schedule our sight seeing, but the plan never worked; we arrived at places that were closed, we occasionally got lost, and never achieved the half of it since the temperature was usually in the eighties or nineties. Ann had located an office called Feedback which places English teachers, an angle she was exploring just in case she could not obtain a passage. It was the perfect time to find such work as the demand is highest during the school holidays which end directly after Mardi Gras. Going on from there we saw the most grisly display of thickened, blackened, and mis-shapen callouses and toe-nails on a board in front of a quack selling little bottles of patent restorative which he offered to demonstrate to us, an offer we graciously declined. In the same street was a large tobacconists, and apart from an amazing range of pipes of all kinds, there stood in the middle of the floor several six-foot high coils of thick, treacly, dark brown rope. It had a lovely aroma and it was in fact chewing-tobacco in different flavours, about a ton of it.

Ann had a variety of local calls to make, so I sat in the square outside the National Library which is a great spot for observing the Cariocas, but is also a great spot for pigeons, since a little old man sits there selling maize kernels to pigeon-fanciers who are then persuaded to pose for their photographs, though the photographers all seemed to have big pouches full of money and did a lot of drinking and not much work, so far as I could tell. Ann and I went next to the Botanical Gardens in Gávea as we had heard of the avenues of 100-foot royal palms, and of the Victoria Regia waterlilies 20 feet across. We visited the Jockey Club Racecourse close by which runs alongside a small lagoon under the brow of several mountains, one being the Corcovado. The 1,200-ton statue of Christ the Redeemer was now lit up, and often on moonless nights appears to float without support as the mountain itself is lost in darkness. We walked on into Leblon, supposedly the cat's whiskers, a jet set playground. Leblon, Copacabana, and Ipanema are neighbouring suburbs, and admittedly the beach is of fine soft sand and is very popular, crowded with healthy young people sporting the barest triangles of cover to satisfy decorum. As for the rest it was very commercialised as the high-rise apartment blocks stand shoulder to shoulder with the mountain range behind, so that only a few buildings secure a view of the seafront. The beach is cleaned up every night by gangs of workmen who work their way from one end to the other with a dust-cart, and meanwhile the joggers and cyclists pass along the fine patterned pavements in the cool (!) of the night. The shops have everything the rich young things can possibly want but at higher prices than anyone else can afford. A great place for Anglophiles in Ipanema is the Lord Jim Pub, an English Tudor-style pub with an old-fashioned British telephone kiosk outside, quaint old horse-brasses, low beamed ceilings with heavy patinas, a bar with dimpled pint mugs and old English beer-pulls. The rooms were decorated with stuffed fox-head trophies, hunting scenes, patriotic poems and pictures, all lit by hurricane lamps. Best of all, the patrons are mostly British and either sat around the treadle-tables or else played that best of British pub games, darts. However the painful prices were not British and nor were the barmen who did not understand English.

 We returned to Lapa by bus, but the bus-driver held no regard for life or limb and it took both hands just to hang onto our seats.

CHAPTER EIGHTEEN   BRAZIL

As a pedestrian I had had to leap aside from the path of a 60 m.p.h. bus jumping the lights in Centro on a prior occasion. As we walked down our street, despite the fact that we were together, the prostitutes still tried to lure me, although I showed them no interest and passed them all every evening. We met Sam and Chantal at our usual café evidently having a wonderful time, while back at the hotel Geoff and Frank were trying to help sort out some accommodation for Rolf and Tobin, whose welcome had worn out after three days of tiptop luxury. The last we saw of them, they were making off to sleep on the beach. They were in no danger of catching cold however, indeed the problem was one of keeping cool. One of the most amazing places Ann and I visited was the Imperial Palace in the Quinta da Boa Vista, the Emperor's private park in the São Cristovao suburb. The park contains many imported trees, a zoo, and formal gardens with a view of the city. To my great joy I found my old friend Barry there and we sat in the shade in the Imperial courtyard on cool marble since it was 110 degrees Fahrenheit in the sun that day, while we waited for Ann and Kyoko (from Rein's expedition). The Palace now houses the National Museum, and it took us a couple of days to see as much as was open. The place contains enormous sections on fossils, dinosaurs, South American Indians, Egyptology, anthropology, mineralogy, preserved or stuffed animals, birds, fish and insects, and the lower phyla. Having seen these creatures in all sizes, colours, shapes, and patterns, I will now believe anything is possible in the animal kingdom. Possibly the most interesting exhibit is the Bendego meteor, there with several others, probably the largest ferrous meteor ever to fall to Earth. There was an oil-well fire-fighter's outfit nearby, and we tried on the helmet and found we could see and hear, quite well despite its thickness.

During the first week of our stay in Rio, Carnival fever was hotting up and a stadium was being erected along a section of Avenida Presidente Vargas, the city's longest and widest street (2.8

miles long and 100 yards wide). Bunting and street-lighting in the guise of colourful birds and palms, and powerful flood-lights were also going up in Avenida Rio Branco and Avenida 28 de Setembro. Hundreds of enormous floats were removed from warehouses and studios, and trundled through the streets and lined up ready for use. I found some causing a traffic jam where they could not be driven under a bridge. Many of the themes were grandiose phantasy and made heavy use of silver glitter. There were elephants, coach-and-fours, dragons, giants, working fountains, spinning dance podiums, displays of feather fans, huge vulgar heads and leering faces, and countless other imaginative subjects, all decked out in mirrors, paint, iridescent plastic, and every trick in the book was used to make them scintillate by day and night.

Rio's Zoological Gardens behind the Imperial Palace were a must for us to see. All the usual animals and serpents are there but it has the most impressive collection of colourful birds, cockatoos, conyures, vultures, toucans — just all kinds. Surely the most handsome of all are the vividly coloured king vultures which have unnerving piercing white eyes, orange wattles like turkeys, and bare necks and breasts in the most flamboyant pattern of magenta, powder blue, and pink. There were many animals I had never even heard of, mostly Brazilian species. Ann had great fun making friends with a curious young giraffe, which was a little perturbed at her standing on its pile of hay. On our way back to Lapa we strolled along Avenida Presidente Vargas where for days the floats and decorations had been accumulating and a Carnival fair had sprouted. There were thousands of people milling around, including the ticket touts. Ann bought a ticket from one before another offered her a ticket at half the price. The tickets were for the two nights before Shrove Tuesday for seats in the arquibancadas (the stands) which are zealously policed at the turnstiles to keep out gatecrashers. There was plenty going on for several nights before Shrove Tuesday.

Back at Lapa we bumped into Rein and Jeannette again, both much fatter and healthier than last time we saw them in Tierra del Fuego. Rein had changed a great deal since Panama, and once again was busy working hard on his truck ready for the return expedition to Barranquilla, and was clearly tired. We found Frank and Geoff back at the hotel, where all of us worked as a team pooling our experiences and suggestions. Ann recovered half the money on her ticket by sharing it with Geoff. This was a week of festivities and we soon went out again following the crowds in bright Carnival costumes, worn especially by the children, and arrived at Avenida Rio Branco. The beat of drums was heavy in the air and in the pedestrian precincts along Praça Floriano the crowd was dancing and singing in a great crush of bodies. Transvestites and homosexuals are very common in Rio de Janeiro, and here they made a great capital of their weird proclivities and played to the crowds with impromptu emotional scenes and blatantly explicit sexual gestures. The weirdos and queers have long been a part of Rio's Carnival and thousands of them were dolled up in women's clothing, bridal gowns, bikinis and high heels, overdone make-up, and fancier dresses and costumes. Their campness was well-practised and it gained them the attention they craved as little knots of people gathered around to watch their sick slick antics.
  Ann and I deliberately carried nothing of value on us to thwart the pickpockets, though back in our hotel half my remaining money had already been stolen. We found a high balustrade to sit on though little actually happened until midnight. The drink vendors kept passing by, in competition with the churrascarias and the temporary refreshment stalls. Now and again a small loud band of musicians was the focus of a fluid mass of dancers insinuating its way through the crowd. Police cleared the streets, to absolutely no avail, as within a minute 10,000 more thronged in their wake. Little groups in party costume were here and there,

parts of the parade to come, brightly illuminated by the decorative neon lamps in the form of fruit and flowers and so on. The first parade with floats and samba dancers came through after midnight, advancing in stages to allow the dazzling costumed performers to repeat their set dance routines every 100 feet. The high feather head-dresses and the sheer opulence and extravaganza of it all was full of razzle-dazzle and pageantry. There are three leagues of samba clubs and each uses a different street in an intense competition of dance. The different clubs adopt their own colour schemes and the participants from each club number up to 3,000 and can take half an hour to pass by. Each club has a bateria, or band, composed mostly of drummers, and cohorts of dancing duchesses, colonial gentlemen, clowns, society ladies, stilt-walkers, and an endless variety of comic strip characters and others parading in rows.

The samba processions passed by all night long and well into daylight, when the sun's early rays transformed the splendour of the decorations and exaggerated the tawdriness and colours of the floats and performers. During the night I slipped back to my hotel but was accosted by more prostitutes hanging around on the fringe of the crowd. They too were in costume for the Carnival. The first slipped her arm expertly around me before I was aware of her business, and fell into step with me despite my rebuttals, until we reached an unlit area where she tried a little harder and considerably overstepped the bounds of decency, so I used a more abrupt method to dump her, but was almost immediately caressed by another. Most of the prostitutes were very pretty, sensual, dark-skinned girls in their teens and early twenties; such a waste of humanity, I felt.

No holiday in Rio is complete without a day at the beach. We chose Flamengo beach, taking it in turn to guard our belongings. The beach was one solid mass of happy Brazilians, black, brown, and white, with almost no room between them to swing our arms or thread a path. It was the same from the promenade to 20 feet out to sea for a mile down the beach as far as the marina. Beyond the mass of swimmers the pollution was immediately less and the water much cooler and more refreshing, the only cold water we found in Rio. When Ann went swimming she was constantly molested and rubbed by the men who have no sense of honour regarding White girls. It is all part of their machismo in which they promote their virility and portray themselves as Don Juans. The Rio beach-girls, however, are very liberated regarding their bikinis, which are so minute they threaten to vanish altogether if the trend continues, already down to a few square inches.

Every time we returned to Lapa, more of the group were leaving Rio and we said our farewells. Ann's ticket admitted her to the arquibancadas for the very best of the processions which always falls on the Sunday night before Shrove Tuesday. The next day we went with Frank had and Geoff to a characteristic working-man's churrascaria which Frank highly recommended in the Avenida Mem da Sá. Frank made himself unforgettable as a great trencherman with a talent for picking out good cheap restaurants which served satisfying helpings. This place was typical of Lapa, catering for its locals. It was fairly spartan with three fixed menus on a blackboard in the street, a set price of a dollar fifty and an unlimited amount of food in five courses which was placed on the table for us to help ourselves. Drinks were extra and their range of tropical fruit juices was nearly all new to me, but the fruit was always depicted on the label. I chose tamarind, which turned out quite tart, but when mixed with cane brandy (aguardente de cana) and water made a most refreshing cocktail.

I went to see Frank off later that evening on the shuttle-bus at the domestic Santos Dumont Airport. The quickest way there was across the top edge of Flamengo Park and along the beach with the lights of Niteroi winking over Guanabara Bay. We emerged on the runway by mistake but the buses run all the time and he was soon on his way to the main airport, sad yet excited at the same time. It was the last night of Carnival, and so I returned by way of the Praça Floriano where the crowds were already huge to find out what was scheduled.

Ann and I set out again at midnight, since nothing major seemed likely to happen any earlier, and made our way through the hustle and bustle. The incessant beat of the big bass drums and songs in chorus echoed above the squeals of delight and the chatter and babble around us, and time after time the whacks of plastic bladders whammed against the cobbles exploded like firecrackers. We saw several processions in Avenida Rio Branco as we gradually made our way towards the more spectacular processions gathered ready to dance down Avenida Presidente Vargas for a high-paying audience. The strong electric light hardened the texture of the velvet and expanded polystyrene, and the gauzy drapes and flouncy decorations on the floats, which were predominantly silver, but there was no main theme. We saw double-faced Janus heads, a stork delivering an adult in a nappy, a hybrid grasshopper/bulldozer, supine dead dragons, weird imaginative structures of octopods consuming buildings and chariots or waving microphones, enormous fruit bowls, painted mannequins 20 feet tall in a variety of poses and states of dress. People thronged all around as the club marshals busily lined the dancers up ready for their big moment, and the last minute finishing touches were added to the floats. The most original uniform was a costume of artificial bananas made up into head-dresses and leotards for one troupe of over 100. The more matronly women tended to wear crinolined frocks bedecked with silvery clutter, masses of frills and lifted hems revealing lots of petticoats. I saw only a score or so of topless girls, one with a reticulated python in the processions, as toplessness and face-masks have now been banned, the first for decorum and the second since personal vendettas have for a long time been traditionally resolved at Carnival time, using the anonymity of the disguise to get close to the victim, and so dispatch him. In fact there was a handful of slim glamour girls in one parade nude but for high boots, and a smattering of others all but nude wearing G-strings.

Ambulances and police cars were the only vehicles able to make their way through the crowd at little more than walking speed with sirens wailing. The bright lights in every direction and a city full of noisy Cariocas putting on their annual best had an infectious joy about it. As we went further along the avenue we saw a lot more floats, representing Brobdinaggian tea sets, slippers, butterflies, Roman gods, char-à-bancs, winged angels, caricature heroes, and outsize obscene heads with lolling tongues. A lot of the floats had platforms for dancers often with head-dresses so tall that the wearers could hardly move. There were no more queers here putting on airs and striking diverting poses for the sake of cheap titillation. By waiting till nearly two in the morning we managed to walk straight into the stadium, no longer policed as very tired spectators were leaving faster than others were arriving, some having been there for two or three days.

Hundreds of children took part, probably as much as 10% of the 25,000 performers who danced the samba down the street were children. The last procession contained a couple of amputees, one wanting an arm and the other a leg. They were given terrific applause, particularly the one-legged man who danced along in hops and shuffles in his bright pink top hat and tails. The sheer quantity of feathers was breath-taking, particularly ostrich and pheasant and other full colourful plumes, some dyed brilliant tints. The last parade went by in the direct shafts of gentle morning sunlight, which had a far more dazzling effect than the flood-lights every did. Every parade had its big band of drummers, its bateria, pounding out an irresistible beat on dozens of big drums, side-drums, tambours, and wether bells. In each parade there were the more expert young samba dancers, usually

Coloured who, with a girl between two men, samba danced the sex act in slow time before they broke apart and rapidly executed a dazzlingly quick samba orgasm for five or ten seconds before moving on. There was no end to the curvaceous brown bodies, deliciously uncovered who enthralled us with belly dancing, mimicked by the younger girls who put on the most fanciful display of wiggling.

We left the stadium with our heads full of lights and colours and rhythm and song and walked home through the litter and debris such as only a crowd of 200,000 revellers can create. There was already an army of workmen cleaning up. We paused at the Campo de Santana, a small central park where hundreds of agoutis live in the shade of dense trees. We took in the gentle view through the railings while soft shafts of sunlight and mottled patches of shade lent a tranquility to the empty woodland, with its curious tropical trees, some with a latticework of roots buttressing and surrounding the bowed trunks, and the tall bamboos under which dozens of curious agoutis were walking nervously about on pencil-thin legs.

My time was up and Ann saw me off on the shuttle-bus and continued on her incessant errand to find some way of leaving Rio within her means. The ten-mile ride to the Galeao Airport on Governador Island went through lovely scenery along the shore of Guanabara Bay, but I hardly noticed it. Tony and Margaret, a couple from Rein's expedition accompanied me as far as Miami. It was night-time when our tristar took off and circled the city below, and I easily recognised the streets and districts, as the street lights created sparkling cobwebs, and not far away lightning flashes played in the sky. After Rio all we could see were fairy lights from a score of little towns and villages amid the dark void and the red pulse of the aircraft's fuselage beacons. I had less than a dollar in my pocket but I had begun the expedition in San Francisco with only seven dollars. The Miami customs very nearly refused me entry for lack of funds, but I showed them travel tickets which would take me all over the United States and halfway around the world over the next ten weeks.

SUFFIX

Latin America can provide a real challenge to the adventurous travellers, and whether you go on an organised trip or just take things as they come, it is a great place to rediscover yourself. One great hazard is avoiding sickness, so take precautions before you go. Lumbered with dysentery from Tijuana onwards, I lost weight steadily at a rate of two pounds a week until rest and North American hygiene worked its cure. No-one except Bill managed to stay healthy the whole expedition, so take heed and take precautions. As some of us found out, hospitalisation works out very expensive indeed. Various prescribed medicines are classified as illegal drugs in certain Latin American countries, and are nearly impossible to obtain.

The troubles in El Salvador were already flaring when we passed that country by, but we did not see any hint of the Honduran, Guatemalan, and Nicaraguan aspects of the problem which made international headlines in subsequent months. By the same token the Falkland Islands crisis was still in the future when we were present, and as a basically British expedition we were welcomed with open arms in Argentina. We witnessed for ourselves how the governments of many of these countries dress up their image behind a tawdry militaristic façade; in some cases even the traffic police had flashy uniforms and plaited lanyards.

Despite the risk of disease and inevitable interference resulting from acts of dishonesty or problematic bureaucracy, the great pluses of exploring Latin America outweigh the minuses. For me it was seeing the natural world, country scenery, and wildlife, and for others, especially Bill and Tobin, it was a photographic bonanza. For Frank it was a philosophical expedition, opening his eyes to a totally new hard-nosed world of human suffering and deception. Others managed to sleep their days away and wake up for the group's social life. One thing is sure, no matter what our reasons for going, we left Brazil with broader horizons and a wealth of experience to our credit.

INDEX

Abancay	Peru	202
Acatlán	Mexico	28
Aguas Galientes	Peru	241
Aguas Verdes	Peru	163
Alligator hunt on the Amazon	Ecuador	139
Amotape Mountains	Peru	171
Antofagasta	Chile	276
Apurímac Valley	Peru	203
Arica	Chile	273
Armadillo	Argentina	217
Asunción	Paraguay	390
Atacama Desert	Chile	276
Ayacucho	Peru	202
Baja Californian Desert		15
Baños	Ecuador	145
Bariloche	Argentina	304
Barranquilla	Colombia	42
Belize City		40
Belmopan	Belize	42
Black magic	Brazil	418
Blow-hole La Bufadora	Mexico	15
Boa Constrictor	Ecuador	145
Bogotá	Colombia	93.95
Brahmin bull	Guatemala	62
Brown pelican attacks us		18
Buin farmer	Chile	292
Cacalures	Argentina	383

Caldera	Chile	279
Caleta Olivia	Argentina	357
Camarones	Argentina	360,366
Candle cacti	Mexico	17
Caporja	Guatemala	57
Carnival of Rio de Janeiro		425
Castrovirreyna	Peru	199
Catalina	Chile	278
Catete Palace	Brazil	422
Cauca River	Colombia	109
Cave paintings	Argentina	304
Cayembe	Ecuador	152
Central Valley	Chile	291
Chan-Chan Ruins	Ecuador	196
Chañaral	Chile	278
Chibcha-Muisca Indians	Colombia	92
Chichén-Itzá Ruins	Mexico	36
Chichicastenango	Guatemala	54
Chiclayo	Peru	174
Chimaltenango	Guatemala	56
Chimbote	Peru	179
Chinandega	Nicaragua	71
Chiquimula	Guatemala	61
Christmas		243
Cloud forest	Ecuador	115
Chubut River	Argentina	307
Coca	Ecuador	141
Colorado River	Argentina	378
Comayagüela	Honduras	67
Comodora Rivadavia	Argentina	358
Copán Ruins	Honduras	57
Copiapó	Chile	280
Coquimbo	Chile	283

INDEX

Cost of expedition		10
Cotopaxi	Ecuador	155
Cuenca Valley	Ecuador	162
Cuña Indians	Panama	82, 84
Curitiba	Brazil	408
Cuzco	Peru	208, 238
Darién Gap	Panama	82
Devil's Throat	Brazil	402
Dugout manufacture	Ecuador	127
El Alto	Bolivia	257
El Bolsón	Argentina	315
El Calafate	Argentina	323, 335
Elephant seals	Argentina	371
El Gigante	Colombia	104
El Milagro	Peru	201
El Triunfo	Ecuador	162
Equator		118
Ferry, La Paz-Mazatlán	Mexico	20
Formosa	Argentina	387
Galápagos Islands	Ecuador	154
Gauchos	Argentina	384
Gold-panning	Ecuador	142
Great Central Patagonian Altiplano		319, 357
Gringo Perdido	Guatemala	45
Guanacos	Argentina	313, 335, 343
Guaíra Falls	Brazil	402
Guasaule	Nicaragua	70
Guatemala City		51
Gulf of California		17
Heart of palm	Ecuador	136
Humid Pampa	Argentina	380
Ica	Peru	192
Iguazú Falls	Brazil	401

Inca Highway		214
Inca stonework	Peru	210
Inca Trail	Peru	218
Indian tribes	Brazil	400
Indian tribes	Honduras	65
Indian tribes	Mexico	14
Indian tribes	Panama	82
Indian tribes	Tierra del Fuego	337
Islands of the Sun and Moon	Lake Titicaca	254
Itauguá	Paraguay	394
Ixtlán del Rio	Mexico	22
José de San Martin	Argentina	310
Juli	Peru	250
Juliaca	Peru	245
Jungle hospitality	Ecuador	130
Jungle Mission	Ecuador	140
Kabah Ruins	Mexico	35
Kapok	Guatemala	58
Laja Falls	Chile	294
Lake Argentino		323
Lake Atitlán	Guatemala	51
Lake District	Chile	296
Lake Fagnano	Argentina	343
Lake Izabal	Guatemala	49
Lake Musters	Argentina	311
Lake Nahuel Huapí National Park	Argentina	303
Lake of Blood	Ecuador	115
Lake Petén-Itzá	Guatemala	45
Lake Titicaca		248
Lapataia	Argentina	348
La Paz	Bolivia	260
La Raya	Peru	244
La Serena	Chile	282

INDEX

Liberia	Costa Rica	76
Lima	Peru	81
Limatambo	Peru	207
Locust plague	Mexico	34
Machu-Pijchu Ruins	Peru	233
Machu-Pijchu train	Peru	213, 217, 237
Magellanic penguins	Argentina	360
Magellanic woodpecker	Argentina	334
Mariachis	Mexico	124
Maya weaving	Guatemala	54
Mexico City		23
Military abuse	Guatemala	47
Misahuallí	Ecuador	120
Moche pyramids	Peru	178
Monte Alban Ruins	Mexico	29
Moon Valley	Bolivia	259
Moreno Glacier	Argentina	325
Mosquito Coast	Nicaragua	70
Mount Montserrate	Colombia	96
Mud desert	Argentina	319
Nazca Plateau	Peru	194
Nueva Ocotopeque	Guatemala	64
Old Panama		86
Ollantaytambo	Peru	204
Opal mines	Mexico	22
Otavalo	Ecuador	152
Palenque Ruins	Mexico	32
Panama City		83
Pan-American Highway		15
Panajachel	Guatemala	51
Papallacta	Ecuador	118
Paracas Peninsula	Peru	188
Paraná Plateau	Paraguay	395

Paso Canoas	Costa Rica	79
Pasto	Colombia	109
Patagonian rock hyrax		365
Payachatas Volcano	Bolivia	267, 270
Peñas Blancas	Nicaragua	72
Perito Moreno	Argentina	316
Petén	Guatemala	43
Petrified forest	Argentina	312
Piranhas	Ecuador	137
Pisaq	Peru	213
Pisco	Peru	188, 196
Pomata	Peru	252
Ponta Grossa	Brazil	407
Popayán	Colombia	108
Prostitutes in Rio		416, 425, 428
Puebla	Mexico	26
Puerto Artificial	Chile	277
Puerto Madryn	Argentina	366, 375
Puerto Pirámides	Argentina	373
Puno	Peru	247
Puyehue National Park	Chile	298
Puyo	Ecuador	144
Quito	Ecuador	117, 146, 153
Red earth country	Paraguay	396
Red earth country	Brazil	405, 410
Rescued in Guatemala		61
Rio de Janeiro	Brazil	411
Río Gallegos	Argentina	338, 356
Río Grande	Argentina	342, 353
Rio Grande	Peru	194
Río Pipo	Argentina	345, 352
San Agustín	Colombia	100
San Francisco	U.S.A.	9

San Ignacio	Belize	42
San Ignacio de Loyola	Argentina	388
San José	Costa Rica	75
Sandfleas	Guatemala	64
Sandstorm	Argentina	375
Santa	Peru	171
Santa Lucia Mountains	U.S.A.	11
Santiago	Chile	287
São Paulo	Brazil	409
Scorpions	Mexico	25
Sea-lions	Peru	190
Sea-lions	Argentina	367
Sechura Desert	Peru	168
Sierra Nevada de Santa Marta	Colombia	91
Straits of Magellan		335, 354
Straits of Tiquina	Lake Titicaca	256
Taboga Island	Panama	86
Talamanca Range	Costa Rica	75
Talca	Chile	293
Tambo	Ecuador	160
Tambo Colorado Ruins	Peru	197
Tambo Quemado	Bolivia	267
Teculatán	Guatemala	50
Tegucigalpa	Honduras	66
Tehuantepec	Mexico	31
Tena	Ecuador	143
Tikal Ruins	Guatemala	43
Trujillo	Peru	176
Tulcán	Colombia	111
Tulum Ruins	Mexico	38
Uripa	Peru	204
Ushuaia	Argentina	344
Valdivia	Chile	297

Valladolid	Mexico	317
Valley of the statues	Colombia	134
Valparaíso	Chile	285
Viedma	Argentina	377
Villahermosa	Mexico	31
Viña del Mar	Chile	285
Yerba mate		347
Zipaquirá	Colombia	97

www.ingramcontent.com/pod-product-compliance
Lightning Source LLC
Chambersburg PA
CBHW041955080526
44588CB00021B/2748